A History of Sheffield

1857-1889

'...speed, science and bottom'

Martin Westby

Copyright Martin Westby. All rights reserved.
First published in 2017 by England's Oldest Football Clubs

ISBN 978-0-9556378-1-0

Cover Image. William Ibbitt, West View of Sheffield, 1855.
Courtesy Sheffield Libraries and Archives.
Composed from a Crookes moor viewpoint it shows the marked difference between the heavily industrialised town centre and the beautiful surrounding countryside. By the early to mid-1880s Crookes would be home to four football clubs. The General Infirmary marks the edge of the town to the north and the most southerly point is where The Moor is today. The football player wears a scarlet shirt and white shorts, the first colours of Sheffield FC.

"The season of 1871-2 has been the most brilliant ever known in Sheffield, and the popularity of the game has been greatly increased by the two great contests played at Bramall lane Ground against London. A great portion of the public consider that to be a player only required one to be what is pithily termed in Sheffield 'soft hard,' but this illusion was dispelled on witnessing the above memorable contests, the dribbling shown and play generally affording a convincing proof that to obtain pre-eminence in football a man must be possessed of speed, science, and bottom."

Sheffield Independent 07 May 1872

Bottom.
1. The posteriors: not now in polite or literary use (1794).
2. Capital, resources, stamina, grit (1662).
3. Spirit placed in a glass prior to the addition of water.
4. To knock the bottom out of one, to overcome, defeat. To stand on one's own bottom, to act for oneself, to be independent.

Slang and Colloquial English. From the library of L. E. HORNING, B.A., Ph.D. (1858-1925) Victoria College

SUPPORTING

10% of the book proceeds will be donated to Prostate Cancer UK

Further copies of this book can be purchased from
www.englandsoldestfootballclubs.com

CONTENTS

Introduction	7
Map: The Birth of Sheffield Football	10
Chapter One: The Search for a Universal Playing Code	**11**
Cambridge Rules 1848	14
Surrey Football Club Rules 1849	16
Sheffield Rules 1858	19
Sheffield Rules 1862	22
The Simplest Game Rules 1862	23
Cambridge University Rules 1863	24
Football Association Laws of 1863	28
The Football Annual 1868	35
Chapter Two: Sheffield Schools	**40**
Ecclesall College	40
Wesley College	40
Collegiate School	40
Chapter Three: Sheffield Volunteer Movement	**44**
Tom Vickers	44
Hallamshire Rifles	45
Chapter Four: Sheffield Football Association	**47**
England's First County Association	47
Sheffield New Football Association	48
Chapter Five: The Golden Age of Sheffield Amateur Football 1857-1876	**53**
1857: Sheffield FC	53
1858: Dingley Dell FC	66
1859: Crusaders FC, Forest FC, Mincing Lane FC	67
1860: Hallam FC, Youdan Cup, World's Oldest Football Ground	68
1861: Norfolk FC, Pitsmoor FC, Norton FC	80
1862: Firvale FC, Heeley FC, Mackenzie FC, Milton FC, Howard Hill Steel Bank FC	87
1863: Broomhall FC	101
1864: The Sheffield Great Flood, Leeds FC, Bradford FC	103
1865: United Mechanics FC	104
1866: Oldest Association Football Clubs by Country, Garrick FC, Wellington FC, Chesterfield FC	107
1867: Wednesday FC, Exchange FC, Dore FC	114
1868: Dronfield FC, Brincliffe FC, Engineers FC (Volunteer Movement)	121

1869: Oxford FC, Parkwood Springs FC	124
1870: Attercliffe FC, Surrey FC, Rotherham FC, Perseverance FC, Walkley New Connexion FC, Crookes FC, Thursday Wanderers FC, Gleadless FC, Lockwood Brothers FC, Alliance FC, Talbot FC	127
1871: Kimberworth FC, Millhouses FC, Exchange Brewery FC, All Saints' Night School FC	143
1872: Brightside FC, Norfolk Works FC, Albion FC, Eldon St Jude's FC, Pye Bank FC	148
1873: Worksop Town FC, Owlerton FC, Philadelphia FC, Endcliffe FC, Rawmarsh FC, Sharrow Rangers FC, Holmes FC, Ecclesfield FC	155
1874: Providence FC, Handsworth Woodhouse FC, Carnforth FC, Woodseats FC, Spital FC	162
1875: Elsecar FC, Whittington Moor FC, Staveley FC	168
1876: Darnall FC, Newfield FC, Mexborough FC, Phoenix Bessemer FC	172

Map: Sheffield Football Clubs 1857- 1873 — 177

Chapter Six: The Decline of the Old Order 1877-1887 — 179

1877: Sheffield New Football Association, Barnsley Wanderers FC, Eckington FC, Hunslet FC	180
1878: The start of the Passing Game, Floodlights at Bramall Lane	187
1879: White Cross FC, Zulus FC, Sheffield Wanderers FC, Doncaster Rovers FC	189
1880: Eckington Works FC	194
1881- 1886 Sheffield resists professionalism	195
1887: Barnsley St. Peters FC	197

Chapter Seven: Football Professionalism and the Football League — 200

Lancashire takes over	200
Football Association Challenge Cup Winners	201
The Football League	204

Chapter Eight: Sheffield embraces Professionalism — 208

The near extinction of Wednesday FC 1887	208
Sheffield Rovers FC	208
Looking for a League	210
Sheffield United Cricket and Football Club 1889	211
The Wednesday reach the F.A. Cup Final 1890	215
Sheffield FC to amalgamate? 1890	218
The First United v. Wednesday derby 1890	219
Professionalism wins an F.A. Cup for Sheffield 1896	220

Conclusion	222
Table One: Sheffield Football Clubs	223
Table Two: Sheffield Football Clubs by date of formation	227
Appendix One: Rules Chronology	231
Appendix Two: Classification Rules for English Football Clubs 1857-1889	237
Notes	241
Bibliography and acknowledgements	247
Index	250

INTRODUCTION

In 1857 there was just one Association Football club in the world; Sheffield FC. Seven years later in 1864, the number of Association football teams in the world was just thirty-three and eleven of those came from Sheffield. In 1867 the Football Association discussed entirely dissolving their organisation because of the apathy to their rules in London, however the game was thriving in Sheffield, which boasted sixteen clubs.

According to F.I.F.A.'s 'Big Count' in 2006, 270 million people (four per cent of the world's population) were actively involved in the game of football. England still had the highest number (as it did in 1864) of football clubs in the world but the number had increased in those 142 years from thirty-three to over 42,000. The total number of football clubs in the world in 2006 was 326,430, with Kazakhstan having one more football club than the entire world could muster back in 1864. The Sheffield and Hallamshire County Football Association alone now has over eight hundred registered clubs.

This book covers the most crucial time in the history of Sheffield football: the first thirty-two years when Sheffield led the world and then nearly disappeared under the pressure of professionalism.

Victorian sporting clubs tended to be select organisations for rowing and cricket but by the 1860s and 1870s these were joined by the sports of swimming, Rugby, athletics and increasingly football. The early football clubs would have been run on the same exclusive rules of membership, with invitations required, forms to be filled and subscriptions to be paid. As time progressed, football clubs were started by different organisations, such as churches, works teams and public houses; as their exclusivity diminished, so the rules became more flexible. However, these early clubs were still dominated by the middle classes with working class clubs extremely rare until the late 1880s and 1890s. These amateur clubs would wane as they became increasingly dependent on maintaining income to survive; this usually meant having an enclosed field of play, so that gate money could be charged.

To enable me to write this book on Sheffield football, I had to first analyse the thousands of English football clubs that were founded between 1857 and 1889. This reclassification gave me a framework against which to measure the accomplishments of the Sheffield game. It soon became clear that 2017 is a very important year for Sheffield football and Association football in general:
- Sheffield FC, the world's oldest football club: 160th anniversary
- Sheffield Wednesday FC, England's third oldest League club: 150th anniversary
- The Youdan Cup, the world's oldest knockout Cup: 150th anniversary
- Sheffield Football Association, England's first County Association: 150th anniversary
- First Sheffield Association Challenge Cup Final Tie: 140th anniversary
- Football Association and Sheffield rules amalgamate: 140th anniversary
- Wednesday FC abandon amateurism and turn professional: 130th anniversary

INTRODUCTION

Just one of these events would be sufficient to generate a newly updated history of Sheffield football; seven anniversaries in the same year could not be ignored.

Using research never-before published, the book will explore all ninety-five clubs that existed between 1857 and 1889, when Sheffield led the world of Association football and was the critical factor in the formulation of modern worldwide Laws and regulations.

This book also features other local clubs' early histories from the surrounding area: Leeds, Bradford, Chesterfield, Rotherham, Rawmarsh, Staveley, Elsecar, Kimberworth, Mexborough, Worksop, Barnsley, Eckington and Doncaster. As well as the impact that Sheffield football had on spreading the Association message to its close neighbours, Sheffield clubs helped the game grow in popularity in Lancashire, Nottinghamshire and Lincolnshire. This book is not just aimed at South Yorkshire and Derbyshire football fans, but for anyone who wants to understand the early development of the world's most popular sport. This is the story of a town that started the (foot)ball rolling, but was then nearly subsumed by the growing tide of professionalism emanating from Lancashire.

I run a website called 'Soccerbilia' which specialises in vintage football newspapers, periodicals and magazines carrying a rich contemporary story of how the game and clubs grew; I wanted to use those resources to create a book about the footballing history of the city in which I grew up. In the future, I plan to use this data to release further books on early football in other English locations. The hope is that this book will generate interest in the many small and local clubs and people involved with early Sheffield football, and inspire further research at the local level. In such a data-rich book such as this, I expect people to spot connections that have eluded me and I look forward to hearing about them. I expect feedback and new information will be unearthed and I hope you will post it at the online forum or contact me to discuss your findings.

To support this book and subsequent books I have a website called: **EnglandsOldestFootballclubs.com** which has further resources.

I can be contacted at:
Email: **Martin@EnglandsOldestFootballclubs.com**

THE BIRTH OF SHEFFIELD FOOTBALL

1. **COLLEGIATE SCHOOL**
   Founded in 1835.

2. **WESLEY COLLEGE**
   The Sheffield Gymnasium was built on adjacent land in 1854.

3. **PARKFIELD HOUSE**
   Home of H. W. Chambers where Sheffield FC was officially founded in 1857.

4. **PARK HOUSE**
   Original headquarters of Sheffield FC; a greenhouse at the house owned by Thomas Asline Ward.

5. **EAST BANK**
   First ground of Sheffield FC and from 1866, Garrick FC.

6. **NORFOLK PARK**
   Norfolk FC formed in 1861 and played in Norfolk Park.
   United Mechanics FC also played here from 1865.

7. **BRAMALL LANE CRICKET GROUND**
   Opened first for cricket in 1855 and hosted its football in 1862.

8. **CREMORNE GARDENS** (Later the 'Orphanage')
   Milton FC played here in 1862.

9. **BROOM HALL**
   Broomhall FC formed in 1863 but played at Ecclesall Road South.

10. **HOUNSFIELD PARK**
    The exact location is unknown but was close to Sheaf House and west of river.
    The new home of Milton FC from 1864 and Wellington FC from 1866.

11. **HIGHFIELD**
    The first ground of Sheffield Wednesday in 1867, just to the east of Cremorne Gardens.

12. **SHEAF HOUSE GARDENS**
    Officially opened in 1870 and Wednesday FC moved here from 1877-1880.

13. **OLIVE GROVE**
    Wednesday FCs penultimate ground from 1887 to 1898 before moving to Hillsborough.

1864 map courtesy of Sheffield Libraries.

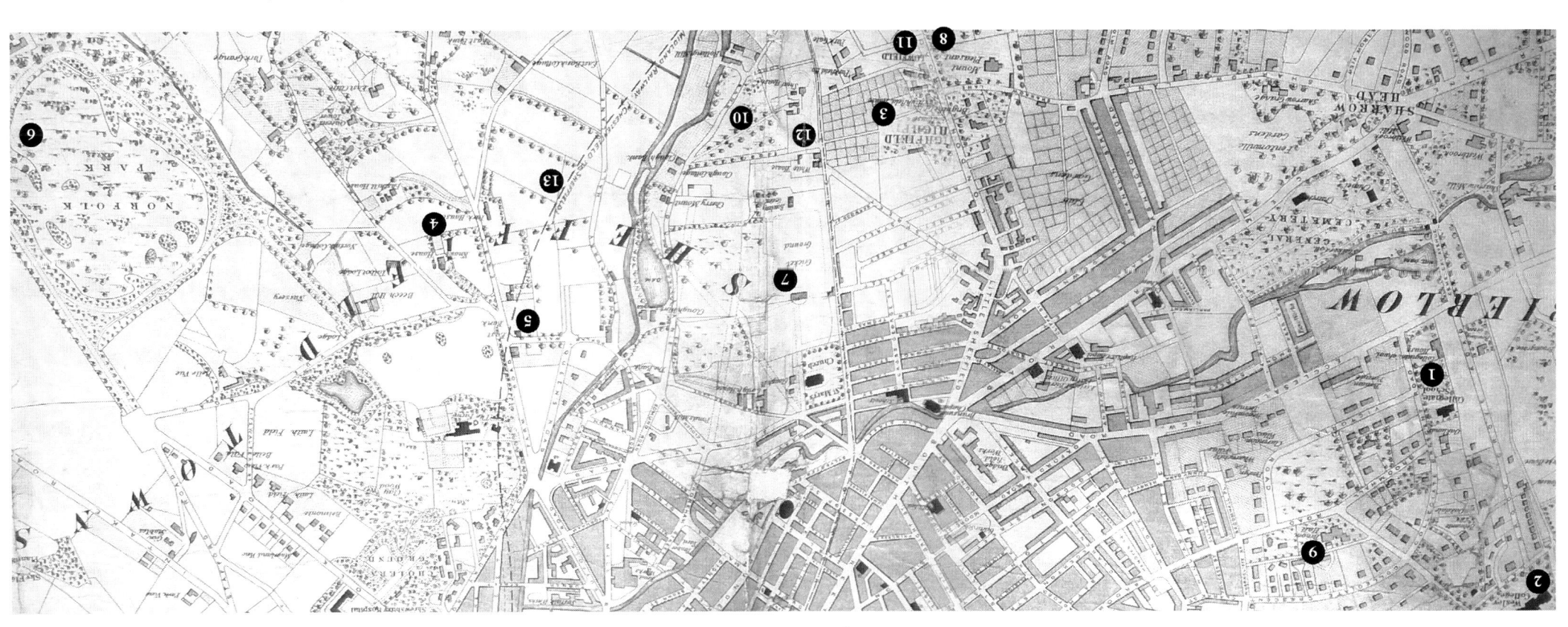

CHAPTER ONE

The Search for a Universal Playing Code

Sheffield had a pivotal role in the evolution of the rules of the Association game, however the first football in England was popular because it had no rules-it was simply an excuse to form a mob and fight with people from within your village (or ideally the village next door). These games were not played by 'Clubs' but by an entire section of any given town or village. The only involvement of 'clubs' were those that were probably used to hit your opponents with during the match! The object of the game was for one side to move a ball from one part of the village to another, whilst another mob tried to achieve the opposite goal. The game took place when people did not have to work, so it happened on annual holidays and in particular, on Shrove Tuesday. Whilst so-called Folk Football or Shrove Football (or probably most accurately Mob Football) was not the 'beautiful game', it was certainly the 'people's game.'

In Anglo-Saxon Britain, the area around Sheffield was known as Hallamshire, a name still in widespread use. In 1609 the Earls of Shrewsbury were the Lords of Hallamshire whose manorial court issued by-laws to stop games of football. Unlike other parts of the north of England there is no long history of Folk Football being played in Sheffield with the earliest reported 'game' played at Bents Green, between Sheffield and Norton in 1793. Back then this would be a grudge match between the two counties of Derbyshire and Yorkshire:

"There were selected six young men of Norton, dressed in green and six young men of Sheffield dressed in red. The play continued for three consecutive days at the arch that was erected at the ground. Those on the Norton side, not being so numerous as those of Sheffield, sent messengers to the Peak and other places in the county of Derby. Then those of Sheffield sent a drum and fife band through the streets of Sheffield to collect more recruits. The fashion then was that all respectable gentlemen, tradesmen and artisans of Sheffield should wear long tails; hence that at the close of the third day's play a general row or struggle took place between the contesting parties. The men of Derbyshire cut and pulled off nearly all the tails from the heads of the gentlemen of Sheffield." [1]

In the first half of the 1800's, Folk Football was considered an unregarded and dying sport mostly due to the increasing industrialisation and urban growth, combined with better law enforcement. For the working class between 1830 and 1870 the only guaranteed national holidays were at Christmas and Easter, not leaving much time for a recreational kickabout. William Hone, in 1838 speaks of 'football and football customs as interesting survivals of past ages than as contemporary pastimes.' [2]

These social changes seemed to influence London and the home counties, but the decline was not so apparent in the north of the country. In July 1831 the Sporting Magazine declared that 'football was the most popular game in a range of northern counties, including Westmoreland, Cumberland, Yorkshire and Lancashire', and in 1842 The Royal Commission on Children in Mines and Manufactories found that football was played widely, but informally, in the West Riding coal fields.

CHAPTER ONE

Folk Football continued in other parts of the north of England during the beginnings of Association football and beyond:
>Laxton, Midlands (1850s)
>Stoneyhurst, Lancashire (1870s)
>Kirkham, Lancashire (1870s)
>Whitby, Yorkshire (1870s)
>Scarborough, Yorkshire (1880s)
>Chester le Street, County Durham (1887 -1900)
>Ilderton, Northumberland (1889 -1900)

Certainly, it continued to flourish in Ashbourne, Derbyshire (thirty-five miles south of Sheffield), where a riot took place in 1860; the newly recruited police force tried to disperse the five hundred or so participants of the Ashbourne Shrovetide Football Match which resulted in 'many of the respectable inhabitants of the town being summoned before the magistrate'; in response, a defence committee was formed and £60.00 was raised to support it.[3] In an analysis of Shrove Football played in Derby in 1846 of the occupations of the 178 players, the vast bulk would be classified as middle ranking and not the expected lower orders. [4]

Sheffield was industrialising fast with the population steadily increasing; at the time of the 1841 census an astounding 60% of British cutlers and 80% of all saw makers worked in and around Sheffield. In the second half of the nineteenth century it would be steel that surpassed cutlery as the major Sheffield industry, whose pioneers were Charles Cammell, Edward Vickers, Thomas Firth, Sir John Brown and Thomas Jessop. In 1851 Samuel Sidney described the industrial environment that would be home to the many working people of Sheffield:

"The town is very ugly and gloomy; it is scarcely possible to say that there is a single good street, or an imposing or interesting public building, - shops, warehouses and factories, and mean houses run zig-zagging up and down the tongues of land, or peninsulas, that extend into the rivers or rather streamlets of the Porter, the Rivling, the Loxley, the Sheaf and the Don." He did however go on to say: "Almost all the merchants and manufacturers reside in the suburbs, in villas built of white stone on terraces commanding a lovely prospect." [5]

This contradiction between the smoky industrial centre of Sheffield surrounded by verdant countryside, is clearly illustrated by the cover of this book. Shrove Football as played by the working people was slowly declining during the 19th century but was increasingly popular among the upper classes in the public school system, as a game to be played in the quad or the school playing field. In terms of violence, there was probably little to choose between two villages fighting for possession of a ball, or two houses at a public school fighting for the ball. Eton old boy G.W Littleton recalled: 'When playing I seldom saw much of the ball but frequently saw and felt the nailed shoes of my adversaries.' [6]

Whilst Folk Football swirled around the people of Sheffield, south and north of them in Derbyshire and Yorkshire, cricket was the early sport of choice with a game played as early as 1771 between Sheffield and Nottingham. Indeed, the Hallam Cricket club is the joint oldest club in the north of England with York, both being established in 1804. Another recognisable footballing name, the Wednesday Cricket club, started in 1820 and the M.C.C. played Sheffield in Darnall in 1825. A general cricket pitch was opened in Hyde Park in 1826 and Sheffield Cricket club was formally founded in 1854, when the Bramall Lane pitch was leased out by the Duke of Norfolk; it would be these cricket clubs, (and many more) that would subsequently start football clubs to keep their players fit during the winter.

It is around this time that the beginning of the separation between the diverse forms of football started to happen, as fermented in the various public schools. The following report from 1866 explains the many differences in rules between the public schools, starting with the differences between the various pitches:

"There are certain principles common, from their simplicity, to all phases of the game. It is played with sides in a 'ground' marked out or enclosed; the object in all is eventually to drive the ball through the 'goal' of the opposing side. The ball is 'out of play' or 'dead' if driven out of the ground, yet not through the goal, and has to be brought back to its place of exit. 'Off side,' 'sneaking,' 'poaching,' 'tagging,' &c., which describe the offence of unfairly passing of the ball from one to another on the same side, are universally forbidden; but beyond these few 'common measures' there is a perplexing variety in the different games." [7]

The criteria for scoring was equally varied:

"Although the ground is always of an oblong shape, the 'goal' varies. In the Winchester game the ground is bounded by canvas screens and ropes, is proportionately narrower than the other grounds, and the whole width of either extremity constitutes 'goal.' In most other games a narrower central space, defined by flags, at either end of the ground is the goal; if the ball passes this line of flags without going between them it is 'behind,' and no goal is won. The Rugbeian system requires the ball to be kicked not only between the goals, but also over a bar, at a certain height from the ground, to win the game. Etonian laws compel the ball to go under a similar line. Most other rules recognise a victory when the ball passes between the flags, at any height from the ground." [7]

Next there is a choice of balls: "The Etonian ball is small and light, suitable for being kept on the ground, and 'bullied' through the forest of legs, where a larger orb might find difficulty in passing. The Harrow ball is about the largest. That used in the Rugbeian style of games is more oval than round, which renders it a favourite where long kicking is practised." [7]

As to the numbers employed in a game: "...eleven or fifteen suffice at Eton and Winchester; tens or even hundreds may engage at Rugby in the great matches, but twenty a side is usual array. In commencing the game at Harrow and Rugby the ball is 'kicked off' from the middle of the ground; at Eton and Winchester the commencement is a 'bully' or 'hot'- all the players en masse, shoulder to shoulder- in the centre of the ground." [7]

Handling the ball was acceptable to all school games but by differing degrees, according to this article:

"'Handing' or 'holding' is altogether prohibited by Etonians. The hands may never be used by them except to stop the ball, keep it down to the feet, or touch in a 'rouge.' The Rugbeian code- the opposite extreme- by a new rule allows the ball to be held even when picked up off the ground; he who has it may, at his peril, run with it into the opposite base, with a view to a 'touch' and 'try at goal,' hereafter to be explained. Harrovians permit a 'fair catch' if the ball is killed, i.e., driven from below the knee, though in its passage it may glance off any other part of the body, provided it does not touch the ground. He who catches may claim a 'free kick' if he calls at once 'three yards,' otherwise he is liable to have his prey knocked out of his hands. Wykehamists allow a 'free' kick from a fair catch, if it can be got; hence in this case they suspend their rule disallowing running with the ball, so far as to afford the catcher the power of, getting his kick with a three yards' run if he can, and also allow 'holding' to stop him for the moment, but the instant he has his course clear, or the ball has been kicked, further privileges of holding or running come to an end." [7]

It would be the debate over whether to allow hacking (the kicking of your opponents) that would define the 1863 debate when the Football Association was created:

CHAPTER ONE

"'Shinning' or 'hacking' is variously allowed or disallowed. The Rugby school of players uphold and countenance it, as a necessary means of forcing the ball through the dense masses that play in such games, and one who runs with the ball may be hacked ad lib, but most other schools taboo it, as unsatisfactory and unnecessary." [7]

The article makes it plain that no school played to anything resembling a modern day 90-minute game:

"Many other differences in the mode of play might be enumerated; and these, of course, all have their effect upon the length of time occupied in each game. Three days may elapse in a great Rugby match before a goal is won. Etonian and Harrovian games are more rapid, and two or three may be played in an afternoon. Winchester games occasionally last only a few minutes; or a dozen can be played in one match." [7]

Some schools predominantly used their hands and some their feet; modern day Association Football evolved from the 'dribbling code' and Rugby Union evolved from the 'handling code.' Rugby League would be formed by a split from Union in 1895 over the issue of professionalism. In Ireland, Gaelic Football is a blend of Rugby and Association and was formalised in 1884. In Australia, a mixture of Gaelic Football and Rugby played on cricket pitches became Australian Rules football. In America, Association was the game first played; this was influenced by the Rugby-playing French Canadians and became American Football. Over time, their game changed from the Canadian rules and there are now two distinct set of rules, completing the seven types of football played around the world today. Of these seven, only Association Football and Gaelic Football play with a round ball, the other five use an ovoid ball. Of course, it is only Association Football of the seven that does not allow handling of the ball, except by the goal keeper. It is interesting that even though in a minority, it is this game based on the 'dribbling code' that has become the global game.

Cambridge Rules 1848

In 1848 two Shrewsbury school boys, would write a set of rules that would start the process towards Association Football. Henry de Winton (1823-1895) was born in Hay, on the Welsh and English border and went to Shrewsbury School. Here he met John Charles Thring and together they went on to further their education at Cambridge. Thring (1824-1909) had been to school at Winchester and went up to St. John's College in 1843. Together with some old Etonians they formed a Cambridge Football Club probably in 1844 or 1845 (or at least before 1846, when Winton graduated). In 1848 they wrote the earliest extant rules of football. An account of the eight hours involved in the drawing up of the Cambridge Rules comes from Mr. H.C. Malden in a letter dated 8 October 1897:

"G. Salt and myself were chosen for the 'Varsity. I wish I could remember the others. Burn of Rugby, was one; Whymper of Eton, I think, also. We were 14 in all I believe. Harrow and Eton Rugby, Winchester, Shrewsbury were represented. We met in my rooms after Hall, which in those days was at 4.pm. Anticipating a long meeting, I cleared the tables and provided pens, ink and paper. Several asked me on coming in whether an exam was on! Every man brought a copy of his school rules, or knew them by heart, and our progress in framing new rules was slow. On several occasions, Salt and I, being unprejudiced, carried or struck out a rule when the voting was equal. We broke up five minutes before midnight. The new rules were printed as the 'Cambridge Rules', copies were distributed and pasted up on Parker's Piece, and very satisfactorily they worked, for it is right to add that they were loyally kept, and I never heard of any public school man who gave up playing from not liking the rules. [...] Well Sir, years afterwards someone took these rules, still in force at Cambridge, and with a very few alterations they became the Association Rules."

No copy of the 1848 rules survives but the following set of University Rules, circa 1856, still exists in the library of Shrewsbury School.

The Laws of the University Foot Ball Club

1. This club shall be called the University Foot Ball Club.
2. At the commencement of the play, the ball shall be kicked off from the middle of the ground: after every goal there shall be a kick-off in the same way.
3. After a goal, the losing side shall kick off; the sides changing goals, unless a previous arrangement be made to the contrary.
4. The ball is out when it has passed the line of the flag-posts on either side of the ground, in which case it shall be thrown in straight.
5. The ball is behind when it has passed the goal on either side of it.
6. When the ball is behind it shall be brought forward at the place where it left the ground, not more than ten paces, and kicked off.
7. Goal is when the ball is kicked through the flag-posts and under the string.
8. When a player catches the ball directly from the foot, he may kick it as he can without running with it. In no other case may the ball be touched with the hands, except to stop it.
9. If the ball has passed a player, and has come from the direction of his own goal, he may not touch it till the other side have kicked it, unless there are more than three of the other side before him. No player is allowed to loiter between the ball and the adversaries' goal.
10. In no case is holding a player, pushing with the hands, or tripping up allowed. Any player may prevent another from getting to the ball by any means consistent with the above rules.
11. Every match shall be decided by a majority of goals.

The Cambridge Rules would be involved in the discussions in London when the Football Association was trying to create a universal code in 1863, and their importance is such that the F.A. has since declared that the Cambridge Rules are the oldest and first football rules. (Eton Field Rules do predate Cambridge Rules by some thirty-three years but presumably the F.A. recognised that they had too much in common with the Rugby code). Rule nine is interesting because this is a very relaxed offside rule, allowing forward passing if there are at least three opponents in front of you. This interpretation resembles modern laws but would be ignored by the Football Association in 1863; they would follow the much stricter off side rules devised initially at Harrow School, right up to 1866 when they changed to one more like the Sheffield Rules. Harrow Rules were written in 1853 and stated that it was unlawful to receive the ball from a forward pass which meant that the best way to advance the ball up the pitch towards your opponent's goal was to dribble; this meant that the ball needed to be round, not ovoid. The other alternative was to form your players diagonally down the pitch and then pass the ball backwards along the line from dribbler to dribbler. The first house game of 'footer' at Harrow was played in October 1832 on their clay playing field and according to legend, it was this tricky playing surface that created so many gifted Harrovian dribblers of the ball, who would go on to illuminate the Association game.

Surrey Football Club Rules 1849

Surrey County Cricket Club was founded on the evening of 22 August 1845 at the Horns Tavern, where around hundred representatives of various cricket clubs of Surrey agreed a motion put by William Denison (the club's first secretary) that a Surrey club be now formed. The Surrey Football Club was formed in September 1849 as an offshoot of the Surrey Cricket Club and all the various cricket clubs that played at the Kennington Oval. If the football club had continued playing and evolved into an Association Club, it would be recognised as the world's oldest football club, (instead of Sheffield FC), by some eight years. In a process that would be repeated many times over by Sheffield cricket clubs in the future, Surrey County Cricket Club looked to football to be the 'winter game' that could help their players keep fit throughout the year:

"THE SURREY CLUB- KENNINGTON OVAL. - The numbers of this and of other clubs on this ground will hold their first winter weekly meeting on Wednesday next, at eight o'clock, when arrangements will be made for the formation of a foot-ball club, which it is intended to carry on during the winter and spring months. It has therefore, been requested that the members will muster in strong force upon the occasion." (8)

In the following month of October 1849, the club laid out its agenda:

"THE SURREY CLUB. On Wednesday, the first 'weekly' winter meetings of this club was held at the Oval, where there was a numerous attendance. In the course of the evening Mr. Denison, who occupied the chair on the occasion, stated that they were well aware that by means of the devotion of the Oval to the purposes of cricket the formation of a county club had been accomplished, and that they had been enabled in four years to resuscitate the game in Surrey so far as nearly to have placed her within that brief period in her former high position as a cricketing county. But there was another healthful vigorous game for which certain parts of Surrey had in bygone days been somewhat celebrated- namely, 'foot-ball.'" (9)

Interestingly, the article lays out the early history of football:

"Some 60 years ago there was a gymnastic society, which had been established by gentlemen who were natives of Westmoreland and Cumberland, for the cultivation and practice of their favourite sports 'wrestling' and 'foot-ball.' The first named of those sports the society had carried on upon the bowling green attached to the Belvedere Tavern at Pentonville: but the latter game was practiced upon Kensington Common, where matches for small and large sums were played in the course of each year: the last of these contests had taken place in the summer of 1789, when twenty-two gentlemen of Cumberland for one thousand guineas; after a severe contest the gentlemen of the former county proved victorious. This was the last great match that was made, for, as several of her leading members retired from business, and went to live, some in the north and two in Gloucestershire; the 'Gymnastic society' was dissolved. Since that period, except on two or three days in the year, the wrestling and foot-ball play continued to dwindle, until at length Good Friday became the only day upon which they were brought into operation. Of these exhibitions, Kennington Common still remained the scene for many years. At last, however, the wrestling was taken to private grounds, amongst which were those attached to a tavern at Kentish Town, then to the Byre Arms, St John's Wood, and at Highbury Barn, and eventually at Copenhagen house, where the matches were played in the present year. The football playing had been abandoned in consequence of the want of room at the places where the other game had been taken to, and the result was that its practice had been discontinued in the neighbourhood of the metropolis. The only locality where the game could now be said to exist near to London was that of Kingston." [9]

Specifically, membership of the new club was limited only to the cricket clubs that used the Oval ground:

"Well, then, as the Surrey Club had resuscitated cricket at the Oval, he was anxious that that body should restore the equally healthful game of foot-ball: also so that district (hear, hear): with that view he had drawn out some rules, which he would now admit for the approval of and adoption by that meeting. By the first of those rules it would be seen, he proposed that the members of the Foot-ball club should be confined to those gentlemen who belonged to one or other of the cricket clubs which met at the Oval (hear, hear). The rules were then read, and having been approved of, Mr. F. Noad moved that they be adopted. Mr. White seconded the notion, which was then unanimously agreed to. The days for practice are every Wednesday and Saturday (the weather permitting), commencing in the first week in October, and then ending in the last week in April in each year. The gentlemen enrolled themselves as members." [9]

The rules the club members subscribed to were as follows.

Surrey Football Club Rules

1. *The Club to only consist of such gentlemen as are members of the Surrey Cricket Club, Surrey Paragon Cricket Club, South London Cricket Club and the Union Cricket Club.*
2. *That subscriptions of five shillings to any of the above named gentlemen shall entitle him to all the privileges of Surrey Football Club. That the money so subscribed shall be appropriated to the defrayal of the expenses of the club, namely, of balls and ropes, and the payment of a person who shall keep them in a proper condition. The members shall dine together at the end of the season, and any surplus in subscriptions which may then be on hand, after the payment of expenses shall be applied to such dinner.*
3. *That the days for practice (weather permitting) shall be every Wednesday and Saturday in the afternoon, commencing on the week of October and continuing until the last week of April, in each year; the play to begin at 3'o clock…*
4. *That the side shall consist of not more than 22 each, but if that number shall not be in attendance then of any smaller number to be arranged by those present.*
5. *That wilful kicking shall not be allowed.*
6. *That the ball shall be tossed up in the centre of the ground, and the game determined in favour of that side which shall first kick the ball over the "goal ropes" of their opponents. Should the ball be kicked over the fence on either side of the ground, then the ball, when regained, shall be tossed up in the centre of the ground, in line with the place where it went out.*

Away from the gentlemanly pursuits of Surrey cricket and football in the 1840s, the working men of Sheffield had much more serious things to think about than whether there would be enough surplus subscription money to provide a decent dinner at the end of the season. The working conditions were horrendous in the town's factories; a book written in 1844 details the hardships:

CHAPTER ONE

"By far the most unwholesome work is the grinding of knife-blades and forks, which, especially when done with a dry stone, entails certain early death. The unwholesomeness of this work lies in part in the bent posture, in which chest and stomach are cramped; but especially in the quantity of sharp-edged metal dust particles freed in the cutting, which fill the atmosphere, and are necessarily inhaled. The dry grinders' average life is hardly thirty-five years, the wet grinders' rarely exceeds forty-five. Dr. Knight, in Sheffield, says: 'I can convey some idea of the injuriousness of this occupation only by asserting that the hardest drinkers among the grinders are the longest lived among them, because they are longest and oftenest absent from their work. There are, in all, some 2,500 grinders in Sheffield. About 150 (80 men and 70 boys) are fork grinders; these die between the twenty-eighth and thirty-second years of age. The razor grinders, who grind wet as well as dry, die between forty and forty-five years, and the table cutlery grinders, who grind wet, die between fortieth and fiftieth year.'" [10]

Dr. Knight continued with the following description of the course of the disease called grinders' asthma:

"They usually begin their work in the fourteenth year, and if they have good constitutions, rarely notice any symptoms before the twentieth year. Then the symptoms of their peculiar disease appear. They suffer from shortness of breath at the slightest effort in going up hill or up stairs, they habitually raise the shoulders to relieve the permanent and increasing want of breath; they bend forward, and seem, in general, to feel most comfortable in the crouching position in which they work. Their complexion becomes dirty yellow, their features express anxiety, they complain of pressure on the chest. Their voices become rough and hoarse, they cough loudly, and the sound is as if air were driven through a wooden tube. From time to time they expectorate considerable quantities of dust, either mixed with phlegm or in balls or cylindrical masses, with a thin coating of mucus. Spitting blood, inability to lie down, night sweat, colliquative diarrhoea, unusual loss of flesh, and all the usual symptoms of consumption of the lungs finally carry them off, after they have lingered months or even years, unfit to support themselves or those dependent upon them. I must add that all attempts which have hitherto been made to prevent grinders' asthma, or to cure it, have wholly failed.' All this Knight wrote ten years ago; since then the number of grinders and the violence of the disease have increased, though attempts have been made to prevent it by covered grindstones and carrying off the dust by artificial draught. These methods have been at least partially successful, but the grinders do not desire their adoption, and have even destroyed the contrivance here and there, in the belief that more workers may be attracted to the business and wages thus reduced; they are for a short life and a merry one. Dr. Knight has often told grinders who came to him with the first symptoms of asthma that a return to grinding means certain death, but with no avail. He who is once a grinder falls into despair, as though he had sold himself to the devil..." [10]

The morals of the young people of Sheffield were also a cause for concern in 1844:

"Immorality among young people seems more prevalent in Sheffield than anywhere else. ... The younger generation spend the whole of Sunday lying in the street tossing coins or fighting dogs, go regularly to the gin palace, where they sit with their sweethearts until late at night, when they take walks in solitary couples. In an ale-house which the commissioner visited, there sat forty to fifty young people of both sexes, nearly all under seventeen years of age, and each lad beside his lass. Here and there cards were played, at other places dancing was going on, and everywhere drinking. Among the company were openly avowed professional prostitutes. No wonder, then, that, as all the witnesses testify, early, unbridled sexual intercourse, youthful prostitution, beginning with persons of fourteen to fifteen years, is extraordinarily frequent in

Sheffield. Crimes of a savage and desperate sort are of common occurrence; one year before the commissioner's visit, a band, consisting chiefly of young persons, was arrested when about to set fire to the town, being fully equipped with lances and inflammable substances." [10]

Whilst the working classes were working and playing hard, Sheffield business was booming; the Sheffield region produced 90% of British steel and nearly half the entire European output. It was estimated in 1871, Brown's and Cammel's alone exported to the United States about three times more than the whole American output.[11] Exercise and sport were considered to be a solution to the poor living standards of Sheffield and one of the major steps that would have a long-term impact on sport in Sheffield was the building of Bramall Lane Cricket ground on January 30th 1854:

"A public meeting was held at the Adelphi Hotel, Arundel Street, on Monday Evening, to consider the offer made by his Grace the Duke of Norfolk, of the appropriation of a piece of ground to the purpose of a public cricket ground. Amongst those present were Messrs. T. R. Barker, M. J. Ellison, R. F. Skelton, J. P. Burbeary, J. P. Prest, W. Prest, &c. Mr. Ellison was called to the chair." [12]

It is fascinating to see at this meeting, the presence of 'W. Prest' because three years later he would be instrumental in the next stage of the evolution of the rules of football. On 24th October 1857 Nathaniel Creswick (1831-1917), a solicitor and William Prest (1832-1885), a wine merchant, formed 'Sheffield Foot-ball Club.' Creswick and Prest's occupations confirm that they were certainly upper middle class but tellingly, an analysis of founding members showed that it was almost devoid of former public school men. [13] The Sheffield Daily Telegraph described the club in 1867: '...as almost exclusively of the middle class.' Intriguingly however, Prest's brother Edward, was at St John's College, Cambridge, where he was an exact contemporary of John Charles Thring. Indirect knowledge of the Cambridge game may therefore have influenced the overall shape of the Sheffield rules. [14]

What follows is from a Sheffield FC club manuscript written in 1907:

"After season 1857-8 the Hon. Sec. Nathaniel Creswick and committee drew up printed rules, regulations and laws for the club, and from these is to be seen that game was half rugby and half association." [15]

Sheffield Rules 1858

Based on the original manuscripts from the club, the rules were produced, at the earliest, in March 1858 after their first season of football, and were written down officially in 21 October 1858 at the club's first A.G.M.

1. *The kick off from the middle must be a place kick.*
2. *Kick out must not be more than 25 yards out of goal.*
3. *A fair catch is a catch from any player provided the ball has not touched the ground or has not been thrown from touch and is entitled to a free-kick. (Revised in the course of the meetings to read: Fair Catch is a Catch from any player provided the Ball has not touched the ground and has not been thrown from touch and entitles a free kick).*
4. *Charging is fair in case of a place kick (with the exception of a kick off as soon as a player offers to kick) but he may always draw back unless he has actually touched the ball with his foot.*

CHAPTER ONE

5. Pushing with the hands is allowed but no hacking or tripping up is fair under any circumstances whatever. (Revised in the course of the meetings to read: Pushing with the Hands is allowed but no Hacking (or tripping up) is fair under any circumstances whatsoever).
6. No player may be held or pulled over.
7. It is not lawful to take the ball off the ground (except in touch) for any purpose whatever.
8. Knocking or pushing on the Ball is altogether disallowed. The side breaking this Rule forfeits a free kick to the opposite side. (Extensively revised in several stages in the course of the meetings, finally reading: Holding the Ball (excepting in case of a free kick) is altogether disallowed).
9. If the Ball be bouncing it may be stopped by the Hand (not pushed or hit) but if rolling it may not be stopped except by the foot (extensively revised in several stages in the course of the meetings, and eventually expunged - see below).
10. (New Rule 9.) No Goal may be kicked from touch nor by a free kick from a catch. (Revised in the course of the meetings to read: A Goal must be kicked but not from touch nor by a free kick from a catch).
11. (New Rule 10). A Ball in touch is dead. Consequently, the side that touches it down, must bring it to the edge of touch, & throw it straight out at least six yards from touch.
12. Each player must provide himself with a red and dark blue flannel cap, one colour to be worn by each side.

The amended version of these eleven rules (with the original laws 6 and 9 removed, and the addition of the new law agreed on the 28th of October 1858) was then printed for the use of club members, as had also been agreed. The 'manuscript minute book' from May 1858 to early 1859 and other documents were sold by Sotheby's for £881,250.00 in July 2011. This archive was sold to an anonymous telephone bidder and it has not since re-emerged; either it has been locked away for investment purposes, or perhaps it will reappear as a spectacular element of a future major footballing event.

Sheffield FC's first Honourable Secretary (Hon. Sec.), William Chesterman kept the club records at his works, which were demolished in the Great Flood of 1864, when two hundred and fifty lives were lost in Sheffield; almost impossibly these documents survived and were recovered later. [16] (Later in 1880 William Chesterman, by now Master Cutler, lost a second business premises, when the Bow Works, Pomona Street, was destroyed by fire.)

There are conflicting accounts for the inspiration of the rules but in 1907, at the club's Silver Jubilee, Nathaniel Creswick gave a speech saying 'that they had written to Eton, Harrow, Winchester, Westminster, Rugby and some others, and a lot of different rules they obtained.' The record of the speech notes that this comment 'prompted laughter.' [17]

Footballing rules for gentlemen may have been gaining prominence but if the wrong types of people played football in public they were still likely to be stopped by the authorities. The following is a report of an illegal game played in Wentworth about ten miles north of Sheffield:

"Playing at football on the turnpike – James Collier, Charles Jessop, and Benjamin Birks were charged with playing at football on the turnpike road in the village of Wentworth, on the night of Monday the 5th June. Constable Airey said there were from twenty to thirty young fellows playing and he warned them to desist, but they took no notice of him... Mr. Whitfield, for the defence, said they had always been used to play in the streets and did not know they were doing wrong – Fined 2s.6d. each and costs." [18]

Back down south a few weeks after Sheffield Football Club had published their rules, a letter was published in the 'The Portico', the in-house magazine of Harrow School:

"FOOTBALL. TO THE EDITOR OF THE PORTICO. EDITOR, —You would favour me much if you would insert in your next number of The Portico this short letter. Would it not be much better if there were settled rules and laws for the game of football, —such as have been, for many years past, founded for the game of cricket? Rules which public schools, universities, and the few clubs that there are at present, might follow; which might be kept with the greatest strictness, and adhered to by all players. At the present time the rules of no two public schools, in this game, at all agree; in fact, I do not hesitate in saying that, at different schools, the game is often entirely different, and would scarcely be recognized by a boy going from one to another. Hence, in the winter, the public schools are united by no annual or even casual match; nor are the universities able to join in this sport, as in cricket, with public schools. Now why should not this game be universal? And why should the rules of it remain different and unaltered at every school? I sincerely wish that the laws could be changed, for boys would play with much more spirit and energy if they knew that there was some important match to be won every year; and therefore it seems to be a pity that every opening should not be given towards the advancement of this manly game, and the making it more universal than it is at the present time. It is not improbable that if general laws were founded, more clubs would be formed in different parts of the kingdom; and the game, in course of time, would become of as much note as cricket is at the present time. Perhaps some would say that football could never be sought so much as cricket; but I think they would find that if those who have both enjoyed, and were skilled in this game during their stay at a public school, had more opportunity of playing in the remainder of their life, no doubt the game would become very popular; and I think that the establishment of fixed laws would be a great assistance towards its general advancement. I hope that this letter may agree with the opinions of some of your readers, and that this game may soon become more universal, —a consummation which has been, and always will be, the ardent desire of

A LOVER OF FOOTBALL, THE PORTICO, VOL. II, No. XIII. —JANUARY 1, 1859."

It is romanticism on my part, but it would be very appropriate if this letter had been penned by Charles W. Alcock, who would graduate from Harrow in 1859, form Forest FC (the third oldest football club in the world, later becoming the Wanderers FC) and go on to be the most influential man in the development of Association football. Certainly, he had a very similar florid style of writing in his future career of journalist and writer of match reports. Whoever the correspondent, his prescient view that football would be improved by having 'some important match to be won every year,' pre-dates the launch of the Football Association Cup by some twelve years.

Another public request for a unified code came in a letter also in 1859 from Fred Lillywhite (Cricketer and Sports Outfitters) to the editor of 'Bell's Life in London and Sporting Chronicle':

"Mr. Editor: It is my intention to publish, in the next edition of the Guide to Cricketers, the laws and rules of all the sports of athletic games which are enjoyed in this country. Among them, of course, will be football: therefore, if Eton and Rugby, as well as other colleges and schools, would form themselves into a committee and arrange that one code of laws could be acknowledged throughout the world, it would be a great benefit to all, as is the case with cricket. Yours, etc., Fred Lillywhite. 2 New Coventry Street, Leicester Square." [19]

Buying an actual football from Lillywhites was a serious investment in 1859:

"Footballs, 10s. 6d., 12s.6d., and 15s. each. ...Apply John Lilywhite's Cricket Warehouse, 5 Seymour Street, Euston Square, N.W." [19]

(Fred and John Lillywhite were cousins of the Alcock brothers and John Forster Alcock (brother of Charles) would attend the inaugural meeting of the Football Association on the 26th October 1863)

The discussion about the standardization of the football rules became heated and led to the 'Bell's Life in London and Sporting Chronicle' declaring in 1859:

"We have received many other letters on this subject from public schoolmen, but they are so mixed up with abuse of each other that we consider them better unpublished, and the correspondence closed. The inference seems to be that it will undoubtedly be unadvisable for different schools to meet at this game. We should have seen with some pleasure some proposition for a generalisation of the rules, but there seems no disposition to concession on any side." [20]

In spite of these requests to standardise the game rules, the row rumbled on, as a correspondent to 'Bell's Life in London' wrote in 1861, football's 'rules are as various as the number of places in which it is played'.

From 1861 to early 1863, J.D. Cartwright of 'The Field' started printing various public school football codes to maintain the agenda of a common code and discussed their relative merits. Meanwhile in Yorkshire and seemingly oblivious to the furore, Sheffield FC continued to hone the playing rules they had devised three years prior and in 1862 they published a much more sophisticated code which was adopted by the ten Sheffield clubs which had by now sprung up.

Sheffield Rules 1862

1. The kick from the middle must be a place kick.
2. Kick Out must not be more than 10 yards out of goal.
3. A Fair Catch is a catch from any player provided the ball has not touched the ground or has not been thrown from touch and is entitled to a free-kick.
4. Charging is fair in case of a place kick (with the exception of a kick off as soon as a player offers to kick) but he may always draw back unless he has actually touched the ball with his foot.
5. Pushing with the hands is allowed but no hacking or tripping up is fair under any circumstances whatsoever.
6. No player may be held or pulled over.
7. It is not lawful to take the ball off the ground (except in touch) for any purpose whatever.
8. Holding the ball (except in the case of a free kick) or knocking or pushing it on with the hand or arm is altogether disallowed.
9. A goal cannot be obtained by free kick or catch.
10. When the ball is in touch, the side that first touches it must bring it to the edge of the touch at the place where it went in, and throw it straight out at least six yards, and it must touch the ground before it reaches any player.

11. A "Rouge" is obtained by the player who first touches the ball after it has been kicked between the rouge flags, and when a rouge has been obtained one of the defending side must stand post two yards in front of the goal sticks.
12. No rouge is obtained when a player who first touches the ball is on the defending side. In that case it is a kick out as specified in law 2.
13. No player who is behind the line of the goal sticks when the ball is kicked behind, may touch is in any way, either to prevent or obtain a rouge.
14. A goal outweighs any number of rouges. Should no goals or an equal number be obtained, the match is decided by rouges.
15. If, in playing a match, half the specified time shall expire without a goal being obtained, the sides shall change goals; the kick off being from the middle, as at the commencement of the game. In practice matches one hour shall be the limit.
16. In setting out the ground, the goal sticks must be placed 12 feet apart, and the cross bar 9 feet from the ground. The rouge flags must be placed one on each side and in line with the goal, and 12 feet distance from the goal.
17. Each player must provide himself with a red and dark blue flannel cap, one colour to be worn by each side during play.

(A 'Rouge' is a touch down or try across the rouge line that extended twelve yards either side of the goal and was used to settle low goal scoring games. Goals outweighed rouges but were used if the game finished in a tie.)

By 1859 Charles Thring was an assistant master at Uppingham Grammar School, where his brother Edward was headmaster; he tried again to establish a shared set of regulations that could encourage games between different schools and launched a more specific set of rules than his previous effort, entitled 'The Simplest Game.'

The Simplest Game Rules 1862

1. A goal is scored whenever the ball is forced through the goal and under the bar, except it be thrown by the hand.
2. Hands may be used only to stop a ball and place it on round before the feet.
3. Kicks must be aimed only at the ball.
4. A player may not kick the ball whilst in the air.
5. No tripping up or heel kicking allowed.
6. Whenever a ball is kicked beyond the side flags, it must be returned by the player who kicked it, from the spot it passed the flag-line in a straight line towards the middle of the ground.
7. When a ball is kicked behind the line of goal, it shall be kicked off from that line by one of the side whose goal it is.
8. No player may stand within six places of the kicker when he is kicking off.
9. A player is out of play immediately he is in front of the ball and must return behind the ball as soon as possible. If the ball is kicked by his own side past a player, he may

not touch it, or advance, until one of the other side has first kicked it, or one of his own side, having followed it up, has been able, when in front of him, to kick it.

10) *No charging is allowed when a player is out of play.*

'The Simplest Game' rules were used in an eleven a side game between Old Harrovians and Old Etonians at Cambridge in 1862. Playing that day was Charles W. Alcock for the Harrow team. [21] Whilst Charles did not officially attend the inaugural Football Association meeting in 1863 his brother John, and fellow Harrovian, certainly did. Charles Thring amended 'The Simplest Game' rules again and these were then known as the 1863 Cambridge University Rules which would eventually be presented at the fourth meeting of the fledgling Football Association in 1863.

Cambridge University Rules 1863

1. *The length of the ground shall not be more than 150 yds. and the breadth not more than 100 yds. The ground shall be marked out by posts and two posts shall be placed on each side-line at distances of 25 yds. from each goal line.*
2. *The GOALS shall consist of two upright poles at a distance of 15 ft. from each other.*
3. *The choice of goals and kick-off shall be determined by tossing and the ball shall be kicked off from the middle of the ground.*
4. *In a match when half the time agreed upon has elapsed, the side shall change goals when the ball is next out of play. After such change or a goal obtained, the kick off shall be from the middle of the ground in the same direction as before. The time during which the game shall last and the numbers in each side are to be settled by the heads of the sides.*
5. *When a player has kicked the ball any one of the same side who is nearer to the opponent's goal line is OUT OF PLAY and may not touch the ball himself nor in any way whatsoever prevent any other player from doing so.*
6. *When the ball goes out of the ground by crossing the side lines, it is out of play and shall be kicked straight into the ground again from the point where it first stopped.*
7. *When a player has kicked the ball beyond the opponents' goal line, whoever first touches the ball when it is on the ground with his hand, may have a FREE kick bringing the ball straight out from the goal line.*
8. *No player may touch the ball behind his opponents' goal line who is behind it when the ball is kicked there.*
9. *If the ball is touched down behind the goal line and beyond the line of the side-posts, the FREE kick shall be from the 25 yds. post.*
10. *When a player has a free-kick, no-one of his own side may be between him and his opponents' goal line and no one of the opposing side may stand within 10 yds. of him.*
11. *A free kick may be taken in any manner the player may choose.*
12. *A goal is obtained when the ball goes out of the ground by passing between the poles or in such a manner that it would have passed between them had they been of sufficient height.*

13. *The ball, when in play may be stopped by any part of the body, but it may NOT be held or hit by the hands, arms or shoulders.* *

14. *ALL charging is fair; but holding, pushing with the hands, tripping up and shinning are forbidden.* *

*These are the two controversial rules that would come to define the Football Association debate in 1863.

It was early 1863 when the debate over standardising the rules of football re-emerged once again in the letters pages of the London newspapers; this time it was from Ebenezer Cobb Morley (1831-1924), a London solicitor, proposing 'an association of football clubs, to allow matches to be organised under an agreed code of rules.' At the same time as writing to the newspapers, Morley (who was not a public school boy) wrote to the major public schools receiving only the same lukewarm response as Fred Lillywhite had received four years earlier. (One would have thought Morley, a Yorkshireman from Hull would have been aware of his compatriots in Sheffield, who over five years earlier had published their own Sheffield Rules, but he didn't contact them.) Six years, almost to the day, from when Sheffield FC was formed, the London Football Association was founded.

Ebenezer Cobb Morley
Image courtesy of the National Football Museum

On Monday 26 October 1863, a meeting was arranged with the object of establishing a code of rules for the regulation of football. Ebenezer Morley was the acting secretary at the meeting as well as a representative of Barnes FC; the acting chairman was Arthur Pember representing N.N. Kilburn. Pember was born in Lambeth, London; he had an interesting career which included barrister and New York Times journalist. What is striking is that this was not a meeting of old men discussing the relative merits of ancient rules, but a group of young men looking to move away from the confusion of the past. The meeting went ahead with thirteen clubs represented all from the London area and a representative from Charterhouse School, at the Freemason's Tavern in Great Queen Street, near to where Holborn tube station is now. (This location might indicate that the prominent movers and shakers of the early football movement worked in this area which would suggest the legal, accountancy and financial fields. It was also a known rendezvous for old Harrovians, as an anniversary meeting took place on the 4th July 1860 at the Tavern, chaired by the Archbishop of York with Sir Robert Peel in attendance.)

The October 1863 meeting is portrayed from a modern perspective as a seismic moment in the evolution of the Association game but I think that the outcome of the Freemason's Tavern meeting was a political victory for the ball-dribbling fraternity and the matter remained far from settled. Whilst creating the Association code they wanted (Cambridge Rules), they alienated the Rugby clubs, who went from strength to strength from that point; it wasn't until 1871 and

CHAPTER ONE

the introduction of knockout football (in the form of the F.A. Cup) that Association football started to take off in its own right. History has always insisted that twelve clubs attended the Freemason's Tavern but I have found a newspaper report that states a thirteenth club (Dingley Dell FC) was also present. Interestingly a later book states: 'and it is recorded that there were several other gentlemen present interested in the subject, but who, although players, did not definitely represent any Club.' [22]

The thirteen clubs and their delegates were:

1) **Perceval House,** Dartmouth Row, Blackheath. Mr. George William Shillingford (4 October 1844- 27 July 1896). Age at meeting, 19. Secretary. A proponent of hacking who would leave at the fifth meeting.

2) **Kensington School,** Mr. William John Mackintosh (14 July 1845 - 16 November 1923). Captain. Age at meeting, 18.

3) **Crystal Palace,** (no relation to the modern League Club), Mr. James Turner (6 December 1839 - 27 July 1922). Age at meeting, 24. A Crystal Palace player throughout the 1860s right up to the first F.A. Cup tournament, he was F.A. treasurer 1864-68, attended the F.A.'s jubilee dinner in 1913 and was presented with a silver casket as one of only three surviving members of the original meeting. Mr. Francis Day (Feb/March 1838 -12 March 1886). Secretary. Age at meeting, 25.

4) **Barnes FC,** Ebenezer Cobb Morley (16 August 1831- 20 November 1924). Captain. Age at meeting, 32. Attended the F.A.'s jubilee dinner in 1913 and was presented with a silver casket as one of only three surviving members of the original meeting.
Mr. Thomas Dyson Gregory (19 July 1835- Jan-Mar 1908). Secretary. Age at meeting, 28.

5) **Surbiton,** Mr. Theodore Bell (30 July 1840 - 7 November 1923). Born and educated at Uppingham, where he was captain of football 1857/58. Although he represented the short-lived Surbiton club at the first meeting of the F.A. and signed them up for membership, he was better known as a rower and was for many years was the secretary of Kingston Rowing Club. A solicitor, he established a legal practice in Epsom and London. He was Clerk to the Justices in Epsom, and also to the Commissioners of Taxes. Age at meeting, 23.

6) **Blackheath,** Mr. Frederick Henry Moore (1839- 2 April 1934). Captain. Age at meeting, 24. Francis Maule Campbell (1843 - 30 December 1920). Secretary. Age at meeting, 20. Elected treasurer of the F.A. at its first meeting, he took the Rugby playing schools out of membership after the sixth meeting and had no further involvement. He was a founder of the Rugby Football Union in 1871.

7) **Blackheath Proprietary School,** Mr. William Henry Gordon (30 March 1845 - 1 January 1929). Captain. Age at meeting, 18.

8) **Crusaders,** Mr. Herbert Thomas Steward (9 November 1838 - 9 September 1915). Age at meeting, 24. Architect and Surveyor.

9) **Forest (Leytonstone)**, John Forster Alcock (1841- 31 March 1910). Captain. Age at meeting, 22. Left Forest FC in 1864 when the Club changed its name to the Wanderers FC.
Mr. Alfred Westwood Mackenzie (24 May 1840 - 6 April 1924). Hon. Secretary. Age at meeting, 23. Attended the F.A.'s jubilee dinner in 1913 and was presented with a silver casket as one of only three surviving members of the original meeting.

10) **No Names (Kilburn)**, Mr. Arthur Pember (9 July 1835 - 3 April 1886). Age at meeting, 28. Captain. Barrister and Journalist.

11) **W.O., War Office** (now known as Civil Service FC), Mr. George Twizell Wawn (1840 - 17 April 1914). Age at meeting, 23. Clerk Third Class.

12) **Charterhouse School**, Mr. Bertram Fulke Hartshorne (26 October 1844 - 31 December 1921). Captain. Age at meeting, 19-his birthday! The only public school representative at the first meeting.

13) **Dingley Dell**, according to the Sportsman newspaper a Mr. Bell represents the Dingley Dell club at the inaugural meeting of the F.A. on the 26th October 1863:

"Pursuant to a notice, a meeting of an influential character of the place at the Freemasons' Tavern on Monday, the object of the promoters being to decide upon some plan of action for bringing about a definite code of laws for the regulation and adoption of the various clubs which indulge in this exciting and health promoting winter amusement. There was a large mustering of the captains and officers of the metropolitan football club present, amongst whom were the following: - Mr. Morley (Barnes), Messrs, Campbell and Moore (Secretary and Captain of the Blackheath), Mr. Pember (N. N.) Mr. M. K (unintelligible-must be Mr Mackenzie) (Forest), Mr. Bell (Dingley Dell), Mr. Wawn (War-Office), Mr. G. Shillingford (Percival House. Blackheath), Mr. J. W. Alcock (Leytonstone), and Mr. B. F. Hartshorne (Charterhouse). &c." [23]

Unfortunately, Mr. Bell remains a mystery as he is not listed as playing for them in Dingley Dell match reports. As the 'Sportsman' report only names nine clubs and one of the missing clubs is Surbiton, then there is also the possibility that 'Dingley Dell' was a typo for Surbiton FC and their representative Mr. Bell.

It would be the decisive fifth meeting on the 1st December 1863 that would settle the future of both the Rugby and Association game permanently.

Clubs present:

Crystal Palace, Messrs F. Urwick and J.L. Siordet.

Barnes FC, Ebenezer Cobb Morley, captain, and Mr. P. D. Gregory, secretary.

Blackheath, Mr. Frederick Henry Moore, captain and Francis Maule Campbell secretary.

Forest School Walthamstow, Messrs J. Morgan and J. Bouch jun.

Wimbledon School, Mr. A.E. Daltry.

Blackheath Proprietary School, Mr. W. H. Gordon, captain.

Forest (Leytonstone), John Forster Alcock, Captain and Mr. A.W. Mackenzie, Hon. Secretary.

No Names (Kilburn), Mr. Arthur Pember and G. Lawson.

The meeting was heavily influenced by a letter from Sheffield FC. The Secretary dealt with matters of correspondence which included a long communication dated 30th November from the Mr. William Chesterman, club secretary of Sheffield FC. He enclosed a subscription for enrolment but also put forward the Sheffield point of view that: '...the Association's proposed rules permitting running with the ball and hacking were directly opposed to football and were more suggestive of wrestling.' [24]

Ebenezer Morley responded for the group now calling themselves the Football Association:

CHAPTER ONE

'...if we have hacking, no one who has arrived at the age of discretion will play at football and it will be entirely left to school boys.' [25]

Twelve clubs and seven schools agreed and paid their guinea membership fee to join the Football Association. Eight clubs were from the London area: Barnes, N. N. Kilburn, Forest, Crystal Palace, War Office, Surbiton, Crusaders and Blackheath, and they were joined by four others who had heard about the meetings through the press: Lincoln, Aldershot, Royal Engineers (Chatham), and Sheffield FC. The schools were Blackheath Proprietary School, Perceval House, Forest School (Walthamstow), Wimbledon School, Kensington School, Royal Naval School (New Cross) and Uppingham.

In a retrospective magazine article in 1891, Charles W. Alcock said:

"The first meeting for the purpose of forming a legislative tribunal held in the autumn of 1863, was primarily as successful as its best wishers could have desired. There was every chance of a set of laws which would embrace all the divergent interests on one platform. Unfortunately, the prospects of a fusion were not realised. But still one cannot help an expression of regret that a more determined effort was not made to harmonise the differences, so as to admit of the adoption of a uniform game for the use of every footballer." [26]

The final laws as decided on 8th December 1863 were as follows.

Football Association Laws of 1863

1. The maximum length of the ground shall be 200 yards, the maximum breadth shall be 100 yards, the length and breadth shall be marked off with flags; and the goal shall be defined by two upright posts, eight yards apart, without any tape or bar across them.

2. A toss for goals shall take place, and the game shall be commenced by a place kick from the centre of the ground by the side losing the toss for goals; the other side shall not approach within 10 yards of the ball until it is kicked off.

3. After a goal is won, the losing side shall be entitled to kick off, and the two sides shall change goals after each goal is won.

4. A goal shall be won when the ball passes between the goal-posts or over the space between the goal-posts (at whatever height), not being thrown, knocked on, or carried.

5. When the ball is in touch, the first player who touches it shall throw it from the point on the boundary line where it left the ground in a direction at right angles with the boundary line, and the ball shall not be in play until it has touched the ground.

6. When a player has kicked the ball, any one of the same side who is nearer to the opponent's goal line is out of play and may not touch the ball himself, nor in any way whatever prevent any other player from doing so, until he is in play; but no player is out of play when the ball is kicked off from behind the goal line.

7. In case the ball goes behind the goal line, if a player on the side to whom the goal belongs first touches the ball, one of his side shall be entitled to a free kick from the goal line at the point opposite the place where the ball shall be touched. If a player of the opposite side first touches the ball, one of his side shall be entitled to a free kick at the goal only from a point 15 yards outside the goal line, opposite the place where the ball is touched, the opposing side standing within their goal line until he has had his kick.

THE SEARCH FOR A UNIVERSAL PLAYING CODE

8. *If a player makes a fair catch, he shall be entitled to a free kick, providing he claims it by making a mark with his heel at once; and in order to take such a kick he may go back as far as he pleases, and no player on the opposite side shall advance beyond his mark until he has kicked.*
9. *No player shall run with the ball.*
10. *Neither tripping nor hacking shall be allowed, and no player shall use his hands to hold or push his adversary.*
11. *A player shall not be allowed to throw the ball or pass it to another with his hands.*
12. *No player shall be allowed to take the ball from the ground with his hands under any pretext whatever while it is in play.*
13. *No player shall be allowed to wear projecting nails, iron plates, or gutta percha* on the soles or heels of his boots.*

(Gutta percha* was a naturally occurring latex or rubber from Malaysia that would strengthen football boots).

Up to Law 8 there is a lot of common ground with Rugby football but the initial response in the press in 1863, from the Rugby fraternity was not favourable:

"This brings me to the last and most important charge, the charge of hacking or shinning. Our game is barbarous because it permits hacking. For my own part, sir, this is the point above all other concerning which I am most confident that we are in the right. I do uphold hacking because it develops that quality of which every Englishman ought to be most proud- his pluck. I know sir, it is objected that he ought to learn pluck by the use of his fists. I admit the correctness of this objection in theory, but I deny its possibility in practice. We are too phlegmatic a nation to use our fists for nothing, to fly into a passion without any cause. This cause is supplied in football. If your readers had seen players appearing on Big Side day after day, either in house matches or school matches, carrying the ball gallantly through, scrimmage after scrimmage, till they could hardly stand, perhaps they would be inclined to admire hacking more than they do at present. In all this I am not speaking of purely vicious hacking but: I am not even speaking of hacking such as our house displayed in a memorable scrimmage some years ago, after we sustained an unexpected reverse, when for five minutes both sides ignored the existence of anything but their own hostility, and the two best forwards of our house severally hewed their way four times through the enemy's ranks, kicking (I need hardly say) something else than the ball. Yet even this last-named instance is not wholly indispensable. Surely it is better if one does lose one's temper to show it in this way then in any other, and I will venture to say that we are all the better friends, and fought all the more stoutly together at the Two House match, for that very encounter. Besides, sir, there can be no doubt that the character of hacking is very much exaggerated. It looks and sounds very much worse than it really is. I have known capital players to go through them. They better than all others can tell, as far as Rugby is concerned, with what justice our greatest general declared that the field of Waterloo was won on the playgrounds of England. I must again apologise for my presumption in venturing to speak thus authoritatively on this subject: I need hardly say I should not venture to do so did I not feel that I am expressing the sentiments of many Rugbeians. I hope that I may have succeeded in persuading some of your readers to look at the football question from another point of view. - Yours, &c, New College, Dec 1863" [27]

CHAPTER ONE

(A few years after falling out over the hacking question, Blackheath and Richmond banned hacking in 1865 and 1866 respectively.)

For all of Pember and Morley's efforts, the new laws still allowed handling the ball. A ball could be caught with the hands before it bounced and the catcher was allowed to take an unimpeded kick (similar to a mark in Rugby or Australian Rules). It also still included a Rugby style offside law that said that men had to be behind the ball when it was kicked. It is unthinkable to imagine a modern-day game where no pass can be played forward. The new laws made it crucial to have a good dribbler in your team; if you kicked the ball forward effectively all your team mates were immediately offside, so the only way to advance down the field was by dribbling, whilst your teammates 'followed up' to take over the dribbling duties when the first player lost the ball. The later 1867 'three man' rule which said that the receiving player was not offside if three opponents stood between him and the goal line meant that the passing game could start to evolve. The change did not greatly enhance goal scoring and Sheffield Football Association introduced a one-man offside rule which encouraged more passing into the game, the so called 'combination' method. (see Appendix One)

Ebenezer Morley was clearly excited at the success of the creation of the new laws. Four days later on 12th December his Barnes team played Alcock's Forest team and lost 1-0 although "there was some talk about the rules and we regret to say some little temper displayed." [28] Ebenezer Morley then organised the first match played under Association Laws, (Richmond FC to play his Barnes team) eight miles away from where they had been agreed at Limes Field, Mortlake on 19 December 1863. Thus, the first ever match to take place under Football Association Laws would ironically be between two teams who would both eventually go on to embrace the Rugby code.

An official show game for the new laws was arranged for Battersea Park on 9 January 1864; the members of the opposing teams for this game were chosen by the President of the F.A. (Pember) and the Secretary (Morley) and included many well-known footballers of the day, who had been selected by Charles W. Alcock. Interestingly in the full transcript of the game (below) a Mr. Chambers from Sheffield FC plays in the game. Harry Waters Chambers was the owner of Parkfield House (the modern address is unknown) where the inaugural meetings of Sheffield FC took place in 1857. He was an attorney's clerk by trade who was also a player, board member and Hon. Sec. for twenty-two years, who only missed four games in this entire period.

Note that this official first game included fourteen players per team; it would take until 1870 for most clubs to accept the eleven a side norm:

"The first match played actually under the new Laws of the Football Association took place on Saturday Jan.9 in Battersea Park amongst the members of the various clubs now forming the association. The sides were chosen by the Messrs. Alcock and Pember (both capital players) and as the president and secretary 'on this occasion only and for their joint benefit' took opposite sides. We class them thus. *(Players' teams added by author).*

The President's Side:
A Pember *(No Names Kilburn)*, CW Alcock *(Forest)*, HW Chambers *(Sheffield FC)*, AM Tebbut *(Forest)*, Gray *(Club Team unknown)*, Drew *(Club Team unknown)*, RG Graham *(Barnes)*, WJ Cutbill *(Forest)*, A Morten *(No Names Kilburn)*, J Turner *(Crystal Palace)*, Morris *(Crystal Palace)*, Renshaw *(No Names Kilburn)*, Leuchers *(Barnes)*, A Scott *(Club Team unknown)*

The Secretary's side:
EC Morley *(Barnes)*, JF Alcock *(Forest)*, CM Tebbut *(Forest)*, A Lloyd *(Crystal Palace)*, C Hewitt *(Club Team unknown)*, GT Wawn *(War Office)*, JP Phillips *(War Office)*, Innes *(Barnes)*, McCalmont *(Barnes)*, Needham *(Club Team unknown)*, H Baker *(No Names Kilburn)*, AJ Baker *(No Names Kilburn)*, Hughes *(Club team unknown)*, Jackson *(Forest)*." [29]

The article continues, with a special mention for the Sheffield representative:
"Where all played well, individual mention hardly within reasonable scope but Messrs. Pember, Hewett, Morley, Chambers and both the Alcock's especially distinguished themselves. Mr. Chambers the able representative of the Sheffield Football club gave a capital taste of his quality. The President's side after some spirited play obtained two goals, the final kick in each instance provided by Mr. CW Alcock. In the evening the members dined together at the Grosvenor Hotel, Pimlico under the presidency of Mr. A Pember 'Success to football, irrespective of class or creed' was heartily drunk and a most agreeable evening was passed." [29]

The first Association Laws match to be played between two Association football clubs was played in Kilburn with the No Names beating Barnes 3-0 in a 15-a-side match on the 30th January 1864. In an F.A. meeting in September 1864 it was announced that the Association now numbered eighteen including Sheffield FC, but this was going to be the Football Association's most difficult period. At a meeting dated 28 October 1864, no business was conducted and the next meeting was not for another sixteen months on 22 February 1866. The Football Association's Laws had still not achieved the universal popularity its authors had hoped for, most clubs preferring their own rules and customs. Barnes, C.C.C., Charterhouse School, Crusaders, Crystal Palace, Hitchin, N.N. Kilburn, Wanderers, Wasps, and West Kent, were all members of the F.A., and were all supposed to know, to understand, and to play, the Association Laws, but they would cheerfully vary them, or even ignore them altogether in favour of some other (obscurely local) code. However, they played just enough matches to keep the game alive, the prevailing mood is summed up by letter to the Press in January 1864 from someone calling himself 'An Old Boy', claiming that:

"...the Football Association was a failure because it lacked the authority which would come from the Public Schools. He felt it had been foolish of the promoters to hold their inaugural meeting at a time when it was practically impossible for the representatives of the leading schools to be present. It was therefore presumptuous to ask all football clubs to take up membership." [30]

The criticism kept coming in the same year for the perceived failure that was the Football Association, even from proponents of the no hacking rules:

"RULES OF FOOTBALL. MR. EDITOR: As the time for football draws near persons who feel an interest in the game begin to wonder whether any steps will be taken to have a universal code of rules drawn up for the use of all clubs. I think that there can be very little doubt that the association which was formed last year for that purpose has been a failure, as whenever I have heard its rules spoken of among football players, it has invariably been in a contemptuous manner.... I may be told that no pluck is required to play a game where no 'hacking' is allowed. I say that there is the same amount of pluck and perseverance required to play it properly as was ever displayed in any of the other games. If by pluck be meant capacity to bear pain and the excitement attendant on the chance of injuring yourself for life, then I say why choose the game of football to display that quality. Why not roll up your sleeves and fight it out like Englishmen,

CHAPTER ONE

instead of kicking each other's legs like a parcel of foreigners. What I consider the equivalent to such pluck, as it is termed, is endurance, which is as much required in the Charterhouse game as in any other.... – Yours, &c NO HACKING." (31)

Whilst the F.A. tried in vain to introduce their rules to new clubs, Sheffield Rules continued to thrive 'up north' and indeed evolve further from the F.A. code in 1866. In spite of this, Sheffield FC publicly continued to support the F.A., notably when it suggested that a Sheffield team should come down to the capital and play a match against an F.A. team in March 1866. This match was played at Battersea Park on 31 March 1866 and was won decisively by two goals and four touchdowns to nil by the home team: "The game was a very hot one; although Sheffield were over matched, many of the Londoners were badly knocked about." (32)

At this match, Charles W. Alcock claimed the unfortunate distinction of being the first man ruled offside in an official Football Association fixture. This game is also known as the first time that a specific ball was nominated and the leather 'Lillywhites's Number 5' ball was the ball of choice. (In the later discussions surrounding the setting up of the F.A. Challenge Cup it was also agreed that the 'Lillywhites's Number 5' should be used in all Cup games.)

On 30th January 1867, the following piece appeared in 'Sporting Life', where for the first time we hear about the foundation of the Sheffield Football Association, formed to liase with the London F.A. over the games rules.

"FOOTBALL IN SHEFFIELD (FROM A CORRESPONDENT). It may not be generally known that Sheffield holds, or ought to hold, a very prominent position in the football world. Perhaps in no other town in the kingdom (London, of course, excepted) is the game played to anything like the extent to which it is in Sheffield. There are now fourteen clubs in the town, almost every cricket club having a football club connected with it." (33)

My research for the end of 1866 also shows fourteen clubs in existence, showing that this correspondent for the 'Sporting Life' was well informed. I was unable to categorise the origin of two of those clubs (Fir Vale and Broomhall) absolutely, but based on his comment I have put them down as formed by existing cricket clubs.

An accolade never mentioned in the long list of Sheffield FC's achievements is in the field of athletics. Before 1858, 'Athletic Sports' events had been conducted by the military and some schools but never in an 'open' context. I have not found British Athletic sports meetings earlier than the one run by Sheffield FC in April 1858. The Amateur Athletic Association did not form until 1880:

"The oldest of the three is the 'Sheffield Football Club,' established in 1857. The others have been established since then at different times, up to and including 1866. Sheffield may also fairly claim to have been amongst the first towns in the kingdom to hold athletic sports, for the Sheffield Club held their first meeting of this kind so far back as April 4, 1858. To such an extent have athletic sports taken root in Sheffield, that there are now ten or twelve of these meetings during the year, and at the last sports of the Sheffield Club, held in May, 1866, upwards of 7,00 spectators were present, a fact which testifies to the popularity of the athletic sports in Sheffield." (33)

Having got all his dates correct so far, it is very interesting for our 'Correspondent' to claim that the Sheffield Rules were in existence in 1857, a year earlier than other records suggest:

"The Sheffield clubs play to a code of rules which was framed in 1857, and has been since then but slightly altered. The chief points in which these rules differ from those played in other towns are the total absence of the 'off-side' rule, and the strictness with which striking the ball with the hand is prohibited. The penalty for an infringement of this rule is a free kick to the opposite side. It is quite refreshing to a lover of 'foot'- ball to hear the universal shout of 'Foul!' which goes round a football field in Sheffield when any player so far forgets himself as to strike the ball with his hand. The consequence of this strictness is that 'dribbling' is brought to considerable perfection. Carrying the ball is also prohibited, and, in point of fact, it is the aim of the Sheffield clubs, as much as possible, to play the game of football, and the use of the hands, in any way (except to obtain a free kick from a catch), is discouraged." [33]

Our 'Correspondent' makes clear the dislike in Sheffield of the old offside rule but insists Sheffield's scientific approach to football is the better for its absence, as too with ball handling:

"The off-side rule has been played in Sheffield, but was universally disapproved of. It was found to be the cause of much discontent, and produced a most unsatisfactory state of things, it being so difficult, in the excitement of a close match, to distinguish what players were 'off,' and what 'on' side. As we believe will always be the case, it added materially to the intricacies of the game without a corresponding benefit. It was, therefore, abandoned, and now, as formerly, the only restriction upon the position of any player in the field is, that he must not be nearer to his adversaries' goal than the nearest of the defending side. There are other points of difference of minor importance which the Sheffield clubs would be prepared cheerfully to concede, but upon the points of off-side and handing the ball they would be inflexible, believing, as they do, that the game can be better and more scientifically played without them. Both have been tried in Sheffield, and both have been found to militate seriously against the game." [33]

It would be fascinating to know who this 'Correspondent' was, as he speaks with authority when setting out a manifesto to bring the codes of Sheffield and London together:

"At the same time, Sheffield would be prepared to sacrifice a great deal for the sake of obtaining a uniform code of rules. This is peculiarly the case with the Sheffield Club, which has now for several reasons been in the habit of playing matches with other towns. In the season 1864-5 this club played two matches with Lincoln and two with Notts. In the season 1865-6, the same matches were played, with the addition of one with London, and in the present season matches have been arranged, and partly played, with Lincoln, London, Manchester, and Notts. It is most unsatisfactory that a different game should have to be played at each of these places, and we hope the day is not far distant when this will be remedied. May we suggest a step in this direction? Let each town that possesses a football club do as Sheffield does. Let them arrange matches with other towns. They will then learn the deficiencies of their own rules, and the excellences of those played by their adversaries, a mutual benefit will be derived, and so the labour of reconciling the differences which exist will be materially lightened. An association of the Sheffield clubs has recently been formed, upon the basis of the General Football Association. The governing rules are practically the same, being only slightly altered to suit local circumstances. No playing rules have as yet been adopted, the meeting establishing the association having been adjourned until after the meeting of the General Association in February. It is to be hoped that such alterations may then be made in the existing code of the Association laws as will enable the clubs of this great football centre of the North to play the same rules as their southern brethren." [33]

The very positive message above from Sheffield football is completely at odds with the mood at a meeting of the London Football Association just thirteen days later; only six people attended the 12th February 1867 F.A. Annual General Meeting and the Association discussed whether it should dissolve itself. However, one of those attending, was Sheffield FC's indefatigable Hon. Sec. William Chesterman; he brought with him a letter of support and encouragement for the F.A., not just from his own club but the recently founded Sheffield Association, which

CHAPTER ONE

represented all the fourteen clubs that played regularly under the Sheffield rules, representing in excess of 1000 members. (My research in fact suggests there were sixteen clubs in 1867). It was good that there was other business to be discussed at the 1867 F.A. Annual General Meeting because it reads as if the downbeat Mr. Morley may have asked for a vote from the six clubs for a dissolution; instead of the recent 150-year birthday celebration, the F.A. might have only existed for four years, cutting the party short by some 146 years:

"Mr. MORLEY said he was a little discouraged at the paucity of attendance that evening, when he remembered that at the commencement of the association in 1863 they had a crowded room, and much more enthusiasm was displayed by those who attended in the interest of the pleasant pastime of football than had ever been shown since. The only way he could account for it was the supposition abroad that the Football Association had accomplished the objects for which it was established, and that there consequently was no further need of its services. When they first met the great dispute was respecting 'hacking', both parties discussed the question; the objectors to hacking prevailed and the others retired. They then formed a code of rules, which was of a great improvement upon anything in existence and thought it had been of great advantage to London players; they were very pleased to find that the rules had been adopted in Sheffield, the great stronghold of football in England, where the games were pursued with much energy and success. They therefore acknowledged the benefits conferred by the association and upheld it, as was abundantly testified by the presence of Mr. Chesterman, of the Sheffield Club, at the meeting that evening who had no doubt been deputed by them to act. Some had stuck to the rules, some had not, and clubs who played association rules declined to accept challenges for matches that were to be played on other terms. He confessed he should like to see more clubs represented at the meeting, but the difficulty was how to get the different clubs to take the pains to frame amendments and send them for discussion at the general meeting in order that they might be advertised in proper time. He thought they should seriously consider that night, whether it were worthwhile to continue the association or dissolve it; if after discussion they considered they had made rules perfect, what was the utility of meeting again to do nothing? They had devoted time, patience and trouble to give these rules to the public and he thought the public could now go on by themselves until another association was requisite. However, they had for discussion that evening amendments proposed by three clubs, Sheffield, the Wanderers and the Barnes Football Club." [34]

Did the formation of the Sheffield Football Association in January 1867 and the message they conveyed down to London with William Chesterman, provide the 'bottom' the Football Association needed to maintain the Association game?

The 20th April 1867 'Field' newspaper reviewed the 1866/67 football season; it said that around 180 matches had been played in the London area, which compared to the comparatively feeble state of the game in 1860 when only two clubs (Crusaders and Dingley Dell) played external fixtures. Clearly London was struggling with its newly formed code to capture the imagination of the ever-growing number of football clubs. Reinvigorated by Sheffield's support, at the September 30th 1867 F.A. Committee meeting, the Secretary was directed to announce a County match and requested captains of Clubs wishing to take part to contact him. The committee also agreed that the one guinea subscription could be waived 'in the event of any Club being prevented joining by that subscription.' [35]

In 1868 a new publication was launched that brought much needed detail to the Association football story.

The Football Annual 1868

The records for early F.A. meetings and minutes are not thorough and what there are, urgently need digitising. The most reliable football record for this early period are the Football Annuals started in 1868, originally entitled as John Lillywhite's Football Annual, edited by the F.A. Secretary, Charles W. Alcock and 'Published with the sanction of the Football Association.', priced at 1s.6d. After the first edition, Charles W. Alcock parted ways with his cousin John Lillywhite and it became his sole responsibility, together with a new publisher and a lower price:

"The Football Annual for 1869, edited by C. Alcock is now ready, price one shilling, thirteen stamps post free. Orders may be sent to the Publisher, SPORTSMAN Office, Boy-court, Ludgate hill, E.C. Trade supplied. - ADVT." [36].

In each edition, Honorary Secretaries were invited to apply for forms which had to be returned before May in each year; these included information such as when the club was formed, where the club ground was situated and whether they played by Association or Rugby rules, so it included all Football Clubs, whether Association or Rugby Clubs. This meant that the records were self-reported and they were only as exact and honest as the Hon. Sec. filling them in, however I don't think it was the Victorian way to lie or exaggerate foundation dates. Human error means that sometimes the foundation dates can fluctuate over the thirty-year period covered by this book, but I have always deferred to the first entry listed as being the most likely to be correct as it is closer to the actual event and less susceptible to fading memories. The Football Annual ran for 40 years until 1908.

The first edition of the Football Annual in 1868, five years after the launch of the Football Association, included a list of all football clubs that had submitted their details to John Lillywhite. At just eighty-four pages it covered a summary of the 1867/68 season, the various Laws and a list of clubs, be they Association or another code. The Annuals were thin paper covered books and designed to fit into a jacket pocket, which is why so very few survived; the ones still rarely found have been bound after the publication. There are eighty-five clubs listed for 1868 and three of those are from Scotland (Annan, Edinburgh Academicals and Glasgow Academicals). Of the remaining eighty-two English (no Welsh) clubs, fifty-one are described as 'Clubs in and around London' and thirty-one are described as 'Provincial.' Just five years after the formation of the F.A. and the choice of code is as fragmented as ever and Rugby is by far the most popular code:

Charles W. Alcock
(Association Football and the Men who Made it 1905)

CHAPTER ONE

Rugby:	38
Association:	23
Sheffield:	13
Special:	4
Mixture:	2
Harrow:	1
Marlborough:	1

In London, the preference for Rugby is even more pronounced; of the fifty-one clubs in London just fifteen are Association, thirty are Rugby and six are other types. Whilst provincially eight clubs play Rugby, two play other types, thirteen play Sheffield Rules and just eight play Association out of the total of thirty-one, so outside of London the Sheffield Rules lead the way.

The Sheffield clubs in the 1868 edition of the Football Annual are described as the 'grinders', with Charles W. Alcock as editor, commenting:

'Most enthusiastic supporters of football they boast of 13 clubs. (I may add that the rules of the Sheffield Association bear close affinity to those of the Football Association-Ed)'

Sheffield and the F.A. would ultimately merge their rules in 1877 and Harrow Chequers, the one club playing by Harrow rules, would also embrace the Association game, so one can say that in 1868 there were thirty-seven (or soon to be) Association football clubs. Of these, five were schools, two athletic clubs and one a military outfit. The breakdown of the forty-six non-Association clubs (of all types) showed sixteen were schools or colleges (including military), six hospitals (all in London) and two athletic clubs (in Birmingham and Manchester). If the schools, college and military of the thirty-seven Association clubs of 1868 are excluded, just eight of the clubs still exist today, two of which play Rugby: Barnes and Sale. Of the remaining six survivors, one is from London, Civil Service, and the remaining five all come from within 45 miles of each other: Sheffield FC, Hallam FC, Wednesday FC, Notts County FC and Nottingham Forest FC.

The Sheffield Football Association discussed the uniformity of rules on the 10th October 1871 and in particular their reluctance to stop catching the ball; because of the town's famous hills many of their grounds were situated on steep gradients. Not being able to catch a ball to stop it going out of play for a long while, was a serious local concern:

"The one thing to be regretted in football is the want of uniformity of rules. To remedy this a number of Associations have been formed, the most prominent of which is the London Association, who solicit the support of the clubs to play their rules. An Association has also been formed in Sheffield for that and other purposes, consisting of a large number of clubs who abide by the code of rules issued. These have been so far rather unsatisfactory, as at each succeeding annual meeting alterations are proposed and carried. The annual meeting for this season takes place tonight at the Adelphi Hotel, and it would be well for the footballers to muster well and issue rules which are likely to be permanent, when the support of other clubs can be confidently solicited. The one absorbing topic for discussion tonight is the rule as regards to catching. Opinions are pretty evenly divided on the subject, and much may be said on each side of the question. There is no doubt that the non-catching rule is the most scientific, but if it is not at all suitable to the majority of the grounds in this neighbourhood, the hilly nature of them frequently carrying the ball out and delaying the play. This argument is also used the other way, the opponents of catching declaring that football was made for the foot and not for the hands. Should the meeting decide to abolish catching, the rules will then be similar to the London Association, with the exception of the off-side, one as regards three men. This although desirable, will not be considered, as the metropolitan body are very stiff-necked, requiring all the concessions to come one way. A significant fact, however, is a decision arrived at by the South Derbyshire Association-which numbers between 600 and 700 members- to the effect that they will play Sheffield Association Rules if catching is relinquished. The same may be said of the Nottingham body." [37]

Three days later on October 12th 1871, Mr. Houseman, the Hon. Sec. of the South Derbyshire Football Association, attended a meeting of the Sheffield Football Association, offering to enrol their eleven clubs into the Sheffield Association from Derbyshire, if they abolished catching the ball; they eventually passed this by twelve votes. The Chairman introduced Mr. C. W. Houseman, Hon. Sec. of the "south Derbyshire Football Association" to the meeting:

"In a telling and fluent speech, he- Mr. Houseman- informed his hearers of the interest taken in football in Derby, and the determination of the body of which he was the hon. Sec. to join the Sheffield Association, should that body decide to abolish catching. They had been solicited to join the Metropolitan Association, but on trial of the respective rules, had decided almost to a man in favour of Sheffield. He said they numbered 11 clubs, and concluded by asking them to well consider the question at issue, not only the Derbyshire Society but the Nottingham Forest Club, he believed would join and swell their ranks… Mr. J. Pashley then proposed and Mr. T. J. Anderson seconded that catching be abolished. An amendment in direct opposition to this was then made by Messrs. W. Littlehales and T. Rycroft. An animated discussion ensued, the supporters of catching urging that the grounds in Sheffield and neighbourhood were unfit for the non-catching rule, on account of their hilly nature. To this the other side responded that this was not a purely local subject, as was seen by the remarks of Mr. Houseman, and that in time a universal code might be adopted. On being put to the meeting, the non-catching rule was carried by 44 to 36." [38]

It's interesting to see that Houseman thought at the time that he could also count on the Nottingham Forest Club joining the Sheffield Association. At the same meeting comes the following:

"Some correspondence was then read between the Hon. Sec. and Mr. Alcock, the hon. Sec. to the London Association, from which it appeared that last year the 'London Wanderers' issued a challenge to play any team in the world. This was accepted by the Sheffield Association, but no answer was vouchsafed until early this season. It was to the effect that the match must be played through the London Association, who were then immediately challenged to play home and home matches, and home and home rules, the latter of which they decided to do on moral grounds. They arrogate to themselves the position of law-makers, evidently assuming themselves to be infallible. Mr. Alcock, however, said he could bring a team down of his own choosing, which was accordingly accepted…. Votes of thanks to the retiring officers and chairman, concluded business of the meeting." [38]

Clearly the Football Association may have been 'stiff-necked' but that did not apply to Charles W. Alcock, who was instrumental in December 1871 in taking a team of London based players (against the wishes of the F.A. Committee) to play a team assembled from Sheffield Association players at Bramall Lane on December 2 1871. The reason the F.A. committee was against the match, was because the game would be played under newly updated Sheffield Rules. It was Alcock's pragmatism that ensured the two codes did not compete against each other, which would have been another drag on the game's development. Charles W. Alcock felt that although they lost by 3 goals to 1 they did not disgrace themselves, as they had only had seen the rules within a few minutes of arriving at Midland railway station. London was a man short and John Shaw, the co-founder of Hallam FC, made up their numbers.

CHAPTER ONE

The team lists were:

Sheffield:

J. Marsh, J.C. Clegg, W.E. Clegg, W. Lockwood, Jnr., T.C. Willey, G.H. Sampson, A. Wood, W.H. Carr, C. Mills, J. Hollingworth, H. Ash.

London:

C.W. Alcock *(Wanderers)*, C.J. Chenery *(Crystal Palace)*, Percy Currey *(Crystal Palace)*, P.B. Soden *(Crystal Palace)*, P. Revitt-Carnac *(Harrow Chequers)*, R.C. Welch *(Harrow Chequers)*, Conrad Warner *(Upton Park)*, C.W. Stevenson *(Wanderers)*, P. Weston *(Barnes)*, E. Weston *(Barnes)*, J.C. Shaw *(substitute)*

Charles W. Alcock's pragmatism was rewarded when he oversaw the amalgamation of the two sets of rules in 1876 under the F.A. banner. When the Sheffield Football Association published its 'Rules of Football' for their 1875/76 season they could list forty-six associated clubs, and the twelve published laws; these were by then closely in line with those of the F.A., containing most of the elements that are familiar in modern Association football. It was not until 1877 that Sheffield fully adopted the F.A. laws, which by that point had already absorbed certain clauses from the Sheffield code.

Of the twelve subsequent changes that were made to the F.A. Laws in the 1860s, eight originated in the Sheffield Rules. The crucial change came in 1866, in the same year that Charles W. Alcock (Wanderers FC) and Charles Clegg (Sheffield Association) joined the F.A. committee, which was when forward passes become permitted, as long as there were three defending players between the receiver and the goal. Finally, forward passing was introduced to the game which had been a rule in the Sheffield game since 1863. Catching the ball in any circumstance (apart from the goal keeper) was now also illegal.

Sheffield FC had joined the F.A. back in 1863 but had continued to play under its own rules. The final barrier to the two codes joining was whether a throw-in could be thrown in any direction (London Laws) or at right angles (Sheffield Rules). With Sheffield's acceptance of this rule, finally the two codes amalgamated in 1877:

"The Sheffield Association has decided to join with the Football Association in the adoption of the Clydesdale amendment with regard to the throw from touch. This union makes one code for association players in England, so that at last, after many attempts, the Football Association and Sheffield have Amalgamated, a step that will be greatly conducive to the advancement of the dribbling game. [39]

In spite of this amalgamation the membership numbers for the Football Association stayed low for over ten years, until the launch of the F.A. Cup in 1871 transformed their fortunes.

By 1906 the Football Association could claim over 7,500 affiliated clubs, approximately fifteen times the number of clubs claimed by the Northern Union and Rugby Football Union combined. It also had 578 teams in the Army, where it was the only recognised code until 1907, and 180 Navy sides. [40]

Just before the First World War, the Football Association had 12,000 clubs affiliated (300 professional), representing between 300,000 - 500,000 players. The total number of clubs in England, including those affiliated to County F.A.s, is now estimated to be 29,000. (Some clubs have many 'teams').

Today the Football Association is often accused of not modernising its structures; the 19th century topics explored in this book - public schools, military and the County Associations - feature as prominently now at the F.A. as they did back in Victorian times. It has a three-part governing structure: board, council and shareholders. The board is the executive branch and has four representatives apiece from the professional and the national (amateur) game. Those eight are joined by two non-executive directors plus the F.A. Chairman and the F.A. Chief executive. The council has 122 members, a number which is increasing all the time because when a councillor reaches 20 years of service and is also 72 years old, he (usually a he) remains on the council as a vice president and is joined by whoever replaced him. The oldest current councillor is Doug Insole aged 90 who played in the Amateur Cup final for Corinthian Casuals in 1956. There are 43 County F.A. representatives, 28 vice presidents, 16 professional game representatives and others representing both Oxford and Cambridge Universities, all three wings of the military and two for schools (one for the state sector and one for the independent sector). The following all have one member apiece: players, fans, managers, referees and disabled, plus two for inclusion (diversity) representatives. Then there are 1,100 votes available to the shareholders, the fans (Football Supporters Federation) has just one vote whilst the large county F.A.s have more than 40 votes. For any change to happen at the Football Association it needs a majority on the board and the council, and three quarters of the shareholders.

In March 2017, Football Association chairman Greg Clarke said he would quit if the organisation could not win government support for its reform plans which seek to:

- Establish three positions on the F.A. board reserved for female members by 2018
- Reduce the size of the board to 10 members
- Add eleven new members to the F.A. Council so it 'better reflects the inclusive and diverse nature of English football'
- Limit board membership to three periods of three years
- Introduce term limits for FA Council membership

CHAPTER TWO

Sheffield Schools

Public schools had taken up football as a way to keep the boys occupied when the masters wanted a break; this left the prefects to manage the in-house school rules football games, which were as varied as there were schools. Eton and Harrow schools favoured the dribbling game with a tight offside rule and Westminster and Charterhouse played a game that specifically excluded handling the ball; this forced players to pass the ball with their feet which increasingly allowed the forward pass, known as 'passing on.'

As an example of the differences between schools' rules, goal dimensions could be as varied as:
- Harrow (base) - Posts 12 feet high and 18 feet apart
- Eton - Posts 7 feet high and 11 feet apart
- Winchester (worms) - The full width of the pitch

In this early period, there were only three fee-paying schools in Sheffield: Wesley College, Collegiate School and Ecclesall College. The latter appears the least interested of the three in playing external opposition at football on their grounds at Newbourne Park. On the 30th November 1870, Ecclesall College played football against 'Mr. Howarth's', which they won by one goal to nil. The only other information offered is that the Ecclesall captain was 'Hardy'. [1]

No records exist of any early football being played at Wesley College or Collegiate School until as late as 1862. Wesley College was a proprietary grammar school situated in six acres on Glossop Road, built by subscription in 1839 at a cost of £15,000. In 1868 Wesley College was described as having a chaplain, a head and second master, and thirteen other teachers, and has accommodation for 250 boarders. [2] The first game code found in the press for Wesley College is March 1874, when they played Huddersfield College, by the Rugby Union rules. In March 1876, they beat Brincliffe FC by five goals to nil, in what would have been an Association code game.

The Collegiate School would have the most influence on Sheffield football. When analysing the English schools to see when they first started playing the 'dribbling' or Association code, I found that the list of the oldest eight educational establishments were predominantly from the south of England, with one from Derby, in the Midlands:

	Name of Establishment (Year of foundation)	First record of Association type football being played (Reference source)
1	Eton College (F. 1440)	1815 - present (In House School Rules)
2	Aldenham School (F. 1596)	1825 - present (In House School Rules)
3	Harrow School (F. 1572)	1832-1927 (School Records) Association football was banned at Harrow School from 1927 until 1977
4	Cambridge University (F. 1209) General games played on Parkers Piece	1839 (Cambridge FC)

5	Derby School (Derby Grammar School) (F. 1160)	1840-present (Football Annuals)
6	St. Mark's College (merged with St. John's College, Battersea 1881) (F. 1841)	1842-present (Soccer's Missing Men" by Mangan and Hickey)
7	Shrewsbury School (F. 1552)	1842-present (Annals of Shrewsbury school 1899 G. Fisher Page 406)
8	Westminster School (F. 1179)	1846-present (Football Annuals)

In ninth place and for the first time in the north of England, is the Sheffield Collegiate School, situated on a site of 3½ acres. It was founded 1835, in new buildings on the corner of Ecclesall Road and Collegiate Crescent, which is now the Grade II listed part of Sheffield Hallam University.

Research shows the earliest that football would have been played at the Collegiate School is in 1847, with the appointment of a Mr. Trown as drill master, when the most basic provision of physical exercise began.[3] Presumably from this point until 1857, football of some kind must have been played, because Nathaniel Creswick and sixteen others of Sheffield FC's initial membership of fifty-seven, were old boys of the Collegiate school. The same research that threw light on Mr. Trown, analysed the educational background of all the staff who taught at the school, looking for a link to a 'ball-dribbling' background to explain Sheffield FC's subsequent development. It discovered only a Reverend G. Sandford (who attended Shrewsbury School) and he had left before the school's football had become particularly organised.[3] This research is complemented by the earlier research of Percy M. Young who said that an A.C. Ainger, whose name appears in the Wall Game lists of Eton, was an assistant at Collegiate School from 1864 to 1866.[4] A mystery surrounds Sheffield FC's early use of the word 'rouge' for scoring which can only be found in Eton school and occasional Cambridge games. Certainly A.C. Ainger was at Eton school in 1865 [5] so he may well have been the inspiration. Alternatively, the adoption of 'rouges' may have been picked up during Sheffield FC's early games against the military, who could have had some Old Etonians in their ranks.

Whilst unclear what kind of football was played at the Collegiate School, it certainly created some kind of shared sporting experience for that group of seventeen students to make their membership of Sheffield FC seem a logical progression in 1857; and surely Nathaniel Creswick would have played his first football here? The other Sheffield FC founder, William Prest lived nearby at this time on Collegiate Crescent, so did they play together at the Collegiate School in the early 1850s on those 3½ acres?

I researched the headmasters of the period to see if any fresh clues could be gleaned from their background. The Reverend William Stanford Grignon from Brighton College was the new headmaster in 1853.[6] Brighton was certainly not a centre for the dribbling game in this period, as Sussex was an early centre for the Rugby game. Reverend Grignon had attended the more Association-friendly Trinity College, Cambridge, but there is no research showing what game was played at the school in this period. Reverend Grignon had moved on two years later and the College's advert for a new principal, showed that they did not feel the need to extol its games curriculum but rather its new laboratory and a need for a religious man.[7] The vacant position was filled in 1855 by Reverend E. D. Ward, M.A., another man with seemingly no great sporting background.

CHAPTER TWO

Whatever the route, by May 1859 there is a Collegiate Football Club and at the Athletic Sports day for the football club members, Creswick and Prest were officiating the proceedings, with Creswick as judge and Prest as one of the stewards.[8] At this time Creswick and Prest were still only in their late twenties, so must have been held in high regard by the Collegiate School, either because of their background with the school, or because of their achievements with Sheffield FC since 1857. In 1861 another new Principal was required as the Reverend E. D. Ward had left for St. John's Wood Proprietary School, London. This time there was no focus on the need for a religious man for the job, but he did have to be a Graduate of Cambridge or Oxford.[9]

By 1868, Collegiate School had a principal and eight other masters looking after 100 scholars who had each paid £25 for a year's education.[10] Like Wesley College, the first external game of football I have found the Collegiate playing is by the Rugby code. The game was against York Athletic Sports and Football Club in 1862; the reason they are not included in this book's main classification is because they were Sheffield's only football club that would ultimately embrace Rugby. Founded very early in 1861, they were never listed as a member of the Sheffield Association, nor were they included in early editions of the Football Annual, but they did play early games of an unknown code against Sheffield FC.

The first sign of the Collegiate School moving towards the Association game is in 1863 with a first match report of a game against Mackenzie FC, when their Rugby skills are still apparent. Mackenzie FC won by one goal and one rouge to nothing and whilst they were:

'...decidedly the stronger' team, the 'Collegiate gentlemen displayed their usual talent in gaining a great number of free kicks from catches.'[11]

The Collegiate School enjoyed academic success but ultimately lacked sound finances and was taken over by Sheffield Grammar School in 1884, to become the Sheffield Royal Grammar School in 1885. In 1905 Sheffield City Council acquired both Sheffield Royal Grammar School and Wesley College and amalgamated them on the site of the latter, changing the name to the King Edward VII school.

In 1887 the Collegiate School team made the final of the Sheffield Association Challenge Cup, losing 2-1 to Wednesday at Bramall Lane. By this point there were two competing Football Associations in Sheffield, but it is still impressive for a school team to play against the likes of Billy Mosforth and their other seasoned players. The match appears to be something of a Clegg family affair, with 'L.J' playing for the school, whilst Charles and William officiate:

"**Wednesday:**
J. Smith, goal: J. Hudson (capt.), and E. Brayshaw, backs; T. E. B. Wilson, A. Beckett, and J. W. Dungworth, half-backs; J. Watson, M. Naylor, W. Mosforth, W. Needham, and T. E. Crawley, forwards.

Collegiate:
W. F. Beardshaw, goal; W. Robinson and L. J. Clegg, backs; H. B. Willey, F. E. Baines, and A. B. Wood, half-backs; G. A. Parker, D. Davy, G, H, Aizlewood, A. C. Liddell, and W. T. Wright, forwards. Umpires, Messrs. W. E. Clegg and T. Tomlinson. Referee, Mr. J. (Charles) Clegg."[12]

Closer inspection of the Collegiate School team reveals they were fielding some Sheffield FC members, presumably old boys who were becoming disgruntled at the club's reluctance to engage against the local teams and only play in inter-County games. At this point the two clubs were the two last bastions of the amateur ethos in Sheffield and close relations had clearly developed between Collegiate School and Sheffield FC, because in 1888 they merged. The meeting to finalise the amalgamation on the 23rd March was chaired by Harry W. Chambers; the outcome was not a foregone conclusion with the question 'evoking considerable discussion,' but in the end, it was decided it would be advantageous with the 'prevailing opinion being that two amateur teams of the character could not exist in the town.' [13] At the same meeting, it was also decided by the newly invigorated Sheffield FC to stop playing only out of town matches and pit themselves once again against the other Sheffield teams. They had acquired the use of Lockwood Brothers ground for practice and they anticipated 'a large influx of members.' [13]

It seems that the merger also helped Sheffield FC remain solvent, who, like many other amateur clubs by the late 1880s, were beginning to feel the pinch:

"By 1885 the club found itself unable to pay the bill for the construction of a new grandstand, and it was probably only an amalgamation with the football branch of the Collegiate Cricket club which kept Sheffield FC afloat." [14]

(Chapter Five covers England's Oldest 'State' School Football Club, in the form of 'All Saints' Night School FC,' founded in Sheffield in 1871.)

CHAPTER THREE

Sheffield Volunteer Movement

In the late 1850s, there was consternation that Napoleon might invade Britain. In the Sheffield Times October 3 1857, a campaign was started for 'Sheffield Volunteers', with the aim of procuring, within a month, five hundred suitable men to join the Army. This was an early incarnation of what we would later call the Home Guard, which was composed mostly of part-time rifle, artillery and engineer corps. The difference was that in most cases these regiments that started off voluntarily, would usually evolve into a full time military outfit. Several thousand people attended an event that was run at Newhall Gardens consisting of military and athletic exercises, with prizes of £1 for successful competitors. The exercise was later proclaimed a success with fifty men enlisted into the full-time Army as a result. Two years later in 1859 Napoleon III invaded northern Italy and a larger Volunteer movement was triggered, on a county by county basis. On 12 May 1859, the Secretary of State for War, Jonathan Peel, issued a circular letter to Lieutenants of Counties in England, Wales and Scotland, authorising the formation of Volunteer rifle corps, and indirectly starting a recruiting ground for many embryonic football clubs:

"From one end to the other the country rings with the proceedings of volunteer corps. The movement makes decided and steady progress. In London, large subscriptions have been raised, and the number of effective riflemen daily increases. In the country districts and in Scotland corps of rifle and artillery volunteers are increasing every day. Peers, squires, farmers, merchants, give money, time, practising grounds, and exhort the youth to enrol. Even Manchester is raising a strong corps. Nottingham and Norwich, relatively small places, are, however, in public spirit on a par with Manchester, and muster as many men. The City of London and the rest of the metropolis ought to raise a force in proportion to their population, and exceed the force of any county in the kingdom. Great as the progress has been much yet remains to be done."[1]

The first external game Sheffield FC played was against the local military in December 1858, when they met and beat the locally garrisoned 58th regiment; there had always been a history of inter-military football matches, so it was logical that when the Volunteer Regiments started, football games were viewed as a way to keep the men interested and more importantly, fit. Other important English football clubs, like Notts County FC (1862), Macclesfield FC (1872) and Northwich Victoria FC (1874) owe a great deal to the Volunteer Movement for their formation. That same influence cannot be claimed completely for Sheffield football, but on analysing the personnel involved with the new movement, a clear link to Hallam FC was revealed.

Tom Vickers

Tom Vickers, the man credited as a co-founder of Hallam FC, was involved from the start in the Volunteer Movement. In a newspaper article dated 21st May 1859, is an inspired method of recruitment for the Sheffield Volunteer Rifle Corp, devised by the Lord Lieutenant of the Riding, Wilson Overend, Esq.:

"… That gentleman immediately took the means to commence a movement for organizing a local corps. He put himself in communication with the Football Club, and the various cricket clubs, and arranged with Mr. Jackson, the Chief-constable, to have a list lying at the Town-hall for any persons who thought proper to join the corps to subscribe their names." [2]

As part of the regulations Volunteers were expected to:

"… bear the expense of their own arms and accoutrements, this might prevent some from joining the corps who would do so if unattended with expense; and probably a subscription will be set on foot to defray the expense of the accoutrements for those who are unable to do so for themselves. Several gentlemen have promised handsome subscriptions for this object." [2]

Wilson Overend, Esq. made it clear:

"… that these corps are liable to be called out for active service only in case of actual invasion, or appearance of an enemy in force on the coast, or in case of rebellion arising out of either of these emergencies." [2]

The movement was motivating the local gentry and the article finished with a list of the gentlemen who had already signed up. Vickers was thoroughly involved, together with his fellow delegates, William Prest and Nathaniel Creswick who had formed Sheffield Football Club two years earlier in October 1857, as well as Harry W. Chambers the club's Hon.Sec.:

"Wilson Overend, W. A. Matthews, Marcus Flockton, Wm. Cooke (cutler, Hodgson-street), N. Creswick, Wm. Prest, J. K. Turner (Columbia-works), T. E. Vickers, Albert Vickers, Frederick Fowler, G. T. Rodgers, Joseph Rodgers, jun., John Denial (Cemetery-road), John Geo. Hewett (accountant, High-street), Fred. Swift (tobacco manufacturer), Samuel Newbould, C. T. Baines (wine merchant), G. Moseley (surgeon dentist), H. W. Chambers (attorney's clerk), Charles Smith, M.D., C. E. Broadbent, Geo. Hardesty (iron merchant), John Brown (Atlas-works), Robert Jackson (Master Cutler), Hy. Chapman (book-keeper, Marsh-gate, Doncaster), Henry Webster (solicitor), and John Newbould (solicitor)." [2]

A week later on the 28th May, there was another meeting of 'persons favourable to becoming members of the Volunteer Rifle Corps' and from the good attendance a committee was appointed:

"Messrs. Harvey, H. Webster, Blackwell, Dr. Charles Smith, Joseph Rodgers, T. E. Vickers, N. Creswick, T. Pearson, W. Prest, and other gentlemen, to draw up a memorial, embodying the views of the corps, for presentation to the Secretary at War, by Mr. Overend, at his proposed interview." [3]

Three weeks later on 11th June, a further meeting was held:

"A meeting of the persons who have joined the rifle corps was held on Monday evening, at the Bramall lane Cricket Ground, to receive the names of those persons who were willing to commence drill at once, and to make arrangements as to the time at which the drill should take place. Six gentlemen gave in their names as ready to commence drill. A sergeant has been engaged to conduct the drill, in the place of Mr. Jones, who had previously promised to undertake the office, but who has been unavoidably prevented from doing so. It was agreed that a deputation should wait upon General Peel to obtain information on various matters connected with the formation of the corps. On Wednesday morning, the deputation, introduced by Earl Fitzwilliam, and consisting of Mr. Overend, deputy-lieutenant; Mr. J. Rodgers, Jun., Mr. S. Newbould, and Mr. T. E. Vickers, had an interview with Gen. Peel, at the War department." [4]

Hallamshire Rifles

Our three footballing protagonists all became officers on 28th June 1859 of the newly named 'Hallamshire Rifles', who would practice their drill at the Collegiate School:

"A general meeting of those who have joined the rifle corps of Sheffield and the neighbourhood was held at the Town-hall yesterday evening; Wilson Overend, Esq., in the chair. The meeting was held for the purpose of swearing in the members, arranging for drill, and electing officers.

CHAPTER THREE

Drill was fixed to take place every evening at the Collegiate School Ground, at seven o'clock. The following officers were elected: - Captains: 1st Company, S. Newbould; 2nd Company, T. E. Vickers. Lieutenants: 1st Company, N. Creswick; 2nd Company, Wm. Prest. Ensigns: 1st Company, Josh. Rodgers; 2nd Company, A. Vickers. Sergeant-Majors: 1st Company, - Gorrery; 2nd Company, Wm. Harvey. Sergeants: 1st Company, North, Terry; 2nd Company, W. W. Renton, -Denial, Corporals: 1st Company, Cook, Wheatley, Riley, C. G. Smith; 2nd Company, Gibbs, H. Branson, E. Drury, M. Flockton. This selection is of course only a nomination, the appointment of all the officers being at the discretion of the Lord-Lieutenant of the Riding." [5]

As officers together in the Volunteer movement, Nathaniel Creswick and Tom Vickers had a falling out at a meeting over the conduct of a Major William Overend which had resulted in Creswick resigning. In response, Vickers described Creswick's statement as an 'entirely concocted composition.' [6] Could this public disagreement in late 1860, in some way have formed a rift that led to the formation of a rival football club to Sheffield FC? Pure hypothesis of course on my part, but it does exactly coincide with the formation date of Hallam FC. Until this point Tom Vickers had been a member of Sheffield FC and after such a public falling out, it may have been difficult to continue in the same team; forming a rival organisation may have seemed an attractive proposition.

By May 1861 Sheffield had three Volunteer Corps and when two guns (32 pounders) arrived at Midland station they all assembled for the first time together to march them back to headquarters. The 58th Regiment sent their band over to lead the procession, which was led out by the Artillery Volunteers with Captain N. Creswick on horseback in charge, followed by the Engineer Volunteers led by Captain Mitchell and finally came the Hallamshire Rifle Volunteers led by Captain T. Vickers. Also mounted were Captain Prest, Captain Cockburn and Mr. S. Parker (Surgeon). The 500 men formed four abreast and marched through the Sheffield streets which were so crowded by onlookers as 'to impede the march of the Volunteers.' [7]

Volunteer Football was first played at Hyde Park, Sheffield, in November 1861 between the 4th West Riding Artillery Volunteers and the West York Engineer Volunteers, to raise money for the funds of the Corps by charging a 6d admission fee. [8] There were three Volunteer Football Teams - the Engineers, the Artillery and the Rifles - based in Sheffield, which in 1872 amalgamated. [9] Before that there are many match reports in the press of Engineers FC playing regularly against the other Sheffield clubs. At a 'Grand Volunteer Review' held in York for the northern counties, there were 20,000 men present, including 300 from the Sheffield Artillery and 350 from the Hallamshire Rifles; [10] by 1882 a North of England Football Volunteer Association had been founded.

In the 1873 Football Annual, the 'Artillery and Hallamshire Rifles' appear as a listing; these were the descendants of the 1859 Sheffield Volunteers, so they were still clearly enjoying their football. In 1883, the War Office re-titled the Hallamshire Rifles as the 1st (Hallamshire) Volunteer Battalion, and together with the York and Lancaster Regiment they raised two 'Active service Battalions' who had fought with regular forces in the Boer War. In 1908, on the reorganisation of the Volunteers into the Territorial Force, the Hallamshires were re-designated the '4th (Hallamshire) Battalion, the York and Lancaster Regiment TF'. In recognition of their war service, King George V decreed in 1924 that the '4th' be dropped from the title and henceforth they should be known as 'The Hallamshire Battalion'.

CHAPTER FOUR

Sheffield Football Association

"There can be little doubting that the development of modern football relied heavily on the creation of networks of clubs, whether we consider the Sheffield clubs, the eleven founder clubs of the Football Association, or the development of powerful County associations that followed thereafter." [1]

England's First County Association

The Sheffield Football Association started in Sheffield 150 years ago in January 1867, with 1,000 members and sixteen clubs; it was formed primarily to respond to the changes made to the playing rules recently altered in London by the Football Association. Its support helped strengthen the London body at a crucial time when the F.A. was struggling to attract clubs to become affiliated to the organisation. It would not be until the introduction of the F.A. Cup in 1871 that the Football Association membership truly began to take off. Birmingham F.A. was the second County Association but it did not form until nine years later in 1876. (The received wisdom is that the Birmingham F.A. was founded in 1875, but my research shows that it was in fact the following year).

"SHEFFIELD FOOTBALL ASSOCIATION. The annual meeting of the various Sheffield clubs forming the above association, which had been adjourned in order to allow time for consideration of the rules adopted by the metropolitan clubs, was held at the Adelphi Hotel on Wednesday evening last, the 7th inst.; H. W. Chambers, Esq. (honorary secretary of the Sheffield club), president of the association, in the chair. The clubs of Sheffield were well represented, as many as thirteen clubs sending representatives. After the preliminary business, the rules as lately adopted by the London association were taken into consideration, and the amendments proposed by the representatives of the thirteen clubs duly discussed. After a long and protracted discussion, a code of rules was formed." [2]

Five years later in 1872, the Sheffield Football Association membership had increased:

"The Association now consists of sixteen clubs, representing several thousand members, and in addition to these South Derbyshire Association have joined, adopting the Sheffield code, and as they number nearly a thousand members it will be seen that a powerful organisation is forming and gradually increasing in the Northern and Midland counties." [3]

The introduction of Cup competitions was a critical reason for the success of Association football, starting with the F.A. Cup in 1871, followed by Sheffield Football Association launching the first County knockout competition in 1876. The powers behind Rugby and cricket did not like these kind of competitions; the cricket authorities were worried about the effect it would have on the emerging county structure and there was a general feeling of disquiet by the middle-class Rugby players of not being able to choose your opponents - they wanted to avoid the potential ignominy of a defeat to a perceived 'lesser' team. The following report shows that such views persisted as late as 1887:

CHAPTER FOUR

"The support given to the Association game is no doubt attributable to the fact that Challenge Cup competitions take place under Association rules, and thus a twofold object in winning is secured. The victory in a tie is not only an end, it is also a means to an end - one step further towards securing the Cup. The so-called Cricket Championship - an honour called into being by Irresponsible persons - was not to be commended, because it tended to transfer the interest which should be felt in each match to the decision of the last series, and it seems to us that the Association Challenge Cups are open to a little objection. The Rugby Union has never espoused this form of competition; while it has set its face against the legislation of professionalism." [4]

For many years, the most derogatory comment gentlemen amateurs could direct at the successful Lancashire Association clubs as they started to dominate the F.A. Cup, was that they were 'pot-hunters.' Charles W. Alcock, whilst instrumental in the introduction of the F.A. Cup, was very active in dissuading the M.C.C. not to introduce knockout cups in cricket. The Youdan Cup was the world's first knockout Cup in 1867 and was not started by an Association, but by a Sheffield music hall impresario (the Youdan Cup story is covered in more depth in Chapter Five). The Sheffield Association Challenge Cup started at the same time as the one started by the Birmingham F.A., becoming England's first County knockout tournaments. The Scottish F.A. launched its national Scottish Cup in 1873 and the Welsh F.A. followed suit in 1877.

Twenty-five teams entered the inaugural Sheffield Football Association Challenge Cup in 1876. (Sheffield FC chose not to enter the competition presumably to continue to focus on inter-county matches). To qualify clubs had to first join the Association at a cost of 5 shillings. The rules were an interesting insight into where the Sheffield game was by this point:

"No individual shall be allowed to play for more than one competing club, but the members of each representative team may be changed during the series of matches if thought necessary. The play in each contest is to last an hour and a half, and the average circumference of the ball to be from 27 to 28 inches…The first and second ties are to be played on the grounds of the respective clubs, the captains of the clubs drawn together tossing for choice, and in case of a drawn match the loser of the first toss is then to have his choice of ground, and so on alternately. The third and following ties are to be played at Bramall lane or such other ground as the committee shall hereafter determine. In the final ties two umpires and a referee will be appointed by the committee, none of whom shall be members of either of the contending clubs…That the cup does not become the property of any club, but shall be competed for annually…The association will present to the winners of the final tie in each year 12 silver medals." [5]

Harry W. Chambers was the first President of the newly founded Sheffield Football Association in 1867; he held this post for two years until he was replaced in 1869 by John Charles Shaw, a position he would hold for 14 years until 1882.

Sheffield New Football Association

The old order of the Sheffield Football Association was challenged on April 2nd 1877, 140 years ago this year, when the Sheffield New Football Association was established. This was a protest organisation because of Sheffield Football Association's decision not to allow any club under two years old to become a member:

"FORMATION OF A NEW FOOTBALL ASSOCIATION. Mr. Frederick Sanderson writes: The first meeting of delegates representing the clubs forming a new football association was held in the Temperance Hall, on Wednesday night, Mr. Frederick Sanderson, president pro tem., in the chair. The number of clubs joining was further increased, and there is every prospect of the movement being successful. The name of the association and its rules, together with the laws of the game of football, were considered, and drafted into form, to be recommended for adoption to the general meeting of members, which will be held at an early date. Mr. B. Hemsworth, hon. Sec., was unanimously elected treasurer; pro tem. The meeting closed with a vote of thanks to the chairman." [6]

It would change its name in 1881 to the Hallamshire Football Association and by the 1880/81 season it had more clubs than the Sheffield Football Association. (These fledgling clubs are covered in more depth in Chapter Six). This situation persisted until the end of the 1886/87 season when a merger of the two Associations was negotiated by Charles Clegg.

The following table shows the history of the two Associations from 1876 to 1889.

Football Season	Name	Sheffield Association Challenge Cup	Officers of The Sheffield Association	Expansion	Notes
1876/77	Sheffield Association	Sheffield Association Challenge Cup Final Wednesday 4 Heely 3 (after time had to be extended half an hour to allow a decision to be arrived at) Bramall Lane	J. F. Hall Hon. Sec. President J. C. Shaw		In the 1876 Football Annual (season 1875/76) the 'Sheffield Association' has 33 clubs with a total of 4,933 members
1877/78	Sheffield Association	25 clubs entered Sheffield Association Challenge Cup Final Wednesday 2 Attercliffe 0 Bramall Lane	W. Pierce Dix Hon. Sec. President J. C. Shaw	Sheffield New Association. Played a 12 club competition on formation. Pye Bank 1 Rising Star 0. (After playing three drawn matches)	Sheffield Association rules amalgamated with the Football Association on 28 April 1877
1878/79	Sheffield Association	31 clubs entered Sheffield Association Challenge Cup Final Thursday Wanderers 3 Heeley 1 Bramall Lane	W. Pierce Dix Hon. Sec. President J. C. Shaw	Sheffield New Association Challenge Cup Final Rising Star 4 Pitsmoor Christ Church Club 1	A total of 76 clubs
1879/80	Sheffield Association	36 clubs entered Sheffield Association Challenge Cup Final Staveley 3 Heeley 1 Sheaf House	W. Pierce Dix Secretary and Treasurer President J. C. Shaw	Sheffield New Association Challenge Cup Final. The winners proved to be Burton Star Club. (30 clubs)	
1880/81	Sheffield Association	29 clubs entered Sheffield Association Challenge Cup Final Wednesday 8 Ecclesfield 1 Bramall Lane	W. Pierce Dix Secretary and Treasurer President J. C. Shaw	Sheffield New Association Challenge Cup Final Intake 2 Burton Star 0 42 clubs entered. (49 clubs in total) Hon. Sec. James Ward	This means that across both rival associations a total of 78 clubs existed Appendix Two - my research has 76 clubs at the end of 1880

CHAPTER FOUR

1881/82	Sheffield Association	18 clubs entered Sheffield Association Challenge Cup Final Heeley 5 Pye Bank 0 Bramall Lane	J. R. Harvey Hon. Sec. President J. C. Shaw	Sheffield New Association changed its name to the Hallamshire Football Association	39 clubs entered Hallamshire Football Challenge Cup (41 clubs in total) Intake 1 Dronfield Exchange 0 This means that across both rival associations a total of 59 clubs existed Appendix Two - my research has 70 clubs at the end of 1881
1882/83	Sheffield Association	Sheffield Association Challenge Cup Final Wednesday 2 Lockwood Brothers 1 (Replayed Final) (Uknown number of Cup entrants)	J. R. Harvey Hon. Sec. President J. C. Clegg (J. C. Shaw retired due to the pressure of being regularly called away on business)		Hallamshire Football Association Challenge Spital 3 Owlerton 0 (35 clubs in total) David Haigh (Hon. Sec.)
1883/84	Sheffield Association	Sheffield Association Challenge Cup Final Lockwood Brothers 2 Heeley 0 (Replayed Final) Bramall Lane (Unknown number of Cup entrants) (S.F.A. didn't report their season's results to the 1884 Football Annual)	J. R. Harvey Hon. Sec. President J. C. Clegg		Hallamshire Football Association Challenge Cup Eckington 4 Clinton 3 (aet) (after the first game ending in a 2-2 tie and after extra time) (22 clubs in total)
1884/85	Sheffield Association	Sheffield Association Challenge Cup Final Lockwood Brothers 2 Park Grange 0 Bramall Lane (Unknown number of Cup entrants)	J. R. Harvey Hon. Sec. President J. C. Clegg		Hallamshire Football Association Challenge Cup Staveley 2 Eckington 1 (18 clubs in total) David Haigh (Hon. Sec.)
1885/86	Sheffield Association	Sheffield Association Challenge Cup Final Mexborough 2 Heeley 1 Old Forge Ground, Brightside Lane ('a quagmire')	J. R. Harvey Hon. Sec. President J. C. Clegg		Hallamshire Football Association Challenge Cup Staveley 3 Eckington 2 23 clubs entered Cup David Haigh (Hon. Sec.)

1885/86 continued		(Unknown number of Cup entrants) (S.F.A. didn't report their season's results to the 1884 Football Annual			
1886/87	Sheffield Association	Sheffield Association Challenge Cup Final Wednesday 2 Collegiate 1 Old Forge Ground, Brightside (Unknown number of Cup entrants)	J. R. Harvey Hon. Sec. President J. C. Clegg		Hallamshire Football Association Challenge Cup Eckington 3 Chirton 1 David Haigh (Hon. Sec.)
1887/88	Sheffield & Hallamshire Association	Sheffield & Hallamshire Association Challenge Cup Final Wednesday 3 Ecclesfield 2 Bramall Lane 'Wednesday winning both the Challenge and Charity, and Carbrook Church the Junior Cup.' David Haigh (Hon. Sec.) (Unknown number of Cup entrants)	David Haigh Hon. Sec. (Sheffield & Hallamshire Association) President J. C. Clegg (Sheffield & Hallamshire Association)	The two rival associations amalgamate	'The wisdom of this (amalgamation) was proved in the results of the Asscociation matches. Close upon 60 clubs have entered the association this season.' David Haigh (Hon. Sec.) (It's actually 54)
1888/89	Sheffield & Hallamshire Association	Sheffield & Hallamshire Association Challenge Cup Final Rotherham Town 2 Staveley 1 Bramall Lane (Unknown number of Cup entrants)	David Haigh Hon. Sec. President J. C. Clegg		

Analysis of the Football Annuals shows the early pre-eminence of the Sheffield Football Association; no competing county had more football clubs than Sheffield, until the 1882/83 season when the Lancashire F.A. overtook them with eighty-four clubs, against Sheffield's sixty-four. (In the same season, Birmingham F.A. had sixty-three).

There is no doubt that the influence of the County Football Associations waned from the late 1880s onwards as the increasingly professional clubs could not see the importance of County selection nor saw the imperative of succeeding in County competitions. Playing international games for your country rather than your county, took on more importance and whilst the county identity remained important at school and amateur level for many years, this too slowly declined.

Thirty-two clubs entered the 2016/17 'Senior Challenge Cup in association with BlueFin' as it is now known; Hallam FC and Sheffield FC were both knocked out at the quarter final stage.

CHAPTER FOUR

The year 2017 represents the 150th anniversary of local County Football Associations, because the first such organisation, the Sheffield Football Association, was formed in 1867.

English County Football Associations still host 'County Cups' held at a sub-regional level, which are open to all affiliated members of the County F.A.s, but there are no national plans to commemorate this important footballing institution, in this significant year. Sheffield Association marks not only its 150th this year but also its 130th anniversary as the Sheffield and Hallamshire Association.

The Sheffield Football Association team.
The Illustrated Sporting and Dramatic News 14th March 1874. Image courtesy of Sheffield FC.

The 1874 engraving above is the earliest known image of Sheffield footballers. It was commissioned to capture the Sheffield Football Association team that played against the London Football Association (captained by Charles W. Alcock) on the 3rd January 1874, played at the Oval. The game ended in a scoreless draw and the eleven Sheffield players were (team names added by author); John Marsh (Capt.) *(Wednesday)* J.C. Clegg *(Wednesday & Albion)*, W.E. Clegg *(Wednesday & Albion)*, W.H. Stacey *(Wednesday)*, W.H. Carr *(Owlerton)*, A. Wood *(Gleadless)*, R. Gregory *(Albion)*, Buttery (If 'T' Buttery *Millhouses & Zulus*), Sellars *(Norfolk?)*, W. Wilkinson *(Brightside)*, B. Tingle *(Oxford)*. Unfortunately, the actual who's who was not elaborated on but presumably the captain is sat in the middle with the ball. In the search for the two Clegg brothers, my guess would the third and fifth from the left on the back row, as the two men with similar features. The two men in hats are unknown, but likely candidates could be John Charles Shaw (Sheffield F.A. President) and Harry W. Chambers (Sheffield F.C. Hon. Sec.)

CHAPTER FIVE

The Golden Age of Sheffield Amateur Football 1857-1876

1857

Queen Victoria's reign had commenced twenty years earlier (20 June 1837) and would not finish for another forty-four years (22 January 1901). In June 1857, the first sixty-two Victoria Crosses were presented for valour in the Crimean war. The Prime Minister was Whig (Liberal) Henry John Temple, 3rd Viscount Palmerston, from 6 February 1855 till 19 February 1858. Together with France, the UK declared war on China in the so-called Second Opium War and the Anglo-Persian war had come to a close. Elsewhere, colonial problems started with a vengeance in the Indian Rebellion. Thomas Hughes' Rugby-based novel 'Tom Brown's School Days' was published, in America the National Association of Base Ball Players was formed and Oxford won the 14th Oxford and Cambridge Boat Race. Robert Baden Powell, Edward Elgar and Joseph Conrad were born in this year. It was also the year when the term 'muscular Christianity' [1] was first mentioned, which can be defined as a Christian commitment to health and manliness. The movement was reflected in an increasing interest from churches to set up their own football clubs.

'Football is a grand game for developing a lad physically and also morally, for he learns to play with good temper and unselfishness, to play in his place, and to play the game, and these are the best of training for any game of life.' Baden Powell; 'Scouting for Boys,' 1908

Of course, we celebrate the year 1857 for the launch of Sheffield FC.

Sheffield Foot-ball Club (Sheffield, Yorkshire October 24th 1857-Present)

- Oldest Sheffield Football Club
- Oldest continuously running Association Football Club in the world
- Sheffield & Hallamshire Senior Cup Winners: 1993/94, 2004/05, 2005/06, 2007/08, 2009/10
- F.A. Amateur Cup Winner: 1903/04

Origin: School Alumni (and Cricket and the Volunteer Movement). Sheffield FC joined the F.A. on 8th December 1863; however, the Sheffield Football Association did not fully embrace Football Association Laws until April 1877.

If you want to stand on the hallowed ground where Association football was first played, then you need to find the B&Q store on Queens Road in Sheffield and you will not be far away. It is only about half a mile away from Bramall Lane; try to imagine the more picturesquely named Strawberry Hall Lane where Sheffield FC first played. It was also sometimes described as Mr. Turners Field, Eastbank, but more regularly plain 'East Bank'; if tempted to stage a commemorative kick about in the B&Q car park, make sure you ask permission first.

CHAPTER FIVE

Historically, an earlier foundation date of 1855 has appeared for Sheffield FC, notably as listed for the first F.A. Amateur Cup in 1893/94, when they were listed as Sheffield 1855. I think this incorrect date came about from Charles W. Alcock, who gets the date wrong and promotes his club incorrectly in place of Sheffield FC, in the following 1905 article:

"The Sheffield Club was formed in 1855, its neighbour Hallam Club, two years later…its antiquity is beyond dispute but whether it was the first to organise seriously with a view to a regular programme of football, is however, a little open to doubt. The first club to work on a definite basis with the distinct object of circulating and popularising the game, I am inclined to think, was a club known as the Forest Club." [2]

This incorrect date is repeated by Richard Sparling as late as 1926: 'The Sheffield Club is the oldest existing football club in the world, and the minute books go back to 1855.' [3]

The table below is a condensation of the facts gleaned from the Football Annuals from 1868 to 1889 and I have repeated this analysis for all the Sheffield clubs from this period. The table shows that the consistency of the foundation dates was not helped by the changing Hon. Secs., who made mistakes over the course of the twenty years of self-reporting to the Football Annual, when even the preposterously early foundation year of 1854 was suggested for seven years by W. A. Matthews.

Football Annual	Ground	Foundation Date	Hon. Sec.	Members	Colours
1868	East Bank	September 1867	Harry W. Chambers	299 Amount of subscription: 2s. 6d.	Scarlet
1869	East Bank	September 1867	John Denton	330	Scarlet
1870	East Bank	1857	John Denton	330	Scarlet
1871	East Bank	1857	Harry W. Chambers	330	Scarlet
1872	East Bank	1857	Harry W. Chambers	330	Scarlet
1873	Brammall Lane *	1857	Harry W. Chambers	330	Scarlet
1874	Brammall Lane	1857	Harry W. Chambers	330	Scarlet
1875	Brammall Lane	1857	Harry W. Chambers	230	Scarlet
1876	Brammall Lane	1857	Harry W. Chambers	230	Scarlet
1877	Brammall Lane	1857	W.R. Wake	230	Scarlet
1878	x				
1879	Bramall Lane Cricket Ground	1854	W. A. Matthews	315	Scarlet and black
1880	Bramall Lane Cricket Ground	1854	W. A. Matthews	205	Scarlet and black
1881	Bramall Lane Cricket Ground	1854	W. A. Matthews	Reporting stopped in 1881 edition	Black
1882	Bramall Lane Cricket Ground	1854	W. J. Beardshaw		Black
1883	Bramall Lane Cricket Ground	1854	W. J. Beardshaw		Black and scarlet
1884	Bramall Lane Cricket Ground	1854	W. J. Beardshaw		Black and scarlet
1885	Old Forge Ground (Changing at the Steam Clock Inn)	1854	W. J. Beardshaw		Scarlet and black
1886					
1887		1857	W.W. Liddell		Half red and black
1888	Bramall Lane	1857	H.B. Willey		Half red and black
1889	Bramall Lane	1857	H.B. Willey		Half red and black

* Not a typo but how Bramall Lane was originally spelt

Sheffield FC held its early team meetings at the Falcon Inn, 15 Flat Street, Sheffield.

What was it about Sheffield FC, created by Nathaniel Creswick and William Prest, that made it the world's first recognised football club as opposed to any of the other competing clubs? A team from Thurlstone was playing in Yorkshire as early as 1841 and there were as many as seven teams playing in the same year in Lancashire. The difference between Sheffield and other fast industrialising areas seems to be that the Sheffield's ambitious middle classes, whether in industry, church or military, seemed to be very attracted to all sports, but particularly cricket and athletics; they were looking at new ways to keep fit all-year-round which included gymnasium membership and the game of football. In Lancashire at the same time there was more interest in the Rugby game and there is a persistent online claim for a foundation date of 1857 for Liverpool FC; this could equal the claims from Sheffield FC, as the games of Rugby and Association were barely distinguishable at this point. However, according to the 1873 Football Annual, Liverpool FC was founded in 1866. Looking at the press reports there is certainly a Liverpool FC playing Rugby in November 1857 but they cease at some point before 1866 and the current Liverpool St Helens club started in 1866. Obviously, the Football Annuals did not exist in 1857, in the same way that they did not for Sheffield FC, but when Sheffield had the option to submit their foundation date they listed 1857, whereas Liverpool FC chose to list 1866:

"This club (*Liverpool*) enjoys the distinction of a long and honoured career dating its origin to about the same time as its oldest rival, the Manchester Club (*1867*)." [4]

Sheffield FC didn't just want to play, it also wanted to create a standardised set of rules that other clubs would want to copy and then it combined that with managing to stay in existence, so that a narrative about the club was formed. It also helped to have local newspapers keen to report on the sport and finally it paid (historically and financially) to have the foresight to keep the original paperwork safe, especially at times of natural disasters like the flood of 1864. There were no football reporters; the newspapers were dependent on the players themselves submitting the reports, which as one might expect led to many post-match disputes. By 1876 the self-reported match reports had become a torrent:

"Correspondents are informed that the waste-paper basket awaits all scores of Saturday matches which reach this Office so late as TUESDAY MORNING. Our stock of waste-paper is also increased by scores written on both sides of the paper, or in pencil. Printed scoring-sheets may be had at any stationers for a trifle." [5]

Sheffield FC's nickname quickly became the 'Gentlemen'; in the February 18th 1928 edition of the All Sports Weekly J.A.H. Catton reminisced (slightly preposterously) about Sheffield FC:

"A friend of mine told me some thirty years ago that the 'Gentlemen' used to play with kid gloves on their hands and carried a coin in each palm –this being not only a device to keep their hands clean but to keep them from touching the ball, as if they did so they would lose the coin."

In the late 1860s unskilled workers, would be earning around 4 shillings a week and skilled workers maybe double that, so Sheffield FC's annual subscription of 2s. 6d. would have represented two or three days' income. The subscriptions would not be totally beyond a working man but the problem would be the absence of an invitation to join and the lack of leisure time for a game of football. It would be Lancashire where the sport became the game of the working man and this would be where professionalism would grow, to the initial disdain of the men of Sheffield FC. In spite of the activity going on in the London and Essex area, by the second half of the 19th century Sheffield was acknowledged as the footballing centre of the world. By 1875 the Athletic News reported that: 'The town of Sheffield is proverbial all over England as the most sport loving place in the country.'

CHAPTER FIVE

Hyde Park in Sheffield was the centre of the early sporting activity in 1856:

"On Saturday last, Messrs. John Kenyon and Co. gave an entertainment to their workmen, about 300 in number, at Hyde Park Cricket Ground, which was specially engaged, and a large tent from Derby was erected as a dining room. Cricket, football, rifle shooting, jumping, &c., were the amusement of the early part of the day, and at three o'clock the company sat down to an excellent dinner. Mr. Gardener and family drove upon the ground, and were received with enthusiastic cheers. After dinner, Mr. Skelton occupying the chair, and Mr. S. Gardner, Jun., the vice-chair, various toasts were given. At eight o'clock tea was provided, which was followed by dancing, kept up with great spirit until half-past eleven." [6]

It is interesting to note that in spite of Sheffield becoming a footballing hot spot and Hyde Park representing their oldest establishing sporting venue, very few football clubs were ever to call it their home. The other booming sports in Sheffield at this time are pedestrianism (competitive walking for a prize), Nurr and Spell (a bat and ball game) and cocking (cockfighting). Nurr and spell was played as early as 1831 (as well as an early football game):

"Nurr and Spell – A match at Nurr and Spell will come off at Hyde park, Sheffield, tomorrow; and in the afternoon a match at football will take place." [7]

Big money cockfighting was reported on in 1844:

"Cocking – On Monday, Tuesday, and Wednesday last a main was fought at Sheffield, between John Cousins and Joseph Ratcliffe, for £2 a battle and £50 the main. Cousins setter for himself, and Harry Booth, of Staleybridge, setter for Ratcliffe. 8 mains 9 byes; second day, Cousins 5 mains and 2 byes. Ratcliffe 1 mains and 1 bye; third day, Cousins 8 mains and 3 byes, Ratcliffe 1 main and 0 bye. Total – Cousins 34 battles and Ratcliffe 13." [8]

In 1847 a challenge mile race was offered in the national press:

"The proprietor of Hyde Park, Sheffield, intends to give a handsome silver cup, value of 20 sovs, for a mile race, to be run, in heats, open to the world. The men entering to choose a party to see a fair handicap on the Thursday before the race. Those not satisfied with the handicap, will have their entrance money returned. The race to come off on Monday, June 28th, 1847. Entrance, 7s. 6d.; second man to save his stake. Entrance on or before Thursday, the 24th of June, by two o'clock. The cup can be seen on and after Monday next, at Mr. Samuel Heathcote's, Hyde Park, Sheffield, it being the same cup which has been run for by all the cracks, viz., Manks, Shepherd, Sherdon, Jackson, Byrom, &c." [9]

Nathaniel Creswick, the co-founder of Sheffield FC, the son of a silver plater, lived as a boy at Parkfield House, Highfields before moving to East Hill House around 1844. [10] (In 1857 Parkfield House, was the home of Harry W. Chambers the club's first Hon. Sec. where the inaugural meetings of Sheffield FC took place in 1857). Nathaniel played cricket with William Prest at the Sheffield United Cricket Club (1854) when they were both in their mid-twenties and may well have been interested in the innovation of the same year when a gentleman's gym opened. It is not known if they joined (or even invested in) the Sheffield Gymnasium but due to its location, where they had probably played as boys, they would certainly have been very aware of its instigation:

"Gymnasium – A piece of ground adjoining the grounds of the Wesley College has been taken and a number of gentlemen have subscribed for shares, to erect a Gymnasium, a Rifle gallery, a Racket court, and an American bowling alley. Amid all the stimulants to mental effort which the present day affords, those take but a one-sided view of education who neglects to train the body as well as the mind. And the more the mind is tasked, the greater is the necessity for cultivating to the highest point of efficiency the physical powers, and keeping them by constant and well regulate exercise in full vigour. The design of this Gymnasium is excellent, and we have no doubt it will be appreciated by the public." [11]

Six months later the gymnasium was open and was state of the art:

"Sheffield Gymnasium and School of Arms – We understand that it is intended to open, next week, the buildings recently erected in Clarkehouse Lane, for the Gymnasium and School of Arms. The design of the promoters has been to supply a want felt by the gentlemen engaged in mercantile and professional pursuits, whose engagements render them unable to spare the time necessary to take that amount of muscular exercise which is necessary for the maintenance of health. The building comprises a gymnasium, 90 feet long and 31 feet wide; racket attic, 65 feet in length and 30 feet wide; rifle gallery, 190 feet long; two American bowling alleys, quoit ground, reading rooms, &c. The gymnasium, attached to which are suites of dressing rooms, is stated to be the most complete in its fittings of any similar institution in England. It and the racket court are lighted from the roof, and in the latter is a raised gallery, with seats for the accommodation of spectators." [12]

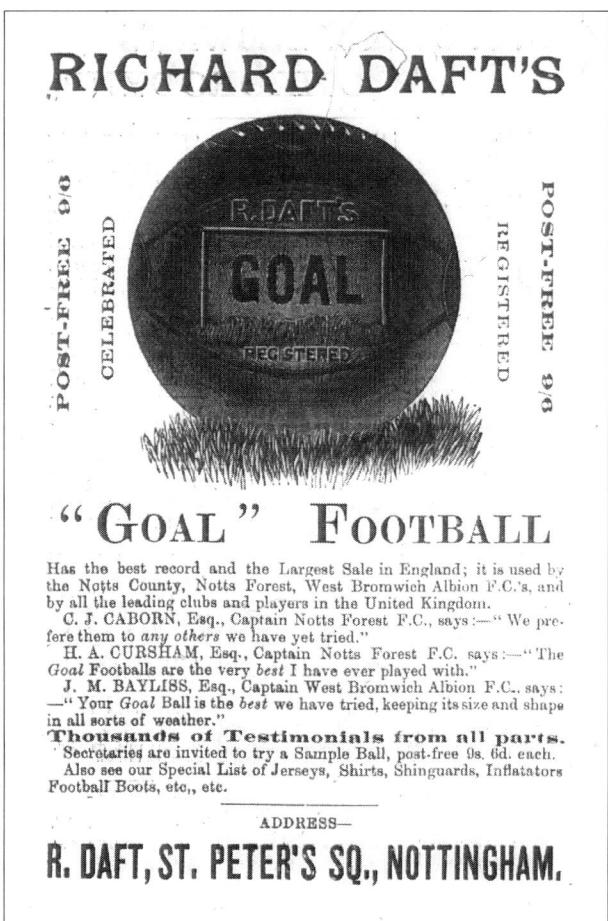

The project was short-lived and the gym was declared insolvent in June 1856; perhaps the gym had provided a place to exercise through the winter and it was thought that playing football would fill the gap, when it closed? Whatever the catalyst, in May 1857 Nathaniel Creswick and William Prest decided to form a 'foot ball' club, but first there was a cricket season to play. William Prest was 92 not out playing for South Yorkshire against Langton Wold [13] whilst Nathaniel Creswick was bowling six wickets for the Hallam Cricket Club. In October 1857 W. Prest was bowled out for 10 whilst playing for the Sheffield Wednesday Cricket club by 'Daft' of the Newark club, a name that would become synonymous with early Nottinghamshire football. After his playing career finished Richard Daft opened a sports equipment shop in St. Peter's Square, Nottingham. This advert is from the 1887 Football Annual, featuring a testimonial from Harry Cursham.

The thriving cricket scene of Sheffield in the 1850's was an important factor in the formation of football clubs, with many early cricket clubs bearing the names of soon to be football clubs, such as Wednesday, Owlerton, Milton, Perseverance, Albion, Pitsmoor, Exchange, Talbot and of course Hallam.

CHAPTER FIVE

Once the cricket season was over, and five months after the football club had first been mooted, the Sheffield Foot Ball Club was officially founded on October 24th 1857 at the home of Harry Waters Chambers, Parkfield House. Harry's son Ernest, a defender for Sheffield FC won the F.A. Amateur Cup with them in 1904 and his other two sons Harry Junior and Geoffrey, both became Club Presidents. In an 1891magazine article, Charles W. Alcock wrote a glowing testimonial for Sheffield FC's Hon. Sec:

"The Royal Engineers, Barnes, the Clapham Rovers, the Crystal Palace Club, the N.N.'s, the Hertfordshire Rangers and the two universities were the principal competitors the Wanderers had to meet in the south; while Nottingham, Notts Forest, Lincoln and Sheffield under the guidance of Mr. H.W. Chambers, the doyen I should fancy of football secretaries, who has directed or helped direct the club for a great part, if not the whole of its life, for now over thirty years, were doing good service in the development of Association football in the more northerly parts of England." [14]

Prest and Creswick were clearly ambitious men: deciding to call their fledgling enterprise Sheffield FC rather than East Bank FC or similar, shows enormous confidence. Other early clubs were going with literary or historical references (Dingley Dell and Crusaders) or their specific local area (Mincing Lane and Forest), but not Prest and Creswick; for them the ploy was to start ambitiously and keep building. The original headquarters was a greenhouse in the gardens of Park House on East Bank Road lent by Thomas Asline Ward, father of the first club president Frederick Ward, and the adjacent field belonging to Thomas Turner was used as their first playing ground, more commonly referred to as East Bank. A descendent of Nathaniel Creswick discovered a diary of his in 2007, which confirms the club's foundation with a single line:

"I have established a foot ball club to which most of young Sheffield come and kick.31st December 1857."

When Sheffield FC sold their archive at Sotheby's the contents were transcribed for the catalogue. It included a letter from N. J. Creswick:

'I remember the first game in Mr. Thomas Turner's field at East Bank and played in it 57.'

In the same archive is recorded that the club had sixty-two members by the end of the first season and in the accounts, is a record of the club paying £2. 6s. for six footballs.

In the early days of the club, football did not feature strongly; the emphasis was on athletics, with the two founders probably the best two performers at the athletics ground of the club at Eastbank in 1858.

"It will be seen that Mr. W. Prest bore away a great number of prizes and in the neatness and finish of his style was certainly beyond all comparison. Mr. N. Creswick's performance in the mile race was, considering the wet grass land, far above average amateur work." [15]

William Prest came first in twelve out of a total of nineteen events: 100 yard flat race, Standing wide jump, Running high jump, Backwards way race, Standing high jump, Hopping race, Hurdle race, Running wide jump, Wrestling, Throwing the hammer, Hop, skip and jump, and the Sack race.

His sporting achievements grew greater in the following month:

"Gentlemen Amateur Pedestrianism at Sheffield. A most exciting and interesting contest came off on Saturday last at Hyde-park Sheffield, between two gentlemen well known in the sporting and cricketing circles. The match, which was a race of 120 yards, had been made some six weeks, and resulted at the celebration of the anniversary of the football club, on which occasion a field day was held by the members."

The gentlemen of the town and assembled to make wagers:

"The weather on Saturday was exceedingly unpropitious, the rain descending heavily until within a quarter of an hour of the starting time. Notwithstanding this drawback, about 200 gentlemen, including Wilson Overend, Esq., deputy lieutenant of the West Riding, and most of the influential gentry of the neighbourhood assembled. The stakes contested for were quite nominal in comparison with the bets which pended the result."

William Prest easily won:

"The competitors were William Prest, Esq, a young gentleman well known to the lovers of the noble game of cricket, and Henry Miller, Esq., of Wadsley House, well known on the Turf. Each went through the requisite training ordeal, and appeared at the mark in excellent condition. Mr. Miller, however, was not so well as his friends could wish, having caught a slight cold a few days prior to the contest. Precisely at three o'clock the amateurs took their positions for the start, which was signalled by the report of a pistol. Mr. Prest was the favourite at the start, as much as 2 to 1 being laid on him at the close. Both gentlemen appeared likely for the task undertaken, and although Mr. Prest had the advantage of height, length and limb, and youthfulness, yet his opponent, who is a compact, muscularly-built young gentlemen, seemed no despicable one. One false attempt was made in the eagerness to get off, the competitors bending to go upon the starter asking if they were ready. Ultimately they re-arranged themselves at the mark, and on a pistol being fired bounded off on even terms and at a tremendous pace. It was said by some of the spectators that Mr. Miller obtained a slight advantage at the start, and that he was a trifle in front for thirty yards. Our opinion, however, was that there was no perceptible advantage in them for that distance. At fifty yards Mr. Prest drew away from his antagonist, and after turning his head several times, won easily, amidst the most vociferous cheering, by half a dozen yards. Mr. Miller ran gamely to the finish, and, notwithstanding his defeat, is far above the average pedestrians. The time so astonished the holders of the watches that they thought the ground run must have been within the prescribed distance, and, consequently, had it measured. It was, however, found correct, and taking into consideration the easy manner in which Mr. Prest won, and the condition of the ground from the recent rains, he has distinguished himself as a first-class runner." [16]

The growing athletic reputation in Sheffield provoked a response in the Leeds Press:

"Athletic Sports – A hint for 'The Gentlemen' of Leeds. To the editor of the intelligencer, Sir, - Will you allow me to suggest to 'the gentlemen' of Leeds, at least to those who are young and active, the propriety of following, in the matter of athletic sports, the example of 'the gentlemen' of Sheffield? Cricket, a fine manly sport, has been hitherto almost the only kind of athletic exercise for the practice of which clubs have been established in this town and neighbourhood; but why should not there be clubs, of societies, or association, for the training of the members in many other excellent physical exercises? Too much of a good thing, as is well known, becomes an evil. Too much cricketing tends to wearisomeness, and does not allow so much scope for the development of physical strength as would be afforded by the practice of several well-known English sports. What 'the gentlemen' of Sheffield have done and are doing may be inferred from the following report, which is copied from a Sheffield paper…. The above account affords so much information, as to the character of the sports and those who practise them at Sheffield that I shall not trespass further on your space than repeating my suggestion to 'the gentlemen' of Leeds to follow the example pointed out. Yours truly, Pedestrian." April 16th 1858." [17]

It would be six years before a Leeds side attempted the Association code which is covered in more detail in the 1864 section.

CHAPTER FIVE

The 1862 edition of 'Pawson's & Brailsford's Illustrated Guide to Sheffield and Neighbourhood,' claims the existence of three local football clubs, which underestimates my analysis by seven clubs (see Appendix Two) :

"...the Sheffield, the Pitsmoor, and the Hallam. In connection with these there are annual sports and athletic games, which, especially those of the Sheffield Club, are attended by the elite of the town."

In 1862, 3,000 people attended the annual Sheffield Athletic Games and by 1867 there would be 7,000 attending. A proficiency at athletic sports was apparently also a good way to meet the ladies, according to a Sheffield Daily Telegraph report about the Sheffield Football Club Athletic Sports Day, that took place at 'Brammall-lane' Cricket Ground in May 1868:

"When the gentlemen-as the members are termed in contradiction to the artisans and tradespeople who compose the other ninety and nine other clubs which flourish in our mist- when the gentlemen turn out to show themselves in the roped and staked arena, the ladies flock in hundreds to witness the conflicts, and the green is fringed with a variegated display of interesting colours. With a forethought and a gallantry becoming men, about to gather together to show their muscle, grand stands overlooking the course were erected, covered with glazed calico, placed in alternate lengths of red, white and blue; and these stands were occupied by ladies, dressed in delicate fabrics, of all the tints and lines of the rainbow, whose faces were radiant with smiles, and the interest they took in the efforts of the athletes to win was apparent from the anxiety they manifested as the struggle for mastery took place, and the lively outburst of sympathetic congratulation that arose upon the conclusion of each event."

Sheffield FC finally found an outside club to play football against in December 1858. They played and beat the locally garrisoned 58th regiment; their full title is, appropriately enough, the 58th (Rutlandshire) Regiment of Foot. The Sheffield team was clearly no upper middle class pushover, as according to a late report in The Week 13th February 1892, two of the soldiers suffered fractured ribs.

Two years later, on December 17th 1860, they played the same opponents as outlined in the first ever match report for Sheffield FC:

"Sheffield v 58th Regiment. This match, which had been delayed for some time, owing to the unfavourable state of the weather, was played on Monday last at the barrack ground at Hillsborough. Considerable interest was caused by the fact that the regiment has amongst its officers several gentlemen who were formerly noted players at the public schools, and it was thought the townsmen had at last met with their match. The game was throughout conducted in a thoroughly good-tempered and friendly manner, and the pluck and stamina exhibited on both sides was undoubted. For some time the garrison had a slight advantage, but after an exciting struggle of more than two hours, the civilians scored a hard-won victory, the result being as follows: Sheffield one goal and 10 rouges, 58th Regiment one goal and five rouges." [18]

(Rouges echo the Eton game rules and it is probably here that Sheffield FC decided to adopt them.)

Nine days later there was a new football club for Sheffield FC to play, called Hallam and Stumperlow, and on Boxing Day 1860 Sheffield FC played their first Sheffield derby:

"Sheffield Football Club v Hallam and Stumperlowe Clubs – this match was played on Wednesday upon the Hallam Cricket ground in the presence of a large number of spectators. Owing to the severe weather several players were absent from each side, but the spirit exhibited by those who were present prevented the game from flagging or becoming uninteresting to the observers, who were extremely liberal with their plaudits on the successful 'charge' or quiet 'dodge', and equally unsparing in their sarcasm and country 'chaff' on the unfortunate victims of the slippery ground or the 'pure' scientific. The day was beautiful and the 'uniform' of the men contrasting with each other and the pure snow had a most picturesque appearance. The Sheffielders turned out in their usual scarlet and white, whilst most of the country players wore the blue garment of the Hallam Club. It would be invidious to pick out the play of any particular gentlemen when all did well, but we must give the palm to the Sheffield players as being the most scientific and also more alive to the advantage of upsetting their opponent. No serious accidents, however, occurred – the game was conducted with good temper and in a friendly spirit – and when darkness closed upon the scene, the Sheffield club, notwithstanding their inferior numbers, counted two goals to nothing, and went home fully satisfied with their victory." [19]

Sheffield FC and Hallam FC played again a year later in support of charity, though it sounds as though the tackles were not of a charitable nature:

"Great Football Match at Sheffield. The Sheffield Football Club arranged a match with the Hallam Club, the proceedings of which was to benefit that admirable institution the Sheffield Public Hospital and Dispensary. The game, which was played by fourteen (playing by eleven side rules would not become the norm until 1870) on each side, took place at Hyde Park on Saturday. The sides were composed of the following gentlemen-

Sheffield:
Captain W. Creswick, Artillery Volunteers, captain of the field; Captain W. Prest, Hallamshire Rifle volunteers, Messrs. W. Baker, J. Appleton, H. Chambers, J. Dixon, Robert Favell, W. Turton, J. Wild, A. Wightman, T. Gould, T. Moore, M. Hall, and David Sellers.

Hallam:
Messrs. J. C. Shaw, captain of the field; F. Vickers, J. Snape, G. H. Waterfall, Wm. Waterfall, F. Warburton, B. Elliott, Alfred Waterfall, Geo. Elliott, A. Hobson, A. W. Pearson, J. W. Pye Smith, H. Moore, and Captain Vickers. [20]

The game was throughout played spiritedly, and many were the noble exploits, skilful dodges, long drops, and beautiful runs obtained. The ball was kicked off by the captain of the Hallam team at 1.45 pm. An hour and a quarter's extraordinary heavy and fierce play ensued before a score was made. Ultimately the Sheffield gentlemen, by the assistance of T. Moore, scored a goal, although the ball was not kicked through. The mettle of the Hallam party was up at fever height and notwithstanding that some were rashly inclined there was some excellent play shown. At the expiration of another half hour, Captain Vickers managed to kick the ball through the goal, which placed the game equal. Before the termination of the succeeding half hour's play, the Hallam fourteen scored another goal and won the match. The spectators numbered between 600 and 700, and from their loud and frequent cheering, evidently enjoyed the sport. Many casualties, however, occurred, and for the safety of the players, it would indeed be much better if a great deal of the tripping up, 'hacking', pushing with the hands, and wild and indiscriminate kicking were avoided. The receipts amounted to about £15, which sum will be handed over to the public Hospital and Dispensary." [20]

By 1866 Sheffield FC started advertising their Athletic Sports Days for Gentlemen amateurs as far away as the London press; this must have been a commercial success as a half-crown entry fee was charged to compete against other elite athletes and spectators were charged for admission.

CHAPTER FIVE

"SHEFFIELD FOOTBALL CLUB, THE NINTH ANNUAL ATHLETIC SPORTS will be held on Monday, the 7th of May, at the Brammall-lane Cricket Ground, when the following events will be thrown open to all Gentlemen Amateurs, viz: -

- Flat Race, 3 Miles.
- Running High Jump.
- Flat Race, 150 Yards.
- Putting the Stone, 24lb.
- Flat Race, 1 Mile.
- Running Wide Jump.
- Flat Race, 440 Yards.
- High Jump with Pole.
- Walking Race, 1 Mile.
- Football Race, once around the course.
- Steeple Chase, about 650 Yards, over 12 Hurdles and 2 Water Jumps.

Entrance fee, 2s 6d for each event. Forms of entries, which must be returned on or before April 2, and other particulars, may be had on application to W. CHESTERMAN, Hon Sec, Sheffield." [21]

It is clear from the revenue details published (in a 1926 book) for the year of 1866 that the Athletic sports days were generating a substantial income for the club's coffers:

"In that particular year (1866) Sheffield Club had 260 members and the year's receipts amounted to £450, so that it was really stronger than it is today" (1926)." [22]

Football popularity in Sheffield grew to such an extent that a knockout competition, the Youdan Cup was staged in 1867 (more of which later in this Chapter). An enormous crowd of up to 3,000 people gathered for the final with each spectator paying 3 pence entry; this was the highest profile football match ever staged in Sheffield and an early indication of the phenomenal attractiveness of the game as a spectator sport and thus its financial potential. Sheffield FC declined to participate in the Youdan Cup, because at this time it was trying to limit its commitment to local matches in favour of inter-county fixtures (which began in 1865), rather than playing the other Sheffield teams. I can find no record of Sheffield FC playing another Sheffield team from early 1867 until 1870, when they played a new gymnastic club, with the Clegg brothers playing for the gymnasium side:

"It is a matter of pleasure to have to record the Sheffield Club again facing a local team, their opponents being an eleven chosen from the Sheffield United Gymnastic Club. On tossing the Gymnastic Club won, and decided to kick towards Sheffield. Some lively play ensued, but eventually W. Marsden scored a goal for the Gymnastic Club by excellent play. After ends had been changed one of the Sheffield Club (J. Whelan) kicked the ball straight for the enemy's goal, but unfortunately for them, the umpire was in the way, and unintentionally stopped it. A goal was claimed, but of course not allowed. After a short time, the Gymnastic Club scored a second goal, W. E. Clegg having the honour of kicking it. The Sheffield team now warmed to their work, playing with pluck and determination, and about ten minutes to time were rewarded by a goal, cleverly worked round from the corner, where it was nearly 'in touch.' The match was concluded in favour of the Gymnastic Club by two goals to one. Players' names: Sheffield Club – H. W. Chambers (captain), W. Lockwood, A. S. Denton, J. Whelan, F. Whelan, G. Marsden, A. Matthews, T. Willey, A. Hoole, F. Fretson, and T. Firth. Gymnastic Club: J. Marsh (captain), J. C. Clegg, W. E. Clegg, J. P. Donovan, F. Barber, A. Hill, and S. Ward. Umpires: J. Deans and

THE GOLDEN AGE OF SHEFFIELD AMATEUR FOOTBALL 1857-1876

S. Chambers. Considering the extremely heavy state of the ground, the play on both sides was remarkably good." [23]

(Whilst Sheffield United FC would not appear until 1889, the 'United' name was a common moniker in Sheffield with both a Sheffield United cricket team and the above Sheffield United gymnastic club.)

The report above is another mention of the Cleggs and as their name will come up a lot in this book, an introduction is needed for these two influential brothers, John Charles Clegg (known as Charles) and William Edwin Clegg. Charles Clegg would eventually rise to the very top of the football establishment, but he was first known as a fine exponent of pedestrianism:

"John Charles Clegg, who was the most distinguished amateur pedestrian in the world in his time, was born at Sheffield on the 15th June, 1850, so that he is now in his twenty-sixth year. In height he stands 5ft. 10 ½ inches, and weights about 10st. 11lb. As regards his personal appearance, very few people would take him to be an athlete, for although he enjoys good health, and is as sound as a bell in wind and limb, yet he looks too pale and studious to impress anyone with the idea that running was his forte. But when stripped he is the model of a flyer; and although he never carried himself so gracefully as his contemporaries, Clague and Blaxter, his style of running was greatly admired, having a long, low, sweeping stride, which showed to great advantages when his favourite distance, a quarter of a mile, at which, fit and well, he was invincible, and several good judges have not hesitated to affirm that he was a match for the celebrated professional, Richard Buttery. Be that as it may, the Sheffielders' appearance in public, and having since joined the noble order of Benedicts, he has announced his intention of finally retiring from the running path. He has always been self-trained, and is of a particularly abstentious disposition, never indulging in tobacco or intoxicating liquor in any form. We regret that in the above brief outline of his performances we have not been enabled to do anything like justice to the best amateur quarter-miler that ever trod a running path." [24]

Charles (15/6/50-26/6/37) and William (21/4/52-22/8/32) were both solicitors by trade; both played for Sheffield FC, Sheffield Football Association, Wednesday FC, Albion FC and England and both acted as Umpires in important games. William was the most famous Sheffield politician called Clegg, until a certain Deputy Prime Minister came along in 2010. After hanging up his boots, William Clegg became Lord Mayor of Sheffield as well as president of Wednesday and Vice President of the Sheffield Football Association.

Charles Clegg was a devout Methodist and an activist for the Temperance League, regularly using the phrase 'nobody gets lost on a straight road.' A tough no-nonsense man, once when a young player had been brought before him in a disciplinary meeting for ungentlemanly remarks to a referee, Clegg asked what had been said. The player responded: 'Well, I said 'I've shit better

John Charles Clegg
(Association Football and the Men who Made it 1905)

CHAPTER FIVE

referees'. 'I see,' said Clegg. 'All right, I'll tell you what I'll do. I'll give you a week to prove you can do just that. But if you can't, I'm afraid you'll have to pay a £1 fine.' [25] He was a fierce proponent of the amateur game and strongly against all forms of professionalism. Over time he mellowed and oversaw Wednesday's transition to professionalism and was involved in the foundation of Sheffield United in 1889, a club designed to be professional from the start. Charles was chairman of Wednesday and of the Sheffield Football Association and the most powerful man in English football between 1890 and 1919 in his capacity at the Football Association as the first and longest-standing chairman. He refereed both the 1882 and 1892 F.A. Cup Finals and in 1899 became chairman of Sheffield United; he became President of the club in 1924. He was knighted in 1927 and his club Presidency only lapsed on his death in 1937.

Early Sheffield football was of a very physical nature with many players getting seriously injured. Sheffield led the way in players' protection by forming a mutual society as early as 1867. Five years later and the society's annual report was concerned by a reduction in players not paying their subs:

"Football Players' Accident Society – The annual general meeting of this society was held at Mr. Armfield's, Adelphi hotel, on Monday night, when the retiring officers, Messrs. Dignam, president; G. E. Ince, vice-president; T. Rycroft, treasurer; and J. Webster, honorary secretary, were unanimously re-elected... The Secretary read the accounts for the past season, which showed that the sum of £25. 16s. 9d. was invested in the Savings' Bank, and £2. 14s. 1d. in the hands of the treasurer... The President (Mr. Dignam) then read the following account of the number of members, the amount of subscriptions, and sums paid for accidents, since the formation of the society in 1867, viz –

	No. of Members	Subscriptions			Amount paid		
		£.	s.	d.	£.	s.	d.
1867-8	151	7	11	0	8	8	0
1868-9	141	7	1	0	6	12	0
1869-70	162	8	2	0	8	8	0
1870-1	184	9	4	0	6	18	0
1871-2	178	8	18	0	4	4	0
	816	40	16	0	34	10	0
Average	163. 1						

This statement shows that the society has not been supported by the football players of Sheffield as it should have been; and also that, had it not been the kindness of Mr. Youdan and other friends the society would have been defunct, the expenses, printing, &c., having been much more than the difference between the amounts received for subscriptions and those paid to members for accidents." [26]

Ultimately the Football Players' Accident Society kept going for thirty years, until December 1897, when it was dissolved as the modern game took over and players stopped paying their subs; the residual balance of £68. 8s. 5d was donated to the Royal Hospital.

In terms of trophies, Sheffield FC's early decision to play only inter-county games, limited their tangible success and it would not be until 1993, that they won the Sheffield and Hallamshire Senior Cup. As likely favourites at the time of the Youdan Cup in February 1867 they might have looked back on the decision not to participate with regret. Whilst Sheffield FC never won the F.A. Cup, the city did contribute the actual trophy. The first trophy, awarded from 1872 to 1895, was made by Martin, Hall & Co, of solid silver and was just eighteen inches high. Based at Shrewsbury Works, Broad Street Park, Sheffield with showrooms in Sydney, Birmingham and Glasgow, the firm exhibited at the 1851 Great Exhibition, the International Exhibition (1862), the Sydney Exhibition (1879), the Melbourne Exhibition (1881) and the 1915 British Industries Fair. It cost £20 to make, featured a figure of a footballer on the top and was popularly known as the 'Little Tin Idol'. Wanderers FC (previously Forest FC) won the Cup three years running in the 1870s and under the rules of the competition they were entitled to keep it, but they decided to hand it back to the F.A. on the understanding that no other team would retain it if they won it three times in the future. The last winners of that first trophy were Aston Villa in 1895; five months after their triumph at the old Crystal Palace, it was stolen from the William Shillcock football outfitters shop in Newtown Row, Birmingham. It was on display there and was never recovered, despite the offer of a £10 reward and is generally thought to have been melted down to make counterfeit half-crown coins.

Sheffield FC did not enter the F.A. Cup proper until 1873/74 where they met fellow debutants Shropshire Wanderers. The first game ended goalless at Bramall Lane and the replay on the 17th November 1873 also ended without any goals being scored:

'At the dinner, afterwards it was arranged to decide by tossing which side should claim the victory, when fortune favoured Sheffield.' [27]

This remains the only tie in F.A. Cup history to be settled by the toss of a coin. After beating the Pilgrims in the second round, Sheffield FC lost to Clapham Rovers in the third round at a match played in Peterborough. Their next actual game played in the F.A. Cup after some scratched matches and walk overs, was in the 1875/76 season where they came up against Wanderers (the eventual winners) in the third round at the Oval on the 29th January 1876:

"The Sheffield forwards, notably Cursham, Sorby, Mathews, and Wylle, made desperate efforts to retrieve the fortunes of the day, but every attack was repelled by the Wanderers' backs, and the end of an hour and a half found the Wanderers in possession of a hard-earned victory, by two goals to none. Considering that they played one less than their adversaries during the second half of the game the Sheffielders played up pluckily and well, and no doubt the journey they had undertaken in the morning did not tend to infuse any great degree of spirit into their play. For the Wanderers F. Heron played up well from first to last, and Lindsey and Birley were most effective backs. The players were: - Wanderers: F. H. Birley (captain) and F. T. Green (half-backs), W. Lindsey and A. H. Stratford (backs), W. D. Greig (goal), Hubert Heron and C. H. Woollaston (upper side), F.B. Maddison and T. B. Hughes (centres), J. Kenrick and F. Heron (lower side). Umpire C. W. Alcock (Wanderers – Sheffield: M. J. Billson (captain) and W. R. Wake (backs), W. E. Clegg and T. C. Willey (half-backs), H. W. Chambers (goal), J. C. Clegg, A. W. Cursham, J. Mathews, H. Sorby, R. A. Sorby, and J. G. Wylie (forwards), Umpire F. J. Whelan (Sheffield), Referee J. Kirkpatrick (Civil Service)." [28] (The Wanderers would knock them out again at the quarter final stage two seasons later.)

Sheffield FC- F.A. Cup Record 1871-1888

1873-74	1	Shropshire Wanderers	H	0-0
	1r	Shropshire Wanderers	H	0-0 Sheffield won on toss of coin
	2	Pilgrims	H	1-0
	QF	Clapham Rovers	N	1-2 at Peterborough
1874-75	1	Shropshire Wanderers	A	SCR

CHAPTER FIVE

1875-76	1	Shropshire Wanderers	H	W/O
	2	Upton Park	H	W/O
	QF	Wanderers	A	0-2
1876-77	1	Trojans	H	W/O
	2	South Norwood	A	7-0
	3	Royal Engineers	A	0-1
1877-78	1	Notts County	A	1-1
	1r	Notts County	H	3-0
	2	Darwen	H	1-0
	3	Bye		
	QF	Wanderers	A	0-3
1878-79	1	Grantham	H	1-1
	1r	Grantham	A	3-1
	2	Nottingham Forest	A	0-2
1879-80	1	Queen's Park (Glasgow)	H	W/O
	2	Sheffield Providence	H	3-3
	2r	Sheffield Providence	A	3-0
	3	Bye		
	4	Nottingham Forest	A	2-2 Sheffield disqualified after refusing to play extra time.
1880-81	2	Darwen	H	1-5
1881-82	2	Sheffield Heeley	H	0-4
1884-85	3	Notts County	A	0-5
1885/86	2	Notts County	A	0-8
1886/87	1	Notts Rangers	H	0-3

Sheffield FC's last appearance in the first round of the F.A. Cup was at home on the 15th October 1887 against local rivals Lockwood Brothers, losing 1-3. Sheffield FC resolved to remain amateur in the face of the rising tide of professionalism and by 1891 had realised that it would never again be able to compete against the professional clubs. It suggested to the F.A. the inauguration of a purely amateur Cup and even offered to pay for the actual trophy. This request was ignored but with Sheffield's Charles Clegg's growing influence at the F.A., it was launched in the 1894/94 season. Sheffield FC's finest moment would come ten seasons later when they beat Ealing in the final 3-1 to win the F.A. Amateur Cup on the 4th April 1904; appropriately the Cup was presented to Sheffield FC by Charles W. Alcock.

Sheffield FC currently (2016/17) play in the Northern Premier League Division One South (8th tier of the football pyramid) at the Coach and Horses Ground in Dronfield, Derbyshire on the boundary with South Yorkshire. Sheffield FC is one of only two clubs to hold the 'Order of Merit', the highest honour awarded by the world's football governing body F.I.F.A. – the other club being Real Madrid.

1858

In 1858 a 13.76 tonne bell was recast in the Tower of Westminster, but a new Big Ben chime did not distract sufficiently from the 'Great Stink'; the stench of sewage from the River Thames was so strong that business in Parliament was affected, and the curtains on the river side of the building were soaked in lime chloride to overcome the smell. The leading article in 'The Illustrated London News' commented that: 'We can colonise the remotest ends of the earth; we can conquer India; we can pay the interest of the most enormous debt ever contracted; we can spread our name, and our fame, and our fructifying wealth to every part of the world; but we cannot clean the River Thames.'

Fortunately, Isambard Kingdom Brunel's S.S. Great Eastern (the largest ship built to date) was launched on the River Thames before the smell started. Charles Darwin and Alfred Russel Wallace announced a theory of evolution by natural selection, whilst Charles Dickens embarked on his first professional tour, giving readings from his works. Richard Francis Burton and John Hanning Speke become the first Europeans to 'discover' Lake Tanganyika and John Hanning Speke carried on in the same year to 'discover' Lake Victoria, the source of the River Nile.

No second football club was formed in Sheffield in 1858. The only club to grace this year was London's Dingley Dell FC, whose name clearly reflects the popularity of Charles Dickens; this makes it the second oldest football club in the world. The inspiration for this team's name was from Dickens' first novel 'The Pickwick Papers', serialized as early as 1836, which featured a brief description of a cricket match between the All-Muggleton team and the Dingley Dell Cricket Club.

The Dingley Dell Football Club played against school teams between 1858 and 1864 and was a 'private club side made of public schools from various foundations.' [29] This makes Dingley Dell the forerunner of the so called 'scratch team' or 'pick–up team' (a team composed of players who normally play for different sides). A lot of early southern Clubs operated under this system, so it was quite usual to find players playing for different clubs, such as Swifts FC, Gitanos FC and Remnants FC, sometimes in the same week.

Because Dingley Dell played an amalgam of rules 'The Field' newspaper (15 March 1862) thought it should publish its rules to help create a universal code: 'It would be a favour to the lovers of football if they would publish a copy of their rules, since they seem admirably adapted to form the basis of a general code. Why should not the Dingley Dell club do for football what the M.C.C. has done for cricket?' Dingley Dell did not take up the challenge which would have significantly altered football history in 1862, a year before the Football Association held their inaugural meeting. In the same 1862 article, 'The Field' described Dingley Dell the as the best club of the season, apart from the public schools.

1859

The only press in respect of football in 1859, is all about the various public school teams playing by their various codes and a high-profile military match which was played at Lords:

"FOOTBALL AT LORD'S. Lord's Cricket Ground (which is now in beautiful condition, the heavy horse-roller being in constant use) presented a very animated appearance on Tuesday last, a great number of the Foot Guards having assembled to witness a match at football between the 2nd and the 3rd battalions of the Grenadier Guards - 25 on each side, headed by two of their officers, Capts. Coulson and Jarratt, and after a severe contest of three hours, terminated in favour of the 3rd battalion. The beauty of the day drew together a large assemblage of spectators." [30]

No new Sheffield clubs were formed again in this year but three clubs were formed in

CHAPTER FIVE

London: the Crusaders FC, Forest FC and Mincing Lane FC. Like Dingley Dell, all were from the Home Counties. Crusaders and Forest share the position of equal third oldest football club in the world, as they joined the Football Association on the same date in 1863.

Forest FC are as influential in the story of Association football as Sheffield FC, firstly because Forest FC became the legendary Wanderers FC, that won the F.A. Cup on five occasions and secondly because of the name most associated with the club, that of Charles W. Alcock. In a magazine article from 1891 he said:

"The creation of the Wanderers out of the remnants of the old Forest Club was the commencement of practically a new era in the Association game. Composed exclusively of old boys from the leading schools, the Wanderers exercised a very healthy and stimulating influence in the early days of Association football. Its constitution gave it for the first time a monopoly of the most highly trained players and it attracted into its ranks the pick of the various elevens as soon as ever the completion of the Public Schools curriculum gave them an opportunity of belonging. Eton supplied not a few of those who made the name of Wanderers familiar as a household word in the earlier days – Hon. A.F. (now Lord) Kinnaird, Alec Bonsor, Edgar Lubbock, and AC Thompson, Quentin Hogg and others will be well remembered by those who can recall the first years of the Association Cup. Harrow was chiefly represented by CW Alcock, M.P. Betts and E.E. Bowen, a master *(teacher)*.

Westminster furnished perhaps the best exponent of pure dribbling in R.W.S Vidal; Winchester sent F.H. Birley and W. Lindsay; Lancing, C.H. Wollaston; Charterhouse, C.E. Nepean. Edward E. Bowen (1836-1901) educated at Blackheath School and Trinity College Cambridge (1854-57) and was a master at Harrow from 1859-1901." [31]

1860

Two clubs came into existence in this year - a second club in Sheffield and the first club from the Midlands, Congleton FC; this is a controversial club, as their claimed 1860 foundation date comes ten years later from the 1870 Football Annual. The only other corroboration is a football match that was played in Congleton, December 1860, between the Volunteers and the Townsmen on the drill ground. Did this football club continue? If so there are no more supporting press reports until 1875, when they added the 'Rovers' suffix. Due to the inclusion in the Football Annual, the club is included in my national classification.

The second club formed in Sheffield was Hallam FC.

Hallam (and Stumperlow) FC (Sheffield, Yorkshire 1860 – Present)

- Second Oldest Sheffield Football Club

- Second Oldest Football Club in the world still in existence

- Sheffield & Hallamshire Senior Cup Winners – 1950/51, 1961/62, 1964/65, 1967/68

Historically Stumperlow (occasionally spelt Stumperley) was part of the village of Hallam; Stumperlow Hall was less than a mile from Sandygate ground.

Origin. Players from another club and the Volunteer Movement. Hallam FC was formed from players from Sheffield FC and as discussed earlier, the reason could have been a falling out between Tom Vickers and Nathaniel Creswick in the Volunteers.

In the official history of Hallam FC:

"It is believed that Captain T. Vickers (a member of Sheffield FC) and John Shaw also a member of Sheffield FC, were the prime movers in establishing the Hallam Football Club." [32]

The official Hallam FC website states:

"John Shaw as founder and captain of Hallam FC and after the formation of Hallam Cricket club in 1804 by the then landlord of the Plough Inn, the club blossomed until by the 1850s it had in excess of 300 members. It was the wish of these members, many of whom were familiar with the team football being played by Sheffield FC, formed in 1857, to create a less exclusive club led by cricketers and thus in 1860, Hallam FC was born."

Both Shaw and Vickers appear to have had an on-off relationship with Hallam FC and their involvement with the club is not featured in either of their obituaries. Because of the long-established Hallam Cricket club (1804), and the potential for it starting its own football club, I investigated the Hallam Cricket Club's archive which includes financial accounts for the club from 1857 and also a list of members dated 1857. The latter includes a Mr. Shaw, but no initial is recorded. There is no reference to the name Vickers in this list. The minutes were examined from 1859, the first meeting being dated 28th February. Most of the minutes are very short, sometimes only three or four lines of text. The exceptions to this are records of annual meetings when elections of officers were held. The last record of minutes is dated 1st January 1866. Unfortunately, there was no mention of the Hallam Football Club in any of the minute records, and no names were found for Shaw or Vickers with the exception of the 'Mr. Shaw' named in the membership list of 1857.

John Charles Shaw, born in Penistone, was aged 27 in the 1861 census and was described as a widower with two sons George and John aged six and two. He lived in Fulwood, Sheffield, and his occupation was law stationer (a person who makes handwritten copies of legal documents). John Shaw married Anne Waterfall in July 1861 and by the 1881 census his occupation has changed to Political Agent. One of his wife's uncles, William Waterfall, would later have a very public falling out with Sheffield FC's founder, Nathaniel Creswick. (see later)

In my research, I have never been able to corroborate John Shaw as an earlier player for Sheffield FC, but by 1860 he is the Hon. Sec. of Hallam FC, a position he held until 1863, when he would have been thirty-three years of age. Then all the footballing newspaper reports stop for Shaw and are replaced with reports of his competition in athletic events. In 1864 he became a committee member for Sheffield Football Club. [33] By 1868 Shaw was Vice President of the Sheffield Football Association and in 1869 he became President, a position he would hold for 14 years until 1882. From 1870 he was also Hallam FC President a position he held until 1874. In 1875 Shaw was appointed the organising secretary for the Conservative Party for England and Wales. He did play in a one-off match for Thursday Wanderers FC in November 1876, which may have been a statement of intent against perceived professionalism in the game (more later). When he retired from the Presidency of Sheffield Football Association in 1882, he cited the pressure of work as the reason.

An enigma in the Hallam FC story is the persistent suspicion that the club started earlier than today's history books state. The universally accepted December 1860 foundation date for Hallam FC is questionable because other data points towards a much earlier date. In the 1868 Football Annual, for all the other Sheffield clubs, these foundation dates are always initially correct and are supported by the Sheffield press reports. The earliest press for Hallam is 1860 but the 1857 foundation date is repeated every year in the Football Annuals until 1880 (when the entries cease) without correction for Hallam FC (see below). It seems hard to imagine in the close community of Sheffield football, that a book likely to be in many a gentleman's pocket, could list an incorrect date for twelve consecutive years without someone from Sheffield FC pointing out the error. In July 1860, a cricket match was played between All England and an Eighteen of Hallam; both Creswick and Prest played for the Hallam side,[34] so clearly all the men involved with both clubs knew each other well. Percy Young, who wrote the first record of Sheffield football in 1962, has the Hallam foundation date as 1857 [35] presumably based on the 1868 (and the subsequent twelve) Football Annuals. 1857 is the date in Charles W. Alcock's Football Annual and is requoted in the 1907 book 'Association Football and the Men who made it' on page 39. In my research for this book I discovered an earlier article from 1894 by Mr. Leonard Cooper (former captain of Oxford University AFC). These recollections are slightly questionable as the article was written thirty-four years after the events in question:

"Lecture on Football. On Thursday evening Mr. Leonard Cooper, late captain of the Oxford University Association Football Club, delivered a lecture on 'Football' to St. John's Longsight, Literary and Debating Society. Mr. Cooper, after a short historical account of football said: Outside the schools and universities, into which former schoolboys introduced the dribbling game, Sheffield appears to have been the pioneer of Association football, two clubs being founded there in 1857, one of which still exists, though its glory has to a large extent departed." [36]

This 1894 article adds to the riddle by stating that one of the 1857 clubs no longer exists; this does not tie in with the dates for when Hallam FC was defunct for a year. The 1857 date is repeated in a talk given by Mr. H.V. Stott, an English referee:

"More important was the forming of the Sheffield and Hallamshire clubs in 1857. These two clubs, the first of their kind in the provinces, were established simultaneously. Yorkshire men, true to the sporting instincts of the county of broad acres, also began to take an interest in football." [37]

More evidence for an earlier formation date comes from when Sheffield FC sold their archive at Sotheby's, when the contents were transcribed for the catalogue. In a file of correspondence there is a letter dated 2 March 1928 from John N. Deansfield to Henry Chambers, on the subject of the club's origins:

'I believe John Charles Shaw a Penistone man and who before going to Sheffield…was in my father's office at Penistone and regularly played football in one of my father's fields. *Soon after* the formation of the Sheffield Club he went to reside at Sandygate and formed the Hallam Club.'

What counts against the above evidence is that it is forty-eight years after the events in question. Another document in the Sotheby's lot was a letter from John Shaw himself to J.C. Bingham on 18 October 1907:

"For many years we had to arrange alphabetical sides to make the games interesting. Subsequently I started a club at Hallam, inducing many Sheffd (sic) Club members to join, for the purpose of getting a team to play against the old club. These matches were most interesting and enjoyable and in a few years led to the Wednesday, Pitsmoor and other cricket clubs to form football Clubs-Previous to this we had been able to arrange friendly matches with Officers and men at the garrison, and rough matches they were…"

If his memory is not playing tricks on him, then what's interesting here is the time span for Hallam playing for 'a few years' before the formation of Pitsmoor in 1861; all of this suggests an earlier date than 1860, however I can find no concrete record of Hallam FC playing a game before December 26th 1860. I think a more likely formation date is 1858 or 1859, but for that elusive confirmation the search goes on.

As I hypothesised earlier, if the all modern-day accounts are correct, then late 1860 is the formation date for Hallam Football club; perhaps it was a falling out of personnel that caused a schism between Sheffield FC and Hallam FC.

In the table breakdown from the Football Annuals, the existence of a 2s. subscription fee highlights the fact that this is another club for gentlemen, rather than the working man.

Football Annual	Ground	Foundation Date	Hon. Sec.	Members	Colours
1868	Sandygate	1857	H. Bramwell, Elliot Road, Crookes Moor	150 Amount of entrance fee: Nil Amount of subscription: 2s.	Blue and white
1869	Sandygate	1857	C. Skelton, Upper Hallam, Sheffield	150	Blue and white
1870	Sandygate	1857	C. Skelton, Upper Hallam, Sheffield	150	Blue and white
1871	Sandygate	1857	F. Benn, 116 Bay Terrace, Crookes	200	Blue and white
1872	Sandygate	1857	F. Benn, 116 Bay Terrace, Crookes	200	Blue and white
1873	Sandygate	1857	F. Benn, 116 Bay Terrace, Crookes	200	Blue and white
1874	Sandygate (N.W.)	1857	J.S. Holmes, Plough Inn, Sandygate	200	Blue and white
1875	Sandygate (N.W.)	1857	J.S. Holmes, Plough Inn, Sandygate	200	Blue and white
1876	Sandygate (N.W.)	1857	J.S. Holmes, Plough Inn, Sandygate	200	Blue and white
1877	Sandygate (N.W.)	1857	J.S. Holmes, Plough Inn, Sandygate	200	Blue and white
1878	x				
1879	Sandygate (N.W.)	1857	G. Hall, Plough Inn, Sandygate	200	Blue and white
1880	Sandygate	1857	G. Hall, Plough Inn, Sandygate	250	Blue and white

As already mentioned in the 1857 section, Sheffield FC beat Hallam 2-0 at the Sandygate ground on Boxing Day 1860; here is another report of that game, this time from the Sheffield Independent rather than the Telegraph:

"Sheffield Football Club v Hallam and Stumperlow – An exciting match between these two clubs was played on the ground of the latter on Wednesday. Notwithstanding the severe weather, the players mustered in good numbers, and the game was contested with great pluck and spirit. Eventually, the Sheffield club came off victorious, having obtained two goals, their opponents not having scored." [38] The line-up for that historical game does not appear to be extant but most likely would have included another important name in the Hallam FC story, that of Waterfall. James Waterfall's daughter Annie, married Hallam FC's co-founder John Charles Shaw. George, William and Alfred Waterfall all played for Hallam FC against Sheffield FC in December 1861. (See [39] for more biographical information)

The other co-founder in the Hallam FC story, is Colonel Thomas Vickers though in his October 1915 obituary, he is remembered for his interest in chess rather than football. His main link to Hallam FC is his captaincy of the team in December 1861 but thereafter his name fades from the story. His obituary said:

"Colonel Vickers found great pleasure in sport, and it would be difficult to say whether he loved most to whip the streams of Scotland and Ireland in search of trout or salmon, or to tramp over the moors after grouse. He was also a votary of chess, and has been found occasionally at one of the chess clubs. The St. George's Chess Club and the British Chess Club were his favourite resorts in London. He also had a penchant for art. But perhaps in this department his inclination was in the direction of ceramic art and bric-a-brac, and in his house he had some magnificent specimens of Worcester and Chelsea ware." [40]

Edward Vickers and his father in law, George Naylor had founded 'Naylor Vickers and

CHAPTER FIVE

Company', a steel foundry in 1828. Vickers' two sons Thomas and Albert both joined the business:

"Colonel Thomas E. (1833-1915) and Albert Vickers (1838-1919) ... provided both inspired technical leadership... and equally astute commercial direction. Both men were autocrats by temperament, but neither shunned advice or avoided delegation; each, but particularly Albert, had a marked gift for the selection of talented subordinates." [41]

Tom Vickers served as Master Cutler in 1872, but both he and Albert eventually moved to London. In April 1859 both Albert and Thomas Vickers as well as J.C. Shaw, Prest and Creswick were all competing in the second annual contest in Athletic sports organised by members of the Sheffield Football Club in April 1859:

"Athletic Sports. On Monday, the second annual contest in various athletic sports, among the members of the Sheffield Football Club, took place on their ground, at East Bank. T. M. Richardson, Esq., judge; M. J. Ellison, Esq., clerk of the course. Vaulting. Prize, a pint pewter. There were five competitors out of ten entries. The contest lay between Mr. T. E. Vickers and Mr. W. Prest, who were ultimately declared equal, each clearing 5ft. 5 in. Walking a mile. Thirteen entries; five contested. Mr. R. H. Bonifant, Nottingham, first. Mr. H. Moore, Mr. G. Smith, Mr. J. C. Shaw, and Mr. A. Vickers also started." [42]

Hallam FC's first reported match on Boxing Day 1860 is included in the Sheffield FC section. In March 1861, the two original football clubs met again:

"Football Match - On Saturday a football match was played at East Bank, between 15 of the Sheffield Club and 18 of Stumperlow and Hallam. The goals, three, were all obtained by the Hallam men." [43]

Following a summer of cricket their season resumed:

"Hallam Foot Ball Club. The opening match of the above club will be played this afternoon (*September 1861*) on the Sandygate Cricket Ground. Play to commence at Three o'clock. John C. Shaw Hon. Sec." [44]

"Sheffield Football Club – there will be a match this afternoon (*21st December 1861*) between the match players and the remainder of the Club. Kick off at 2.30pm. The club plays Pitsmoor on Thursday next, at Two o'clock, on the Pitsmoor ground; and Hallam on Saturday, the 28th game at Hyde Park, at One o'clock." [45]

The charity match played between Sheffield FC and Hallam FC in late December 1861 (already reported in the Sheffield FC section), included the following Hallam FC line-up:

"Messrs. J. C. Shaw, captain of the field; F. Vickers*, J. Snape, G. H. Waterfall, Wm. Waterfall, F. Warburton, B. Elliott, Alfred Waterfall, Geo. Elliott, A. Hobson, A. W. Pearson, J. W. Pye Smith, H. Moore, and Captain Vickers." [46]

* An unknown relation of Captain Tom Vickers, or a newspaper typo for his brother Albert?

Hallam FC was not a particularly young team; in 1861 the ages of the players we know were: John Shaw, 31, Tom Vickers, 28, George Waterfall, 40, William Waterfall, 37 and Alfred Waterfall, 35.

The next match report from February 1862 is interesting as it illustrates that the club was divided along class lines; they were admitting artisans and tradesmen and their status was specified as 'players' as opposed to 'gentlemen:

"Hallam Football Club – A very exciting match was played last Saturday afternoon, in front of Stumperlow Hall, between 14 gentlemen and 14 players of the above club. It was evident from the first that the players had no chance whatever against their more active opponents. After two hours and a half of first-rate play, the gentlemen obtained three goals; players, 0." [47]

72

Having fallen out with Tom Vickers in the Volunteers, Nathaniel Creswick had another public falling out in 1862, on December 29th, when Sheffield FC played Hallam in a charity match. The 'Sheffield Independent' report states:

"At one time it appeared that the match would be turned into a general fight. Major Creswick (of Sheffield) had got the ball away and was struggling against great odds with Mr. Shaw and Mr. Waterfall (of Hallam). Major Creswick was held by Waterfall and in the struggle Waterfall was accidentally hit by the Major. All parties agreed that the hit was accidental. Waterfall, however, ran at the Major in the most irritable manner, and struck him several times. He also threw off his waistcoat and began to show fight in earnest. Major Creswick, who preserved his temper admirably, did not return a single blow."

The following week, a letter appeared in The Sheffield Independent, defending the actions of William Waterfall. (William Waterfall was John Shaw's wife's uncle):

"The unfair report in your paper of the football match played on the Bramall Lane ground between the Sheffield and Hallam Football Clubs calls for a hearing from the other side. We have nothing to say about the result - there was no score - but to defend the character and behaviour of our respected player, Mr. William Waterfall, by detailing the facts as they occurred between him and Major Creswick. In the early part of the game, Waterfall charged the Major, on which the Major threatened to strike him if he did so again. Later in the game, when all the players were waiting a decision of the umpires, the Major, very unfairly, took the ball from the hands of one of our players and commenced kicking it towards their goal. He was met by Waterfall who charged him and the Major struck Waterfall on the face, which Waterfall immediately returned."

The Youdan Cup

Hallam FC were the winners of the oldest Football Cup in the world, the Youdan Cup, in 1867. Thomas Youdan appeared in the Sheffield press as early as 1857 as the proprietor of the Surrey Music Hall, organising a free 'Monster Tea Party' for 2,000 women over 60 years of age, held in the cattle market on 600 yards of tables. A charge for admission was made for all, except the old ladies, and the net proceeds went to aid the sufferers of the mutiny in India. His new idea in 1867 for publicity was to exploit the fast-growing popularity of Sheffield football. The publicity for the trophy began in February 1867:

"Mr. THOMAS YOUDAN having offered for COMPETITION, by the Football Clubs of the Town and Neighbourhood, a Valuable SILVER CUP, will award a Premium of One Sovereign to the most original and appropriate Design, which may be sent, under cover, to Daily Telegraph Office, endorsed 'Design for the Youdan Football Cup.' FREDK. CORBETT, Hon. Sec." [48]

The Sheffield Independent announced the winner of the design as a 'Mr. Jarvis of Roscoe Place Works,' [49] which was further elaborated on in the Sheffield Daily Telegraph:

"THE YOUDAN FOOTBALL CUP. - CONTESTS FOR THE PRIZE. - The contests for the cup which Mr. Youdan has offered for competition amongst the local football clubs commenced on Saturday. In order that the cup should be handsome and appropriate in finish and design, a prize was offered for the best drawing. There was a large number of competitors, and Mr, Jarvis, designer, was the successful one. His design was, we understand, slightly modified by the introduction of a small part of another competitor's design, and for this use an additional prize was awarded. The cup will cost about twenty guineas, and the contests for the honour of its possession will be keen and determined. The clubs competing were twelve in number, and

CHAPTER FIVE

lots were drawn to decide in what order they should play. A good deal of interest was manifested in the contests on Saturday, it being understood that each club would be represented by its best players. Those of the spectators who were not familiar with the usages of football players were not a little astonished at the unequivocal, but good humoured, roughness displayed, especially when a 'charge' took place, and it was particularly gratifying to see that, notwithstanding the severe collisions, the heavy tumbles, and the scarred shins, perfect friendliness invariably prevailed; and after a 'charge,' a collision, and a downfall, the prostrated would instantly spring to their feet and resume the game in the heartiest and the most determined and enthusiastic spirit." [50]

The format of the competition was drawn up by a committee and played under Sheffield Rules:

"This day. The Youdan Football Cup. The first series of games for the Cup presented by Thos. Youdan, Esq., to the Clubs of the Town and Neighbourhood, will be played this day, as follows: -

1. – United Mechanics' v. Norton, at Norton. – Referee – Mr. W. I. Bingham. – A 'Bus will leave the Surrey Arms, Granville Street, at Half past One o'clock punctually.
2. – Garrick v. Mackenzie, at The Orphanage – Referee – Mr. J Faith.
3. – Hallam v. Heeley. At Hallam – Referee – Mr. R. Dickinson. – A 'Bus will leave Heeley bridge about one o'clock, and call at the bottom of Ecclesall Road at Half past One.
4. – Norfolk v. Fir Vale, at Norfolk Park. – Referee – Mr. J. Tomlinson.
5. – Broomhall v. Pitsmoor, at Ecclesall Road – Referee – Mr. J Pinder.
6. – Milton v. Wellington, at The Orphanage – Referee – Mr. J. Crapper. Every game to commence punctually at Three o'clock – No waiting for Players allowed." [51]

The competition was also reported in the national press:
"Sheffield – Youdan's Football Cup. The first series of matches played by some of the Sheffield football clubs for the silver cup presented by Thomas Youdan, Esq, to the clubs of the town and neighbourhood took place at Sheffield, on Saturday last, the 16th last, with the following results: - First Draw; 1. United Mechanics v. Norton, at Norton. – Won by Norton by one goal and three rouges to one rouge. 2. Mackenzie v. Garrick, at the Orphanage – Mackenzie won by one goal and two rouges to nothing. 3. Hallam v. Heeley, at Hallam – Hallam won by two goals and two rouges to one rouge. 4. Norfolk v. Fir Vale, at Norfolk Park – Norfolk won by two goals and four rouges to nothing. 5. Broomhall v. Pitsmoor, at Ecclesall road – Broomhall won by two rouges to nothing. 6. Milton v. Wellington, at the Orphanage – Milton won by two goals and four rouges to nothing. The following is the order in which the matches are drawn to be played on Saturday next: -Norfolk v. Broomhall at Norfolk Park; Hallam v Norton, at Norton; Mackenzie v. Milton, at Orphanage (ground of the latter), The rules for guidance of clubs contending for the cup are as follows: - 1. The games to be played by twelve a-side, 2. The games to commence punctually at three o'clock. No waiting for players allowed. 3. That each game be played one hour and a half in the usual way, but at the end of that time a draw takes place the clubs play again to toss for choice of goals, and play on. The first point scored

to decide the game: but if after one hour's play the game still remains a draw, it is adjourned to Monday, at three o'clock. 4. That for each match there be two umpires and one referee the decision of the referee to be final." (52)

The first two rounds were on a knockout basis; however, the final was contested between three teams playing each other in turn. The final between Hallam FC and Norfolk FC was played at Bramall Lane, on 5 March 1867 and attracted 3,000 spectators, each paying 3d admission. Thomas Youdan, ever the business man, had the final played on Shrove Tuesday, when the 'common man' would have a day off work. The throng did not have a great deal to cheer, with the match ending goalless, decided by rouges scored:

"THE YOUDAN FOOTBALL CUP. -The Hallam and Norfolk Football Clubs played the final match for this prize at Brammall-lane Cricket Ground, Sheffield, on Shrove Tuesday. The toss for choice of goals was won by Norfolk, who kicked with the wind, but were unable to score. After playing half time ends were changed, when it was soon evident the Hallamites had the game in their own hands. After half an hour's play the ball was kicked by Elliott, not through the goal, but just over it, and was touched down be Ash in splendid style, after running round two of his opponents before getting to the ball, thus securing a rouge. The Norfolk captain immediately kicked off, thus hoping to secure a goal for his side whilst his opponents were off their guard, but in their haste and confusion they left their goal unprotected, which was taken advantage of by one of the Hallam players securing another rouge, when time was called. Thus, Hallam won scoring two rouges to their opponent's nothing." (53)

No details exist of the how much money Thomas Youdan made from the Youdan Cup but three days after the final match, his room at the Alexander Music Hall was broken into and the vast amount of £70 was stolen in three bags. Perhaps it was this set back that was a factor in the original planned Cup not being made. The promised Youdan Cup should have been presented on the 11th of March but instead a silver claret jug was awarded, as the Jarvis-designed Cup was announced as not being ready on time:

"THE YOUDAN FOOTBALL PRIZE. - During the last three weeks, the members of the local football clubs have been competing for a silver cup, presented by Mr. Thomas Youdan. After a protracted and keen competition, the Hallam club was declared victorious. At the conclusion of this competition it was resolved that the Mackenzie and Norfolk Clubs, who had been beaten by the Hallam, should play for a second prize. Accordingly, the clubs met at Brammall-lane Cricket Ground, on Saturday last, and after a well-contested match- each side in turn appearing to have the best of the game- Norfolk eventually won by one rouge. Last evening representatives from each of the clubs to the number of about forty sat down to dinner at the Adelphi Hotel, Arundel-street. After partaking of an excellent repast, served in Mr. Sampson's usual excellent style, Mr. Councillor Hawksley was called on to preside, while the vice-chair was occupied by Mr. J. Birley. The usual loyal and patriotic toasts having been given and duly responded to, the prizes were put upon the table. They consisted of two handsome cups. The first prize, presented by Mr. Youdan, is a richly-ornamented claret jug, and the second a double-handled goblet. The first prize is not from Mr. Jarvis's design on account of the protracted time which would have been required in its manufacture; but it is understood that Mr. Youdan will present one after that design next year. The goblet is enriched with appropriate figures. After the prizes had been handed round the company, Mr. Sampson very generously 'hanselled' them by filling them and setting them on the table. The chairman being a member of the victorious club, Mr. Birley presented the goblet to the Hallam Club. In doing so, he proposed a vote of thanks to the donor for the handsome gift- a gift which he was sure had been keenly contended for and honourably won." (54)

CHAPTER FIVE

The design by Mr. Jarvis was never completed and the prize remained a claret jug. When Hallam FC hit hard times in 1886 they sold the Youdan Cup, but an antiques dealer in Scotland found it in 1997 and Hallam FC were able to buy back the Cup for £2,000. In 2014 the Youdan Cup appeared on the BBC's 'Antiques Road Show', where it was valued at £100,000. Silver specialist Alastair Dickenson said: 'At first sight it's a fairly standard Victorian claret jug, which would be worth about £800.' But he said he had learnt more about the cup's history, adding: 'We are pretty certain this is the world's oldest football trophy.' As such, I think the value has shifted a bit from my previous valuation. I would expect it to fetch £100,000 - probably more."

Oldest Association Football Cups in the world

1. Youdan Cup (Sheffield) 1867
2. Cromwell Cup (Sheffield) 1868
3. Football Association Cup 1871/72
= 4. Sheffield Association Challenge Cup 1876/77
= 4. Birmingham and District Association Challenge Cup 1876/77
= 5. North Staffordshire Football Association Challenge Cup 1877/78
= 5. Shropshire Association Challenge Cup 1877/78
= 6. Berks and Bucks Association Challenge Cup 1878/79
= 6. Cheshire Association Challenge Cup 1878/79
= 6. Blackburn Football Association Challenge Cup 1878/79
= 7. Basingstoke Association Challenge Cup 1879/80
= 7. Lancashire Football Association Challenge Cup 1879/80
= 7. Walsall and District Football Association (Licensed Victuallers) Cup 1879/80

Outside England there is the Scottish Cup (1873), which is the oldest cup still being presented, and of course we are on F.A. Cup number five in England. The Welsh Association Cup was launched in the 1877/78 season. In terms of Rugby, the earliest trophy is the United Hospitals Challenge Cup of 1874.

By 1870 Thomas Youdan had moved to the Alexandra Opera House in Sheffield:

"ALEXANDRA OPERA HOUSE (Proprietor, Mr. Thomas Youdan). - This gentleman has fallen back to concert hall business, the drama being at a discount this hot weather. The company comprise the Murray family, Charles Clements, a comic, Miss Florence Sanger, a characteristic vocalist, and some performing dogs, under their very able instructor, Mons. Pannoll. There are three charmed monsters engaged at this establishment. Persivani, Sylvester, and Little Dean, acrobats; Sidney Barnes, comic; Miss Ada Maitland, vocalist; and Chapman and Cushman, a pair of tidy negro artists. The stage is admirably managed by Mr. Oliver Cromwell, and the band is all that can be desired under the efficient direction of Mr. Parkin." [55]

Oliver Cromwell, the stage manager mentioned above, had been the manager of the Alexandra Theatre in 1868, and he too launched an eponymous football Cup competition; this time Wednesday FC won the tournament and is covered in more detail in the Garrick FC (1866) section.

Clearly Thomas Youdan's circumstances had changed in the two years since the event but he continued to support the football cause in Sheffield:

"ALEXANDRA OPERA HOUSE (proprietor, Mr. Thos. Youdan; Manager, Mr. W. Brittlebank). - Since our last, Mr. Youdan has given a benefit to the Football Accident Fund, the performance being on this occasion the splendid drama, 'Lady Audley's Secret,' Miss Eliza Thorne sustaining the part of Lady Audley. Mr. J. Fox appeared to advantage as Robert Audley. At the conclusion of the piece, Miss Thorne and J. Fox were loudly called for to receive the plaudits of a large and appreciative audience." [56]

In the mid-1880s, at the same time as Sheffield FC was feeling financial pressures, Hallam FC also hit hard times. In May 1886, a special meeting was called without an agenda becoming public and in October they sold their entire stock of equipment including the Youdan Cup and the club crest:

"CRICKET FIELD, PLOUGH INN, SANDYGATE.TO MEMBERS OF FOOTBALL CLUBS, Mr. ROBERT LOWE is instructed by Hallam Football Club to SELL by AUCTION, in the field, as above on MONDAY NEXT, October 4, at 2.30 o'clock, the whole of the CLUB APPOINTMENTS, &c, comprising two sterling silver cups, four Footballs, Machine for blowing up Balls, four Goal posts and two Cross Bars, Boundary flags, 22 Jerseys, two Bags, large chest, 36 boards, 16ft to 22ft, by 11in., nearly new; 31 Battens, lot Sundry Wood, 50 Shuttle Boards, 1,858 potties, two Mallets, two strong Fencing Ropes, 183 Stakes, various sizes; 20 flakes, the Club's Crest, &c. Shiregreen, October 2, 1886." [57]

Later in the same week Hallam FC was no more:

"It is with great regret I have to record the dissolution of the Hallam Football Club. This old-established organisation is one of the oldest in the district, and has produced some of the most accomplished players under the association rules who have done honour to the town and to the clubs. The Hallam Club stood out as an old land mark, and very many will deplore that, through whatever cause, disbandonment should have taken place." [58]

No specific reason was ever stated why the club disbanded, but it is highly probable for it to have been due to financial difficulties:

"Fifteen clubs will be left in the Challenge Cup competition when those clubs that have tied have settled their differences, and thus seven matches will be played in the second round, and one club will have a bye. It was the intention of the committee that 16 clubs should be let in for the next round, but the Hallam club having ceased to exist, that calculation has been upset." [59]

However, less than a year later in September 1887, the club was back:

"HALLAM v. ST. GEORGE'S ATHLETIC (1st teams). - This match was played at Sandygate on Saturday. After about twenty minutes' even play Hallam scored from a foul through a misunderstanding between the goalkeeper and back; by St. George's played up very well, and Keeling equalised about ten minutes after by a good shot from the right, and at half-time the score was one goal each. After change of ends the game was very well contested, but no other score was made up to call of time, and a very stiff match resulted in a tie, one goal each." [60]

As part of my reclassification of England's early football clubs (Appendix Two) I decided that if a club is defunct for more than a year then any future incarnation is classed as a new club, but in this case Hallam FC maintained its continuous position. Within a month, they travelled a long way north for an unsuccessful away game:

"MIDDLESBRO' v. HALLAM (SHEFFIELD). Played at Middlesbro' in wretched weather before about 600 persons, Harrison kicked off for Hallam, but the visitors were soon put on the defensive, and within ten minutes Fox scored the first goal for the home team. After some give-and-take play R. Wilson registered the second goal for Middlesbro', and another was nearly scored from a corner kick, and was being headed into goal when it was cleverly got out of danger. In fact the second half the play was entirely in the visitors' quarters, with the exception of two intervals, when Kinman and Elliott broke away and had a brilliant run. Four more goals

being added, the game resulted in a victory for the home team. Powell, Elliott, and Kinman played best for the visitors, and all the home team played well.
Result: -
MIDDLESBRO' .... 6 goals.
HALLAM ....0 goals." [61]

The World's Oldest Football Ground

Hallam FC's Sandygate ground is sometimes incorrectly reported as 'the world's oldest football ground,' a poorly defined title that has many clubs competing for the honour and I have tried to address the problem as part of my research for this book. Because Hallam FC stopped playing at Sandygate from 1933 until 1947 it is going to struggle to claim any continuity records.

The accolade of 'oldest Football Ground' is dependent on definition:

1. **1789.** Kennington Common in Surrey featured a football game where twenty-two gentlemen of Westmoreland were backed against twenty-two gentlemen of Cumberland for one thousand guineas in 1789. The first place where football was played. Kennington Common became Kennington Park in 1854 and whilst no early football teams listed it as their ground, the nearby Kennington Oval (1845) was the home of Surrey Football Club in 1849 and both the Civil Service FC and the Harrow Pilgrims FC listed it as a home ground in 1870. In the same year it was the venue for the first ever 'international' football match on 5 March 1870, England against Scotland. It was the home of the F.A. Cup final from 1872 to 1892, when the last game of football was played there.

2. **1802.** Vincent Square, where Westminster school football has been continuously played since 1802, making it the oldest school football ground in the world.

3. **1815.** Eton College where school football has been continuously played since 1815, making it the second oldest school football ground in the world.

4. **1830.** Turton Football Ground, Tower Street, Chapeltown. According to Peter Swain Tottington v Darwen played each other in 1830 (Folk Football) on the ground that Turton FC (Association) started playing on in 1871 and is the current home ground of the Old Boltonians, which would make it oldest non-school, amateur, football ground in the world, still in use today.

5. **1839.** Rugby football was played on Parker's Piece by the Cambridge Football Club formed in 1839 by Old Rugbeians, making it the first ground to feature the Rugby code.

6. **1855.** Bramall Lane, Sheffield, completed in 1855, is the oldest major stadium in the world still to be hosting professional Association football matches, with football games starting in 1862.

7. **1860.** Sandygate, Sheffield. The second oldest existing non-school Association Football Ground in the world 1860 (cannot claim continuous use by Hallam FC as they disbanded for a year in 1886 and stopped playing there between 1933 and 1947). (Mansfield Town FC make a claim for 1861 and their Field Mill ground, which I cannot substantiate).

8. **1870.** Reigate Priory FC claim the oldest existing amateur ground with one club in England, with continuous use of the cricket pitch since 1870. However, York Road,

Maidenhead United's ground is acknowledged by F.A. and F.I.F.A. as having the oldest football ground continuously used by the same club since 17th February 1871; there is a blue plaque to that effect saying 'York Road is believed by the F.A. to be <u>the oldest senior football ground continuously used by the same club.</u>'

9. **1877.** Racecourse Ground, Wrexham. <u>The world's oldest international football stadium that still hosts international matches,</u> having hosted Wales' first ever home international match in 1877. (Wrexham FC played their home games in the 1881/82 and 1882/83 seasons at the Recreation Ground),

10. **1877.** Stamford Bridge is <u>the oldest ground still being played on in the Premier League</u> as Mincing Lane played there in 1877, but Chelsea FC did not move in until 1905. In terms of continuous occupation, then the oldest Premier League ground is Burnley's Turf Moor, under my reclassification rules of earlier foundations (Appendix Two), then it was actually formed as Rugby playing Burnley Rovers in 1874, which played at Turf Moor at the time.

11. **1878.** Deepdale (Preston North End). <u>The second oldest existing League ground with one club in the world 1878.</u> (First oldest if you discount Burnley).

An accolade that cannot be taken away from the Sandygate ground is that it hosted the first ever (practice match) of Sheffield United in August 1889, featuring some expensive Scottish imports, (match report in Chapter Eight).

In John Shaw's obituary of 1918 there is no mention of his involvement with Hallam FC:

"FIFTY YEARS' WORK FOR CONSERVATISM. It is with much regret that we announce the death of Mr. John C. Shaw, one of the best known Conservative agents in the country, and one of the most notable organisers of the nineteenth century, which occurred at Moseley, near Birmingham, after a short illness. His name deserves a permanent place in the history of political organisation. As chief organiser for the whole of the country, he accomplished many remarkable things for the Conservative Party, and some of the results he obtained were almost startling. Mr. Shaw, who was about 86 years of age, was chief officer of the Midland Union of Conservative Associations for 26 years, retiring at the age of 80." [62]

Besides being unsure of his age at death they are also not sure of the foundation date of Sheffield FC:

"Before going to Birmingham, he had had a long and successful career in Sheffield, his native place. He belonged to the family of Shaw, of Attercliffe, and was articled to the late Dr. Shaw, his uncle, afterwards entering the legal profession, and finally choosing politics for a career. In the early days, he was a well-known athlete, achieving distinction as a cross-country runner, and occupying a leading position in organised football. He was one of the regular players of the old Sheffield Football Club, established in 1855, or 1856, and for 16 years held the presidency of the Sheffield Athletic Association." [62]

I think the reporter has also mixed up the non-existent Sheffield Athletic Association with the Sheffield Football Association, of which he was President for 14 years.

"In his early days, Mr. Shaw was connected to the legal profession, and his first political work was done while he was still in the law. After the Sheffield flood of 1864, he was engaged under Mr. J. Newbould, solicitor to the Flood Commissioners, to deal with compensation claims. The work was on a tremendous scale, and Mr. Shaw had no fewer than 30 clerks working under him. At the same time, a by-election was in progress in the town, and Mr. Shaw was pressed to render what assistance he could. This proved the immediate stepping-stone to his long career as a professional politician. After being secretary and treasurer of the Redistribution Association, for the whole of the Southern Division of Yorkshire, and holding local political positions, he was appointed, about the year 1875, organising secretary for the Conservative Party for the whole of England and Wales. He occupied this position for 10 years, during which he was responsible to the Whips for the efficiency of the Conservative organisation." [62]

It seems as if John Shaw did as much for the cause of Conservatism as he did for Hallam FC:

"Modern Party organisation practically owes its existence to Mr. Shaw. His work was of the real pioneer character, and he was the first to adopt methods which are now in universal use. In 1885, leading Conservatives from all over the West Riding met at Wakefield to entertain Mr. Shaw to luncheon, and to present him with a purse containing £200, a silver salver, and an illuminated address, in recognition of his valuable work. When he resigned his secretaryship of the Midland Union in 1912, he was presented at Birmingham with an address and a cheque for £1,120. Under the principal Conservative agent for the country, he had been sub-agent for the ten Midland counties for 20 years, and had also held the honorary secretaryship of the Union for 26 years." [62]

1861

This is the year the American Civil War broke out, which in turn caused the Lancashire cotton famine, (when the cotton supply to Europe ceased completely), leading to mass unemployment. Lancashire, which had imported three quarters of all cotton grown on southern plantations (1.3 billion lbs), now found that 60% of the county's mills closed down.

The deprivation caused in Lancashire made headline news and indirectly led to the first ever football match to be played at Bramall Lane in December 1862, between Sheffield FC and Hallam FC, to raise funds for the jobless Lancashire mill workers.

Bestselling books of this year, Tom Brown's School Days (1857) and the follow up book, Tom Brown at Oxford (1861) were integral to the growing ideal of 'Muscular Christianity'.

Five more would-be Association football clubs started in 1861, one each from Lincoln and Middlesex and three more for Sheffield. A report from this year deliberately sought out the worst aspects of Sheffield, making for gruesome reading, concluding:

"The rest of these investigations prove that, although Sheffield possesses a medal of honour conferred at the hands of the Emperor of the French, it is as devoid of the decencies of civilisation as it was in the Dark Ages." [63]

Norfolk FC (Sheffield, Yorkshire December 1861-1881)

- Equal Third Oldest Sheffield Football Club
- Equal Eighth Oldest Football Club in the world

Origin – Cricket, named after the park where they played.

The Duke of Norfolk owned a considerable area of land in Sheffield known, logically enough, as Norfolk Park; in the 19th century this extended from its current location all the way towards the city centre, including Bramall Lane. The Duke of Norfolk's plan to lease eight acres of his land to create a cricket ground in the Bramall Lane area was first discussed at a meeting on January 30th 1854, a meeting that William Prest, the co- founder of Sheffield FC, attended. Michael J. Ellison was the Duke's agent, who in time would become President of Sheffield United:

"Proposed Formation of a New Cricket Ground. A public meeting was held at the Adelphi Hotel, Arundel Street, on Monday Evening, to consider the offer made by his Grace the Duke of Norfolk, of the appropriation of a piece of ground to the purpose of a public cricket ground. Amongst those present were Messrs. T. R. Barker, M. J. Ellison, R. F. Skelton, J. P. Burbeary, J. P. Prest, W. Prest, &c. Mr. Ellison was called to the chair. The Chairman said he supposed they were all aware of the object of the meeting. He thought there could be but one option of the desirability of obtaining, if they possibly could, a really good ground for practicing the healthy and enjoyable game of cricket. When the Duke of Norfolk was last in the neighbourhood, he (the Chairman) asked his father to name to his Grace the circumstances in which they were placed in regard to the cricket ground in Sheffield, it being inaccessible in situation, and not always kept in good order, and to state that if his Grace would allot a space of ground for the purpose, they should be able to raise sufficient money to make a cricket ground which should be a credit to the town. The Duke fell in with the suggestion, and desired him (the Chairman) to look out for a suitable situation. He had done so, and he thought the most desirable was one in Bramall lane. They should there be able to have a ground of nine acres in extent, and which might be made at a comparatively small expense. The Duke would give them a lease for 99 years for the land upon which they should build the pavilion, but owing to the strict nature of the family settlement, he could not give a lease for that portion which would be required for the formation of the ground. The rent for this portion would be £5 an acre. That was not what lawyers would call a beneficial rent, and the Duke was precluded from granting leases except at a beneficial rent. It would, however, be held sacred to the purpose during the life of his Grace, and he had no doubt that so long as it was conducted in a proper manner, it would remain so. It would be for the meeting to consider how the money which was necessary for the formation of the ground should be raised, and also to appoint a committee to receive applications for shares, and also to draw up a report as to the most desirable manner in which the ground should hereafter be managed. He had roughly estimated the cost of the undertaking at from £1700 to £2000, which included the erection of the pavilion, the fence walls, and the levelling of the ground. The money might have been raised in their own club, but it was thought that a greater interest would be taken in it by the town, if shares were distributed amongst cricketers generally who chose to take any risk in it." [64]

The Bramall Lane cricket ground opened on May 1st 1855 with a match played between the first eleven and twenty-two selected from the 'Sheffield', 'Wednesday', 'Broomhall', 'Milton', 'Caxton', and 'Shrewsbury' clubs (with a 3d admission). By 1857 the Norfolk Park Cricket Club was playing at Bramall Lane as well; in all probability, it was the Norfolk cricket club that formed the football team. Later football match reports have Norfolk FC playing their home matches at Norfolk Park [65] and Norfolk Park is listed as its ground in the 1868 Football Annual (together with the 1861 foundation date), so presumably Norfolk FC could not afford the rent for Bramall Lane and had to move.

As mentioned earlier the first football game at Bramall Lane took place seven years after the ground opened, on December 29th 1862, between Sheffield FC and Hallam FC to raise funds for the jobless in Lancashire. Admission was 3d (still) but this time reserved seats were 6d. There must have been a fair number of Bramall Lane cricket shareholders because the pre-

CHAPTER FIVE

match publicity asked them not to claim their usual free admission.

The first match report found for Norfolk FC is from 1863:

"Football – The closing match of the Norfolk Football Club was played at Norfolk Park on Saturday last. The sides were chosen by Messrs. J. Roberts and A. Skinner, and after playing a splendid game of two hours, the result was a draw, each party obtaining a goal and a rouge. The members have played ten matches since the latter part of January, and won seven, lost two, and drawn one." [66]

In 1865 Norfolk FC played to an unknown code against Leeds FC (1864):

"Leeds football club. – The return match with the Norfolk football club of Sheffield will be played in the new portion of the Leeds Royal Park, on Thursday, the 28th instant. Play to commence at two, to conclude at half-past four in the afternoon. Admission by the Lion Entrance, 3d. Practice upon the Moor to-day, commencing at three in the afternoon. J. G. Hudson, Hon. Sec." [67]

By referring to a 'fifth anniversary' the following 1867 article suggests a later 1862 foundation date for Norfolk FC, but the 1868 Football Annual is very specific:

"Norfolk Football Club. The fifth anniversary of this club was held at Bramall Lane, yesterday, when from 6000 to 7000 persons assembled to see the sports. E. Round, Esq., as judge; and Mr. R. Bunting as clerk of the course. The first event was the 120 yards' handicap, in three heats, which were won by Burgin, Banks, and Barraclough. About thirty started, and in the final running off Barraclough was first, Banks second and Burgin third. Time, 12 sec… In the running long jump over a hurdle, Grayson at the first attempt topped the hurdle, and in the next went a cropper over it, and shook himself seriously; nevertheless, he managed to come in second, Simmonite being first." [68]

The Football Annuals show Norfolk FC's membership to be thriving for the first few years of existence:

Football Annual	Ground	Foundation Date	Hon. Sec.	Members	Colours
1868	Norfolk Park (SE)	December 1861	H.F. Bryars	240	Grey and blue
1869	Norfolk Park	1861	H.F. Bryars	270	Grey and blue
1870	Norfolk Park	1861	H.F. Bryars	270	Grey and blue
1871	Norfolk Park	1861	H.F. Bryars	160	Grey and blue
1872	Norfolk Park	1861	John Pashley	160	Grey and blue
1873	Norfolk Park	1861	R.C. Marsden	120	Grey and blue
1874	Norfolk Park	1861	R.C. Marsden	120	Scarlet, blue cap
1875	Norfolk Park	1861	R.C. Marsden	120	Scarlet and white
1876	Norfolk Park	1861	R.C. Marsden	120	Scarlet and white
1877	Norfolk Park	1861	G. Cropper	120	Scarlet and white
1878	x				
1879	Norfolk Park	1861	G. Cropper	120	Scarlet and white
1880	Quibell's Field, near Hyde Park	1860	G. Cropper	100	Scarlet and white

By late 1873 they were playing at Bramall Lane against Chesterfield:

"Norfolk Club v Chesterfield. This match was played on Monday afternoon at the Bramall lane Ground. The weather was fine but cold, and between 200 and 300 spectators put in an appearance. The ground was in splendid condition, and Norfolk having won the toss, took advantage of a westerly wind to kick with their backs to Bramall lane." [69]

Norfolk FC won by three goals to nil and the team line-ups were:

"Norfolk - T. Banks (captain), W. Barraclough, G. Clarke, T. Dixon, W. Platts, F. Sellars, J. P.

Donovan, W. Orton, G. Anthony, W. H. Booker, C. Ingleson, G. Bowling, T. Round. Umpire, J. White. Chesterfield – W. Stanton (captain), K. Marriott, G. E. Whomersley, G. Linley, G. Blanks by A. Gratton, R. Green, J. Smith. Umpire, C. W. Rollinson." [69]

Norfolk FC never played in the F.A. Cup but were the losing finalists to Hallam FC in the 1867 Youdan Cup. (See the Hallam FC section for the match report). On the internet, there are uncorroborated claims that when Norfolk FC was playing away at Nottingham Forest in 1878, a whistle was used for the first time by the umpire. In fact, I found a Mr. Brown suggesting the idea, six years earlier in 1872:

"Mr. Brown, in the recent match, Sheffield v Nottingham Forest, made a valuable suggestion, to the effect that each umpire should be furnished with a whistle, which he should blow in case of granting an appeal for a foul; as, in the event of a dispute, the players cannot be certain what his decision is. Of course, on the whistle being blown, play would at once cease. At present some cry 'foul', and others 'play on' so the players are uncertain what the umpire's decision really is. Before another season this will be a very proper subject for discussion by the Association." [70]

The first treasurer of Nottingham Forest in 1865 was William Brown so it would be serendipitous if he could be credited with the whistle blowing idea, as well as being a founder member of the club. It is thought that the use of a whistle by a referee did not become commonplace until nearly twenty years later in 1891, when the official moved on to the actual field of play and would have to stop play by some means or another; a whistle was deemed more effective than a flapping handkerchief.

The last press report I have found for Norfolk FC is in 1881; naturally enough, a club's demise does not feature as strongly as their creation and the early end of Norfolk FC is not explained. The mid 1880s was a difficult time to be an amateur club, but 1881 is early, considering the fact that the previous year they still had 100 members paying their subscriptions; this coincided with their move away from Norfolk Park to Quibell's Field, near Hyde Park, so perhaps finding a place to play was the problem, or that the rents required no longer made it viable. The key to survival in the coming period would be securing an enclosed space so gate money could be charged.

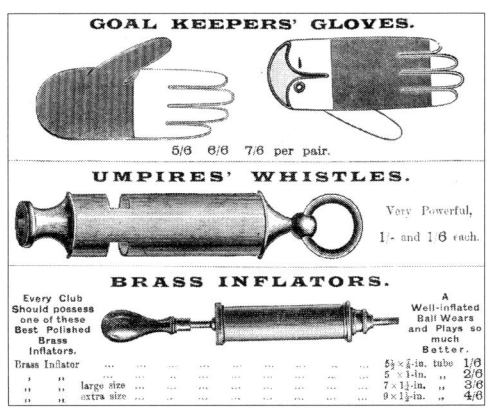

Advert from Football Annual
courtesy of the National Football Museum

Pitsmoor FC, (Sheffield, Yorkshire November 1861-1887)

- Equal Third Oldest Sheffield Football Club
- Equal Eighth Oldest Football Club in the world

Origin – Cricket Club. Another club for subscription-paying gentlemen in the mould of Sheffield, Hallam and Norfolk. In 1861 Pitsmoor was an affluent village to the north of the town centre.

CHAPTER FIVE

The foundation of the football club was announced by the press:

"Pitsmoor Cricket Club announce their intention to form a foot ball club (at a meeting on November 7th). J. Brown. Sec." [71]

Pitsmoor FC's Hon. Sec. in February 1867 was Thomas Clarke of 52 Harvest Lane, Sheffield, which was updated by the 1868 Football Annual in the following year:

Founded: 1861
Number of members: 264
Club Ground: Pitsmoor
Amount of entrance fee: Nil
Amount of subscription: 2s 6d
Code: Sheffield Association
Hon. Sec.: G. Fowler, Bay Horse, Pitsmoor
Colours: White

The 1869 Football Annual repeated the facts from the 1868 edition except that the membership had gone down to 165 members. This remained true for 1870 but in the 1871 edition, their last entry shows the membership down to a 100 and the Hon. Sec. as W.C. Birks, Barrel Inn, Pye Bank.

Pitsmoor was undisputedly the best team in Sheffield in 1863, having beaten all opposition, whilst Sheffield FC's star had waned, drawing two games and losing the rest:

"Pitsmoor Football Club – This club played their closing match of the season on Saturday last. Sides were chosen on the field by Messrs. Stones and Cadman, and after some good play Mr. Stones' side were victorious, making one goal and one rouge against one rouge. The members of this club have been very successful this season, having played thirteen matches against the best clubs of the town, and defeating all of them in one game, and some both in the first matches and the return, so that, considering this is but their second season, the club has every reason to congratulate itself on the position it holds amongst those who admire the healthy and vigorous game of football. The annual sports will finish the season, and will take place shortly. Every preparation is being made in order to give them as much interest as possible. Sufficiently good prizes have been offered to induce the competitors in the different events to do their best; and no doubt, from the well-known capabilities of the members in running, leaping, &c., their friends will be able to spend an agreeable hour or two with them on the above named occasion." [72]

In 1866 they were still capable of beating Sheffield FC, with the match making the national press:

"Pitsmoor v. Sheffield – On Saturday, eleven each of these clubs met on the Pitsmoor Ground, to try the respective strength of both, and were witnessed by many gentlemen and players of various clubs in Sheffield, &c. After a well-contested game the Pitsmoor eleven came off victorious, securing one goal and two rouges to Sheffield's one goal." [73]

"Pitsmoor v Mechanics (Sheffield). The first teams of the above clubs played a match at Pitsmoor on Saturday last (1868), which resulted in a draw. The sides were as follow: - Pitsmoor: G. Fowler (captain), T. Heaton, G. Simpson, J. Simpson, J. Harris, H. Rollitt, W. Wardley, W. Carr, C. Roberts, G. Rogers, W. Waterfall and P. Cadman – Mechanics: J. Marsh (captain), J. R. Deans, J. Brennan, J. White, J. Jenkinson, B. Hammond, J. Lee Thompson, Varley, Charlesworth, and two others. Referees, J. Bradley, and J. Rodgers." [74]

Pitsmoor FC never played in the F.A. Cup but took part in the Youdan Cup in 1867 and were still operating in 1887 (A.G.M.).

Norton FC (Sheffield, Yorkshire 'About'1861- 1878)
- Fourth Oldest Sheffield Football Club
- Ninth Oldest Football Club in the world

Origin: Cricket. Norton remained part of Derbyshire until 1901, but they were early members of the Sheffield Football Association. Norton FC does not receive a mention in the Football Annuals until 1870 and then unfortunately without a foundation date or the team's colours; all we know is that they played in Norton with 50 members and the Hon. Sec. was George Rodgers. It is the 1872 Football Annual where Hon. Sec. Fred Morton quotes the foundation date as 'About 1861 and the strip is green'.

There is a very long standing cricket club in Norton run by George Barker from the Cross Scythes Public House at Four Lane Ends as this advert from 1826 shows:

"NORTON CRICKET GROUND. GEORGE BARKER respectfully returns his sincere thanks to his Friends for the past favours, and begs to inform them, that he has lately enlarged his Ground, which will be ready for playing on, on Monday first, and continue open every lawful day during the Season, except on Thursdays. G. B. has always on hand a superior Stock of Wines, Spirits, &c.; and by keeping every article of the best quality, and using his utmost endeavours to give satisfaction, flatters himself with a continuance of public favour. N. B. Dinner and Tea parties attended as usual." [75]

A year later in 1827 Norton Cricket Club played other clubs for large wagers:

"CHALLENGE, FOR FIFTY SOVEREIGNS. THE NORTON and HEELEY CLUB hereby Challenge the HALLAM CLUB to play them a MATCH at CRICKET for 50 SOVEREIGNS, either at the Hyde Park or Darnall Grounds, on condition that two Sheffield Gentlemen shall be the Umpires. The Public are most respectfully informed, that a CRICKET MATCH for 11 Sovereigns, will be played at Cross Scythes, on Monday next, the 15th inst.:- WOODSEATS against COAL ASTON and DRONFIELD. N. B.- Should the above Challenge not be accepted, the last Match for the Season will be played at Cross Scythes, by the Members of the Club, on Monday, the 22nd inst." [76]

In 1853 Norton Cricket Club was playing at Oakes Park against a team with the interesting nickname of the "Etonians":

"Norton v. Gleadless – On Monday, a match was played in the Oakes Park, between the Norton and Gleadless clubs. The ground was honoured by the presence of numerous admirers of the game, and, owing to the cricketing notoriety which the Gleadless Dons had hitherto maintained (with one exception, when they were recently defeated by Norton), the odds appeared in their favour. The Norton players, however, were not to be discouraged by chaffing; neither did the fame of the 'Etonians' lower the Nortonites in the estimation of their friends. After allowing their rivals every advantage in the selection and nomination of players on both sides, it will be seen by the following result of the match, that the Norton cricketers beat their competitors in one innings." [77]

'The Oakes' at this time was the family residence of Francis Westby Bagshawe Esq. D.L. a J.P. in Norton. (Unfortunately, I have not been able to establish a personal family connection, but the Westby family remains optimistic!). By 1861 Oakes Park would be the home ground of Norton FC.

The 1861 foundation date is confirmed with a match report from that year, which was nearly an early five-a-side game, based on the number of players who had shown up to play:

"Yesterday, a match was played on the Sheffield ground between three of the most celebrated

CHAPTER FIVE

players of the Sheffield Football Club, and six of the Norton Club. After two hours, exciting play the Norton players proved the victors. Goals as follows: Norton, 4: Sheffield, 0." [78]

A year later in 1862 they played Hallam FC at home:

"The return match between the above clubs was played on Saturday last, at Norton, in the grounds of F. W. Bagshawe, Esq. (Oakes Park) the superior strength of the Norton team soon told on their opponents, though they played in the most plucky manner. The game was spirited and well contested. It resulted in an easy victory for the Norton players, who succeeded in scoring four goals to Hallam's nothing." [79]

A Derbyshire Times newspaper report from 2 January 1864 noted a scheduled game between Chesterfield and Norton football clubs:

"We understand that the Chesterfield and Norton football clubs will play a game on the turnpike en route from Sheffield to Chesterfield. This day. Norton Football Club. The first practice meet will take place today on the Norton Ground – Kick off, Three pm. T. Bramall, Hon. Sec." [80]

Norton FC played Sheffield FC at their East Bank ground on the 11th February 1865, which is described as played by the 'the old rules.' [81]

Undoubtedly Norton FC's biggest ever match was in the Youdan Cup on the 23rd of February 1867 against Hallam FC, the eventual winners. After a draw the two clubs played again two days later, in front of an amazing crowd of 3,000 spectators:

"Hallam v. Norton. The match between these two clubs was played on the ground of Norton Club, which is distant about five miles from Sheffield, and resulted in one of the closest and most exciting games ever witnessed at football. The result of two hours and a half hard play on Saturday was, that neither side had been able to score, a sufficient proof of the equality of the contest. According to the rules formed for the regulation of matches played for the Youdan's Cup, published in THE SPORTSMAN of the 19h inst., play had to be renewed on Monday last, the 25th, at 3pm. After a second long-protracted fight, and another game as well contested as the first, the match was finally decided in favour of the Hallam by one rouge, cleverly secured by H. Ash. As a proof of the great interest excited in Sheffield by these contests for the Youdan's Cup, we may mention that the match between the above clubs was witnessed by nearly three thousand spectators. For the Hallam Club, T. Armitage, G. Jones, J. Dale, and S. Gilbert, while for the Norton Club, J. Linley, F. Morton, Jackson, and H. Butterly greatly distinguished themselves. The following is a list of the players: Hallam Club: J. C. Shaw (captain), H. Ash, W. Adsetts, J. Dale, J. Bradbury, G. Jones, T. Armitage, J. Bownes, S. Gilbert, A. Hobson, G. Elliott, and H. Branwell (goal-keeper). Umpire, Mr. J. Bradshaw. Norton Club: F. Morton (Captain), J. Linley, W. Jackson, J. Jackson, T. Birch, R. Kilner, S. Needham, H. Butterly, C. Mills, G. Osborne, John Shaw, and James Shaw. Umpire, Mr. T. Downing, referee, Mr. W. J. Bingham." [82]

Norton were members of the Sheffield Football Association but they also looked south to Derbyshire for football games. The 'South Derbyshire Football Association' formed in March 1871, was by 1873 named 'Derbyshire Football Association'; they played a game of 'Town versus County' and a number of players from Sheffield clubs from the southern side of the city played, including Norton, Gleadless and Heeley. In August 1871, a report was featured on Norton Football Clubs' '7th Annual Athletics Sports', which took place in Mr. John Lister's Field, off Derbyshire Lane and 'were well and fashionably attended.' [83]

Norton FC stopped appearing as a club in the Football Annual in 1875 but played on for a few more years until at least 1878; in 1901 the parish of Norton was incorporated within the city of Sheffield.

1862

It seems that mob rule still occasionally operated in Sheffield in 1862, based on this insight from the press; a grave robbing sexton and a mob looking for retribution. A sexton is an officer of the church who has responsibility for the buildings and grounds:

"An extraordinary riot took place at the Wardsend Cemetery, Sheffield, in consequence of a report that the sexton had been in the habit of disinterring bodies and disposing of them for dissection. The mob forcibly entered the house formerly occupied by the sexton, but recently furnished, in part of the use of the officiating clergyman, where they demolished the furniture, windows, doors, &c. They next proceeded to the house of the sexton, which they set on fire, and thus utterly destroyed the house and its contents. The damage done to the sexton's house was estimated at £500. The Rev. John Livesey, the incumbent was tried at the York Assizes on the 24th of July, for making a false entry of burial and for giving a false certificate; was found guilty, but without any fraudulent intent, and was merely nominally sentenced to three weeks' imprisonment. Isaac Howard, the sexton, was indicted for disinterring bodies, found guilty, and sentenced to three months' imprisonment. Howard afterwards obtained £200 from the county, for damage done to his house." [84] Ten football clubs started in 1862, three from the Home Counties, one from Lincolnshire, five more from Sheffield and the world's oldest League football club, Notts County FC.

Firvale FC (Sheffield, Yorkshire 1862-1893)

- Equal Fifth Oldest Sheffield Football Club
- Equal Thirteenth Oldest Football Club in the World

Origin: Cricket. With so many football clubs playing in Sheffield presumably at some point the origin becomes nothing more than football achieving critical mass in a specific area, particularly as Pitsmoor was then the adjoining village to Firvale. I have put cricket as the club's origin because an article written for the Sporting Life on Wednesday 30 January 1867, said that 'There are now fourteen clubs in the town, almost every cricket club having a football club connected with it.' (The article is repeated in full in Chapter One). It is striking that in 1868, in such a small geographical area, a total of 400 gentlemen were members of the two clubs; a subscription fee of 2s. 6d. suggests that Firvale FC was indeed a club for gentlemen. I could not find an existing Fir Vale cricket or athletics team prior to 1862; Firvale FC never played in the F.A. Cup but did enter the 1867 Youdan Cup, losing to the eventual finalists, Norfolk FC in the first round. The first match report I found was from 1864:

"Fir vale football cub. The members and friends are respectively informed that the opening match will be played this day, on the Fir Vale Ground. Kick off at 2pm. H. Peck, Hon. Sec." [85] In 1865 the Club secretary was W.H. Jarvis, 4 Burngreave Place, Pitsmoor and an analysis of the Football Annuals shows J.W. Gillatt had replaced him by at least 1868.

Football Annual	Ground	Foundation Date	Hon. Sec.	Members	Colours
1868	Pitsmoor	1862	J.W. Gillatt	136	White and red
1869	Pitsmoor	1862	G.D. Davy	120	White and red
1870	Pitsmoor	1862	G.D. Davy	120	White and red
1871	Pitsmoor	1862	J.V. Nutt	120	White and red
1872	Pitsmoor	1862	J.V. Nutt	120	White and scarlet
1873	Pitsmoor (N.E)	1862	J.V. Nutt	120	White and scarlet

CHAPTER FIVE

1874	Pitsmoor (N.E)	1862	F.J. Sayer	123	White and scarlet trimmings
1875	Pitsmoor (N.E)	1862	F.J. Sayer	135	White and scarlet trimmings
1876	Pitsmoor (N.E)	1862	F.J. Sayer	135	White and scarlet trimmings
1877	Pyper Lane, Pitsmoor	1862	F.J. Sayer	135	White and scarlet trimmings
1878	x				
1879	Pyper Lane, Pitsmoor		H. Firth	135	White and scarlet trimmings
1880	Pyper Lane, Pitsmoor		F.J. Sayer	30	White and scarlet trimmings

Pyper Lane later became Herries Road and according to later press reports, Firvale FC subsequently played three miles away at Newhall Gardens, Pitsmoor. Clearly something happened in 1880 for the membership numbers to crash and the reporting to stop for the Football Annuals, but the club continued to play until 1894.

In Sheffield match reports a new footballing term appears, that of a 'screw kick,' which doesn't appear in other regions until later. The forebear of the modern 'banana kick' is executed by Pinder in the following report for a game against Hallam FC:

"Fir-vale v. Hallam (1st Teams) – This match came off on Saturday last (*1875*) at Sandygate in most bitter cold weather. The visitors took up a very good representative team, and eventually proved too good for the home players by winning the match by two goals to one. Fir-Vale won the toss and took the advantage of the wind, which was blowing very strongly across the field. The ball being set rolling by the Hallam captain it was quickly returned to their territory, and J. Marsden secured the first goal for Fir-vale after about three minutes' play. Ends were now changed, and Hallam tried hard to equalise matters, and after the visitors had played strongly on the defence for about 35 minutes, G. Pinder by a good screw kick put one through for his side, thus making the game equal. At this time the play become most exciting, and some good play was shown by both sides, and in less than 10 minutes Fir-Vale secured their second goal, H. Ellis steering the ball though the posts. Time was then played out without any farther score being made. For Hallam A. B. Slowe, G. Ellis, Pinder, and Middleton played well, as also Simpson, J. Hudson, F. Sellars, and L. Herring for Fir-Vale." [86]

In 1893 Firvale FC were still advertising for players, but from 1894 I can find no more match reports or meetings.

Heeley (Christchurch) FC (Sheffield, Yorkshire 1862 to 1899)
- First Football Club in England to be formed from a church
- Equal Fifth Oldest Sheffield Football Club
- Equal Thirteenth Oldest Football Club in the World
- Sheffield & Hallamshire Senior Cup Winners – 1881/82 (match report in Pyebank)
- Their first appearance in the Derbyshire Football Association Challenge Cup 1884/85

Origin: Church team. Throughout England twenty clubs had been formed by this point, but Heeley FC is the first team to be founded as part of a church, the first embodiment of 'Muscular Christianity' that would fast become a growing nationwide trend. Heeley FC was presumably formed by gentlemen members of a church congregation, as a reaction to the blossoming Sheffield football scene, and still well-to-do enough to be able to afford the 2s.6d. subs. Appropriately, Heeley Parish church, at 151 Gleadless Road, was founded in 1846 from part of St Mary's Parish on Bramall Lane. Nathaniel Creswick, the co-founder of Sheffield FC, is buried in the Heeley Parish church graveyard; perhaps he was part of the congregation back in 1862.

THE GOLDEN AGE OF SHEFFIELD AMATEUR FOOTBALL 1857-1876

The club could not have been solely the province of gentlemen, because by 1868 Jack Hunter was playing for them. Heeley's most famous player John 'Jack' Hunter was born in Crookes in 1852; his father was a table knife cutler and by the 1861 census the family had moved to Highfield. In 1871 Jack followed his father into the cutlery trade. According to the 1881 census, John was married with four children, living at the back of Well Road in Heeley. He played for Heeley (in 1868 aged 16), Providence, Albion and Zulus and won seven caps in total for England, but his biggest success was across the Pennines as player coach for Blackburn Olympic from 1882 to 1887. Despite the Zulu FC appearance money, Jack remained a table knife cutler but interestingly his occupation in the 1901 census was 'professional football trainer'. Under his management, Olympic FC became the first non-southern club to win the F.A. Cup in 1883; a truly seismic moment that signalled that the amateur game had been irrevocably replaced by professionalism. One of the umpires at the Cup Final that day was Pierce Dix who had resigned from the Sheffield Football Association as Hon. Sec. over the professionalism row with the Zulus FC (more about this later in Chapter Six), so the F.A. Cup victory must have been twice as sweet for Hunter. Surprisingly, it was the first time that an all English eleven had won the F.A. Cup, bearing in mind the tournament was now in its twelfth year. The last such 'all-English' team to repeat the feat was Manchester City in 1969 (and it probably will never happen again). Jack Hunter died of consumption aged 51 on 9 April 1903; his pall bearers included Sheffield's Billy Mosforth and Blackburn Rovers' Fergie Suter.

Blackburn Olympic FC. Photograph from 'around May 1882.' Image courtesy of the National Football Museum

According to 'Shooting Stars: The Brief and Glorious History of Blackburn Olympic 1878-1889' by Graham Phythian, Jack Hunter is second left, middle row.

CHAPTER FIVE

From 1873, the Football Annuals included a new piece of information; the location of a dressing room. More often than not this was reported as 'on the ground' but for Heeley FC it was three pubs; the Red Lion (1881), the White Lion (1887) and the Crown Inn (1888), all three within a few metres of each other.

Football Annual	Ground	Foundation Date	Hon. Sec.	Members	Colours	Dressing Room
1868	Heeley, Wellsbrook Park	1862	T. Woodcock		Grey and white stripes	Reporting did not start until 1873
1869	Heeley, Wellsbrook Park	1862	T. Woodcock		Grey and white stripes	
1870	Heeley, Meersbrook Park	1862	T. Woodcock		Grey and white stripes	
1871	Heeley, Meersbrook Park	1862	J.D. Harrison		Grey and white stripes	
1872	Heeley, Meersbrook Park	1862	Richard Gillet		Grey and white stripes	
1873	Heeley, Meersbrook Park	1862	R. Osborne	70	Grey and white stripes	
1874	Heeley, Meersbrook Park	1862	R. Osborne	70	Grey and white stripes	
1875	Heeley, Meersbrook Park	1862	J. Tomlinson	70	Grey and white stripes	
1876	Heeley, Meersbrook Park	1862	J. Tomlinson	70	Grey and white stripes	
1877	Heeley, Meersbrook Park	1862	J. Tomlinson	70	Grey and white stripes	
1878	x					
1879	Meersbrook Park	1869*	J.E. Deans	200	Puce and black hoops - red cap	
1880	Meersbrook Park	1869	J.E. Deans	250	Puce and black hoops - red cap	
1881	Meersbrook Park	1860	J.E. Deans	Reporting stopped in 1881 edition	Violet and black	Red Lion
1882	Meersbrook Park	1860	J.E. Deans		Violet and black	Red Lion
1883	Meersbrook Park	1860	J.E. Deans		Violet and black	Red Lion
1884	Meersbrook Park	1860	J.E. Deans		Violet and black	Red Lion
1885	Meersbrook Park	1860	J.E. Deans		Violet and black	Red Lion
1886	Meersbrook Park	1860	J.E. Deans		Violet and black	Red Lion
1887	Meersbrook Park	1860	Allen Hall		Violet and black	White Lion
1888	Meersbrook Park	1860	Allen Hall		Violet and black in halves	Crown Inn

*The club's foundation date goes haywire when J.E. Deans took over in 1879 and the subsequent dates are all incorrect.

According to my research, Heeley FC's 1868 ground, Wellsbrook Park, appears in no Sheffield records and may have been private grounds. Meersbrook Park is still a park today covering 17 hectares but was originally the grounds to Meersbrook Hall (now the Ruskin Museum), until acquired by Sheffield Council in 1886. The Meersbrook pitch must have had quite a bit of a slope, based on the following match report which describes;

'One goal in as it were a coal pit, and the other on the summit of Snowden.' [87]

The Yorkshire-Derbyshire border was a lot further north than it is in modern times, with the current Sheffield suburb of Heeley forming the Yorkshire boundary. It was defined by the 'Meres Brook', a stream that feeds into the river Sheaf which originates in Gleadless and joins the Sheaf (tunnelled) in Lowfield. Historically this stream formed the boundary between the ancient kingdoms of Northumbria and Mercia. Later, in Victorian times, the Meersbrook river divided the West Riding of Yorkshire from North Derbyshire. In this period, Bramall Lane was just a mile or so south of the Derbyshire border, meaning the following Sheffield clubs could all be geographically classified as Derbyshire clubs: Norton FC, Gleadless FC, Millhouses FC, and Woodseats FC. However, as they were all members of the Sheffield Football Association, I have categorised them all as Sheffield and Yorkshire clubs. In 1921 the Yorkshire-Derbyshire boundaries were extended to include Handsworth and Wadsley and in 1935 they were altered again to include Totley, Dore, Beauchief and Greenhill. In 1974 the ancient Ridings of Yorkshire were dismantled. The earliest match report for Heeley FC I have been able to find is from 1863:

"A friendly game at football was played on Shrove Tuesday, between two elevens of the Hemsworth v. the second eleven of the Christ Church, Heeley, Football club; which, on the ground for the former, resulted in an easy victory for Christ Church." (88) (Hemsworth FC never featured in the Football Annuals or either of the two Sheffield Associations)

In 1864 Heeley FC found somewhere else to play, other than Meersbrook Park:

"This day. Heeley Christ Church Football Club. The members are respectfully informed that the opening match will be played today in the Field adjoining the Tilt. Kick off at three o'clock. F. W. Martin, Hon. Sec." (89) (The Heeley Tilt was a mill on the river Sheaf).

At some point between late 1864 and September 1867 they dropped the 'Christ Church' part of their name:

"Heeley Football Club – A meeting of the above club was held in the National School, on Tuesday night, when the following were elected officers for the ensuing season: Hon. Sec., Mr. Herbert Hurt; treasurer, Mr. Mathew Lee; committee: Messrs. V. Dearden, R. Barringham, J. Martin, J. Jones, R. Gillott, John Elliott, Wm. Ashton, Thomas Woodcock (presumably the club's original Hon. Sec.), and W. Wilson." (90)

By 1867 Heeley FC had become one of the strongest Sheffield teams taking part in the Youdan Cup. They played in the final of the first ever Sheffield Association Challenge Cup (1876/77), at Bramall Lane with 7,000 to 8,000 spectators, narrowly losing to Wednesday by 4 goals to 3. (match report in the Wednesday FC section). In fact, they featured in four of the first six finals between 1876 and 1881, losing three times and winning once in 1881/82, when they beat Pye Bank FC 5-0 (See full match report in Pye Bank 1872) section. I have struggled to find full match reports for Heeley FC until the late 1870s; the following report for 1877, does feature Sheffield Albion's star player Billy Mosforth, but not, unfortunately, Jack Hunter:

"Heeley v. Albion. Played at Meersbrook Park on Saturday. Owing to the popularity which the Heeley Club has attained in the late contests at Bramall-lane a large number of spectators, numbering three or four hundred, assembled to witness the match, and they frequently applauded any unusually spirited play on either side. Heeley was weakened by the absence of Andrews and Hunter, the former playing in a match at Chesterfield for the benefit of the widow and children of the late Mr. Rodgers, and the latter being indisposed. At 3.40, Mosforth having won the toss, Heeley kicked off towards the Chesterfield road, and against a slight breeze which considerably stiffened as the game advanced, but notwithstanding this the Albion defences were soon in peril. This was mainly due to the unselfish passing play of the brothers Tomlinson, who seem to know each other's positions and tactics admirably. Mosforth made a brilliant run down the low side, but he was intercepted by the backs and the ball was soon returned, where but for the timely interposition of Teather, Jun., the Albion flag must have been lowered. F. Brownhill returned to the charge, whose accurate kicking was generally admired – and directed the leather to Beard, but his effort failed. Whittaker, about this time, was frequently applauded for his fearless, lunging back kicking. Albion now raised the siege, and Mackenzie had a try but the ball went outside. J. Tomlinson made a splendid shot at the Albion goal, but the wind carried it about an inch outside the post. A foul was called for and allowed near the Albion citadel, but the advantage was of no fruition. Again Beard had a chance, but the ball grazed the post on the outside. Mosforth, by one of his marvellous runs, took the leather into the vicinity of the Heeley territory, but his final effort went over the bar. He immediately after had another try, but with the same result. Brownhill now distinguished himself by a splendid run all the length of the field, and finally left the ball in charge of Beard, whose aim was too elevated, it once more going over the bar. A few minutes after half-time was called, and Heeley having the wind in their favour, it was conjectured they would soon change the aspect of affairs. This opinion was verified a few minutes after the recommencement. The Brothers Tomlinson's manipulation of the ball completely nonplussed all opponents, and getting within reach, the sphere was propelled direct for the goal. Wright had just got hold to throw it out when Beard rushed up, and the result was a goal for the home team. Wright disputed the goal on the plea that he had managed to scramble it outside the post, but the umpires flag was in favour of Heeley. Mosforth received an ovation for the dexterous manner in which he eluded three opponents. Brownhill worked the ball up to the Albion fortress, but it struck the crossbar and rebounded in front of the goal. A tremendous scrimmage took place, and Wright had his work cut out to save his stronghold, which he did manfully, the ball eventually being put out of danger. England did some useful work for Albion, but his side seemed to lack energy in kicking through. Time was played out without any addition to the scoring, Heeley thus winning a very good match by one goal to nil. The players' names are appended: - Heeley: J. Harrison, J. Thorpe, H. G. Barringham, T. A. and J. Tomlinson, R. Martin, T. Metcalf, F. Broomhill, H. Brown (goal), J. Linley, and W. Beard. Albion: Mosforth (captain), Wright (goal), Whittaker, Jessop, W. Teather, A. W. Teather, Bright, Podoski, W. H. England, R. England, A. Mackenzie, and Robertshaw." [91]

Jack Hunter's reputation was defended in 1880 by Heeley's Hon. Sec., J.E. Deans, after a game between Heeley and Providence for the Wharncliffe Charity Cup, when he was accused of deliberately charging a player in an off the ball incident:

"I should like to call the attention of the public to one or two inaccuracies in your report of the football match, played on Saturday at Bramall lane ground. In the first place, your reporter states there were only about 500 persons present; the fact is, over a thousand paid admissions, which your reporter could have easily have ascertained had he taken the trouble. In the second place, the report says, 'Hunter, who had been charged previously, now charged his opponent most deliberately, and this set a bad example, the man not being near the ball at the time.' The only excuse I can offer for your reporter is that he could not see the positions of the players in the field, or he would not have made such a mistake. The fact is (and I was in a position to see all that took place, being one of the umpires) the ball was not two yards away from the players at the time, and I maintain that Hunter was perfectly justified in charging as he did, which was to prevent the said player getting the ball. Hunter is well known both in Sheffield and all over England and Scotland, wherever football is played, as one of the fairest players that ever kicked a football, and my object in writing this letter is that his reputation should not suffer from a mistake made by your reporter. Yours respectfully J. E. Deans, Hon. Sec. Heeley Football Club. [The attention of our football reporter has been called to the above letter. He maintains the accuracy of his remarks, and states that the ball was at least five, if not ten, yards away from the player when Hunter charged. – ED. S. D. T.]" [92]

(The Wharncliffe Charity Cup was an invitational knockout charity competition, taking the name of its sponsor, the Earl of Wharncliffe, and was designed to raise money for local good causes. It began in 1878/79, ceasing in 1983/84 over a hundred years later; the trophy's first winners were Wednesday when they beat Heeley three goals to two at Bramall Lane.)

When Middlesbrough FC formed in 1876, there was no local Cup to compete for as the Cleveland Association would not be formed until 5th February 1881 at the Swatters Carr hotel in Middlesbrough. Instead they joined the Sheffield Football Association in 1879 and it seems they enjoyed the competition because they were still playing in the 1883/84 season when

Heeley played them to settle second place in the competition:

"The Sheffield Football Association Challenge Cups have this season caused some determined struggles, and although Lockwood Brothers have won the principal cup, the second place in the same competition has not yet been taken. Heeley and Middlesbro' having failed to settle the point on Saturday last, as each scored a couple of goals. The teams will meet again, and the association on Thursday decided that the Heeley team shall, on the next occasion, journey to Middlesbro', instead of the Middlesbro' men coming to Sheffield. Neither club on Saturday last put its full strength in the field, Heeley being very poorly represented." [93] Heeley defaulted the game, presumably due to the travelling distance involved in the replay and the 'Executive Committee awarded the silver medals to the Middlesbro' Club.' [94]

Heeley FC - F.A. Cup Record 1871-1888

Season	Rd	Opponent	H/A	Score
1881/82	1	Lockwood Bros	H	5-1
	2	Sheffield FC	A	4-0
	3	Bye		
	4	Wednesday	A	1-3
1882/83	1	Bye		
	2	Nottingham Forest	A	2-7
1883/84	1	Notts County	A	1-3
1884/85	1	Notts Wanderers	H	1-0
	2	Nottingham Forest	A	2-4
1885/86	1	Eckington Works	H	2-1
	2	Notts Rangers	H	1-6
1886/87	1	Grimsby Town	H	1-4
1887/88	1	Attercliffe	H	9-0
	2	Owlerton	A	0-1
1888/89	1	Walsall Town Swifts	A	1-5

The mistaken Heeley FC foundation date (of 1860 rather than 1862) quoted by the club's Hon. Sec. J.E. Deans, that appeared in the 1881 Football Annual, is repeated in this 1891 article:

"Heeley Football Club Concert. The above old-established football club, who date their existence as far back as 1860, held their annual 'smoker' on Wednesday night in the Bramall lane Pavilion, the large room of which was lent for the occasion by the proprietors. Members and friends to the number of nearly 200 attended, and thoroughly enjoyed an excellent entertainment. Songs were sung by the following gentlemen, all of whom were most cordially received: Messrs. J. Robertson, A. S. Platts, W. A. Spooner, W. A. Studdart, J. Mack Clarke, H. Lawrence, and J. Ryan. Mr. C. H. Howlett gave several songs in good style during the evening, accompanying himself on the guitar and mandolin. Messrs. Mordaunt and Brown were greatly appreciated in their duet with the banjo and the piano; while the former also rendered two or three humorous songs capitally. Mr. J. Hearne recited the 'Quack Doctor' in inimitable style; and Mr. T. M. Byron gave a short ventriloquial entertainment, which was received with applause. In all respects the entertainment was a success, and under the presidency of Mr. Chas. Stokes a thoroughly enjoyable evening was spent." [95]

Heeley's president 'Chas.' or Charles Stokes is an interesting man who was also influential at Milton FC, and especially at Wednesday FC and Sheffield United FC (more about him later in Chapter Eight).

The 1860 foundation date continues to be mentioned and is expanded to make Heeley FC, incorrectly, England's second oldest football club in 1896:

"Heeley Football Club. Last evening at the Waggon and Horses Hotel, Gleadless Road, the Heeley Football Club held its annual general meeting. The club claims to be second to Sheffield Club as the oldest established association code organisation in England, having been founded in 1860, and still sticks to amateurism. Last season's work shows the following results: - Matches played 28, won 20, lost 6, drawn 2, goals for 93, against 32; income £27 3s 0d; expenditure, £23 19s 10d. This leaves the club with a balance in hand of £3 3s 1 ½ d. The statement of accounts was read and passed, and the following officials were elected for the ensuing season: President, Mr. Charles Stokes; vice president, Messrs. A. Hall, W. H. Swain, H. Wragg, J. Thraves, W. Elvidge, J. Berley, R. Gillott, C. Roberts, J. R. Wheatley, W. Adams, C. Ashmore, G. C. Brownell, P. W. Brownell, E. Brooks, H. Berley, I. Swallow, and I. C. Jones; treasurer, Mr. Allen Hall; hon. Secretary, Mr. R. R. Bentley, 337, Gleadless Road; assistant Hon. Secretary, Mr. J. Clarke; committee, Messrs. M. E. Wragg and I. C. Jones, delegate to Sheffield Association, Mr. R. R. Bentley, delegate to accident society, Mr. J. Craven. The ground of the club is the Ball Inn, and those closely connected anticipate good season." [96]

Sheffield United chose Heeley FC to be their first Sheffield opponents following their first game in Nottingham, on the Sheaf House ground on the 14th September 1889.

By 1899 there was a second team in Heeley called Heeley Friends FC and by the following year it seems to be the only team left in Heeley; in the absence of clear press announcements and an absolute date for their demise, I have set 1899 as Heeley FC's final year and hope for future research to categorically set the date of its finish.

Mackenzie FC Sheffield (Sheffield, Yorkshire October 1862-1872)

- Equal Fifth Oldest Sheffield Football Club
- Equal Thirteenth Oldest Football Club in the World

Origin: Cricket- There is a cricket team of the same name that decided to form a football club in October 1862:

"MACKENZIE CRICKET CLUB. - The closing match of the present season of the Mackenzie Cricket Club was played at the Bramall lane ground on Monday. Sides were chosen by J. Sorby and Thomas Hodgkinson, and after a good contested game, ended in a draw, time being called when the last pair were at the wickets, with 18 runs to win. After play the members and friends assembled to a substantial repast at Mr. Henson's, confectioner, Sheffield moor, and, supper being over, a statement was read by the President showing the present condition of the club and the successful season just terminated, as, out of seventeen matches played, ten have been won, six lost, and one drawn. Arrangements were announced or the commencement of the foot-ball club, in connection with the cricket club, on Saturday next. Toasts and songs were then resorted to, and the company separated well pleased with their day's sport." [97]

I cannot find a business name or a pub in Sheffield with the name 'Mackenzie' around which the cricket club might have formed. We know that their first strip included a plaid cap which would suggest a Scottish link and there is a Mackenzie Crescent in the Broomhall district of Sheffield which was a few hundred yards from the former Sheffield Collegiate School. Another interesting alternative theory regarding the choice of name, is that the chief benefactor of the early Sheffield Wharncliffe Charity Cup's full name was James Archibald Stuart-Wortley-Mackenzie. [98]

Only a year after formation in 1863, they had a very successful season, had nearly a hundred members and Thomas Hodgkinson was now President:

"Mackenzie football club – On Wednesday night the annual meeting of the members of the above club was held at their committee room, Thomas street, when the following gentlemen were elected as officers for the ensuing season: President, Mr. T. Hodgkinson; vice do., Mr. T. Corthorne; treasurer, Mr. G. Thorpe; honorary secretary, Mr. R. Dickenson, committee, Messrs. F. Barber, T. Fisher, J. Sorby, C. Moore, H. Wigfull, T. Greaves, H. Webster, W. Higgins, A. Leonard, and H. Packard. From the committee's report for the last season, it appeared that the club had been very successful, having won twelve matches out of fourteen; and every success is to be anticipated for the coming season form a club numbering upwards of 100 members." [99]

Football Annual	Ground	Foundation Date	Hon. Sec.	Members	Colours
1868	Myrtle Road		Thomas Hodgkinson, Clough Bank	500	Plaid cap, pink shirt
1869	Myrtle Road		A. Wragg, New George Street	300	Plaid cap, pink shirt
1870	Myrtle Road		Walter Ellin, George Hotel, New George Street	150	Plaid cap, pink shirt
1871	Myrtle Road	1862	C. Lowe, George Hotel, New George Street	150	Plaid cap, pink shirt

Myrtle Road is part of Heeley but about a mile further north of Meersbrook Park, which would also be the home ground of Wednesday FC from 1871-1877. The football was played in the Ball Inn Recreation ground, south of Myrtle Road, the only flat piece of land, in the area, now taken up by Myrtle Close, Drive and Crescent. The Ball Inn (not to be confused with the Crookes' Ball Inn) was situated at 230 Myrtle Road before it was turned into apartments. Mackenzie FC never played in the F.A. Cup but competed in the inaugural 1867 Youdan Cup. The 500 members reported in 1868 Football Annual is by far the greatest number of any club reported so far. In 1864 Mackenzie FC played the 'Gentlemen' again:

"Sheffield Football Club v. Mackenzie Football Club. – On Saturday, last a match took place between the above-named clubs on the ground of the former, at East-bank, the Sheffield nominally playing 11 against 16 of their opponents. The 'kick-off' took place about two o'clock, and was continued for hours. At the commencement of the game the Sheffielders (who lost the toss) had several of their number absent, and with difficulty defended their goal against such great odds at 7 to 16, and at that period the Mackenzie players succeeded in obtaining rouge. After some time, more of the Sheffield men coming on the ground, the sides more equal, and on the change of goals at half play, the Sheffielders having now the slope of the field in their favour, generally managed to keep the ball in the vicinity of their opponents' goal, but time was called before either side could claim a goal, and the match, which was fairly and good temperedly played on both sides, ended up by one rouge to the Mackenzie Club to nothing to their opponents. A large number of spectators were on the ground, and manifested great interest in the amusement." [100]

In 1865 the club was in rude financial health:

"On Tuesday, April 18th the members of the Mackenzie Football Club, held their annual dinner at the house of Mr. George Thorpe, Thomas street. Mr. Riley, Garrick Tavern, was called to the chair. Mr. Riley presented the prizes to the successful competitors. The report of the secretary was to the effect that the last season had been a successful one; over £70 balance

CHAPTER FIVE

would be placed in the bank to the credit of the clubs, after giving £5 each to the Infirmary and Dispensary. The most pleasing event of the evening was the presentation of a silver plated cup to Mr. Hodgkinson, subscribed by the members of both cricket and football clubs, in recognition of his past and untiring services. The cup bore the following inscription: 'presented to Thomas Hodgkinson, by the Mackenzie Cricket and Football Clubs as a mark of esteem and for his untiring efforts in the arduous duties of honorary secretary.' Mr. Hodgkinson thanked the subscribers in a few appropriate remarks." [101]

Mackenzie FC played Sheffield FC on 28th October 1865 and 'played the offside rules.' [102] Two years later, in 1867, Mackenzie FC played Garrick FC on their home ground at Myrtle road, Heeley:

"The Mackenzie-ites were declared the winners by one goal and two rouges to their opponents one rouge. This is the third match which the Mackenzie have played with Garrick this season, the former winning every game. On the part of Mackenzie, the play of W. Wright, W. Jackson, and C. Mills (forward) was good. J. Jenkinson and T. Banks (half back) also distinguishing themselves. J. E. Deans, W. Furniss, J. Dale and Donovan worked hard for Garrick, as did also Hepworth. The Mackenzie goal was well kept by C. Webster. The following are the names of the players; - Garrick: T. Rycroft (captain), W. Haley, W. Deans, J. Witherford, J. Wilmer, T. Pursehouse, and C. Howson. - Mackenzie: J. Jenkinson (captain), C. Webster, W. Ellin, C. Mills, W. Jackson, W. Barraclough, T. Banks, W. Cheetham, E. Carrington, W. Wright, W. Shaw, and H. Maitland." [103]

Milton FC (Sheffield, Yorkshire November 1862- 1870)

- Equal Fifth Oldest Sheffield Football Club
- Equal Thirteenth Oldest Football Club in the World

Origin: Cricket Another gentlemen's club but with the added interest that this short-lived club was instrumental in the formation of Notts County FC, the world's oldest League football club.

Football Annual	Ground	Foundation Date	Hon. Sec.	Members	Colours
1868	Heeley	1862	J. Rowbotham, New Inn, Ecclesall Road, Sheffield Moor	Upwards of 180	Black and yellow
1869	Abbeydale Road	1862	C. Stokes, jnr. Myrtle Road, Heeley	140	Black and yellow
1870	Abbeydale Road	1862	C. Stokes, jnr. Myrtle Road, Heeley	140	Black and yellow

(Milton FC's first ground was at Cremorne Gardens)

Milton Cricket Club was thriving in 1854 and must have been the instigator of a football team of the same name; presumably it took its name from the nearby Milton Arms pub in Highfields. In the White's directory, the Milton Arms was at 81 London Road and in 1862 Samuel Eaton ran it as a beer house. Milton FC never played in the F.A. Cup but competed in the inaugural 1867 Youdan Cup, beating Wellington FC in the first round but then losing to Mackenzie FC in the second round. Charles Stokes represented the club in October 1869 at the Sheffield Football Association, but it is not listed as a member of the Sheffield Association from 1871. Even as a short-lived club it certainly had an interesting story, both in its choice of ground and its influence on the development of Notts County FC.

The evidence used by Notts County FC in respect of their foundation, is in fact a misreported newspaper article about Sheffield's Milton FC. The official Notts County FC website quotes as evidence for their 1862 foundation date:

"The opening of the Nottingham Football Club commenced on Tuesday last at Cremorne Gardens. A side was chosen by W. Arkwright and Chas. Deakin. A very spirited game resulted in the latter scoring two goals and two rouges against one and one.' - The Nottingham Guardian from 28 November 1862." (104)

On further research the original article reads with a differently named club and is still incorrectly placed in Nottingham:

"Football. – The opening of the Milton Football Club commenced, on Tuesday last, at Cremorne Gardens, Nottingham. Sides were chosen by William Wainwright and Charles Deakin; a very spirited game was played, which resulted in the latter gaining two goals and two rouges, against one goal and one rouge. The first kick of the ball was made by an old gentleman, 89 years of age. After the games the members adjourned to the Milton Arms, Highfields, and spent a convivial evening." (105) Nottinghamshire Guardian. Friday 28 November 1862

A third, and different version of the same match report, which this time comes from 'The Sporting Life' states:

"CREMORNE GARDEN GROUND. - The opening day of the Milton Football Club took place at the above pleasantly situated grounds on Tuesday, when there was a tolerable attendance of the members. Sides were chosen by Mr. W. Wainwright and Mr. Charles Deakin, and a most spirited game ensued, which resulted in the latter going two goals and two rouges to their opponents' one goal and one rouge. A convivial evening was afterwards spent at the Milton Arms, Highfields, whither the players betook themselves at the close of the play. A pleasant and prosperous season is anticipated." (106)

The general confusion caused by the three contradictory reports is not helped by the presence of a second Cremorne Gardens in Nottingham but we know that the Cremorne Gardens in the quotes, are in respect of Sheffield because the two players, mentioned above are Sheffield Milton FC players, as evidenced in the article below:

"Milton Football Club – The annual meeting for the election of officers, &c., took place at Mr. Wainwright's, Milton Arms, Little Sheffield, On Wednesday, when the following officers were elected: President J. Goddard: vice-president W. Saunders n; treasurer, W. Wainwright; hon. Secretary, J. Rowbotham; committee, Messrs. G. E. Ryalls, S. Gould, R. Lilleyman, H. Hawke, C. Howsley, T. Martin, T. Goddard, S. Deakin, A. Taylor, S. Thorp, T. Lane, and R. Smith." (107)

The 152-year old confusion with the Notts County foundation date seems to stem from the fact that the launch of a Sheffield-based football club, Milton FC, was covered in the Nottingham press rather than locally. Darrin Foss (108) suggests that perhaps members of the Volunteer rifle corps (known as the 'Robin Hoods,' who formed the early playing staff of Notts County) attended the match as spectators and were inspired to form a proper club of their own. They had been playing a form of football in the winter since 1859 as a way of keeping fit. It was usual for newspapers to accept reports from the public, so one of the volunteers could have written the report and handed it in to the Nottinghamshire Guardian. However, that does not explain the addition of the word 'Nottingham,' which has clearly confused historians ever since. If the match played in late November 1862 was the inspiration to form Notts County FC, then for a formation date of 1862 to be possible they only had six weeks from watching a Milton FC game to instigating a club, which does seem ambitious.

The inspiration for the 'Cremorne Gardens' name comes from a famous pleasure gardens in London where high-wire demonstrations took place. Sheffield's Cremorne Garden playing area was also known locally as the 'Orphanage,' and in February 1867 Garrick FC played Mackenzie

FC in the first round of the Youdan Cup here. It was centred on the London Road area (also known as Little Sheffield) and is only around 200 metres away from Bramall Lane. It is also very close to 'Highfields' and in some reporting, the names seem interchangeable. Cremorne Gardens also provided the inspiration for a nearby pub, also used now by pre-match Blades, called 'The Cremorne' located at 185 London Road.

The next match report found in 1863 has Milton FC playing 'workmen' which suggests the game is trickling down from the 'gentlemen' to the 'players':

"A friendly game at football was played at Cremorne Gardens, on Monday, between twelve of the workmen of Messrs. W. and H. Hutchinson, Norfolk Street, and twelve of the Milton Football Club. The game was well contested, though under great difficulties, owing to the wetness of the ground. Messrs. Hutchinson's men, however, were the victors by two rouges, and the Milton Club nil." [109]

Highfields was the first ground of Wednesday in 1867, before they moved to Myrtle Road in 1870; in November 1877, they moved back to an area a few hundred yards away from the old Cremorne Gardens called Sheaf House Gardens:

"New Ground for the Wednesday club – This important football club have just taken Sheaf House Ground, and their cup tie against Exchange Brewery will be played there next Saturday.

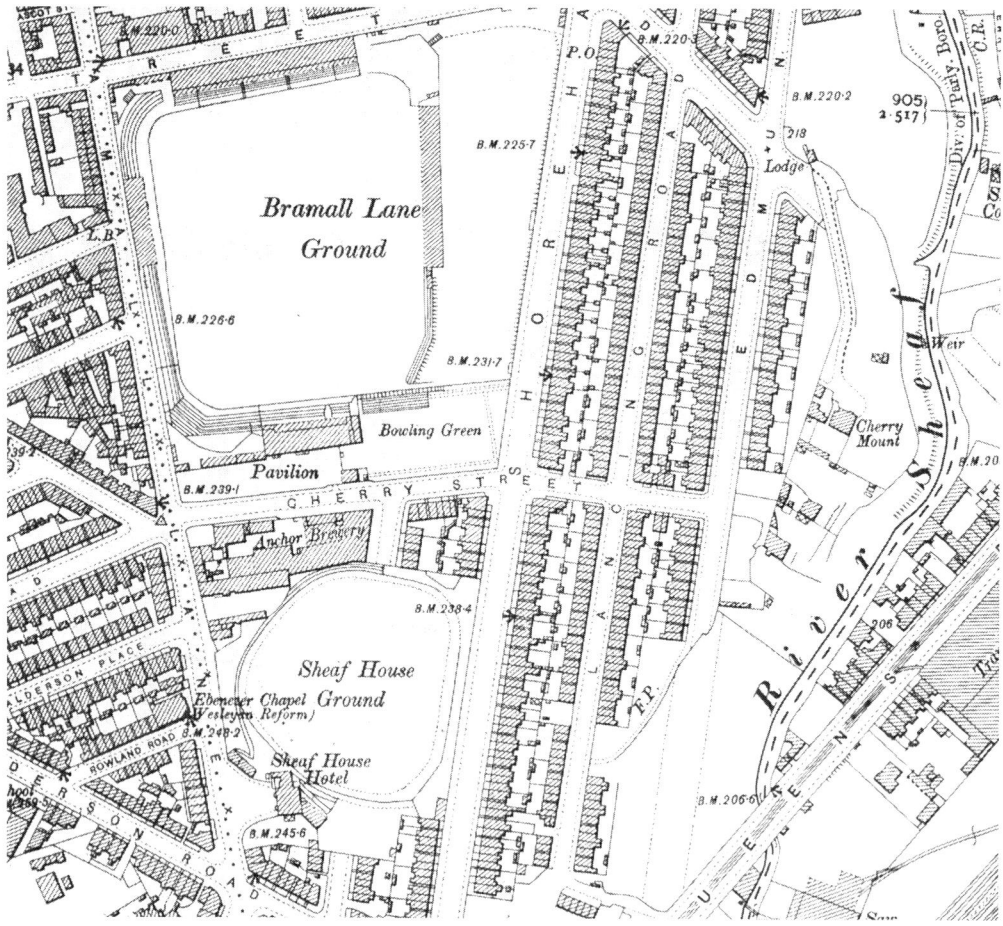

Circa 1903

Mr. Garrick, the enterprising proprietor of Sheaf House, has already carried out great enlargements and improvements in the ground, and he intends sparing no expense to render it one of the best in Yorkshire for both cricket and football. Centrally situated as Sheaf House is, there can be no doubt that the ground will receive a large share of patronage from local clubs." [110] (In an earlier article the proprietor is called 'Garrick', which is a typo for Mr. R. Garratt).

Sheaf House Gardens was directly south of Bramall Lane on the other side of Cherry Street and was the full-time home of Wednesday from 1877 to 1880.

Today the site of the Sheaf House ground is home to the Anchor Point Apartments, but the Sheaf House Hotel is still there on Bramall Lane offering thirsty fans a pint before United matches; and marks one of the corners of the now non-existent old ground at 329, Bramall Lane. Back in 1870 it was harder to get a drink; when Richard Garrett applied for a drinks licence for the Sheaf House and gardens, he found himself opposed by a familiar name, Mr. Clegg, but it is not clear which of the teetotal solicitor brothers this is, Charles or William. "Richard Garratt, Bramall lane, was supported in his application by Mr. Baker, barrister (instructed by Mr. D. Wightman). Mr. Clegg opposed, on behalf of the Rev. C. E. Lamb. It was intended to throw open the grounds surrounding the house. Mr. Clegg said the intention of the Legislation in granting beer licences was to supply the wants of the neighbourhood, and not to provide recreation grounds. The applicant no doubt intended to have some kind of amusements in the house, and he (Mr. Clegg) contended that it was very dangerous to call a number of young people together and supply them with drink. An application of a similar kind had been made for the Cremorne Gardens, which were not far from the applicant's house, and the neighbourhood was up in arms against it. The house was not required, as last week a certificate was granted to Mr. Gregg for a large house in the neighbourhood, which was in a direct line from the railway station; and the applicant had admitted that there were other houses for the sale of drink in the immediate locality. He submitted that the house was not required. - Granted." [111]

The drinks license was granted and by December 1870, Sheaf House was open, featuring pleasure grounds, vineries and greenhouses and a charming promenade. There was no admission charge to the gardens, all the income was generated by the 'wines, beers and refreshments.' Mr. Garratt's other stream of income was generated by renting out the sports field and it remained Wednesday's main 'home' ground until 1880. Most of Wednesday's home matches in the early 1880s switched to Bramall Lane but due to the cost of hiring it they would still use Sheaf House, until eventually, their new ground, Olive Grove, opened in 1887.

The Sheaf House ground was still flourishing in 1889 with a crowd of 2,200 watching a game between the newly formed Sheffield United FC and Heeley FC; many different sports were played at the Sheaf House ground until June 1909, when it closed. By 1864 Milton FC were playing at Hounsfield Park which I have not been able locate in Sheffield history books, but from the route of a paper chase, described below, Hounsfield Park appears to be close to Sheaf House:

"Milton Football Club – For the amusement of the Milton Football Club members a paper chase was run on Shrove Tuesday *(1865)*, which ended satisfactorily to all present, there being upwards of a thousand persons present to witness the chase. The start was from the Old Nursery, Highfields, and got on the chase near the Havelock Inn, near Heeley; passed Mr. J. Appleyard's farm, Upper Heeley, to Newfield Green, near Leas Hall Wood, then to Far Lees Hall Wood heading to Mr. Addy's farm, then to Hemsworth Common to Gleadless Common, then to Manor House, then to Bellevue Field to Norfolk Park, then to East Bank, over the river

CHAPTER FIVE

Sheaf, to Hounsfield Park, and finished on the Old Nursery, Highfields, near the Milton Arms, to the delight of the thousand persons present. The distance of the chase was about seven miles, which was completed in one hour by the foxes (Messrs. Robert and R. Butterley), and in one hour and ten minutes by the hounds." [112]

"Football – Milton v. Mackenzie – The first match of the Milton Football Club was played on Saturday last (1864), on the ground of the former, lately called Hounsfield Park, and some spirited play was exhibited on both sides (some excellent sport for the lookers-on). After about an hour's play in the Milton scored a goal to their opponents' nothing, so the match ended in favour of the Milton Football Club. The manner in which the referees, W. Heath and T. Hodgkinson, acted, cannot be too highly spoken of." [113]

"Milton Football Club. – A general meeting of the above club was held at Mr. J. Fowler's, Milton Arms, Highfield, on Tuesday last (1869), when the following officers were elected for the ensuing football season: President, Mr. J. Lain; Vice President, Mr. J. Goddard; hon. Secretary, Mr. Charles Stokes, jun.; treasurer, Mr. James Powler; a committee, Messrs. B. Wilson, Charles Houseley, J. Stacey, F. Marshall, C. Siddall, A. Taylor, H. Hawley and J. Wright." [114]

Howard Hill Steel Bank FC (Sheffield, Yorkshire November 1862-1864)

This enigmatic club was never listed as a member of the Sheffield Association nor included in early editions of the Football Annual (due to its omission, I have not included it in my full national classification of all English football clubs) but it appears in the local press and consequently is in this book.

- Equal Fifth Oldest Sheffield Football Club
- World's first pub team

Origin: Public House. Steel Bank is an area, situated between Heavygate Road, Slinn street, Western Road and Springvale Road, so whilst sounding like a workplace foundation, it is more likely named after the Howard Hotel on Steel Bank, presumably the place the players met to drink and change before and after a match; thus, making them the world's first pub team. Anne Marples, the Crookes historian, tracked down the exact location of the Howard Hotel to the top corner of Birkendale view, so technically in Walkley, and just outside of the district known as Steel Bank:

"Football – The opening match of the Howard hill Steel bank Football Club was played on Tuesday (1862). Sides were chosen by Messrs. Proctor and Ibbotson. After some good play, Ibbotson's side obtained three goals to Proctor's one. After the match the players dined together." [115]

By 1863 they had added cricket to the club's activities:

"The Howard Hill Cricket and Football Club held their general meeting at the Howard hotel, Steel bank, on Monday last. The President, Mr. Peter Law, occupied the chair. Mr. Robert Ibbotson, hon. Secretary read over the report of the club, which, it appears, has now been established a little under six months, and now numbers about seventy members. The gentlemen in the neighbourhood have contributed most liberally to the support of the club, which is now in a position to complete the ground. A committee was chosen for the cricket season. Votes of thanks to the officers were passed." [116]

Thanks to the generosity of the gentlemen in completing the ground, by later that year they had 120 members:

"HOWARD HILL CRICKET AND FOOTBALL CLUB. - The closing match at cricket in connection with the above club was played on Monday last, on the Howard Hill ground. After the match the members and friends sat down to an excellent supper at the Howard Hotel, under the able presidency of S. Berry, Esq. After the usual loyal and patriotic toasts had been given and duly honoured the secretary, Mr. R. Ibbotson, read the report, from which it appeared that this young club numbers upwards of 120 members. Sixteen matches have been played during the season; and from its past success, there is every prospect that under proper management the club will become one of the most flourishing in the neighbourhood. The following gentlemen were appointed officers in connection with the Football Club for the ensuing season: - President- S. Berry, Esq: vice-president- Mr. W. Mountain: Treasurer- Mr. W. Wright; Hon. Secretary- Mr. E. Woolhouse." [117]

Despite its success, by 1865, Howard Hill Steel Bank FC had dropped football and was just playing cricket.

1863

Just five Association clubs were founded nationally in this year, including the first military club (Royal Engineers FC), the first Lancashire club (Hulme Athenaeum FC) and the oldest hospital club (St. Bartholomew's Hospital FC, better known for its Rugby playing), plus one Sheffield club. Obviously, this is also the year of the foundation of the Football Association in London and it seems the repercussions from the Freemason's Tavern had spawned a form of the game across the channel:

"A number of English gentlemen living in Paris have lately organised a football club, to which is to be added athletic indoor exercises of a gymnastic character. The football contests take place in the Bois de Boulogne (a large park in Paris) by permission of the authorities, and surprise the French amazingly." [118]

As well as the Football Association, another great sporting institution was born in this year; on 8th January, the Yorkshire County Cricket Club played its initial first-class match against Surrey at The Oval on 4, 5 and 6 June 1863. The return fixture was played at Bramall Lane, their first home match, in July 1863. As well as juggling his football commitments, Charles W. Alcock was the secretary of Surrey Cricket Club from 1872 to 1907.

Broomhall FC (Sheffield, Yorkshire October 1863-1880)

- Sixth Oldest Sheffield Football Club
- Equal Sixteenth Oldest Football Club in the World

Origin: Cricket. There was an existing Broomhall cricket club from as early as 1850 and I have put cricket as the club's origin because of an article written for the Sporting Life on Wednesday 30 January 1867, which said that 'There are now fourteen clubs in the town, almost every cricket club having a football club connected with it.' [119] Broom Hall is a listed building now, used as offices situated near the city centre and just a few yards from the then Collegiate School; perhaps the original house had some parkland they could initially practice on, but the ground they ultimately decided to play on was three miles away on Ecclesall Road.

Broomhall FC never played in the F.A. Cup but competed in the inaugural 1867 Youdan Cup; they appear in the Football Annual from 1868 until at least the 1880 issue and were stalwarts of the Sheffield Football Association from the very beginning. In 1868 Broomhall FC

CHAPTER FIVE

was charging 2s.6d. to subscribe, so it is likely to be (yet again) for well-to-do middle class gentlemen. Clearly the Crown and Anchor pub (situated in what is now 218 Fitzwilliam Street) was also an integral part of the club:

"Broomhall Football Club- the first general meeting of this club took place on Wednesday evening, at Mr. James Dixon's, Crown and Anchor, Bright Street, when the following gentlemen were appointed officers for the ensuing season: President, John Tomlinson; vice-president, R. Bunting; secretary, H. Mather; treasurer, James Dixon; committee, E. Watts, S. Roffy, J. Wheatley, T. Gaunt, A. Elliott, and J. Gaunt." [120]

Football Annual	Ground	Foundation Date	Hon. Sec.	Members	Colours
1868	Ecclesall Road (south)	October 1863	John Westran	150	Black and white
1869	Ecclesall Road (south)	October 1868	William Westran	188	Black and white
1870	Ecclesall Road (south)	October 1868	George Stanyard, Crown and Anchor, Bright Street	188	Black and white
1871	Ecclesall Road (south)	October 1868	George Stanyard, Crown and Anchor, Bright Street	188	Black and white
1872	Ecclesall Road (south)	October 1868	John E. Deans	150	Black and white
1873	Ecclesall Road (south)	1868	Chas. Mills Crown and Anchor, Bright Street	150	Black and white
1874	Ecclesall Road (south)	1868	Chas. Mills Crown and Anchor, Bright Street	150	Black and white
1875	Ecclesall Road (south)	1868	Chas. Mills Crown and Anchor, Bright Street	150	Black and white
1876	Ecclesall Road (south)	1868	Chas. Mills Crown and Anchor, Bright Street	150	Black and white
1877	Ecclesall Road (south)	1868	Chas. Mills, 5 Washington Road	150	Black and white
1878	x				
1879	Sheaf House	1863	Chas. Mills, Penley St	90	Black and white
1880	Sheaf House	1863		100	Black and white

A wag had fun with Broomhall FC's dress code in 1866:

"Football Club Sports. To the editor – As I am not in the habit of attending athletic sports, which seem to popular in connection with football clubs just now, I am obliged to appeal to you to settle certain curious problems which have presented themselves to my mind, suggested by the advertisement of the Broomhall Football Club. I have there read, to my horror, that 'competitors are required to wear loose shirts and trousers.' Am I right in making the shocking inference that at some of the sports competitors have worn tight shirts and no trousers? I cannot quite decide which would present the more imposing spectacle – an athlete with tight shirt but minus the garments usually deemed indispensable among civilised communities, performing with the leaping pole, or one who, while clothing his nether man in a graceful attire, should yet be seen clearing hurdles with his shirt-tails floating gaily in the breeze – as 'required' by the Broomhall Football Club. If their sports cannot be made attractive without a resort to such demoralising proceedings, I think the authorities ought to interfere and put them down – Yours (with averted face), The Ghost of Mrs. Grundy." [121]

One of the chief characteristics of Sheffield football pitches was their steepness and it seems the Crookes FC ground in 1876 had the extra hazard of a quarry next to it:

"A serious accident occurred yesterday at Crookes to a young man named William Lawton, who resides with his parents in Bramall Lane. He is a member of the Broomhall Football Club, a team from which was yesterday playing the Crookes club on the ground of the latter. Beyond one of the boundary lines is a stone quarry about twenty feet deep. The ball was sent in that direction, and in his eagerness to stay its progress he followed it to the very edge of the quarry. There he attempted to stop it, but he slipped, and fell over into the quarry. He pitched on the side of his head. He was picked up in an unconscious state, and was taken to the Infirmary, where it was found his skull was fractured. Though the accident happened about half-past three in the afternoon, the unfortunate young man had not recovered consciousness when inquiries were made late last night. Slight hopes are entertained of his recovery." [122]

1864

The Great Flood
No new Sheffield football clubs were formed in this year, no doubt as a result of the Great Flood, an unparalleled disaster that (with the exception of maritime disasters) was the greatest loss of life in the Victorian era in Britain. On the night of 11 March 1864, assisted by a strong south-western gale, the newly built dam, known as the Dale Dyke Dam in Bradfield Dale near Low Bradfield on the River Loxley, collapsed while it was being filled for the first time, killing at least 270 people:

"Six hundred and fifty million gallons of water roared down the Loxley valley and into Sheffield, wreaking death and destruction on a horrific scale. Individual experiences were infinitely tragic, pathetic, and sometimes bizarre. The first to drown was a two-day-old baby boy, the oldest a woman of eighty-seven. Whole families were wiped out; one desperate man, trapped upstairs in a terrace house, battered his way through five party walls to safety collecting thirty-four other people as he went; a would be suicide, locked in a cell, decided, as the flood poured in, that he no longer wished to die; one poor old man drowned alongside his sleeping companion - a donkey; a husband put his wife and five children on a bed on which they floated until the water went down.' After about thirty minutes the flood gradually subsided leaving a trail of destruction more than eight miles long: it was later described as 'looking like a battlefield'. In addition to the massive loss of life; total or partial destruction occurred to 415 dwelling houses, 106 factories/shops, 64 other buildings, 20 bridges and 4478 cottage/market gardens." [123]

Of the existing eleven Sheffield football clubs that have already been discussed, all survived the flood because as seen from the map on page 177 they are all, except two, situated south of the city centre and were left untouched:

"The full fury of the flood seems to have spent itself on the district lying between the junction of the Loxley and the Rivelin and the Neepsend bridge. The scene of the devastation is awful, un-paralleled. A populous district has been almost obliterated from the face of the earth. Solid and substantial buildings, workshops, rows of houses, bridges, everything that opposed the course of the flood, yielded before its overwhelming might as though it were built of paper. All were whelmed beneath the mighty rush of the waters. But with deep sorrow we have to relate that the loss of property, incalculable as it at present is, sinks into insignificance when it is compared with the awful loss of human life that has taken place. Persons who are familiar with the district will know that between Hillsbro' bridge and Malin bridge there stood several long rows of cottage houses, inhabited by workmen of the mills and their families. With a few exceptions, the flood has either wholly or partially demolished these rows of dwellings. In many instances even their foundations are obliterated by the furious rush of the waters. Standing at the junction of the Loxley and the Rivelin, we saw only a few scattered houses, the walls and windows burst in by the flood, standing to mark to locality of the once popular village." [124]

CHAPTER FIVE

The year of 1864 saw only seven football clubs form nationwide; outside England however, on the 22nd October 1864, Wrexham FC sprang into life, making it sixth oldest Club in world still in existence. Also, this year the first three 'old boy' clubs started, which would all be very influential in the dissemination nationwide and beyond of Association football: Old Harrovians FC, Old Etonians FC and the Old Carthusians FC. Two of those seven clubs formed in England came from other parts of Yorkshire; **Leeds FC** briefly tried their hand at Sheffield Rules in 1865, before converting to Rugby in 1874 as Leeds Athletic FC:

"LEEDS FOOTBALL CLUB. - On Monday last (November 1865), fourteen members of the above club went to Sheffield to play fifteen of the Norfolk Football Club in that town. Mr. G. F. Curzon, of the Leeds Express, and Mr. W. Skinner president of the Norfolk Club, were the respective umpires. The match was played in Norfolk Park, and lasted half an hour and a quarter, at the end of which time Sheffield had obtained a goal and two rouges, Leeds players being unpractised in the Sheffield rules, nearly all of which were different from those which guide their own play on Woodhouse Moor. But we cannot help recording the really scientific play with the Sheffield men backed each other up, a point in which Leeds was visibly deficient, although perhaps the individual kicking of the latter was superior. Several of the best of the Leeds Club were absent, for reasons best known to themselves. After play was over, a sumptuous repast was partaken of at the Adelphi Hotel, Norfolk-street, and a pleasant evening spent." [125] In December 1865 year the same two clubs played the return match in the 'the new portion of the Leeds Royal Park, on Thursday, the 28th instant.' [126]

Leeds Athletic FC renamed themselves as the Yorkshire Wanderers in 1881but quite quickly disbanded in 1883. It would not be until 1904 that Leeds City FC was formed from the remnants of Hunslet FC (1877), which would play Association football. In 1919, Leeds City FC was wound up by the Football League, due to illegal payments and the current Leeds United was born.

The other Yorkshire football club formed in 1864 was **Bradford FC**, which from the start was also an out and out Rugby playing outfit. As discussed in Chapter One, the 1860s saw two football codes struggling for their own identities and were indistinguishable from each other, until clarification came in the form of the R.F.U. in 1871. The reason Rugby playing Bradford FC feature in my overall list of Association clubs is because it played the Association code the longest. It played Rugby for forty-three years as Bradford RFC before changing to Association for sixty-seven years (as Bradford Park Avenue FC). Its move to the Association code was characterised locally as the 'Great Betrayal'; in response in 1895, a new Bradford Northern Rugby League team was born, which in 1995 became the Bradford Bulls FC.

1865

In August 1864, as the American Civil War neared its close, the first large cotton consignment arrived in Britain, and Lancashire employment started to return to normal by 1865. Unperturbed by trade fluctuations the population of Sheffield grew rapidly throughout the 19th century and Sheffield became a city in 1893:

1801 60,095	1811 69,275	1821 84,540
1831 112,408	1841 134,599	1851 161,475
1861 219,634	1871 277,794	1881 335,953
1891 388,089	1901 451,195	

At its peak, in 1951, Sheffield's population numbered 577,050 and currently stands at 563,749 residents. A sense of the grim working conditions in Sheffield can be gleaned from the following 1865 report of a factory accident:

"THE FATAL ACCIDENT BY MACHINERY The adjourned inquiry into the circumstances attending the death of Mary Ann Staniforth, aged eleven years, whose parents reside in Trinity street, took place at the Town Hall on Thursday afternoon, before J. Webster, Esq., Coroner. The accident by which deceased lost her life occurred on Friday, the 20th of January, at the cutlery establishment of Messrs. Hides, Hollis Croft. The inquest was opened on the 27th, and adjourned to allow the jury an opportunity of visiting the room where the accident happened. Mr. A. C. Branson attended to watch the case on behalf of the friends of the deceased, and Mr. Chambers, Jun., appeared for Mr. Hides. The first witness called was John William Staniforth, of Trinity street, brother of the deceased, who said he had a room and power at Messrs. Hide's. His father and the deceased worked there also. He had a key of the room and no one had a right to enter without his permission. Mr. Hides or his engine tender could go in to attend to the machinery. There was a shaft through the room, from one end to the other. Both ends of the shaft were protected, but it was not protected in the middle where his sister's clothes became entangled. He did not see how her clothes were caught. When he first saw her she was lying on the floor naked, and her clothes were spinning round the shaft. She had been working there nearly ten months. There were six working in the room, but his sister was the only female. The shaft was not boxed off when he took the room, and to his knowledge it never had been protected. He had not removed the boxing and broken it up. Both himself and his father had asked Mr. Hides to box off the machinery, but he refused to do it. When the accident happened he was asked, and he told them to do it themselves. It was Mr. Hide's duty to box it off. The fly wheel was under their room, and they were in constant danger of their lives." [127]

Eight Association football clubs formed nationally in 1865, all from the south of England, with the exception of Nottingham Forest FC and one club from Sheffield. Nottingham Forest played by Sheffield Rules, according to the Football Annuals from 1869 until 1872, and are the second oldest League club in England.

United Mechanics FC, (Sheffield, Yorkshire September 1865- 1877)

- Seventh Oldest Sheffield Football Club
- Equal twenty-fourth Oldest Football Club in England
- World's first football club to be called 'United'

Hanover United FC (later Polytechnic FC) founded in 1876, [128] incorrectly claim the accolade for the first football club with 'United' in their name, in fact United Mechanics FC takes the prize. Of course, Sheffield United is the first ever Football League club called 'United' (1892), beating Newcastle United by one year (1893), Burton United (1901) by nine years and Manchester United (1903) by eleven years. (Manchester United's earlier incarnation, Newton Heath FC, entered the Football League in 1892).

Origin: Work place. The second oldest workplace listed as an origin for a football club nationally, after the London civil servants of the Civil Service FC, and despite the 'United Mechanics' name these are well-to-do business men, not the working class. This is a collective of engineers from various works getting together to play sports; they had a long-established cricket club of the same name from 1864. The Football Annuals below show that J.E. Deans, Heeley's long standing Hon.Sec., also fulfilled the same role for the 'Mechanics' in 1869.

CHAPTER FIVE

Football Annual	Ground	Foundation Date	Hon. Sec.	Members	Colours
1868	Norfolk Park (SE)	September 1865	William Whittles, St. Phillips Road, Sheffield	140 Amount of subscription: 2s 6d	Blue and white cap
1869	Norfolk Park (SE)	1865	J.E. Deans	254	Blue and white cap
1870	Norfolk Park (SE)	1865	James Lee (Lee and Reanes), Eldon Street, Sheffield	150	Blue and white cap
1871	Norfolk Park (SE)	1865	James Lee (Lee and Reanes), Eldon Street, Sheffield	150	Blue and white cap
1872	Norfolk Park (SE)	1865	James Lee (Lee and Reanes), Eldon Street, Sheffield	150	Blue and white cap
1873	Norfolk Park (SE)	1863	James Lee (Lee and Reanes), Eldon Street, Sheffield	250	Amber and white

Strangely for such a thriving club, it is not mentioned again in subsequent Football Annuals and the Mechanics never entered the F.A. Cup. In 1861 William Whittles was presented with testimonial gifts for his long service as both secretary and president of the original United Mechanics cricket club. [129] The first report found for the football club in 1865 has William Whittles as their first Hon. Sec.:

"UNITED MECHANICS' FOOTBALL CLUB. The OPENING MATCH will be played in Norfolk Park on SATURDAY next, the 24th inst. Kick off at 2.30 p.m. WM WHITTLES, Hon. Secretary." [130]

"FOOTBALL. - BROOMHALL v. MECHANICS. - On New Year's Day (1866) these clubs played in Norfolk Park. Broomhall again won, getting one goal and one rouge. Mechanics did not score." [131]

Following the trend of Sheffield football clubs before them, United Mechanics also ran an Athletic sports day, with a nod towards the Volunteer Movement:

"Mechanics' Cricket and Football club. Athletic sports, at Bramall Lane Cricket ground, Sheffield, about the Middle of April (1876). Prizes will be given for the following events: Military flat race, 1000 yards. Open to the Military stationed in the Barracks, the Yeomanry Cavalry, and the Volunteers of Sheffield and twenty miles round. To Run in Drill order, without accoutrements – Entrance, 1s each. Flat race, Half mile – Entrance 1s. 6d each. Flat race, Quarter mile – Entrance 1s. 6d each. Open to members of all football and cricket clubs in Sheffield and Neighbourhood. All entries to be made no later than Monday, March 4th, to W.M. Whittles, Hon. Secretary." [132]

It seems that Sheffield FC's innovation of running Athletic Sports days back in 1858 was beginning to lose its shine ten years later:

"Mechanics' Football Club Sports. The annual sports of this rising club took place at Bramall lane yesterday (1868). The ground was only thinly attended, possibly because the public are (very naturally) getting weary of athletic sports. The events were brought off punctually under the superintendence of – Starter, Mr. W. Skinner; judge, Mr. G. E. Swift; clerks of the course, Messrs. J. W. White and W. Bartholomew; and an efficient staff of stewards. The sports commenced with a handicap flat race, 120 yards, in heats. – Ten came out in the first heat, which, after a good race, was won by G. Cousens, 8 yards, who ran all his opponents to a standstill; time, 121 secs." [133]

In 1872 the 'Mechanics' was Sheffield's most successful football club:

"UNITED MECHANICS. - From being amongst the least successful a few years ago, this indefatigable club has gradually advanced until it now holds the premier position as regards the results of matches, which stand as under: - Total played 24; won, 15; lost, 3; drawn, 6." [134]

1866

The National Olympian Association staged the first National Olympian Games field events at the Crystal Palace in South London, where a young W. G. Grace, aged eighteen, won the 440 yards' hurdles. Grace was a fine all round sportsman and played twice for the Wanderers FC, once against Crystal Palace on 25th November 1871 at the Oval and he scored against Clapham Rovers on the 9th March 1872. It was in the latter match when W. G. Grace took the ball off his teammate Charles W. Alcock in front of goal and took a shot himself, an event Alcock described as 'the most blackguard thing that happened to me during a long sporting career.' [135]

Lausanne FC was formed this year in Switzerland by British visitors; in 1863 the game had been exported to France, so the missionary work had continued eastwards. It seems the Lausanne FC players (perhaps when their Swiss employment finished), returned home to London in 1867 and continued playing under their original name, in the slightly less glamourous confines of Peckham.

Oldest Association Football Clubs by Country

I have covered the difficulties of definition, when trying to attribute the oldest football ground, earlier in the book. The first foreign Association football clubs should not be defined by when British tourists first showed up with a football. To my mind a club has to be started by the indigenous people, which creates the following list for Association playing extant clubs:

1) England – Sheffield FC. 1857
2) Wales – Wrexham FC. 1864
3) Scotland - Queen's Park FC.1867
4) Argentina - Club Mercedes. 1875
5) Denmark - Kjøbenhavns Boldklub.1878
6) Switzerland- St. Gallen. 19 April 1879
7) Netherlands - Koninklijke HFC. September 15th 1879
8) Northern Ireland- Cliftonville Football & Athletic Club. September 20th 1879
9) Belgium- Royal Antwerp FC. 1880
10) Portugal - Associação Académica de Coimbra. 1887

(This topic is an ongoing discussion at my Facebook page – please join the debate at www.facebook.com/WorldsOldestFootballClubs)

In light of the awful working conditions, it is surely no surprise that in the 1860s Sheffield had become one of the UK's leading centres for trade unionism. Relations between employers and employees had deteriorated to such an extent that between 1866 and 1867 the workers had become very militant; this led to the so-called 'Sheffield Outrages.' In August 1867, an official enquiry looked at the 'Outrages' and in particular the act of 'rattening', where Unions would take away workmen's property to coerce them into joining a Union or to go on strike. The enquiry found that out of the sixty trade unions in Sheffield, thirteen had committed the crime of rattening. As time passed the outrages became increasingly desperate:

CHAPTER FIVE

"This morning at about 25 minutes past one, an attempt was made to blow up with gunpowder Joseph Martin, a saw handle maker, who lives at 76, Broad-lane. Martin being, in consequence of the badness of trade, out of employment, had taken work at Messrs. Spear and Jackson's, whose saw handle hands are now out on strike. A stone bottle, filled with gunpowder and bits of steel- a rough grenade, and having the cork bored for a fuse, was hurled against one of the bed-room windows of Martin's house. It appears to have missed the glass, for it bounded back, and fell on the pavement." [136]

In 1866 five Association clubs were founded in England, including one in Chesterfield and another two from Sheffield.

Garrick FC (Sheffield, Yorkshire October 1866 -1886)

- Equal eighth Oldest Sheffield Football Club
- Equal twenty-seventh Oldest Football Club in England

Origin: Public House. The Garrick Hotel was in Sycamore Street, Sheffield and W. Riley was the Hon. Sec. Garrick FC is therefore the world's second oldest pub team, after Howard Hill Steel Bank FC. The Adelphi Hotel and the Garrick Tavern were adjacent and both are no more, having been replaced by the Crucible Theatre in 1971. (The Adelphi is where the Sheffield Football Association and Wednesday FC were both founded in 1867).

Garrick FC was an extremely prosperous club; in comparison to Pitsmoor FC which had 264 members paying 2s 6d in 1868, Garrick had 400 members paying 2s. and matches were on the same ground as Sheffield FC. Unskilled workers would be earning around 4 shillings a week at this time; could it be that this pub was also convincing lots of working class men to part with two or three days' pay to belong the football club for the year, or was this still the province of Sheffield middle classes? Working hours had been limited by the 1850 Factory Act, to sixty hours per week, with the working week ending earlier at Saturday lunchtime. Over time this meant that, with Sundays set aside for church, the main leisure time for working men was Saturday afternoon:

"Skilled workers in the manufacturing trade were the first to receive a Saturday half holiday, and those towns dominated by single manufacturing industries were the first able to make use of the Saturday afternoon. Some firms were closing at 1.00pm as early as the 1850's in London and Birmingham. By the 1860's skilled and lower middle class workers in the railways had followed suit. The Factory Act of 1878 gave all factory workers the same right. Unskilled workers and shopkeepers and their assistants, by contrast, were more likely to have to work through. In Birmingham, the 1pm finish was general by the late 1870's, reaching noon in 1890, the effect on Saturday soccer was major. The area only had 20 district soccer teams mentioned in the press in 1876 but 155 in 1880. In areas like Liverpool, with its low proportion of skilled workers, or the north east with its heavy industry, Saturday half days were uncommon until the mid-1880s……. In Birmingham between 1876 and 1884 about 9 % of reported soccer teams were named after workplaces." [137]

Was the booming football scene in Sheffield becoming a game for all men? Men with time on their hands looked for local things to do and the rising popularity of football meant either playing or spectating. These men were more mobile due to the boom in railway building; in 1845, 2,441 miles of railway were open and 30 million passengers were being carried. Between 1861 and 1888 the track mileage grew by 81% and the traffic carried by 180%. Not only was the network increasing, but the speed of the trains at 50 m.p.h. meant the journey from Sheffield to London was a mere four hours. Football clubs could consider playing 'foreign' opposition more easily and the rail expansion would ultimately facilitate games being played right across England in the new national Football League, when it was eventually formed in 1888. Local transportation dramatically improved in Sheffield in 1872, with the Tramways Act of 1870, which came into force in 1872; the Sheffield horse tramway began with the first destinations catering to the industrial districts of Attercliffe, Carbrook, Brightside, Heeley, Nether Edge and Owlerton.

The Sheffield press described Garrick football club as 'newly formed' in April 1867 and they started in the time-honoured way with an Athletics competition at Bramall Lane.

Football Annual	Ground	Foundation Date	Hon. Sec.	Members	Colours	Code
1868	East Bank 'One and a half miles from Midland Station'	October 1866	W. Riley, jun., Garrick Hotel, Sheffield	400 Amount of entrance fee: Nil Amount of subscription: 2s	Red white and blue	Sheffield Association
1869	East Bank	October 1866	W. Riley, jun., Garrick Hotel, Sheffield	350	Red white and blue	Sheffield Association
1870	East Bank	October 1866	W. Riley, jun., Garrick Hotel, Sheffield	350	Red white and blue	Sheffield Association
1871	Endcliffe or Shallow Vale (Sharrow Vale)		J. Riley and J.L. Ward, Garrick Hotel	400	Red white and blue	It stated that this club is not a member of the Sheffield Association but still listed the details and the fact that they played by the Sheffield Association rules. By 1873 their ground was reported to be near Broadfield Bar, Abbeydale Road, Sheffield.

In 1867 they divided the club members up into two teams, differentiated by coloured caps for a training match - an interesting strategy, pre-dating modern use of tabards and bibs:

"THE GARRICK FOOTBALL CLUB, SHEFFIELD. The opening match of the above club was played on the club ground, at East Bank on Monday last, when sides were chosen by W. Riley, jun., who commanded a team distinguished by blue caps, and W. Harrop led a party of blue and red caps. A very spirited game took place, the play of F. Sanderson and C. Mills, on the part of the Blue and Reds, being really first class, as also was that of J. Deans and G. Marriott on the part of the Blues. After two hours' spirited play the Blues proved the winners, having scored one goal and one rouge to one goal obtained by their opponents." [138]

Garrick FC played in the first round of the Youdan Cup losing 1-0 to Mackenzie FC at a game played at Cremorne on the 16th February 1867; it remained in the Sheffield Association until 1875.

"GARRICK v. MECHANICS. THE first teams of the above clubs met on Monday last, December 30 (1868), on the Garrick Ground, but, as will be seen from the score, the Mechanics were greatly over-matched, the Garricks scoring three goals and five rouges to their opponents'

CHAPTER FIVE

nothing. The play of the Garrick men left nothing to desire. Subjoined are the names of the Garrick players: - J. Dale, C. Lee, W. Mills, G. Stanyard, T. Rycroft, J. E. Deans, R. Buttery, H. Ash, A. Rayner, J. West, J. Jenkinson, G. Jones, W. Furniss." [139]

Garrick FC played the Wednesday in the final of the Cromwell Cup at Bramall Lane on the 15th February 1868. The idea of the tournament was to match up four clubs, described in the press as 'junior clubs', who had to be no more than two seasons old:

"The Cromwell Cup was the second ever football competition and was named after Oliver Cromwell, the stage manager of the Alexandra Theatre which was on Blonk Street. Oliver Cromwell was, incidentally, interested in the Garrick Club, which had its headquarters at the Garrick Hotel in Sycamore Street, a famous old theatrical house in days gone by. Garrick was reported to be the best team in Sheffield, and it was believed they would win the Cromwell Cup. Four clubs entered: Garrick (two seasons old) Wellington (two seasons) Wednesday and Exchange (one season). The draw paired Wednesday and Exchange and Garrick and Wellington. Considerable excitement prevailed, for after Wednesday had defeated Exchange, on the Mackenzie club's ground on February 1st 1868 by 4-0, the Garrick, apparently became alarmed, for it is recorded that the following Saturday when they had to play Wellington at Norfolk park, they introduced seven members of the Hallam club to join them. Garrick, even so, triumphed by only one rouge, the sole score of the game. The Wednesday, who by the way, had adopted blue and white for their colours, played Garrick in the final at Bramall Lane on February 15th, and it was the first game the Wednesday had played for which an admission fee was charged. There were 600 spectators." [140]

Garrick FC lost 1-0 in injury time to the first ever use of the 'Golden Goal' concept. The match was scoreless and it was decided to continue until the first score was registered and after ten minutes Alf Wood of Wednesday scored the winner.

In 1870, a relationship was forged between Garrick FC and Hulme Athenaeum FC (Manchester). The latter, formed in 1863, is Lancashire's oldest club and I think England's first truly working class football club; it fits well with my hypothesis that Garrick FC was also not uniquely a middle-class organisation for gentlemen, but a team for the working man:

"Football – Garrick (Sheffield) v. Hulme Athenaeum (Manchester) – two teams of 15 a side, selected from each of the above clubs, met, on Saturday last, on the ground of the latter (which is situated in Withington Road, Hulme) to contend for the honour of supremacy. The friends of both teams mustered strongly on the occasion, and all expressed the opinion that it was one of the best contested matches ever played in Manchester. The game commenced about three o'clock and was continued till about half past four pm, when the last kick in the match decided it in favour of the Hulme club by one goal to nothing. Both sides played with uncommon spirit, but the home team had rather the best of the play throughout. When all played well it would be invidious to particularise. The names of the Garrick team are as follow: - J. E. Deans (captain), J. Riley, R. Lilleyman, G. Robertson, Walter Mills, C. Cole, E. Beeley, W. B. Harrop, H. Gill, J. L. Ward, G. Leek, E. Hatherly, W. Horton, J. Banks, F. Furniss. We understand it is the intention of the Hulme gentlemen to come to Sheffield for the return match in about three weeks." [141]

The two teams played again in 1872: "Football – Garrick v. Hulme Athenaeum. – this match, played at the Alexandra Park, Manchester, on Monday last, was one of the most exciting character, and ended in a draw, neither side scoring. The following were the respective players on both sides: Garrick: R. Lilleyman (captain), T. Riley, F. Furniss, W. Horton, W. Ward, J. L. Ward, J. Burton, F. Butler, G. Fearn, J. J. Banks, W. Stacey, W. Fearnshough, F. Calton, K. Flint, and G. Leek. Hulme Athenaeum: T. Barlow (captain), E. Powell, C. F. Pickering, G. T. Pickering,

W. Kidson, J. G. Sanderson, C. Morton, T. Nall, W. Groves, T. Riley, W. Faggart, G. Groves, A. Groves – Milnes, and J. Norbury." (142)

Garrick FC slowly withdrew from playing football against local Sheffield teams and instead played Rugby against another club from Manchester in 1870, the Free Wanderers FC:

"Garrick Football Club – On Saturday a match was played between the first fourteen of the Garrick and the first fourteen of the Lancashire Free Wanderers, on the ground of the latter, at Didsbury. The rules were strict rugby, and therefore entirely different from those played by the Garrick, but, nevertheless, the Sheffielders proved quite equal to their opponents, both in point of speed and endurance. The game was one of the best contested ever witnessed, and it was only about five minutes before the time appointed for concluding the fame that the Wanderers, by a first-class rush, secured a touch-down, which ultimately ended in a goal for their side, and the match consequently ended in a victory for the Wanderers by one goal to nothing." (143)

The press reports then dry up and Garrick FC may have stopped playing from 1878, but it appears again in February 1886 for a very special theatrical event:

"Pantomimists in the football field. Many big gatherings of people have taken place at Sheffield's famous athletic arena in Bramall lane, but seldom, if ever, had it been crowded to the extent it was yesterday afternoon, when a team of Pantomimists appeared there in character to play football …and so the match – Sheffield Pantomime Players versus the Garrick Club, in aid of the Children's hospital and Totley Orphanage – came off yesterday. At eleven o'clock in the morning Sheffield was enveloped in a smoke-laden fog, and even Oscar Wilde, with his knack of finding something to admire in things which to the ordinary observer are unwelcome or unsightly, would have failed to discover, had he been in the town at that hour, anything pleasant – except staying indoors. The prospect then of the football match attracting many people was, to say the least, a dim one but suddenly, as if some real fairy (and not one of your stage ones) knew of the laudable effort to be made to augment the funds of two deserving charities, and had waved her magic wand over black Sheffield, there was a glorious transformation. The sun shone brilliantly, the tall chimneys seemed to be belching forth less smoke than usual, and the afternoon turned out to be one of the finest this year." (145)

The first ever experiment of floodlights in 1878 had attracted an estimated crowd of 20,000 to Bramall Lane (see Chapter Six) and this Pantomimists' game matched that record in 1886. The record attendance for Bramall Lane and Sheffield football, would not be beaten until 1889. (144)

The above article goes on to describe the crowd: "A larger concourse of spectators was thus assured, but the most sanguine could not have expected the monster attendance of people which there was. From a sportsman's point of view the match was a failure, but financially it was a huge success. For half an hour before the time for the kick-off, and a similar period after, Bramall lane presented a very thronged and busy appearance, reminding one of the roads near Doncaster racecourse on a Leger day. Indeed, so great was the crushing at the entrance to the football ground that many, mostly females, turned back. Along the walls of the ground sat working men, the windows of the surrounding houses were filled with people, and on the wooden stand and thereabouts men and women were inconveniently crowded together. Usually, at football matches here, the spectators are confined to one end of the ground, but this event attracted so many would-be onlookers that everywhere (including the centre of the ground, but with the exception of the new pavilion) was occupied by visitors. Of course, only moderate proportions were able to witness the play, and, in one respect, it is a pity the attendance was so great. Many, undoubtedly, were disappointed, and it will be a matter for

CHAPTER FIVE

consideration, in regard to any future similar match, whether or not the charge for admission should be higher so as to reduce the number of spectators. The playground was soon spoiled by the people, and play was frequently stopped by the crowding, and it was not till the arrival of an extra force of police that the game could precede in a satisfactory manner. There is, however, one exceedingly gratifying feature about the match, and that is that it will not only have caused handsome assistance to the two charities named above, but put money into the coffers of another highly deserving institution, the Boys' Working Home. The Pantomimists were, of course, 'the observed of all observers', and doubtless many of the latter were imbued with a spirit of curiosity to see the demons, villains, and merry men of pantomime in the daylight.... it is roughly estimated that upwards of 20,000 people visited the ground yesterday." [145]

(The all-time record attendance for Bramall Lane is 68,287 is for an F.A. Cup match between Sheffield United and Leeds United in the 1935/36 season).

Wellington FC, (Sheffield, Yorkshire 1866-1878)

- Equal eighth Oldest Sheffield Football Club
- Equal twenty-seventh Oldest Football Club in England

Origin: Unknown

Football Annual	Ground	Foundation Date	Hon. Sec.	Members	Colours
1868	Houndsfields Park (SE)*	1866	W. Briggs	150 Amount of entrance fee: Nil Amount of subscription: 2s 6d	Puce and white
1869	Houndsfields Park (SE)	1866	Peter Schofield	280	Puce and white
1870	Houndsfields Park (SE)	1866	Peter Schofield	280	Puce and white
1871	Houndsfields Park (SE)	1866	Peter Schofield	150	Puce and white

* The mystery deepens on the location. Hounsfield Park, (also spelt Houndsfield and Houndsfields) on which Milton FC played and appears in no local research, yet appears to be close to Sheaf House.

Wellington FC played in the first round of the Youdan Cup, losing 5-0 to Milton FC at a game played away at Cremorne on the 16th February 1867. As a 'junior club,' Wellington FC was invited to compete in the four-club tournament called the Cromwell Cup in 1868, but Garrick FC beat them by four rouges to nil in what was effectively the semi-final. Wellington FC stop appearing in the Football Annual from 1879. Wellington FC tried the much-used strategy of an Athletics day at Bramall Lane in 1869, however:

"The attendance was very limited, so much so that the club will hardly net enough to clear expenses. The sport was of a moderate character, and the following gentlemen carried out the arrangements: Judge, Mr. Thomas Nixon; starter, Mr. J. Marsh; and clerk of course, Mr. G. Harrison, aided by an efficient staff of stewards." [146]

A short-lived **Chesterfield FC** also started in 1866 but ceased in 1881. The current Chesterfield FC website has further information:

"Irrespective of when it was formed, this first (Chesterfield) club folded in 1881, largely through lack of interest in anyone taking charge of its small debt. A knot of its players sought to re-establish the side as 'Chesterfield United,' and this side may have played on into the 1890s, although mention of it after its inaugural season (1881-2) is very hard to find. The attraction of the more successful Spital club, who operated on a field near Horns Bridge, drew Chesterfield players away, and those who did not pledge allegiance to either side dissolved into a growing pool of local clubs." [147]

(The current Chesterfield FC dates from April 1919, and was formed from the Chesterfield Municipal FC). A cricket team was playing in Chesterfield as early as 1858 and since Norton FC played football with a Chesterfield team in early 1864, it seems logical that football would have continued to have been played between these adjacent places. However, Norton FC persisted whilst the Chesterfield team match reports ceased. From the 1871 Football Annual onwards, Chesterfield FC (1866), was trying to decide which of the three different playing codes to adopt.

Football Annual	Ground	Foundation Date	Hon. Sec.	Members	Colours	Code	Dressing Room
1871	Recreation ground, Chesterfield	1866	C.W. Rollinson, St. Helen's, Sheffield Road, Chesterfield	100	Blue cap, blue and white jersey and stockings, white trousers	Football Association	
1872	Recreation ground, Chesterfield	1866	C.W. Rollinson, St. Helen's, Sheffield Road, Chesterfield	100	Blue cap, blue and white jersey and stockings, white trousers	Football Association	
1873	New Recreation ground, Chesterfield	1866	C.W. Rollinson, St. Helen's, Sheffield Road, Chesterfield	130	Blue cap, blue and white jersey and stockings, with white knickerbockers	Derbyshire Football Association (the first version 1871)	Under the Grand Stand on the ground
1874	New Recreation ground, Chesterfield	1866	C.W. Rollinson, St. Helen's, Sheffield Road, Chesterfield	150	Blue cap, blue and white jersey and stockings, with white knickerbockers	Derbyshire Football Association (the first version 1871)	Under the Grand Stand on the ground
1875	x						
1876	x						
1877	x						
1878	x						
1879	Recreation	1865	G.E. Edge	120	Blue, white band and badge	Included in the Sheffield Clubs (Sheffield Association)	
1880	Recreation	1865	G.E. Edge	120	Blue, white band and badge	Sheffield Association	

In the 1930s, the incorrect 1866 foundation date is applied to the Chesterfield team of the day:

"Two shillings a year was enough to make you a member of the Chesterfield Football Club in the early days of its existence. Rules drawn up for the 1871-2 season fixed this sum as the annual subscription. The rules declared also, that the season should start in October and end in March, and that players should meet for practice on Wednesdays and Saturdays. These were the first rules drawn up, although the club had actually been in operation since 1866." [148]

A February 1868 match report suggested a formation date of 1867 rather than 1866:

"CHESTERFIELD. -Yesterday, teams from the Chesterfield and Garrick (Sheffield), football clubs, contested for superiority in the Recreation Ground, Chesterfield, and after some spirited play the Garrick gentlemen were returned the victors. Considering that the Chesterfield club has *only been in existence a few months,* they played with admirable skill and pluck." [149]

The first match report with a team list I found for Chesterfield FC is from 1872, when it still had not adopted the Sheffield rules:

CHAPTER FIVE

"Football. Chesterfield v. Brincliffe (Sheffield) – A match was played in the New Recreation Ground, Chesterfield, yesterday, between two teams of the above clubs, in the presence of a large concourse of spectators. The visitors kicked off shortly after half-past two, and for a considerable time kept the ball at the mouth of the Chesterfield goal, but it was frequently staved off in clever style by Roper. The pluckiest of play on both sides continued, and frequent applause greeted first one side and then the other. Ultimately Sampson, with his usual dexterity, secured a somewhat easy goal for his side. Ends were then changed, and a good play was again shown by the majority of those engaged, and a few minutes before time the home team secured a goal, but it was disputed by the visitors on the ground that the ball, which was kicked from boundary by a Chesterfield player, was played a second time before it had been kicked by one of the opposing side; still the Sheffield umpire did not call a foul until the goal was got. Thus the match ended in a dispute. Players: Brincliffe: Messrs. Sampson, Jackson, Wake, Matthews, Stokes, Neill, Vickers, Bowling, Marsden, Webster, Harrison, and Richards. Chesterfield: Messrs. Francis, Calder, Nall, Roper, Riggott, Whomersley, Marriott, Plumbridge, Downey, Donovan, Smith and Charlwood." [150]

Chesterfield FC joined the Sheffield Association in 1879 (possibly sooner) and remained a member in 1880 and 1881 (it didn't join the Sheffield New Association); by 1882 it is not listed in either of the Sheffield Associations. There is no Chesterfield FC in the 1883 or 1884 editions of the Football Annuals. The second incarnation of the Derbyshire Football Association was formed in September 1883 and in the inaugural Cup competition there is only one Chesterfield team, Spital FC, as featured in the 1874 section.

1867

Joining England and Wales with an Association football club is the Queen's Park Football Club, founded on 9 July 1867 in Scotland; more surprisingly, the Buenos Aires Football Club was founded in this year too. I omitted this club from third spot on my list of oldest clubs by country because this is another example of British ex-pats forming a club so that they can play the game they love. In this case, it was Thomas Hogg an owner of a Yorkshire textile factory, originally from Skelton on the outskirts of York. The club continued until 1870 when a yellow fever outbreak killed 8% of inhabitants of Buenos Aires. Sheffield Wednesday, England's third oldest League club, started in the same year,1867, that the Sheffield Association was formed. In total ten Association clubs were founded in England, and three were from Sheffield.

The Wednesday FC (Sheffield, Yorkshire 1867 – Present)
- Third oldest League club in existence (after the two Nottingham clubs)
- Ninth Oldest Sheffield Football Club
- Equal twenty-ninth Oldest Football Club in England
- Wednesday won the Cromwell Cup, their first trophy, in 1868
- Won the inaugural Sheffield Association Challenge Cup in 1876/77 and have won it fourteen times since.

Origin: Cricket. Wednesday Cricket Club was founded in 1816 and the football club was added on September 5th 1867, as a means for the cricket players to keep fit during the winter season (like so many clubs before them):

"SHEFFIELD WEDNESDAY CRICKET CLUB AND FOOTBALL CLUB. - At a general meeting held yesterday, at the Adelphi Hotel, it was decided to form a football club in connection with the above cricket club, with the object of keeping together during the winter season the members of this influential club. The office-bearers were elected as follows: - President, Mr. B. Chatterton; vice-president and treasurer, Mr. F. S. Chambers; hon. Secretary, Mr. Jno. Marsh; assistant, Mr. Castleton; committee, Messrs. John Rodgers, John Pashley, Wm. Pilch, W, Fry, Wm. Littlehales, John White, C. Stokes, and H. Booking. After which above 60 good men were enrolled as members, and this without any canvass, amongst whom are many of the best players in the town." [151]

One name to note from the above founding Committee is Charles Stokes who had already been influential in two other Sheffield clubs and twenty-two years later would be the driving force behind the formation of Wednesday's arch rivals, Sheffield United. It took five weeks till the 12th October, for a practice match to be arranged by J. Marsh, the Hon. Sec. at the top of Bramall Lane, near Highfield, which kicked off at 2.30.

"The club's first ground was near the present Upper Colver Road, it was called high field and the Highfield Library now stands there." [152] The library is still there on London Road, Sheffield S2 4NF, less than half a mile from the present Sheffield United ground. This locates the ground a little to the east of Cremorne Gardens and is probably where St. Barnabas church is now, which was built between 1874 and 1876.

The Wednesday was in no rush to start playing; its first match did not happen until December 31st, over eleven weeks after the first practice match on 12th of October and sixteen weeks after the club's foundation. The match report described its opponents, Dronfield FC, as 'newly-formed' and the game was played 'in a field lent by Mr. S. Baggaly'. Wednesday won by one goal to four rouges from the Dronfield team. [153]

I mentioned earlier that blue and white was adopted for the Cromwell Cup match in February 1868, which is described below as 'hoops' by 1871. In the 1868 Football Annual, the foundation date reflects the practice match rather than the foundation meeting. Unfortunately, none of the Hon. Secs completed the column in the Football Annuals, where you could list your club's dressing room, as that would have given more insight into where they were playing. The only mention is for 1885 when it says that players could change 'on the ground.'

Football Annual	Ground	Foundation Date	Hon. Sec.	Members	Colours
1868	Heeley	October 1867	John Walsh, 21 Eyre Street, Sheffield	170 Amount of entrance fee: Nil Amount of subscription: 2s 6d	
1869	Highfield, Heeley	1867	John Walsh, 21 Eyre Street, Sheffield	260	
1870	Highfield, Heeley	1867	John Walsh, 21 Eyre Street, Sheffield	260	
1871	Myrtle Road, Heeley	1867	John Marsh, Engraver, 35 Randall Street, Highfield, Sheffield	260	Blue and white hoop
1872	Myrtle Road, Heeley	1867	John Marsh, Engraver, 35 Randall Street, Highfield, Sheffield	260	Blue and white hoop
1873	Myrtle Road, Heeley	1867	John Marsh, Engraver, 35 Randall Street, Highfield, Sheffield	250	Blue and white hoop

1874	Myrtle Road, Heeley	1867	John Marsh, Adelphi Hotel	250	Blue and white hoop
1875	Myrtle Road, Heeley	1867	W. Littlehales, 34 Talbot Street	250	Blue and white hoop
1876	Myrtle Road, Heeley	1867	W. Littlehales, 34 Talbot Street	250	Blue and white hoop
1877	x				
1878	x				
1879	Sheaf House	1867	W. Littlehales, 34 Talbot street	250	Blue and white hoop
1880	Sheaf House	1867	W. Littlehales, 34 Talbot street	300	Blue and white hoop
1881	Cricket Ground	1867	W. Littlehales, 48 Charlotte Road	Reporting stopped in 1881 edition	Blue and white
1882	x				
1883	Cricket Ground	1867	J. Hoyland, 25 Union Street		Blue and white
1884	Cricket Ground	1867	J. Hoyland, 25 Union Street		Blue and white
1885	Bramall Lane	1867	J.B. Thompson, Garrick Hotel, Sycamore street, Sheffield		Blue and white

Wednesday's first trophy came just six weeks after their first competitive match, when they won the Cromwell Cup (see match report in Garrick FC section). The gap in their choice of ground in the Football Annuals is solved by the report in the Milton FC section, stating that Wednesday had taken the Sheaf House ground. There is no doubt that the Wednesday would have joined defunct club Thursday Wanderers (1870) and many other Sheffield clubs, had it not sorted out a regular enclosure to play in, first in 1887 and then in 1899:

1867-1870 Highfield
1871-1876 Myrtle Road
1877- 1880 Sheaf House
1881-1884 Cricket Ground (Bramall Lane cricket ground but also at Hunter's Bar)
1885 Bramall Lane
1886 Unknown (Press reports suggest Bramall Lane and Sheaf House)
1887 - 1898 Olive Grove
1899-present Owlerton (the stadium name change to Hillsborough happened in 1913)

The Olive Grove ground opened in September 1887:

"The new ground of the Wednesday Football Club which was opened yesterday, is a great addition to the grounds where the winter pastime may be indulged in under favourable circumstances, in Sheffield. The portion set apart by the rule, measuring 110 yards in length, 70 in width and is surrounded by a cinder path 6ft wide. There is a large shed capable of accommodating about 1000 persons and it is probable that a covered enclosure will before long be erected. The ground has two double entrances- one near the railway from Olive Grove road, and the other from the direction of Myrtle Grove road." [154]

The postcard depicts Olive Grove in 1850.
Image courtesy of "The World's First Football Club, Sheffield FC"

Olive Grove still has a football pitch but is now called the Sheffield Works Department, Sports and Social Club, Heeley Bank Road, S2 3GG. At the time of writing, Sheffield FC is in talks to relocate from Dronfield, Derbyshire, to play at the old Olive Grove ground, which is appropriately only about a mile away from where their first pitch, East Bank, was located.

The first ever Sheffield Football Association Challenge Cup featured the Wednesday in the 1876/77 season:

First Round: Wednesday 3 Parkwood Springs 1
Second Round: Wednesday 1 Kimberworth 0
Third Round: Wednesday 1 Attercliffe 0
Fourth Round: Wednesday 3 Exchange 1
Final Tie: Wednesday 4 Heeley 3

Match report of that first final featured an attendance of between 7,000-8,000:

"The Sheffield Football Association Challenge Cup. Decidedly the most interesting match of the Sheffield football season was that which took place on Saturday afternoon, at Bramall Lane Ground, between those two well-known clubs, Wednesday and Heeley. The contest was the final outcome of the Ties for the splendid silver trophy offered for competition early in the season by the Sheffield Association. The Wednesday and Heeley teams had succeeded in defeating all their previous opponents, and now met to decide as to superiority between themselves. As may be easily understood, the highest excitement was manifested in the result of the struggle, not in Sheffield alone, but in all the football circles of this and the neighbouring counties. It would probably be within the mark to state that between seven and eight thousand spectators must have visited the ground during the afternoon. Many ladies were present – some of them, judging from the warmth of their plaudits, being doubtless relatives or close friends of the players engaged." [155]

The players were – Wednesday: Mr. W. H. Stacey (captain), Mr. J. C. Clegg, Mr. W. E. Clegg, and Messrs F. Stacey (goal), J. J. Lang, F. M. Butler, T. M. Butler, H. Muscroft, J. Bingley, T. Bishop, W. E. Skinner, and E. Buttery. – Heeley: Messrs J. E. Deans (captain), J. Linley (goal), H. J. Barringham, J. Thorpe, J. Hunter T. Leslie, P. Andrews, T. A. Tomlinson, J. Tomlinson, F. Brownhill, R. Martin, and W. Beard. Umpires, Mr. W. R. Wake and Mr. J. W. Barber; referee, Mr. J. C. Shaw.

"Heeley won the toss and Mr. W. H. Stacey, the Wednesday captain, kicked off against the wind, which was blowing pretty strongly. Heeley at once assumed the offensive, and at the call of half-time, they had secured three goals, two of which were accidently put through by Wednesday players, to their adversaries' welcome. With the wind in their favour it was now confidently anticipated by their friends that Wednesday would soon succeed in scoring, though their most sanguine partisans hardly imagined that they would so completely alter the appearance of the game. After some magnificent play, the Wednesday players succeeded in equalising matters. The scene of excitement that followed the last goal beggars' description. The efforts to score now on both sides and thus win the cup were quite terrific, time being almost up. Both of the teams laboured exhaustively till the call of time, but no further score having been effected the match was declared to be a tie. Immense cheering succeeded the declaration of this result. The players now gathered in a group in the centre of the ground, and there was a short parley as to what course should be pursued – whether the match should be played out then, or whether a postponement should take place to a future day, when the contest could be replayed from the start to the finish. The captains of the two teams eventually agreed that the team should antagonise for another half-hour – fifteen minutes each way – and if at the end of that time nothing more were scored, the match be re-played on a future occasion. After some exciting play, Wednesday scored a goal. Time was eventually called, and the Wednesday Club thus became the victor of this magnificent and gloriously contested match – unquestionably the best of this season – by four goals to three." [155]

The 1877 article goes on to describe the celebratory dinner of the same evening where seventy gentlemen attended the Imperial Hotel, Castle Street, including:

"...the players in both teams. Mr. J. C. Shaw (President of the Association) occupied the chair, and Messrs. Skinner and Dickenson sat at the head of the opposite table. Amongst those present were councillors Clegg (two), Mr. W. E. Clegg, Mr. J. F. Hall, Mr. W. R. Wake, Mr. J. W. Barber, Mr. W. P. Dix, Mr. W. H. Stacey, and others – Mr. Shaw made an appropriate speech preparatory to handing over the prizes. He alluded in warm terms to the remarkably gallant contest which had preceded the dinner. He said he considered it one of the closest and most exciting struggles he had ever witnessed, either in the present or any previous season. The players on both sides had shown the best possible spirit, and the match had been satisfactory in every possible way." [155]

John Shaw in his capacity of President of the Association spoke about why the Sheffield Football Association had started the Challenge Cup competition:

"The association", he said, "were desirous of cultivation and encouraging the highest and best principles of the noble winter pastime. They were convinced that football, so far from having the deteriorating effects upon the minds of the multitude which so many of our so-called 'sports' undoubtedly had, was in a very large degree useful as a moral agency – cultivating as it did gentlemanly habits, good temper, coolness, self-denial, courage, and abstemiousness." [155]

The abstemiousness did not last long as the winner's Cup was filled with champagne and passed around, presumably to the dismay of the Clegg brothers. The winners' medals were:

"Composed of silver in the form of a Maltese cross, and each was enclosed in a handsome leather case. The Heeleyites heartily applauded the recipients of the gifts, and the cheering was as warmly returned. The proceedings terminated at later hours after most pleasant entertainment." [155]

The Wednesday - F.A. Cup Record 1871-1888

The Wednesday had a good record in the F.A. Cup in the period ending 1889/90, culminating in losing in the final to Blackburn Rovers FC.

Season	Round	Opponent	Venue	Score
1880-81	2	Blackburn Rovers	A	4-0
	3	Turton	A	2-0
	4	Darwen	A	2-5
1881-82	2	Bye		
	3	Staveley	H	2-2
	3r	Staveley	A	0-0
	3r2	Staveley	N	5-1
	4 S	heffield Heeley	H	3-1
	QF	Upton Park	H	6-0
	SF	Blackburn Rovers	N	0-0 (St John's Rugby Ground, Huddersfield)
	SFr	Blackburn Rovers	N	1-5 (Whalley Range, Manchester)
1882-83	3	Nottingham Forest	A	2-2
	3r	Nottingham Forest	H	3-2
	4	Notts County	H	1-4

1883-84	2	Staveley		A	1-3
1884-84	1	Long Eaton Rangers		H	1-0
	2	Bye			
	3	Nottingham Forest		H	1-2
1885-86	1	Long Eaton Rangers		A	0-2

1886-87 Wednesday did not send in their registration in on time to play in that season's F.A. Cup competition and the beneficiaries were Lockwood Brothers FC, which gained several Wednesday players who still wished to play in some capacity. Having to compete in the qualifying rounds for the first-time, Lockwood Brothers FC reached the first round by beating Long Eaton Rangers 1–0, Cleethorpes 4–1 and Nottingham Forest 2–1 and receiving a bye in the fourth qualifying round. They were finally knocked out in the 5th round by West Bromwich Albion, losing 2–1.

1887-88	3	Bye		
	4	Crusaders	A	1-0
	5	Nottingham Forest	A	4-2
	QF	Preston North End	H	1-3
1888-89	1	Notts Rangers	A	1-1
	1r	Notts Rangers	H	3-0
	2	Notts County	H	3-2
	QF	Wolverhampton Wanderers	A	0-3

Wednesday were losing F.A. Cup finalists in 1889/90, but winners in 1895/96 and both occasions are covered in greater depth in Chapter Eight. It wasn't until the 1920s that the club dropped the definite article and changed its name permanently from 'The Wednesday' to 'Sheffield Wednesday'.

At the time of the book's publication (April 2017), Wednesday seem set to compete in the play-offs for promotion to the Premier League.

Exchange FC (Sheffield, Yorkshire 1867-1896)

- Tenth Oldest Sheffield Football Club
- Thirty-First Oldest Football Club in the World
- Founder member of the Sheffield and District Football League in 1889/90
- Later named Park Grange FC and later reverted to Exchange FC

Origin: Cricket. Exchange Cricket Club was playing as early as 1858, known variously as 'Exchange' or 'Exchange Cricket and Football Club' (not to be confused with a different Sheffield club called 'Exchange Brewery FC').

Exchange FC club played in the Park Hill area, close to the city centre that became a notorious tenement area known as Little Chicago in the 1930s, due to its endemic poverty and violence; it was comprehensively demolished after the Second World War, to be replaced by the Park Hill flats in 1957. The 1871 Football Annual states an 1863 foundation date but this is contradicted by its entry in the Cromwell Cup in February 1868. The tournament was only open to 'junior clubs', which meant they had to be only two seasons (or younger) old. (See details at Garrick FC) This, combined, with the fact that there was no press for Exchange FC until 1869, convinced me to overrule Thomas Johnson and the Football Annual and change the foundation year from 1863 to 1867.

CHAPTER FIVE

Football Annual	Ground	Foundation Date	Hon. Sec.	Members	Colours
1871	Hallam's Farm, Park	1863	Thomas Johnson, Sheffield Arms	120	Scarlet and white
1872	Hallam's Farm, Park	1863	Thomas Johnson, 6 Clough Road	120	Scarlet and white
1873	Hallam's Farm, Park	1863	H. Wilkinson, Hospital Tavern, Park Hill Lane	120	Scarlet and white
1874	Hallam's Farm, Park	1863	T. Fletcher, 59 Pearl Street	120	Scarlet and white
1875	Hallam's Farm, Park	1863	T. Fletcher, 59 Pearl Street	200	Scarlet and white
1876	Hallam's Farm, Park	1863	T. Fletcher, 59 Pearl Street	200	Scarlet and white
1877	Quibell's Field near Hyde Park	1863	T. Fletcher, 59 Pearl Street	200	Scarlet and white
1878	x				
1879	Quibell's Field near Hyde Park	1863	S. Osbaldisston, Harwood Street	150	Scarlet and white
1880	Quibell's Field near Hyde Park	1880	S. Osbaldisston, Harwood Street	250	Scarlet and white

The ground's description, 'Hallam's Farm, Park,' from the Football Annual, at first sounds as though the team played in the Sandygate area, but research shows that a Mr. Joseph Hallam of Park Farm, Cricket Inn Road, Sheffield Park was a needle manufacturer and it must have been his land it played on. The Exchange Cricket club was playing at the nearby Hyde Park in 1863. In 1877 Exchange FC left Mr. Hallam's Farm for the nearby field owned by Mr. Quibell.

The first match report I found for Exchange FC is from 1869:

"The Norfolk met the Exchange at Mr. Hallam's Farm, Cricket road, and after a severe struggle the match resulted in a draw." [156]

Three years later in 1871 more details emerged of some Exchange FCs' player's names:

"Exchange v. Parkwood Springs – the 1st teams of these clubs contended on the ground of the former, at Hallam's Farm, Cricket road. Owing to the unfavourable state of the elements, only about half the number on each side put in an appearance, but with the pluck proverbial to football players determined to have a match. The Exchange team proved victorious just previous to call of time, obtaining a goal, put through by S. Lucas, in a scrimmage. Messrs. C. White, for Parkwood, and J. Martin and Tandy, for Exchange, distinguished themselves by superior play." [157]

In 1873: "Exchange v. Broomhall. First teams – On the same day the above named match was played at Mr. Hallam's Farm, Cricket road, and ended in favour of the Exchange by two goals to nothing. The players who most distinguished themselves were Messrs, J. Beardshaw, C. Mills, C. Malpas, and F. Butler for the Broomhall, and Messrs. G. Anthony, J. Houseley, E. Bowling and F. Sellars on the Exchange side." [158]

The following three clubs, Exchange FC (1867-1882), Providence FC (1874-1882) and Perseverance FC (1870-1882), merged to become Grange Park in 1882 and played in the F.A. Cup 1887, under that name. In 1889 Park Grange FC changed its name (back) to Exchange FC. (The full Park Grange story is at Providence FC)

The three-way merger in 1882 appears strange in retrospect; all three clubs had thriving membership numbers in 1880, with Exchange FC having 250 and Providence FC 110. Perseverance FC seems the smaller outfit with the last reported membership numbers being 100 in 1873. As mentioned previously, the financial viability of a club in the mid-1880s became much more fraught and perhaps membership numbers had been declining.

Dore FC (Derbyshire 1867-1891)
- Eleventh Oldest Sheffield Football Club
- Equal thirty-second Oldest Football Club in England

Origin: Unknown. Dore FC has a much earlier foundation date than the Football Annual suggests, which is understandable given that the Sheffield football scene was booming just down the road. In 1934 the village of Dore moved allegiance from the County of Derbyshire to Yorkshire and became a suburb of Sheffield.

The influence of Sheffield football shows in this February 1868 game between 'Derbyshire' villages, by the fact that are also using the rouge in their scoring:

"The Dronfield and Dore Clubs met in friendly rivalry on Tuesday last, and after an exciting game the former were declared victors, scoring one goal and two rouges to their opponents nothing." [159]

Match reports for Dore FC games over the years were very sparse:

"FOOTBALL- HALLAM V. DORE. - A match between these clubs was played at Sandygate on Monday *(11th March 1868)*. Hallam scored two goals to three rouges; Dore two rouges." [160]

"FOOTBALL. - DORE V. DRONFIELD. - The return match between these two new clubs was played on Saturday last at Dore, and, after a well-contested game *(21st March, 1868)*, resulted in the victory of the former, who scored four rouges to their opponents nothing." [161]

"DORE ATHLETIC SPORTS. The third annual athletic sports of the Dore Football Club took place in a field near the village *(1869)*. The attendance was moderate. Mr. P. Aldred officiated as starter; Mr. W. Taylor and Mr. J. Birley, judges; and the Rev, J. T. F. Aldred as clerk of the course." [162]

According to the 1876 Football Annual, Dore FC was still thriving, with 100 members:
Founded: 1874
Code: Sheffield Association
Number of members: 100
Club Ground: Dore
Hon. Sec.: G. Clarke, 91 Hodgson Street, Dore
Colours: Red and white cap

The above information was duplicated in the 1877, 1878 and 1879 editions of the Football Annual. The last press mention I found for the club: "The members and friends of the old established 'Dore Football Club' met together at the Devonshire Arms, Dore on Tuesday evening." [163] The club was advertising for games later in 1891 then the club appears to cease. Another Dore FC was formed in 1928 by Alfred Worboys. [164]

1868

'Brammall-lane' was in a bad state of repair in January 1868:

"Sir, Allow me through the columns of your journal draw the attention of the authorities to the disgraceful state of the south end of Brammall-lane. It is the only outlet in the town for the large population living on the new land societies at Upper Heeley, and is so deep in mud as to be almost impassable, and there is no gas lamp beyond the middle of Brammall-lane. I sincerely trust that the Highway Committee will take the matter in hand at once, as it is really a great hardship that a population contributing so largely to the borough rates should receive so little

CHAPTER FIVE

attention at the hands of the borough authorities. Yours very respectfully, UPPER HEELEY." [165]

Sixteen Association clubs were formed in this year, eight from the south, two more from Nottinghamshire, one from Norfolk and the 4th Oldest League Club, Stoke Ramblers FC, which later became Stoke City. The official Stoke City website and their club badge states a foundation date of 1863, but my research confirms it was founded in 1868. One club each came from Cambridgeshire and Shropshire and just two clubs from Sheffield commenced in 1868; strictly speaking the first is from Derbyshire, albeit a member of the Sheffield Association.

Dronfield FC (Derbyshire January 1868-1924)

- Twelfth Oldest Sheffield Football Club
- Equal thirty-seventh Oldest Football Club in England

Origin: Unknown. Probably cricket as they had a long-standing club from at least 1853. The Football Annual of 1871 has a foundation date of 1869, which is contradicted by earlier match reports.

According to the 1871 Football Annual:
Founded: 1869
Number of members: 120
Club Ground: Dronfield
Code: Sheffield Association
Hon. Sec.: J. Fisher, Dronfield
Colours: Puce and white

Mr. Fisher appears to have got the foundation date wrong, as a match report suggests their first match was very early in 1868 against a prestigious opponent, also playing their first match:

"Dronfield Football Club – The members of this newly-formed club played their first match on Tuesday against the Sheffield Wednesday Club, in a field kindly lent by S. Baggaly, Esq. The Sheffielders scored a goal in ten minutes. When goals were changed the Dronfielders scored four rouges." [166]

The club website says that Baggaly's field is today located on the corner of Gosforth Lane and Manor Crescent. [167] Like its Derbyshire neighbours, Dore FC, the reporting for early Dronfield FC matches was very basic: "DRONFIELD. - FOOTBALL MATCH. - The Dronfield and Dore Clubs met in friendly rivalry on Tuesday last (1868), and after an exciting game the former were declared victors, scoring one goal and two rouges to their opponents nothing." [168] Wednesday was happy to travel south again, a year after their first match:

DRONFIELD v. WEDNESDAY. - A bus will leave Mr. Armfield's ADELPHI HOTEL, Arundel street, for DRONFIELD, at 12 o'clock punctually. Kick-off at 2 o'clock. JOHN MARSH, Hon. Sec." [169]

Dronfield FC made their first appearance in the Derbyshire Football Association Challenge Cup 1884/85, which started in 1883/84. The press reports stop for Dronfield FC after 1924.

Brincliffe FC (Sheffield, Yorkshire 1868–1881)

- Thirteenth Oldest Sheffield Football Club
- Thirty-Eighth Oldest Football Club in England
- Amalgamated with Endcliffe FC in April 1879

Origin: unknown. The 1872 Football Annual lists a foundation date of 1870 but the press reports confirm an 1868 start:

"BRINCLIFFE FOOTBALL CLUB. - This club, which embraces the districts of Brincliffe and Sharrow, played their first practice match on Saturday last, but, owing to the unfavourable weather, it was only short of duration. The playing ground is on Mr. Ibbotson's farm, at Cherrytree." [170] Mr. Ibbotson's farm at Cherrytree was on Machon Bank Road, Nether Edge:

"Brincliffe Football Club. The general meeting at the above club will be held at the Union Inn, Cherrytree, on Tuesday, the 12th *(1869)* first at 7.30pm for the Election of Officers for the comings Season, and for the transaction of other Business of the Club. All members are particularly requested to attend." [171]

The next match Brincliffe played in 1872 is interesting because it is the first report of a game with the **Engineers FC**; no team of that name is listed in the Sheffield Football Association or the Football Annuals but it was the Engineers Regiment, which formed part of the Sheffield Volunteer Movement at the time:

"Brincliffe v. Engineers (1st Twelves) – This match was played on Saturday on the ground of the latter at Endcliffe and after a spirited and well contested game, the Brincliffe team came off victorious by two goals to nothing. Messrs. G. H. Sampson, Henry Swift, Henry Steel, and Harrison were conspicuous for the Brincliffe club; while Messrs. A. Wood, J. Hand, and Chambers did good service for the military." [172]

Football Annual	Ground	Foundation Date	Hon. Sec.	Members	Colours
1872	Hunter's Bar South	1870	W. H. Jackson, Norfolk Street	120	Scarlet
1873	Hunter's Bar Ecclesall Road	1868	W. H. Jackson, Norfolk Street	80 (Limited)	Amber and black
1874	Hunter's Bar Ecclesall Road	1868	W. H. Jackson, Norfolk Street	80 (Limited)	Amber and black
1875	Hunter's Bar Ecclesall Road	1868	W. H. Jackson, Norfolk Street	80 (Limited)	Amber and black
1876	Hunter's Bar Ecclesall Road	1868	W. H. Jackson, Norfolk Street	80 (Limited)	Amber and black
1877	Hunter's Bar Ecclesall Road	1868	W. H. Jackson, Norfolk Street	80 (Limited)	Black and white
1878	x				
1879	Hunter's Bar Ecclesall Road	1868	W. W. Liddell, 13 Brocco Bank	80 (Limited)	Black and white
1880	Hunter's Bar Ecclesall Road	1868	J. Bradbury, Victoria Road, Broomhall Park	80 (Limited)	Black and white

Charles Clegg continued his habit of turning out for many clubs; in 1875 he played for Surrey FC against Brincliffe and scored a hat-trick. The phrase 'hat-trick' is originally a cricketing term denoting bowling down three wickets in three successive balls but it does not appear to have become part of the Sheffield football vernacular by 1875, as it is not mentioned in the following match report:

"Football. Surrey v. Brincliffe (1st teams) – This, the last match of the season, so far as the Surrey Club is concerned, was played on Saturday at the Farm, before a goodly number of spectators. Play was commenced at four o'clock, Brincliffe winning the toss, and electing to kick with the wind, which was very strong. Notwithstanding the advantage of the wind, in a short time a goal was secured for the home team by a splendid kick from J. C. Clegg. Ends were now changed, and in a few minutes J. C. Clegg obtained another goal for Surrey. Surrey again kicked against the wind, when the splendid back play of Messrs. T. Willey, W. R. Wake, and

S. Dixon was noticeable, and the ball was quickly returned to the Surrey forwards. After some fast play the ball was sent to the Brincliffe goal and F. Proctor cleverly put it through. Surrey, with the wind in their favour, now kept up an incessant battering at the Brincliffe goal, W. E. Clegg several times kicking the ball over the bar, but the fine goal-keeping of W. H. Jackson kept them at bay. About this time J. C. Clegg from the corner kicked the ball through the goal, but owing to it being a free kick, the goal was not allowed. S. Dixon was here noticeable for several grand rushes and charges which he made, upsetting the equilibrium of several of the Surrey men. The ball was again brought in close proximity to the Brincliffe goal and by a piece of cool and scientific play the ball was put through by J. Willey, the goal keeper (W. H. Jackson) being beautifully charged by Donnellan. A short time after play had been resumed the Brincliffe men brought the ball near the Surrey goal, where a foul was given, but no sooner had the ball been touched than J. C. Clegg got possession of it and took it rapidly away in his usual good style, but was quickly followed by S. Dixon and others. A few minutes later, however, he was rewarded by another goal. After about five minutes' more play W. E. Clegg was at last successful in his endeavour to score, thus gaining the sixth goal for Surrey. On ends being changed the Brincliffe men, with the wind again in their favour, made several attempts to retrieve their fortunes, but were disappointed up to within a minute of time, when the ball rolling slowly into the Surrey goal, and the goal keeper missing his kick it went through about three feet, thus scoring the first and only goal for Brincliffe. Time was now called, leaving Surrey the victors by six goals to one. Besides those already mentioned for Brincliffe, Sorby, Payne, and Richards played well; and for Surrey, Messrs. M. Ellison and Parker. The Surrey team was well coached by T. Willey, the captain." [173]

It is interesting to see for the first time, in the above press report, the first mention of a team being 'coached'. Training and coaching was viewed by southern amateur players as an ungentlemanly activity. Jack Hunter took a professional approach to player recruitment and training when he transferred to Blackburn Olympic FC as their player/coach after falling out with Sheffield football establishment over the 'Zulu' affair. Famously Olympic went to Blackpool to train before their semi-final against the Old Carthusians for one week, shocking the Eton establishment:

"So great was their ambition to wrest the Cup from the holders, that they introduced into football a practice which has excited the greatest disapprobation in the South. For three weeks before the match they went into a strict course of training" …" [174]

Jack Hunter's scientific approach paid off when Olympic won the 1883 F.A. Cup in his first season. The Football Association reacted by passing legislation the following year banning such a professional approach; no more than one day's wages per week could now be claimed for time lost through football.

1869

Fourteen Association clubs started in England this year, two of which came from Sheffield.

Oxford FC (Sheffield, Yorkshire October 1869-1884)

- Equal fourteenth Oldest Sheffield Football Club
- Equal forty-sixth Oldest Football Club in England

Origin: Unknown. Its meeting place was the now defunct New Inn, at 108, Ecclesall Road (about half a mile from both Bramall Lane and the Collegiate School), was central to the rest of the Sheffield football scene. In 1871 Joseph Rowbotham was landlord, rather than the J. Ridge quoted in the Football Annual, so perhaps it was the base for any post and for their meetings. A few hundred yards away from New Inn was another pub more appropriately called the Oxford House, at 131-133, Moore Street; maybe this was the inspiration for this thriving club's name?

Football Annual	Ground	Foundation Date	Hon. Sec.	Members	Colours
1871	Ecclesall Road	October 1869	J. Ridge, New Inn, Ecclesall Road	140	Blue and yellow
1872	Ecclesall Road	October 1869	Ben Tingle, New Inn, Ecclesall Road	140	Blue and yellow
1873	Ecclesall Road	1869	Ben Tingle, New Inn, Ecclesall Road	140	Blue and yellow
1874	Ecclesall Road	1869	Ben Tingle, New Inn, Ecclesall Road	140	Blue and yellow
1875	Ecclesall Road	1869	B. Fox 48 Clun Street	140	Blue and yellow
1876	Ecclesall Road	1869	B. Fox 48 Clun Street	140	Blue and yellow
1877	Hunter's Bar	1869	G. Glentworth, 15 Albert Terrace Road	140	Blue and yellow
1878	x				
1879	Hunter's Bar	1869	J. Swallow, 3 St Thomas Street	170	Blue
1880	Hunter's Bar	1869	J. Swallow, 3 St Thomas Street	160	

(In 1870 the President of the club was Mr. Ibbotson)

In 1869 Oxford FC, did not show up for a match and the contrite Hon. Sec. of Oxford FC made his apologies to Fir Vale FC:

"Oxford Football Club. To the editor – On behalf of the committee of the Oxford F. B. C., I beg to state that we are very sorry if we have inconvenienced the Fir Vale players, but owing to our late secretary leaving town and not informing the committee of the match arranged on Saturday last, we knew nothing of it until Friday night last. It being then too late to get a team, our present secretary went to the secretary of the Fir Vale F. B.C, and not being able to see him, left word that we should not be able to play the match on that date. Yours respectfully, John Haigh, Hon. Sec." [175]

Solid cross bars did not become law until 1875 and it is easy to see why they were needed from the report of this 1871 match:

"The ground of the Oxford Club in Ecclesall road was the scene of a contest between the first teams of that club and Norfolk, ending in a draw. During the match a ball was kicked by one of the Norfolk players and struck the cord, but whether under or over was of course left to the umpire to decide, and that was in favour of Oxford. On another occasion the ball was played through the goal by Mr. J. P. Donovan for Norfolk, but the umpire disallowed it on the ground that a foul had been given immediately preceding. The match eventually ended in a draw, neither team scoring." [176]

In the following 1873 Oxford FC game, is the the earliest mention of a headed goal found in a Sheffield match report:

"Perseverance v Oxford – The second teams of these clubs contested their return match on the Oxford ground, Ecclesall Road, on Wednesday. The teetotallers were not long in securing a goal, and on ends being changed were speedily rewarded with a second. The first goal was obtained by good play on the part of J. H. Banks, and the second was "headed" through by T. Heeley. Oxford did not get a goal. A. Cam, for Oxford, kept the goal admirably." [177]

CHAPTER FIVE

Parkwood Springs FC (Sheffield, Yorkshire 1869-1880)

- Equal fourteenth Oldest Sheffield Football Club
- Equal forty-sixth Oldest Football Club in England

Origin: Unknown. Parkwood Springs was a large green area north of Sheffield city centre; it was the subject of a compulsory purchase order in 1973 and is now mostly an industrial area. There could be a link to Messrs Ridge's (Limited) as the Football Annual table below shows; certainly the membership numbers are consistent every year, which may be linked to his work force. Parkwood Springs is just under three miles north of Norfolk Street. The 1871 Football Annual lists a foundation date of 1870, but the press reports confirm an 1869 start.

Football Annual	Ground	Foundation Date	Hon. Sec.	Members	Colours
1871	Parkwood Springs	1870	Ben Hammond, Messrs Ridge's (Limited) Norfolk Street	100	White
1872	Parkwood Springs	1870	Ben Hammond, Messrs Rodgers, and Sons (Limited) Norfolk Street	100	White
1873	Parkwood Springs	1870	Ben Hammond, Messrs Rodgers, and Sons (Limited) Norfolk Street	150	White, with amber and black caps
1874	Parkwood Springs	1870	W. Fern, 6 Burton Street	150	White, with amber and black caps
1875	Parkwood Springs	1870	W. Fern, 6 Burton Street	150	White, with amber and black caps
1876	Parkwood Springs	1870	W. Fern, 6 Burton Street	150	White, with amber and black caps
1877	Parkwood Springs	1870	W. Fern, 6 Burton Street	150	White, with amber and black caps
1878	x				
1879	Parkwood Springs	1866	W. Fern, 6 Burton Street	150	White, with amber and black caps
1880	Parkwood Springs	1866	W. Fern, 6 Burton Street	150	Scarlet and Blue

In the days before official football reporters, if someone from the football club did not send in the reports then the club would not be well reported, and Parkwood Springs FC is very poorly reported. The earliest press mention is from 1869:

"Parkwood Springs Football Club. A meeting of the above club will be held on Monday evening next, at Eight o'clock, at the House of Mr. J. Brough, White Horse Inn, Parkwood Springs, to Elect Officers for the ensuing season. All persons desirous of becoming members are respectfully invited to attend." [178]

Parkwood Springs FC was a vehicle for socialising as well as a football club, holding a musical evening in 1870:

"Parkwood Springs football club – The first annual concert in connection with the above club was given by the members and friends on Thursday evening, at the club-house (Mr. G. Brough), White Horse Inn, Parkwood Springs. Amongst the artistes was Messrs. T. Hibbert, G. Ward, C. Fisher, G. Stewart, H. Long, and William. Mr. Hart presided at the piano-forte. The members appeared to give great satisfaction." [179]

The first match report came in 1873 but without a full team line-up:

"Gleadless v. Parkwood Springs (First team) – This match was played at Gleadless on Monday, and after an excellent contest, was won by Gleadless Club by one goal to nothing. The play of Messrs. A. Wood, J. Houseley, J. Marten, and H. Ward, for Gleadless, was particularly fine. Messrs. W. H. Carr, S. Buttery, C. Addy, and C. Roberts also played remarkably well for the Parkwood springs." (180)

1870

Association football burst into life nationwide with twenty-nine clubs started in this year; only four of them would stand the test of time: Maidenhead FC, Marlow FC, Reigate Priory FC and Ipswich FC (5th Oldest League Club). The official Ipswich Town FC club site has a foundation date of 1878 but under my classification rules, they inherit the earlier date of the Rugby club with whom they amalgamated in 1888 to form Ipswich Town FC.

Sheffield's Midland railway station opened in 1870, meaning that that there was now a direct connection to St Pancras, not that any Sheffield football was played down there in future F.A. Cup finals, before 1890. Ten of the clubs founded nationally this year came from Sheffield and another one from Rotherham.

Christchurch (Attercliffe) FC (Sheffield, Yorkshire 1870-1904)

- Equal fifteenth Oldest Sheffield Football Club
- Equal forty-ninth Oldest Football Club in England
- Founder member of the Sheffield and District Football League in 1889/90

Origin: Church. Formed as Christ Church, playing in Attercliffe in 1870 before changing its name to Attercliffe in the 1873/74 season:

'The club was formerly composed of villagers but now *(1875)* numbers almost all the leading Sheffield players in its ranks.' (181)

Christchurch Attercliffe FC is in the 1871 Annual stating that the club was not a member of the Sheffield Association, but still listed the details and the fact that they played by the Sheffield Association rules. They officially joined in October 1871:

"Application was then made by the Christ Church, Perseverance, and Surrey clubs for admission into the Association, and on being carried, they sent as delegates Messrs, W. Jackson, E. S. Drake, and M. Ellison." (182)

As the village of Attercliffe had a Cricket Club as early as 1856, this may have also contributed towards the club's formation.

Football Annual	Ground	Foundation Date	Hon. Sec.	Members	Colours
1871	Attercliffe	1870	W. Jackson, Attercliffe	70	Blue and white
1872	Attercliffe	1870	W. Jackson, Attercliffe	70	Blue and white
1873	Attercliffe Station	1870	W.H. Jackson, Norfolk Street	120	Blue and white
1874	Attercliffe Station	1870	J. Smith, Attercliffe, Sheffield	120	Blue and white
1875	Attercliffe Station	1870	J. Smith, Attercliffe, Sheffield	120	Blue and white
1876	Attercliffe Station	1870	J. Smith, Attercliffe, Sheffield	120	Blue and white
1877	Attercliffe, near Sheffield	1870	A. Johnson, 11 Church Street,	120	Blue and white
1878	x				
1879	Brightside Lane, Sheffield	1870	G. Denton, Church Street, Attercliffe	200	Blue and white
1880	Attercliffe Station	1870	Joseph Smith, Don Foundry, Sheffield	200	Blue and black

It is not clear where their ground was; the church was at 747, Attercliffe Road and no longer exists as it was bombed in the Second World War. Attercliffe Station was opened in 1870, which was about a mile away from the church and it would have made sense to have a ground next to a railway station. In the 1874 Annual, the ground is described as 'being two miles from Victoria Station M.S. and L.R.' Brightside Lane is less than a mile from the church and was known locally as the Old Forge Ground.

Attercliffe - F.A. Cup Record 1871-1888
1886/87	1	Staveley	A	0-7
1887/88	1	Sheffield Heeley	A	0-9

Middlesbrough FC (1876) entered the Sheffield Association Challenge Cup and made the long journey south to play Attercliffe FC. In the following 1884 press report, Attercliffe lodge an objection against 'Ewbank', questioning whether he was from Middlesbrough or Pontefract:

"The Attercliffe v. Middlesbro' game appeared to be a good thing for the home team up to a very short time of the whistle being sounded, as Attercliffe had put on two goals, one a grand one by Curtis, and another by Pawson. Then, when the Middlesbro' men were deemed to be beaten, they came up in gallant fashion, and by magnificent crossing and judicious all-round play, they put on three goals in an incredibly short time, and won amid hearty cheers. An objection has been lodged by Attercliffe against Middlesbro' being allowed to run into the semi-final on the ground that Ewbank, who has had no small share in the making of the Middlesbro' team, is not now resident in the iron-making centre, but, as a matter of fact, has his head-quarters in Pontefract. The vanquished team of Saturday last do not claim the match, however; they simply ask the committee of the association to consider Ewbank's qualification, and, if they decide in favour of the Attercliffe Club, the latter will gladly avail themselves of the chance of reversing last Saturday's decision." [183]

Later in the same month the objection was overruled:

"FOOTBALL. SHEFFIELD CHALLENGE CUP. The protest which was lodged by the Sheffield Attercliffe Football Club against the Middlesbro' Club, who defeated them in the third round for the Sheffield Challenge Cup, has been over-ruled. The objection was to Mr. Jackson Ewbank not residing within certain limits to entitle him to play with the Middlesbro' team. Mr. Ewbank has been employed in Middlesbro' for some years past, and has been one of the principal members of the club since its commencement." [184]

Surrey FC (Sheffield, Yorkshire 1870-1882)
- Equal fifteenth Oldest Sheffield Football Club
- Equal forty-ninth Oldest Football Club in England

Origin: Church
"Surrey Football Club - At a meeting held last night at St. Marie's schoolroom, Surrey street, it was unanimously resolved on the motion of Messrs. Donovan and Whelan, that a club be formed bearing the above title. By the kind permission of his Grace the Duke of Norfolk, a ground has been obtained at Norfolk Park. A number of noted football players and athletes were enrolled as members, and a prosperous season is anticipated. The election of officers resulted as follows: President, Mr. D. Roberts; vice-president, Mr. C. Abel; treasurer, Mr. F. Whelan; Hon. Secretary, Mr. J. Bradbury. Committee: Messrs. J. P. Donovan (captain), M. Ellison, P. J. Fay, I. T. Thorpe, L. Barmascone, C. Lyons, T. Valentine, and G. Whelan. The opening match will be played on Saturday next, at Norfolk Park." [185]

St. Marie's Catholic Cathedral is situated on Norfolk Row in the Sheffield city centre and was opened in 1850. Three years later St. Mary's (Marie's) School opened on Surrey Street, so it would seem that Surrey FC was linked to the church school. The report also suggests a ground within Norfolk Park, but Farm Bank was on Shrewsbury Road, less than a mile north east of Bramall Lane and not within Norfolk Park as marked on an 1864 map. I would approximate its modern position as the far end of Barnes Court. The Farm was on the southerly edge of the 'Cholera Ground,' where 402 people were buried following an outbreak in 1832; it seems it was once part of Norfolk Park and the Duke donated the unconsecrated land when the death toll was threatening to overwhelm the existing church graveyards.

Football Annual	Ground	Foundation Date	Hon. Sec.	Members	Colours
1871	The Farm	1870	Frank Whelan, Farm Bank	80	Red and white
1872	The Farm	1870	Frank Whelan, Farm Bank	80	Red and white
1873	The Farm	1870	Frank Whelan, Farm Bank, Sheffield	100	Scarlet and white
1874	The Farm	1870	Frank Whelan, Farm Bank, Sheffield	100	Scarlet and white
1875	The Farm	1870	Frank Whelan, Farm Bank, Sheffield	100	Scarlet and white
1876	The Farm	1870	Frank Whelan, Farm Bank, Sheffield	100	Scarlet and white
1877	The Farm	1870	Frank Whelan, Farm Bank, Sheffield	100	Scarlet and white
1878	x				
1879	Queens Road	1868	J. J. Dowd, 91 Fitzwilliam Street	200	White jersey, navy blue knickers
1880	Queens Road	1868	J. J. Dowd, 91 Fitzwilliam Street	200	White jersey, navy blue knickers
1881	Queens Road	1868	J. J. Dowd, 91 Fitzwilliam Street	Reporting stopped in 1881 edition	White jersey, navy blue knickers

The first full match report I have found is from 1873:

"Surrey v. Brincliffe, First Teams – This match was played at the Farm on New Year's Day, when the Surrey Club won by one goal to nothing. It was apparent from the first that the Brincliffe Club were over matched, and they very wisely played excellently, and their rushes at times were very brilliant. Owing to the defensive tactics adopted by the Brincliffe team, it was difficult to signalise individual excellence on their side; the energy, however, displayed by their captain, Mr. G. H. Sampson, and the really excellent goal-keeping exhibited by Mr. W. H. Jackson, were perhaps the most conspicuous. The umpires were Mr. W. E. Able for Surrey, and Mr. Hallam for Brincliffe, and their decisions gave entire satisfaction." [186]

The club was described as 'flourishing' in 1881, but there was no more press after 1882.

Also formed in this year, from outside of Sheffield, is the very complicated story of **Rotherham FC (1870 – 1878)**. It is listed in the 1871 Football Annual as 'Rotherham,' with an 1870 foundation and a ground at Clifton Lane. This first incarnation was as a member of the Sheffield Association; but later Rotherham clubs seemed keener to join the breakaway New Association in 1877:

- Rotherham FC (1870-1878)
- Rotherham Wanderers (1873 -1880?) Joined Sheffield New Association in February 1879
- Lunar Rovers (1875 -1880) Joined Sheffield New Association in October 1879
- Thornhill FC (1877-1925) Became Rotherham County FC in 1905
- Rotherham Town (1877-1925) Merged with Rotherham County in 1925 to become: Rotherham United (1925-present)

Rotherham United claim an official foundation date of 1925 but at other online sites there are suggestions that the current club is linked to the 1870 club:

CHAPTER FIVE

"A team called Rotherham was founded in 1870 which became Rotherham Town. Another team called Thornhill was founded in 1877 which eventually became Rotherham County. Rotherham Town and Rotherham County were amalgamated in 1925 as Rotherham United." [187]

This is important if true, because under my classification this would mean that the Millers could claim 1870 as a foundation date and be the equal 13th oldest English football club, still playing today. The problem is that Rotherham football in the Victorian era was very (very) complicated. The 1871 Annual stated that Rotherham FC club was not a member of the Sheffield Association, but still listed the details and the fact that they played by the Sheffield Association rules and their first ground suggests cricketing gentlemen were involved, as Clifton Lane is still Rotherham Cricket Club's ground.

"Rotherham Football Club. During the past week, several gentlemen in Rotherham have been devoting their energies to a football club *(1870)*, and their efforts have so far been successful, that the opening match was played in a field on the Doncaster Road. Mr. Henry Hart is secretary and there is every likelihood that the club will be well supported." [188]

Football Annual	Ground	Foundation Date	Hon. Sec.	Members	Colours	Dressing Room
1871	Rotherham Cricket ground	1870	R. Hart, Market Place, Rotherham	90	Blue and white	Reporting did not start until 1873
1872	x					Reporting did not start until 1873
1873	Clifton Lane	1870	Charles H. Moss, Rotherham	100	Scarlet and white	On the ground
1874	Clifton Lane	1870	Charles H. Moss, Rotherham	100	Scarlet and white	On the ground
1875	Clifton Lane	1870	T. J. Lloyd, Effingham Works, Rotherham	100	Scarlet and white	On the ground
1876	Clifton Lane	1870	T. J. Lloyd, Effingham Works, Rotherham	100	Scarlet and white	On the ground
1877	Clifton Lane	1870	T. J. Lloyd, Effingham Works, Rotherham	100	Scarlet and white	On the ground
1878	x					
1879	x					
1880	x					
1881	x				Reporting stopped in 1881 edition	
1882	x					
1883	x					
1884	x					
1885	Still listed as plain 'Rotherham' and playing at Clifton Lane	1875	J. J. Thirwell, Nelson Street		Chocolate and light blue	St George's Hall

After the seven-year break between the 1878 and the 1885 Football Annuals, Rotherham FC was not the same club as the 1870 club and it is most likely to have been Rotherham Town FC. I think the following match report from 1873 is about Rotherham FC (1870), confirmed by the presence of a player called Lloyd, who may be the Hon. Sec. mentioned in the above table:

"Sheffield Club v Rotherham – A very interesting match between the above-named clubs was played at Bramall lane ground, Sheffield, on Saturday afternoon. Rotherham won the toss and kicked towards the road, and after playing about a quarter of an hour they secured a goal, which was well kicked by Mr. Lloyd. The home team had then the advantage of the wind and in a short time obtained a goal, the ball being kicked by Mr. Matthews. The remainder of the game was pretty equal, but as the wind was in the favour of the visitors the ball was never in the Sheffield goal. Messrs. J.C. and W. E. Clegg and Willey had some good runs, but were stopped by the fine back play of the Rotherham team. Time was called before any other score was made, consequently the match ended in a tie. In addition to the above-named gentlemen Messrs. Vickers and Fretson played well for Sheffield, so also did Messrs. Hickmott, Booth, and Roberts for Rotherham." [189]

In 1876 a Rotherham works team was launched called Phoenix Bessemer FC which is covered in the 1876 section, and by 1877 even more Rotherham clubs were on the scene:

- Thornhill FC (1877-1925) Became Rotherham County FC in 1905
- Rotherham Town FC (1877- 1925) Merged with Rotherham County in 1925 to become
- Rotherham United FC (1925 -present)

For present day Rotherham United to be able to claim a 1870 foundation date, the original Rotherham FC must have become either Thornhill or Town in 1877 or 1878. Certainly, the match reports for a 'Rotherham' seem to end with a game against Chesterfield; [190] the only clue from this critical time is:

"The progress of the game, however, has been so great in and about Rotherham that players who, of necessity, a few years ago confined themselves to the only club of the town, have this season declared for other teams, thus weakening the senior club committee's choice." [191]

This suggests the new clubs were taking Rotherham FC's players and weakening them, but to the extent of extinction or to relaunch as a newly named club? I can find no press supporting mergers and the team listings are meagre, making confident conclusions impossible. I will leave local historians to keep looking for the link back to 1870 for the Millers.

Rotherham Town FC won the Sheffield Association Challenge Cup two years in succession:

- 1888/89 Rotherham Town 2 – 1 Staveley. Final played at Bramall Lane.

- Replayed final 1889/90: Rotherham Town 1 – 0 Sheffield United. Final played at the ground of the Rotherham Swifts.

Rotherham Town FC was clearly a successful club and would survive into the 20th century, unlike many other local clubs, by following the route of professionalism. But it did not stop a Rotherham vicar in 1895 worrying about the soul of the game:

"A Vicar on Professional Football. Quite right in moderation. On Tuesday, speaking

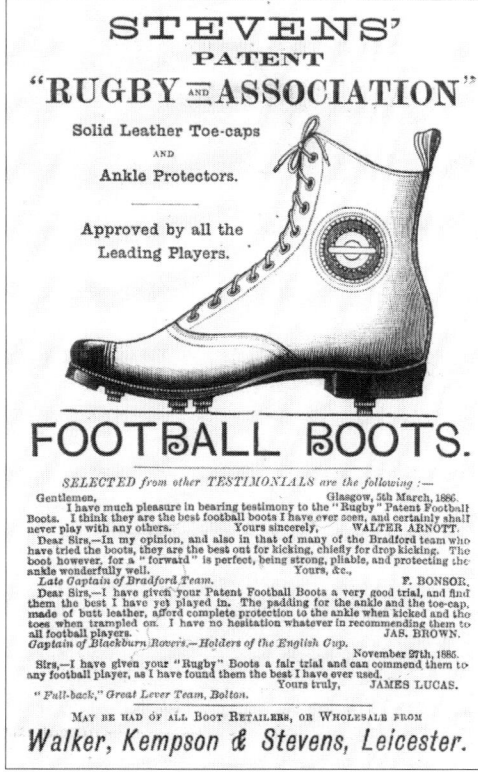

An advert from the 1887 Football Annual

at the opening of a bazaar in aid of the funds of Rotherham Town Football Club, the Vicar of Rotherham (The Rev. W. R. Pym) said he doubted whether the present fashion of football playing was wholly for the best interest of sport. One wanted to avoid the danger of making any sport a commercial transaction or speculation. He had not a word to say against professionalism. There was a large opening for professionals in the football field as well as in the cricket field, but he thought the system of playing matches with teams composed almost wholly or wholly of professionals might not be for the best interests of sport in the long run. If they went in for that it meant that with the club, instead of developing the bone, sinew, pluck and patience of the district, it became a matter of the longest purse. If it became a question of this kind the Rotherham district would not cut a very fine figure against the much more wealthy places." [192]

Perseverance (Temperance) FC (Sheffield, Yorkshire 1870-1896)
- Sixteenth Oldest Sheffield Football Club
- Equal fiftieth Oldest Football Club in England
- Member of the Sheffield New Association 1881

Origin: Temperance. The movement had a cricket team with the same name of 'Perseverance' in 1856 and was supported by Charles Clegg. I am grateful to Mike Bradbury [193] as I could only find evidence of Providence and Exchange merging in 1882 but his research points to the inclusion of Perseverance FC, making it a three-way merger:

"At the start of the 1882/83 season, it seems that the Perseverance suffered an internal wrangle which led to the club breaking up. Their original name was the Perseverance Temperance football club, so when two teams rose out of the ashes of Perseverance-named Sheffield Temperance and Park Grange- this suggests that the teetotallers from the Temperance side of the club remained true to their faiths, whilst the more recent recruits left and helped form the Park Grange (with members of the Exchange and Providence clubs)." [193]

The following three clubs, Exchange FC (1867-1882), Providence FC (1874-1882) and Perseverance FC (1870-1882), merged to become Grange Park in 1882 and played in the 1887 F.A. Cup, under that name. In 1889 Park Grange FC changed its name (back) to Exchange FC. (The full Park Grange Story is at Providence FC)

According to the 1872 Football Annual, Perseverance FC:
Founded: 1870
Number of members: 150
Club Ground: Norfolk Park (SE)
Code: Sheffield Association
Hon. Sec.: E.S. Drake, East Parade
Colours: White

In the following year's entry (1873 Football Annual) its numbers had reduced and they claim that they were founded a year earlier.
Founded: 1869
Code: Sheffield Association
Number of members: 100
Club Ground: Norfolk Park (S.E.)
Hon. Sec.: E.S. Drake
Colours: White with blue star

The first match report I was able to find for Perseverance FC was a return game against the British Workmen's Club at Clough Lane, reported in the Sheffield Daily Telegraph on Monday 04 April 1870. It doesn't 'persevere' very long in the Football Annuals, as there are no more mentions up to and including 1889.

"The Perseverance (Temperance) Football Club. This club held their second carnival at Bramall Lane yesterday *(1871)*. The day, though dull and threatening, held up during the sports, but caused a limited attendance, only about 500 spectators being present. The sports were under the management of Mr. J. C. Clegg as starter, Messrs. R. Higginbottom and J. Short as clerks of the course, aided by a numerous and efficient staff of stewards." [194]

In 1884, Perseverance FC crossed the Pennines to play the F.A. Cup holders in its newly merged incarnation, Park Grange FC; its players probably wished they hadn't bothered:

"BLACKBURN ROVERS v. SHEFFIELD PARK GRANGE. - The National Cup holders were in fine form on Saturday when they met the Park Grange representatives at Blackburn in the presence of a large number of spectators. The visitors only brought ten men, and had to have a substitute. In the first half the Rovers had all their own way, and before half time was called were credited with seven goals. The second half was even more in their favour, 10 goals more being scored, the Rovers thus winning by 17 goals to none." [195]

Walkley New Connexion FC (Sheffield, Yorkshire 1870- 1890)

- Equal seventeenth Oldest Sheffield Football Club
- Equal fifty-first Oldest Football Club in England
- Founder member of the Sheffield and District Football League in 1889/90

Origin: Church. Methodist New Connexion was a Protestant nonconformist church, also known as the Kilhamite Methodists. It was formed in 1797 by secession from the Wesleyan Methodists, and merged in 1907 with the Bible Christian Church and the United Methodist Free Churches to form the United Methodist Church. Walkley New Connexion was also the name of a cricket club from the 1860s. In 1851 it had five chapels in Sheffield but by 1881 it had increased to twelve.

Football Annual	Ground	Foundation Date	Hon. Sec.	Members	Colours
1873	Hillsbro'*	1870	W. J. Bentley. 258 Langsett Road, Sheffield	110	Scarlet and white
1874	Hillsbro'	1870	W. J. Bentley. 258 Langsett Road, Sheffield	110	Scarlet and white
1875	Hillsbro'	1870	W. J. Bentley. 258 Langsett Road, Sheffield	110	Scarlet and white
1876	x				
1877	Penistone Road	1870	W. J. Bentley. 258 Langsett Road, Sheffield	110	Scarlet and white
1878	x				
1879	x	1870	H. J. Bentley. 157 Grammar Street, Langsett Road, Sheffield	70	Scarlet and white
1880	x	1870	H. J. Bentley, Burnell Road, Sheffield	76	Scarlet and white

*In this instance Hillsbro' equates more specifically to Langsett Road in Hillsborough, opposite the Barracks where Sheffield FC played their first 'foreign' match.

The first match report found for Walkley New Connexion FC is from October 1870:

"The opening match of the Walkley New Connexion Football Club was played in a field in

Langsett Road on Saturday last. Sides were chosen by J. W. Bentley and C. Addy, and after an exciting contest of two hours' duration the match ended in favour of the former by two goals, the other side failing to score." [196]

In the next match, also in 1870, Walkley played the Engineers Volunteer Regiment: "Walkley New Connexion v. Engineers (first teams) took place on the ground of the former, on Langsett road. The ground was very heavy from the recent fall of snow. The match was keenly contested by both parties, but the Walkley team proved too strong for their opponents, scoring two goals, the military being unable to score. The goals for Walkley were obtained by T. Mallinson and J. Oates." [197]

Listed in the 1873 Football Annual as 'Walkley' FC, it had a productive 1874/75 season and had dropped the 'New Connexion' suffix, which was in press reports as well:

"Football. The Walkley Football Club – This club has had a very successful season having antagonised on no fewer than 27 occasions, 18 of which were first team contests and nine second. Of the total number played they have won 13, lost but five, and drawn nine. They have scored an aggregate of 43 goals to their opponents 20, a most satisfactory result." [198]

At some point before 1888 Walkley FC moved out to Crookes:

"Walkley football club – The annual dinner and presentation of prizes took place at the Old Grindstone Inn, Crookes, where the club is now established and has its ground, and was a most successful gathering – Mr. Geo. Willey proposed 'Success to the Local Association' and said that given continued good management, the association would be stronger during the ensuing season that it had ever been, notwithstanding a recent secession – In responding, Mr. A. W. Clayton, vice-president of the Association, said he was a strong advocate of unity, and was very pleased that the amalgamation of the two associations, which took place last year, had been productive of increased interest and success. – Mr. Senior proposed the toast of the evening, viz., 'Success to the Walkley club and the health's of the prize winners,' to which Mr. W. Cooke responded, after which the prizes were presented by Mr. Clayton. Songs and recitations were given by Messrs. Clayton, Gregory, Senior, Thorpe, H. Machon, and J. Fisher. Mr. A. Smith was an able accompanist." [199]

(The Old Grindstone Inn, Crookes, is even closer to the Lydgate Lane ground than the Ball Inn, used by Crookes FC, see next)

By the 1889/90 season, Walkley FC was a member of the Sheffield and District Football League and in October 1890 set an unwanted losing record in the F.A. Cup first round by losing 19 nil against Staveley FC. The score line may have been the club's epitaph for I can find no match reports for Walkley FC after that date.

Crookes FC (Sheffield, Yorkshire 1870-1903)

- Equal seventeenth Oldest Sheffield Football Club
- Equal fifty-first Oldest Football Club in England

Origin: Cricket. Based on the assumption that they originally played their football on the Lydgate Cricket pitch.

The ground referred to as 'Crookes' initially meant Lydgate Cricket pitch, which no longer exists but is marked by Lydgate Lane. The list of Hon. Secs. suggests a close link to the Ball Inn (171-173 Crookes, Sheffield S10 1UD). Whether J.C. Hand or F.S. Sellers were the landlords of the Ball Inn or whether it was used as a meeting place for the players is unknown. The pub was built in 1852, five years before a foot ball was kicked around in Sheffield, meaning the chosen name was probably designed to attract sports people of all persuasions. I spoke to Anne Marples, a Crookes historian, who pointed out that the 'Hallamshire Proprietory Bowling Club' was formed in 1863 and is still going strong today, based in Crookes. Interestingly a member of the New Football Association was called Hallamshire FC, formed in 1878 and playing at Lydgate; perhaps an offshoot from the Bowling Club?

Football Annual	Ground	Foundation Date	Hon. Sec.	Members	Colours
1873	Crookes	1870	James Wragg, Crookes	140	White
1874	Crookes	1870	J. C. Hand, Ball Inn, Crookes		White
1875	Crookes	1870	F. S. Sellers, Ball Inn, Crookes		White
1876	Crookes	1870	F. S. Sellers, Ball Inn, Crookes		White
1877	Crookes	1870	F. S. Sellers, Ball Inn, Crookes		White and red

As mentioned in the Broomhall FC section, by 1876 the Crookes football ground skirted a quarry, meaning the club had left the comforts of the Lydgate Cricket pitch. Anne Marples says:

"Although there were several quarries active in 1876, the most likely contender might be the one owned by the Sandersons, of Poplar Farm, on Cross Lane. They owned a lot of land, including a large field stretching from the corner of Cross Lane and Lydgate Lane. Right up to the end of where the children's playground is now. The land not being very profitable, they quarried it out, right down to the bedrock, as the stone there was a hard gritstone, so very valuable for sills, lintels and gateposts (still in evidence around Crookes). When the stone was all quarried out, they installed a ropeworks on the site, as rope was in demand for building the many houses at that time. Afterwards, the site was abandoned, so may have been used for games."

In 1873 Crookes FC were still at Lydgate Lane:

"CROOKES ATHLETIC SPORTS. The annual athletic sports, under the auspices of the Crookes Cricket and Football Club, took place yesterday (*1873*) in the cricket field, Lydgate Lane, Crookes. As it was the village feast, a considerable number of people flocked to the place, and the result was a large augmentation of the club funds. The weather was fine, and good programme was presented. Some of the running was very good, but time would be no criterion on account of the uneven nature of the ground. Mr. F. Harrison was the starter; Mr. W. Reaney, judge; and Mr. J. C. Hand, clerk of the course." [200]

The 1874/75 season was very successful:

"Crookes Association Club – This club has played 24 matches, of which they have won 14, lost 3, and drawn 6 first team contests 8 were won, 2 lost, and 4 drawn. Of the seconds 5 were won, 1 lost, and 2 drawn. In third teams 1 was won and 1 lost." [201]

There was fluidity in the clubs that players played for, in some cases, like the Clegg brothers, on a week to week basis. It was certainly the case in London Association football with players playing when there was a game on, regardless if it was 'their' team or not. In the following 1876 match report a 'J. Hunter' plays well and as previously mentioned, future England international and F.A. Cup winner, Jack Hunter, was born in Crookes; so this could be him helping his local club, when ordinarily his team was Heeley FC?

"Exchange v. Crookes (1st Teams.) – Played at Crookes on Saturday (1876), Exchange having won the toss, J. Hunter, for Crookes, kicked off downhill, when the play at once became very fast, the Exchange men playing well together, and in the short space of twenty minutes had scored three goals, Messrs. Ramsden, Orton, Anthony, and Marples making some splendid runs for them. This roused the Crookes men to renewed exertions, and J. Hunter, G. Clarke, and W. Wragg made great efforts to lower the Exchange goal, but without avail, as just before half time the Exchange men scored again, making four goals to nothing. On changing ends and with the hill in their favour the Exchange men played with renewed vigour, causing their opponents to act on the defensive, and when time was called the Exchange were the victors by nine goals to nothing. On the Exchange side all, without exception, played well, but the play of Messrs. Anthony, Orton, Ramsden, Hanson, E. Marples, and Houseley deserves special mention. On the other side of Messrs. J. Hunter, A. Barlow, E. Mounsey, W. Wragg, O. Wragg, and G. Clarke played best. The goals were kicked by W. Orton three, H. Storey three, T. Thorpe two, and J. Houseley one." [202]

(Bankers FC) Thursday Wanderers FC (Sheffield, Yorkshire 1870-1882)
- Equal eighteenth Oldest Sheffield Football Club
- Equal fifty-second Oldest Football Club in England
- Sheffield's first non-manual working class club
- Sheffield & Hallamshire Senior Cup Winners – 1878/79

Origin: Workplace. Team of bank clerks who became Thursday Wanderers. Began in season1870/1874 as Bankers FC (Football Annual 1874); in season 1875/1882 became Thursday Wanderers (Football Annual 1875).

In 1872 the Bank clerks played the 'Gentlemen' of Sheffield FC and lost 2-0 in a close game:

"The match was played yesterday, on the ground of the Sheffield Club, at East Bank. The weather was favourable for the game, and the ground in very fair order. Players. - Sheffield Club: F. Whelan (captain), A. Marsden, Jun. Willey, C. Chambers, B. Otley, H. Steel, H. Whelan, W. Marsden, A. Badger, and T. Furnell. Bank Clerks: B. Liddell (captain), A. V. Edlin, U. A. Coombe, J. H. Barber, E. Tateham, J. J. Chatterson, J. Green, A. Carlisle, J. Bambridge, W. Widdowson, and the substitute. Umpires, Messrs. Anderson and Dean." [203]

At the 1874 A.G.M., the clerks changed their name but annoyingly without explaining the reason. My (unproved) theory is that the clerks' working practices changed to a half day holiday on Thursdays and they took advantage of it to play their games on Thursdays:

"BANKERS' FOOTBALL CLUB. - At the general meeting of this club, held yesterday evening it was resolved that the name of the club be altered to that of the 'Thursday Wanderers.' The usual officers were elected, and Mr. Liddell was appointed delegate to the association for the ensuing year." [204]

From the Football Annual detail regarding kit colour, the bankers liked to be seen in the red:

Football Annual	Club Name	Ground	Foundation Date	Hon. Sec.	Members	Colours
1874	Bankers	Hunter's Bar	1870	J.H. Liddell, Union Bank	60	Scarlet
1875	Thursday Wanderers	Hunter's Bar	1870	J. Wild, Sheffield and Rotherham Bank.	60	Scarlet
1876	x					
1877	Thursday Wanderers	Hunter's Bar	1870	J. H. Barber jnr. Broomhall Park	80	Scarlet and navy blue
1878	x					
1879	Thursday Wanderers	Hunter's Bar	1874	R.A. Sorby, Park Grange	80	Scarlet and navy blue
1880	Thursday Wanderers	Hunter's Bar	1874	R.A. Sorby, Park Grange	80	Scarlet and navy blue

During my research, I was astounded to discover Thursday Wanderers FC playing against Crystal Palace FC. It seemed impossible that a team of amateurs based in London would travel north to play a team of bank clerks. The reality turned out to be more mundane. 'Thurlstone'

Crystal Palace FC was a team started by John Marsh, an ex-Wednesday player, in the village of Thurlstone, near Penistone. The first match he organised was against his old club:

"Thurlstone Crystal Palace Club (Fourteen) v. Wednesday (Eleven) – Mr. March selected the club he has been so long connected with in Sheffield as the one to open the season with the newly formed one at the little village where he has taken up his residence. About thirty players and friends mustered at the Victoria Station on Saturday afternoon, and arrived safely at Penistone per special carriage. They were met at the station by a representative of the home club, and conducted to a capital field just on the outside of the village. Here upwards of five hundred spectators gathered to witness the new game – to them – of football." [205]

Thurlstone Crystal Palace FC played a match against Thursday Wanderers FC in 1874, but failed to add the 'Thurlstone' prefix in the article, that so confused me initially:

"Thursday Wanderers v Crystal Palace, Thursday's match was played at Thurlstone yesterday afternoon and the Wanderers were victorious. The very high win prevailed and was a great detriment to the game, but not withstanding the Wanderers succeeded in scoring compared to their opponents nothing. The first was from a well-played kick by Wild, which was cleverly headed through posts by J. Willey. The second was got by *(illegible)* who succeeded in running the ball up the field and cleverly in between the goal posts, right over the goal keepers head. Messrs. J. Willey and Messrs. Beardshaw and Fay also played well for them, as did Mr. J. *(illegible)* from the Crystal Palace club." [206]

In November 1876, Thursday Wanderers FC benefitted from Sheffield FC's decision not to compete in the inaugural Sheffield Association Challenge Cup; mirroring their refusal to enter the Youdan Cup ten years previously. The move was a reaction from some Sheffield FC players interested in competing in the new trophy and the club they chose to play for was Thursday Wanderers FC. In the Cup match against Heeley FC, the Wanderers gained from the addition of a veritable who's who of Sheffield FC talent: most notably John C. Shaw playing his first match for a long time, as captain, Harry W. Chambers in goal, W.A. Matthews, A.W. Cursham and the two Sorby brothers.(Arthur William Cursham and his brother Henry 'Harry' were Notts County players by this point, but Arthur had played for Sheffield FC in the F.A. Cup match against Charles W. Alcock's Wanderers, in January 1876).

Balancing the 'importation" of outside help gained by Thursday Wanderers FC, Heeley FC played their own import, Peter Andrews from Glasgow (who together with Jimmy Lang represented Sheffield's first professional footballers). Was it a coincidence that the Sheffield FC players chose to play in a match against a player that to them represented the growing rise of professionalism? From the account of the game it was thrilling match played at Hunter's Bar, with Heeley FC winning by five goals to four.

Thursday Wanderer's FC transformation was not temporary; the quality players from Sheffield FC continued to play for the Wanderers in Cup matches and they imported even more quality, in the person of Ernest Greenhalgh. The club from this point is influenced greatly by the T. H. Sorby and R. A. Sorby, sons of Robert Sorby (Robert Sorby and Sons, Manufacturers and Merchants, Carver Street). The Sorby family was one of Sheffield's longest standing cutlery firms, with Robert Sorby in 1620 Sheffield's first ever Master Cutler. Both T.H. and R.A. Sorby had played for Sheffield FC in the 1875/76 F.A. Cup and by 1879 R.A. Sorby was Hon. Sec. of Thursday Wanderers FC.

Eventually Thursday Wanderers FC won the Sheffield Association Challenge Cup, against Heeley FC in the 1878/79 season, winning by 3 goals to 1, at a game watched by 6,000 spectators; played at Bramall Lane with Charles and William Clegg as umpires, the line-up was as follows:

CHAPTER FIVE

THURSDAY WANDERERS. - M. Ellison (goal), E. H. Greenhalgh (captain), W. Beardshaw (backs), T. C. Willey, J. H. Barber (half-backs), A. W. Cursham, H. A. Cursham, T. H. Sorby, R. A. Sorby, W. A. Matthews, H. Wood (forwards). Umpire, J. C. Clegg; referee, W. Pierce Dix. HEELEY. -A. Harvey (goal), R. Barringham, W. Moss (backs), J. Hunter (captain), T. A. Tomlinson, (half-backs), J. Tomlinson, P. Andrews, J. E. Deans, S. Scaife, R. Martin, J. Wild (forwards), W. E. Clegg, umpire.

The Sheffield press at this point did not seem concerned about the ongoing presence of Peter Andrews, Heeley's paid professional but there was disquiet in Sheffield footballing circles over the importation of three 'visitors' into the Thursday Wanderers team for the tournament. The addition of E. H. Greenhalgh and the Cursham brothers from Mansfield and Nottingham respectively, apparently did not break the rules:

"The club has acted strictly within the rules and nothing can be urged against them; but looking at the competition as members of the Sheffield Football Association, the introduction of members of the London Football Association-who have a challenge cup of their own, for which the three gentlemen named have played – is a question open to debate." [207]

Ernest Harwood Greenhalgh (born Mansfield, 6 March 1849 - 11 July 1922) was an English footballer who played for England as a full back in the first ever international match against Scotland and made 163 appearances for Notts County between 1869 and 1883. Eventually four members of the Greenhalgh family would play for Notts County. Ernest was the first ever player to make 100 appearances for Notts County and he found time to start a football club in his home town in 1870 calling it Mansfield Greenhalgh FC. In May 1894, Mansfield Town FC and Mansfield Greenhalgh FC amalgamated and become Mansfield FC, but had immediate financial difficulties and considered disbanding in 1895; it fought on until eventually ceasing in 1899. I can find no link from this point to the current Mansfield Town FC; it claims on its website to have begun as a team called Mansfield Wesleyans FC, started by Frederick Abraham and Thomas Cripwell, in 1897.

Henry 'Harry' Cursham

Arthur W. Cursham (1853-1884) and Harry A. Cursham (1859-1941) were sons of a vicar who both became England internationals. Arthur played for Notts County between 1876 and 1883 and was also a County cricketer. Henry 'Harry' Cursham also played for Notts County, scoring 208 goals between 1877 and 1891 and is the all-time record goal scorer in the F.A. Cup, with 49 goals; five more than Liverpool FC's Ian Rush.

The coverage in the 31st March 'Sheffield Independent' of the Thursday Wanderers victory in the Sheffield Association Challenge Cup received first billing in the football section with a full column of copy; this is followed by a report on a game between Spital FC v. Nottingham Forest and finally there is a quarter of a column on the F.A. Cup final between Clapham Rovers FC and the Old Etonians. Sheffield chauvinism plays a part of course, but you would think that the national tournament in its eighth year would have been of more interest to the Sheffield readers.

After a lull in the press reports, it seems Thursday Wanderers FC was back in 1882 playing the Old Rossallians. Rossall School was founded in 1844 on the Lancashire coast between Fleetwood and Cleveleys. In this match, Ernest H. Greenhalgh was playing for the opposition rather than

THE GOLDEN AGE OF SHEFFIELD AMATEUR FOOTBALL 1857-1876

the Wanderers and the Cursham brothers continued to 'moonlight' away from Notts County FC:

"Thursday Wanderers v. Old Rossallians. We understand that the revival of the once formidable Thursday Wanderers Football Club is being considered. It may be remembered that in 1878 the club in question carried off the Sheffield Association Challenge Cup, and they were in the habit of playing nearly every Thursday afternoon important matches, which afforded admirers of the game in this district much pleasure. We hear that on Thursday next (to-morrow) the old club meet, at Bramall Lane ground, a team of Old Rossallians and the following sides should afford an excellent match – Thursday Wanderers: W. E. Wake (goal), W. F. Beardshaw, A. T. Dobson, W. Robinson, J. H. Barber, A. W. Cursham, H. A. Cursham, E. Barber, H. Wood, C. E. Sorby, and another. Old Rossallians: F. W. Hotham, J. R. Napier, W. Mason, H. J. Gibson, E. H. Greenhalgh, P. H. Morton, V. Royle, C. P. Wilson, and three others." [208]

Gleadless FC (Sheffield, Yorkshire 1870-1880)
- Equal eighteenth Oldest Sheffield Football Club
- Equal fifty-second Oldest Football Club in England

Origin: Unknown. As mentioned in the Norton FC chapter, the Gleadless cricket team's nickname was the 'Etonians', so there is a very good story in there somewhere for someone to discover.

In 1871 Gleadless were described as 'newly-formed' and were outmatched by their opponents 'field tactics':

"Dronfield v. Gleadless – A match was played at Dronfield on Saturday between two teams of the Dronfield and Gleadless Football Clubs. After about fifteen minutes play the former made a goal, kicked by Geo. Milne, and neither side making another, Dronfield, of course, was the winner. Taking into account that Gleadless was but a newly-formed club, the players acquitted themselves very fairly. They were outmatched by their opponents in field tactics, a quality they will acquire and improve in by experience" [209]

"Gleadless v. Rawmarsh – This match took place on Saturday (1872) on the ground of the former, and ended in a victory for Gleadless, who obtained two goals to their opponents nothing. On behalf of Gleadless Messrs. C. White, H. Ward, J. Jones, and J. Martin, did good service. Messrs. Lancashire, Lourative, Rollinson and Goddard played well for Rawmarsh." [210]

"Gleadless Football Club Athletic Sports. Yesterday afternoon (1873), the annual athletic sports of the above club took place in a field kindly lent by Mr. John Rhodes, of Charnock Hall. About 700 persons were present. The Handsworth Woodhouse Brass Band attended, and, under the leadership of Mr. W. Cooke, played a selection of popular music. Messrs. G. Mottram and W. Jackson were the judges, Mr. J. Plant starter, and Mr. J. Martin clerk of the course; and these gentlemen, assisted by an efficient body of stewards, fulfilled their duties to everybody's satisfaction." [211]

Football Annual	Ground	Foundation Date	Hon. Sec.	Members	Colours
1874	Gleadless	1870	James Martin, Gleadless	98	White
1875	Gleadless	1870	G. Kirk, Gleadless	98	White
1876	Gleadless	1870	G. Kirk, Gleadless	98	White
1877	Gleadless	1870	J. Spottiswood, Deep Pits, Gleadless	98	White
1878	x				
1879	Gleadless	1870	J. Spottiswood, Deep Pits, Gleadless	60	White
1880	Gleadless	1870	J. Spottiswood, Deep Pits, Gleadless	60	White

139

CHAPTER FIVE

There is no specific detail about exactly where the ground was in Gleadless: perhaps the Common? The field lent by the owner of Charnock Hall would be in the approximate area of today's Gleadless library.

Lockwood Brothers FC (Sheffield, Yorkshire 1870- 1888)
- Equal nineteenth Oldest Sheffield Football Club
- Equal fifty-fifth Oldest Football Club in England
- Sheffield's first industrial working class club
- Winners of the Sheffield Association Challenge Cup in 1883/84 and 1884/85

Origin: Workplace. The club was probably founded by George Francis Lockwood the grandson of the founder, and W. Lockwood (possibly one of the brothers?) who played in the match for Sheffield FC against London on December 2nd 1871 at Bramall Lane. George Francis Lockwood had studied at the Sheffield Collegiate school, leaving in 1866. The members were made up of the factory employees of this file steel and cutlery firm (74, Arundel Street); by 1882 the Club had

MESSRS. LOCKWOOD BROTHERS, ARUNDEL-STREET

140 members and they played regular matches against another local firm, Joseph Rodgers and Sons, who were only about a mile away.

There is no mention of Lockwood Brothers FC in early editions of the Football Annual, with the first mention in 1880:

Founded: 1870
Number of members: 137
Club Ground: Hunter's Bar, Ecclesall Road
Dressing room: Noah's Ark, Thomas Street
Code: Sheffield Association
Hon. Sec.: J. W. Coombs, 54 Myrtle Road, Heeley
Colours: Navy blue
Lockwood Brothers belatedly joined the Sheffield Association in 1879. [212]

The 1864 map of Hunter's Bar shows plenty of open space in the immediate area; Mike Bradbury in his book 'Lost Teams of the North' has the ground placed between the two current roads of Bruce and Hiscott. Judging from the 1864 map, this would have been a river meadow skirting south down to the Porter Brook. The pub they met in was on Thomas Street just over a mile away, so perhaps the ground was a bit further north east closer to the pub and their actual factory? It is worth mentioning here that the Collegiate School is around half a mile from their likely ground. The Football Annual mentions then cease until 1887, when they push their foundation date back to 1868. By then they were playing at Ecclesall Road, changing at the Levair Hotel and still playing in blue. Their Hon. Sec. was by then J.A. Frost of the Red Lion Hotel, Charles Street, Sheffield. All this information was repeated for the following year in 1888.

As mentioned in Chapter Four, Lockwood Brothers FC were losing finalists in the Sheffield Association Challenge Cup in 1882/83, but won it 1883/84 and 1884/85.

They first entered the F.A. Cup in 1881:

1881/82	1	Heeley	A	1-5
1882/83	1	Macclesfield Town	H	4-3
	2	Wednesday	A	0-6
1883/84	1	Sheffield FC	H	4-1
	2	Rotherham Town	H	3-1
	3	Staveley	A	0-1
1884/85	1	Sheffield FC	H	0-3
1885/86	1r	Notts Rangers	A	0-4

In the 1886/87 season, Lockwood Brothers FC gained five Wednesday players, who had failed to register for the Cup in time; this gave Lockwood Brothers an excellent run to the F.A. Cup fifth round. This experience contributed to the discontent in the Wednesday camp, which would result in it becoming professional in the following year. (More in Chapter Eight)

	1	Long Eaton Rangers	H	1-0
	2	Cleethorpes	A	4-1
	3	Nottingham Forest	H	2-1
	4	Bye		
	5r	West Bromwich Albion	N	1-2
1887/88	1	Sheffield FC	A	1-3
	2	Bye		
	3	Derby Junction	A	1-2

In spite of the Wednesday F.A. Cup experience, Lockwood Brothers FC remained defiantly amateur, looking for kindred spirits from north of the border. In 1888 they played Clyde of Glasgow at Sheaf House with 1,000 spectators and lost 2-4. The team sheets were:

"CLYDE OF GLASGOW. - W. Chalmers, goal: E. Sawers, R. Buchanan, backs; J. Pollock, J. Drummond, J. M'Laughlan, J. Collins, W. M'Lure, G. Cochrane, R. M'Farlane, and T. Stark, forwards. Umpire, Mr. J. Seaton. LOCKWOOD BROTHERS. - C. Creswick, goal; G. Crawshaw, M. Whithain, backs; L. M'Loughlin, T. Milner, W. Jones, half-backs; J. Sellars, W. Madin, T. Austin, G. A. Shaw, and A. White. Umpire, Mr. W. Harris. Referee, Mr. T. Hardman." [213]

Alliance FC (Sheffield, Yorkshire 1870-1880)

- Equal nineteenth Oldest Sheffield Football Club
- Equal fifty-fifth Oldest Football Club in England

Origin: Temperance. The 'United Kingdom Alliance' was a temperance movement of which William Clegg was a leading proponent, joining Perseverance FC as Sheffield's second teetotal footballing outfit.

According to the 1879 Football Annual –

Founded: 1870
Number of members: 50
Club Ground: Norfolk Park
Hon. Sec.: W.H. Seagrave, 51 Trafalgar Street, Sheffield
Colours: Red white and blue

CHAPTER FIVE

The above details were repeated in the 1880 edition with the exception that the members had gone up to 60.

In 1873 they played a bad-tempered match against a club called 'Garden Street', which never joined a local Football Association. Garden Street still exists in central Sheffield and at the time would have been heavily industrialised.:

"ALLIANCE (TEMPERANCE) v. GARDEN STREET. - A game was played between these clubs on the ground of the former on Saturday, and resulted in favour of Garden street by three goals to one. Two goals were scored by the teetotallers, but one was disallowed. On the part of Garden street, the game was not very friendly towards the teetotallers. Messrs. Horsfield, Swift, Seagrave, and Adams played well on behalf of the Alliance, as did Messrs. Gorrill, Eyre, and the brothers Jennett for Garden street." [214]

The following A.G.M. report from 1879 shows that there was a heavy family involvement from the Cleggs, supporting their favourite cause of Temperance:

"ALLIANCE FOOTBALL CLUB.- At the annual general meeting the following were elected officers:- President, Councillor W. J. Clegg: vice-president, Councillor J. C. Clegg: Mr. W. E. Clegg, Mr. W. N. Swift; hon. secretary, W. H. Seagraves, 51. Trafalgar street; honorary assistance secretary, H. C. Cooke: treasurer, Mr. H. Grafton; committee, Messrs. Parkin, W. B. Wright, J. Cooke, W. Wainman, J.W. Newsome, W. Heeley, H. Owen, and W. Seagraves; delegates to S F. A., Mr. W. N. Swift, and Mr. W. Y. Adams; delegate to Accident Society, Mr. J. V. Hosfield; captain, W. Y. Adams." [215]

Talbot FC (Talbot Street FC) (Sheffield, Yorkshire 1870-1880)

- Equal nineteenth Oldest Sheffield Football Club
- Equal fifty-fifth Oldest Football Club in England

Origin: Cricket. The Talbot Cricket Club was playing as early as 1858 and I have made the assumption that they formed a football club; unfortunately, it is not named in the Football Annual until the 1879 edition, nine years after its stated foundation date.

> According to the 1879 Football Annual –
> Founded: 1870
> Number of members: 65
> Club Ground: Norfolk Road
> Hon. Sec.: W. Tummon, Gell Street
> Colours: Blue and grey
> According to the 1880 Football Annual
> Founded: 1870
> Number of members: 65
> Club Ground: Park Hill Lane
> Hon. Sec.: W. Tummon, Gell Street
> Colours: Blue and grey

Talbot FC was the first Sheffield club to list Norfolk Road as a ground and moved the following year a mile or so north to Park Hill. (Talbot Street is just around the corner from Norfolk Road.)

The earliest press report I was able to find for Talbot FC is for 1873:

"Norton Bible Class v. Talbot Street (1st Twelves) – A friendly game of football was played on Saturday on the ground of the latter, and resulted in a victory for Talbot Street by two goals to one." [216]

By 1875 Talbot FC's playing record was very good:

"Talbot Street Football Club – The closing match of the above club was played on Saturday, in the form of a match between the married and single members, and ended in a tie, each side securing a goal. During the season 27 matches have been played, of which 18 have been won, three lost, one tied, and five drawn." [217]

In 1876 Talbot FC played a new team that had sprung up, called 'Heeley Victoria', another team with no records of joining either Sheffield Association and no press coverage:

"TALBOT STREET v. HEELEY VICTORIA (1st Teams). - This match was played on Saturday, on the ground of the latter at Heeley. Heeley won the toss, and kicked down hill, but the Talbot men found the Heeley players plenty to do to defend their goal. Half time was called, and Talbot street had to kick down hill, and soon obtained a goal, got by W. Tummon. Play continued, and Talbot street soon captured the Heeley goal again. Nothing more was scored up to time, and Talbot street thus won easily by three goals to nothing. For the victors Messrs. T. Hardman, Bros. Wild, J. Bingley, and H. Fletcher played well, and for the losers Messrs. Joe Thorpe, H. Parker, Goodall, and Earnshaw worked hard." [218]

Having listed its details in the 1879 Football Annual, the club match reports ceased after 1880, making Talbot FC one of the more enigmatic of the Sheffield clubs.

1871

In the year that the Rugby Football Union and the Football Association Challenge Cup both started, twenty-eight Association clubs were founded across England, including Reading FC, the 6th Oldest League Club. Of those twenty-eight clubs, just three came from Sheffield and a second club from Rotherham, **Kimberworth FC (1871-1879)**.

Football Annual	Ground	Foundation Date	Hon. Sec.	Members	Colours
1874	Kimberworth	1871	J. Hall, Kimberworth	70	Blue and white
1875	Kimberworth	1871	G. Stansfield, Kimberworth		Blue and white
1876	Kimberworth	1871	G. Stansfield, Kimberworth		Blue and white
1877	Kimberworth	1871	F. Hall, Kimberworth		Blue and white
1878	x				
1879	Kimberworth	1871	F. Hall, Kimberworth	31	Blue and white
1880	Kimberworth	1871	F. Hall, Kimberworth	49	Black and white

The first match report I found for Kimberworth FC was from 1876:

"Kimberworth v. Ecclesfield (1st team) – This match was played on the ground of the former on Saturday last, Ecclesfield won the toss and kicked off with a strong wind in their favour, and after about ten minutes' play secured a goal kicked by Birkhead, quickly followed by another, the ball rebounding from one of the Kimberworth players. After the change of ends the Kimberworthites set to work and quickly secured three goals, kicked by M. Cook, W. Gregory and M. Richardson respectively, thus leaving Kimberworth the victors by three goals to two. Special mention must be made of Messrs. T. Beet, J. Jackson, and Birkhead for Ecclesfield; and for Kimberworth Messrs, T. Corbett, T. Duke, and M. Cook played well." [219]

New leather footballs in this period cost between half a crown and fourteen shillings, so an expensive game of football was played with the iron and steel works side 'Brown, Bayley and Dixon' later in 1876:

CHAPTER FIVE

"Kimberworth v. Brown, Bayley and Dixon – Mr. H. Bayley, hon. Secretary of Brown, Bayley and Dixon's Club, writes: Will you kindly correct the report in your issue on Monday of the above match, played on Saturday on the ground of the former? The match most certainly ended in a draw, on account of the ball bursting eighteen minutes before time, the Kimberworth party not having another ball fit play with. Two were burst during the game. It was fully understood on both sides, when our men left the field, that it was to be considered a drawn match, and for Kimberworth to claim a win under these circumstances is very unfair indeed. If you will be good enough to correct your report in tomorrow's issue, we will be obliged." [220]

Millhouses FC (Sheffield, Yorkshire 1871-1881)
- Equal twentieth Oldest Sheffield Football Club
- Equal sixty-second Oldest Football Club in England

Origin: Unknown. Probably cricket.

Football Annual	Ground	Foundation Date	Hon. Sec.	Members	Colours	Dressing Room
1875	Millhouses	1871	F. Lowe, 46 Woodhead Road	130	Scarlet and black	Robin Hood Inn
1876	Millhouses	1871	F. Lowe, 46 Woodhead Road	130	Scarlet and black	Robin Hood Inn
1877	Millhouses	1871	T. Gill, Banner Cross	130	Scarlet and black	Robin Hood Inn
1878	x					
1879	Millhouses	1871		120	Scarlet and black	Robin Hood Inn
1880	Millhouses	1871	W. Lawton, 70 Bramall Lane	130	Scarlet and black	Robin Hood Inn

In 1872 'Tippler' Shaw played for Millhouses FC, so presumably it was not a Temperance team!:

"MILLHOUSES v. DRONFIELD (1ST TEAMS) These teams met on the ground of the former. Millhouses won the toss, and elected to kick down hill. Some fine screw kicks by J. Wragg soon placed the Dronfield goal in jeopardy, but the 'kick in' failed to put them through. Nothing being scored at half time ends were changed, and both teams set to work in good earnest, Dronfield especially playing with great vigour. The umpire's voice calling time brought a capital match to a close, it being then nearly dark, neither party having scored. For Millhouses: - Messrs. J. Wragg, 'Tippler' Shaw, T. Buttery, L. Jackson, and J. Houseley played exceedingly well; and for Dronfield, Messrs. Cotterill, Naylor, Crump, Bennett, and Champion distinguished themselves." [221]

In the 1873/74 season, Millhouses FC was a hard team to beat:

"The Millhouses Football Club – This rising suburban club had played 21 matches during the past season, of which they have placed 10 to their credit, have lost but 4, and drawn the balance, 7 - a very creditable performance." [222]

In the following 1878 match Tomlinson scored against Millhouses for Heeley with a pitch-long dribble:

"Football. Heeley v Millhouses (1st teams).These clubs met on Saturday at Meersbrook Park, where a numerous company assembled to witness the play. Heeley won the toss, and T. Lawson kicked off for Millhouses. It soon became apparent that the home team were much too good for their opponents, for in about ten minutes J. Wild secured the first goal for Heeley after some nice crossing play by the forwards. Just after this R. Martin scored another goal by a splendid kick from the low side. Nothing further was scored up to half-time, but after changing ends the Heeleyites found plenty of work for the Millhouses backs and goalkeeper, the latter having to use his hands several times in quick succession. After about a quarter of an hour's play Heeley obtained another goal from a free kick, and soon afterwards J. Tomlinson took the ball unaided right from one end to the other, and scored a fourth goal (one of the finest pieces of play ever seen in a football field). Heeley thus won by four goals to nothing. For Heeley, the back play of J. Hunter, U. Moss, and S. A. Tomlinson was particularly good, and the forward play of J. Tomlinson, J. Wild, and R. Martin was excellent. For Millhouses T. Lawson kept goal splendidly, and two of their backs (whose names did not transpire) played in good form." [223]

The following 1878 report alludes to the world's first ever floodlit football match on 14th October 1878, (which is covered in more detail later in the book):

"The Cup tie between Millhouses and Elsecar. To the Football Editor – In reply to John Gill's letter of the 3rd inst., I beg to state that his statement is quite incorrect with reference to the cup tie, Elsecar v. Millhouses. He states that I use my hands underneath the goal line. Certainly, I did use them, but I was fully four yards in front of the goal; and if the electric light had been in use, as at Bramall lane, he might have seen clearly, as he states the umpire could not see without the above. Again, the ball was confined to the Millhouses territory during the last fifteen minutes, and also when the spectators closed in on the ground – Yours, &c., M. Harrison, goalkeeper." [224]

Exchange Brewery FC (Sheffield, Yorkshire 1871- 1880)

- Equal twentieth Oldest Sheffield Football Club
- Equal sixty-second Oldest Football Club in England

Origin: Workplace. Exchange Brewery FC first appears in the 1875 Football Annual alongside Exchange FC (1867), so it is totally different club based in the Burngreave area. Ale and porter brewers, and maltsters, Exchange Brewery, was originally based at 4, Bridge Street in the 1850s but relocated to Fox Street in the Burngreave area of Sheffield.

Football Annual	Ground	Foundation Date	Hon. Sec.	Members	Colours
1875	Fox Street	1871	J. Chatterton, Exchange Brewery	100	Amber and black
1876	Fox Street	1871	J. Chatterton, Exchange Brewery	100	Amber and black
1877	Fox Street	1871	A. J. Crowder, Exchange Brewery	100	Amber and black
1878	x				
1879	Fox Street	1871	A. J. Crowder, Exchange Brewery	50	Amber and black

The 'Volunteers' Engineers FC was still playing football in 1874:

"A well-contested match at football was played on the ground of the Exchange Brewery, Fox Street and Nottingham Street, on Saturday. No goal was obtained until ends were changed at half time. In a very few minutes after, H. Thompson kicked a goal for Exchange Brewery. Afterwards the Engineers got a goal kicked by Bussey. John Nichols kicked a goal for the Exchange Brewery, which was objected to by the Engineer's captain, but the umpire allowed another goal for the Exchange Brewery. Thus, the brewers won by two goals to their opponents' one." [225]

Exchange Brewery FC was Wednesday's first opponents at its new ground at Sheaf House after moving from Myrtle Road in 1877:

"Wednesday v. Exchange Brewery. (Cup tie). It was rather unfortunate for Exchange Brewery that they were drawn in the first round of the Cup ties with such a strong club as the Wednesday. Their most sanguine supporters could scarcely have anticipated victory in the match on Saturday on the new Wednesday ground, at Sheaf house, but that the Brewery team were fully justified in entering the competition there cannot be two opinions, for though they were defeated by five goals to none, they possess many excellent and plucky players, who would have shown to greater advantage against ordinary opponents. Notwithstanding showery weather, a capital attendance assembled to witness the contest. Losing the toss, the Wednesday captain was agreeably surprised on his side being deputed to kick downhill. The reason for this doubtless was that the Brewery party, possessing the heavier physique, their captain thought they would last longer; but it was bad policy nevertheless, as the rain threatened every moment to render the ground soft to work upon, and during the last half drenching showers actually did fall. It is not our intention to enter into details of the play. Suffice it to say that at the start the Exchange men held their antagonists very tight, and at one time appeared about to assume the command. This, however, was only a flash in the pan. Gathering their forces, the Wednesday forwards swooped down upon the opposing host and scored their first goal in a scrimmage. Before the end of half-time three other goals had been secured, F. Butler, Carr, and Mr. J. C. Clegg being the executants. At the change it was thought that the Brewery would at least score, but the anticipation was not realised, as Wednesday fully maintained their own, and actually obtained another goal up hill. Thus they proved victorious by five to none. The Messrs. Clegg, the Messrs. Stacey, Stratford, Bishop, Bingley, and Butler excelled for Wednesday: and for the Brewery, Hudson, White, Bailey, and Fogg. The contending teams were: Wednesday: Messrs. J. C. and W. E. Clegg, Messrs. W. H. and F. Stacey, F. Butler, H. Muscroft, E. Buttery, W. H. Carr, T. Bishop, E. L. Stratford, and J. Bingley. Exchange Brewery: C. Hudson, W. Bailey, G. and J. Taylor, E. Parkin, G. Barker, J. Greenwood, C. White, F. Fogg, G. Haslam, and G. Solkend." [226]

All Saints' Night School FC (All Saints' Victoria FC) (Sheffield, Yorkshire 1871- 1883)

- Twenty-First Oldest Sheffield Football Club
- Sixty-Fifth Oldest Football Club in England
- A member of the Sheffield New Association by 1881, as All Saints Wanderers FC
- England's Oldest 'State' School Football Club

Origin: School. The All Saints' school opened in 1871 in Ellesmere Road [227] and by January 1872 housed 300 boys, 300 girls and 300 infants. [228] At some point the night school part of this school formed a football club; the Football Annual has an 1871 foundation for the club but this could have been a reference to when the actual school formed rather than the football club, so I have given them the benefit of the doubt.

Throughout England, many other earlier football clubs were started by old boys from various *public schools* after they left school; Forest FC and Harrow Chequers FC, were both started by old boys from Harrow school. In 1841 St. Mark's College (Chelsea, London), an Anglican Teacher Training College, became the *first state college* to form a football team; followed in 1870 by Saltley Teacher Training College FC, which carries the accolade of the first football team in Birmingham. Sheffield's All Saints' Night School FC is different because it is a state school not a state college that formed a football team. This modest club from 1871 is the first state school football club I have found formed in England. The second state school (non-public) football club didn't begin until 1876 when the Hanover United FC formed. This London outfit was the brainchild of two very famous names from Victorian football: Quintin Hogg and A.F. Kinnaird (later Lord Kinnaird). Quintin Hogg played for Wanderers, Old Etonians, Civil Service and

Hanover United, and won an F.A. Cup runners up medal for the old Etonians in 1876. Arthur F. Kinnaird played for both the Old Etonians and the Wanderers FC; he appeared in nine of the first eleven F.A. Cup finals between 1873 and 1883, the most of any player in the history of the competition, and was on the winning side on five occasions. Kinnaird and Hogg started the 'Ragged School & Mission for Boys' in York Place, (formerly Of Alley, off the Strand) using their own money in 1864; their philanthropic venture eventually evolved into a social and athletic club called the Junior Hanover Athletic, then Hanover United FC and finally Polytechnic FC. Another state school football club started in 1876 was Goldthorn FC, better known nowadays as Wolverhampton Wanderers; either way, Sheffield's All Saints' Night School FC beats both clubs by a good five years.

The following report states that the All Saints' Night School FC merged with Burngreave Victoria in 1876:

"ALL SAINTS' VICTORIA FOOTBALL CLUB. - At a meeting in All Saints' school, at which members of the All Saints' Night School and the Burngreave Victoria football clubs were present, it was decided that these two clubs amalgamate, and that they hence forth be known as All Saints' Victoria. The following were elected officers for the ensuing season: - President, Mr. John S. Watson; vice-presidents, Messrs. Henry J. Hobbiss and P. F. Cadman; treasurer, Mr. John B. Toyne; hon. secretary, Mr. George Batty, 44 Earsham street, Spital hill: committee: Messrs. J. Peck, George Oxley, Henry J. Carr, John Bingham, John Bardill, J. Whittington, George Innman, and Charles Green." [229]

The first match report I found for the school is from 1875, and covers a match played at Carwood Lane; this address no longer exists, but modern day Carwood Road is nearby:

"ALL SAINTS' NIGHT SCHOOL v. ALL SAINTS' CLUB (with six scratched). - Played at Carwood lane, and a well contested game ended in a tie-each side scoring a goal. That for the school was kicked by Norton, while Thompson performed a similar service for the club. The play of G. Batty, Holleyhead, Elliot, and Robinson, for their respective sides was very good." [230]

In 1875, struggling to get a team up for a Monday match, they combined with Pye Bank:

"Norfolk Works (mixed team) v. All Saints' Night School and Pye bank. - A match having been arranged between Norfolk Works 2nd team and All Saints' Night School, and the six of All Saints finding it difficult to get a team of their own for a Monday match, it was arranged that they should get a team where they could, and Norfolk Works played a mixed team. Therefore the match was played on Monday at Brightside-lane, and after a very evenly contested game resulted in a draw, neither side scoring. The play of the united team was very good. The same can be said of S. Charles, C. White, W. Loukes, W. Allen, J. Gardiner, and R. Longwell for Norfolk Works." [231]

"All Saints' Victoria v. Pyebank, 2nd Teams – Played at Hallcar Lane on Saturday (1876). Pyebank won the toss, and All Saints' put the ball in motion and after a pleasant game All Saints' were declared the victors with two goals to one. The play of both teams was very good, but that of E. Bennett, J. R. Gibson, J. Chance, J. Holleyhead, and J. Bardill, for All Saint's; and J. T. Reaney, J. Simpson – Leavesley, T. Marsden, and J. Carrier, for Pyebank, deserves special mention." [232]

All Saints' Victoria FC's ground is listed in the Football Annual as Hallcarr Lane which also no longer exists, but it shows in early directories as being in the district of Brightside. The only similar sounding road in the right area is Hallcar Street which is half a mile away from Carwood Road.

According to the 1879 Football Annual –

CHAPTER FIVE

Founded: 1871
Number of members: 100
Club Ground: Hallcarr Lane, Sheffield
Hon. Sec.: G. Batty, 72 Petre Street, Sheffield
Colours: Red and navy blue

The 1880 Football Annual has the same information except that All Saints' Victoria FC's membership had gone down to 80 members and it was playing at Grimesthorpe, Sheffield, with a new Hon. Sec. called G.C. Allat of 8 Clun Road, Sheffield. The following is the first press mention to include a full team line-up for an All Saints' game in 1881:

"ATTERCLIFFE v. ALL SAINTS' VICTORIA. This match was played at Brightside lane on Saturday. The weather was bitterly cold, and the attendance but small. The ground was very slippery and covered with ice in several places. Both sides were men short and had to engage several substitutes. Attercliffe had but two of their regular team playing, but were supported by one of their old members, A. Malpas, one of the Wednesday Cup team. The other side had also secured the services of several men, members of other teams, and although they were probably as a body the best players, Attercliffe ultimately won by one goal to nothing, secured for them principally by a well-centred ball by Malpas to Allen, who shot the ball through cleverly. Malpas, Hibberd, and Jackson did excellent service for the victors, as did also W. Hall and several on the other side. The names of the players are appended: - All Saints' Victoria: G. Booth (goal), J. Holleyhead, J. Clarke, B. Bennett, G. Robinson, C. Green, W. E. Jaquee, A. Booth, C. Hall, W. Hall, and J. Stevens. Attercliffe: A. Jackson (goal), A. Malpas, G. Barber, F. Johnson, T. Morrell, H. Shephard, R. B. Allen, R. Hibberd, T. Charles, F. Johnson, ad J. Emanuel. Umpires, Messrs. H. Fletcher and J. Jallands. Referee, Mr. G. C. Allflat." [233]

1872

Twenty-One English Association clubs started in 1872, of which only five still ply their skills today: Macclesfield FC, Kettering FC, Bury St Edmunds FC and Kidderminster FC. The fifth team of 1872 that is still extant, was a team made up of active students; Oxford University A.F.C. (O.U.A.F.C) was the first school or college team to really make a mark in Association football. According to the 1885 Football Annual its ground was 'The Parks' (where the Centaurs, the University second team still play their matches today) and their dressing room was the King's Head public house. The O.U.A.F.C would become by far England's most successful school or college team by dint of winning the F.A. Cup in 1874 and finishing the competition as runners-up in 1873, 1877 and 1880.

Of those sixteen long defunct teams of 1872, five came from Sheffield.

Brightside FC (Sheffield, Yorkshire 1872 -1879)
- Twenty-Second Oldest Sheffield Football Club
- Seventy -second Oldest Football Club in England

Origin: Unknown. There had been a Cricket club in the area since at least 1868.
The first match report I found for Brightside FC was from 1872:
"AN ELEVEN OF ATTERCLIFFE CHRIST CHURCH v. FIRST OF BRIGHTSIDE. - These teams also met, and after a good match Christ Church won by 1 goal to 0, kicked by W, H.

Football Annual	Ground	Foundation Date	Hon. Sec.	Members	Colours	Dressing Room
1874	Brightside	1872	J.F. Hall, Norbury, Pitsmoor	100	Yellow, red cap	
1875	Brightside	1872	W. Wilkinson, Grimesthorpe	150	Yellow, red cap	
1876	Brightside	1872	W. Wilkinson, Grimesthorpe	150	Yellow, red cap	
1877	x					
1878	x					
1879	x					
1880	Mill Lane, Brightside	1872	S.J. Robinson, Brightside Works	80	Scarlet and dove	Bridge Inn

Jackson, Messrs. Widdowson and Ash played well for Attercliffe, and Messrs. Wilkinson and Hudson showed promising play for Brightside." (234)

It seems their ground is more specifically located at Blackburn Meadows:

"Brightside v Heeley (1st teams) – The above contest took place on the Brightside ground at Blackburn Meadows*, on Saturday last *(1874)*. Up to half time neither side could gain any advantage, but when the ends were changed Heeley immediately obtained a goal, which fell to the credit of A. Wood. Brightside now went at it with a will, and in less than five minutes they not only scored a goal but took away the posts, such a strong rush being made; H. Ash passing the ball through for his side. For Brightside, H. Ash deserves especial mention; also Messrs. Wilkinson, Hall, and Hanson played well; and for Heeley, Messrs. A. Wood, J. Hunter, J. Osborne, and W. Beard, did good service. The match ended in a tie. The home team had the best of the game, but Heeley played two men short." (235)

"Heeley v. Brightside (1st Teams) – These clubs contested on the ground of the latter at Blackburn Meadows, on Saturday *(1874)*. Brightside won the toss, and kicked with a slight breeze, and this was the only advantage, as the ground is quite level. In about ten minutes S. Scaife secured a goal for Heeley, and soon after the change of ends J. Bird secured a second for the same side. Brightside now put forth their utmost efforts, but Heeley added two more goals, kicked respectively by A. Wood and S. Scaife. They thus won by four goals to none. For Brightside, W. Wilkinson, E. F. Fay, G. Proctor, H. Firth, and R. Hall played well; and for the winners, A. Wood, W. Godfrey, F. Brownhill, and J. E. Deans were conspicuous for excellence." (236)

* Blackburn Meadows is an area of land just inside the Sheffield city border at Tinsley and became the location of the main sewage treatment works for the city in 1884. Blackburn Meadows is around three miles away from the district of Brightside.

Norfolk Works FC (Sheffield, Yorkshire 1872- 1877)

- Equal Twenty-third Oldest Sheffield Football Club
- Equal seventy-third Oldest Football Club in England

Origin: Workplace. No connection to Norfolk FC (1876) but instead a works team from Thomas Firth and Sons Limited which was a Steel Castings Manufacturer based at Norfolk Works, Savile Street East, Sheffield. The company had formed in 1842 and by the 1870s had moved into the armaments market. All the built-up guns (artillery with a specially reinforced barrel) made at the Royal Arsenal, Woolwich, were lined with a steel tube; this tube was derived from a solid cylinder or ingot, supplied from the works of Messrs. Firth and Sons :

"The casting of the tube for the enormous gun was carried out at these works on Friday week in the most successful manner. The ingot is made of crucible steel, and required for its construction 628 crucibles, each containing 70 pounds of metal, the total weight being thus

CHAPTER FIVE

very nearly 20 tons. The casting occupied 42 minutes, and employed 194 men. The ingot measures 42 inches in diameter and 13 feet in length." [237]

According to the 1875 Football Annual –
Founded: 1872 Code: Sheffield Association
Number of members: 50
Club Ground: Newhall
Hon. Sec.: W. Allen, Norfolk Works
Colours: Blue and white hoops

The above details were repeated in the 1876 edition and the only change in the 1877 Annual was that the the Hon. Sec. was G.H. Firth of the Norfolk Works. Thomas Firth fathered ten children so 'G.H' could well be a relation. They played at Newhall which is a district just north east of the city centre and, based on the match reports, was near Brightside Lane. At the 1875 A.G.M. the man elected President of the club was none other than Thomas Firth himself:

"Norfolk Works Football Club – at the annual meeting of the above club the following officers were elected for the ensuing season – Thos. Firth, Esq., president; John L. Firth, Esq., vice president; G. Milnes, treasurer; C. Biggin, hon. Secretary; G. Gardener, delegate for the Association; J. Bagshaw, delegate for the accident fund, and a committee of eight." [238]

"Norfolk Works v. Exchange Brewery (1st teams) – Played on Saturday (1876), on the ground of the Norfolk Works Club, Brightside Lane, and resulted in an easy victory for the home team by three goals to none, the home team playing a splendid game throughout. Fogg, G. Taylor, J. Coup, and Shreadgold played well for the visitors. O. White, G. Oxley, J. Gardner, J. Roebuck, and Barker played well as forwards, and O. Carr made some well-judged kicks in the backs for the home team." [239]

Albion FC (Sheffield, Yorkshire 1872 – 1880)

- Equal Twenty-third Oldest Sheffield Football Club
- Equal seventy-third Oldest Football Club in England

Origin: Unknown. 'Albion' was a very popular name; there was a long-standing cricket club from 1856 and a brewery. 'About 1870 the Ecclesall New Road was beginning to develop and the first buildings of note were the Albion Brewery and, nearby, the Soho Brewery; just two of the dozens of breweries in the Sheffield area.' [240] There was also half a dozen Sheffield pubs and hotels that went by the name of the 'Albion' in the Victorian era. Albion FC's first strip listed below shows that the club clearly had a sense of humour or had perhaps been drinking at one of the pubs.

Football Annual	Ground	Foundation Date	Hon. Sec.	Members	Colours
1875	Ecclesall Road	1872	W.P. Dix *, Assay Office, Fargate	50 (limited)	White and white hoops
1876	Ecclesall Road	1872	W.P. Dix, Assay Office, Fargate	50 (limited)	White and white hoops
1877	Ecclesall Road	1872	C.M. Bright, 340 Glossop Road, Sheffield	50 (limited)	Blue and white hoops
1878	x				
1879	Abbeydale Road, Sheffield	1872	C.M. Bright, 340 Glossop Road, Sheffield	50 (limited)	Black, white anchor on breast
1880	Abbeydale Road, Sheffield	1872	W.T. Teather, Nottingham Street, Sheffield	50 (limited)	Black, white anchor on breast

* W. Pierce Dix liked to keep busy; he was the Hon. Sec. of the Sheffield Football Association in 1877 and later the treasurer. My subjective opinion formed of Pierce Dix during the course of my research, would not suggest a drinking man with a sense of humour, so a cricket or a hotel origin is probably the more likely.

In 1872 Albion FC played Ecclesall College FC:

"ALBION v. ECCLESALL COLLEGE. - Played at Ecclesall on Saturday and resulted in favour of the Albion Club with four goals against two. The goals were kicked for the Albion by Messrs. Dronfield (2), England and Mosforth; for the Ecclesall College by Messrs. Munro and Murray." (241)

Clearly an ambitious and confident club, Albion FC made the long journey north in 1876 to play Alexandra Athletic at the Queen's Park ground, Glasgow. (242) The next interesting press report is from the 1879 season when the Albion club members were divided into two teams by marital status to provide a pre-season training game:

"Albion Football Club. The opening match in connection with this club was played on Saturday last to inaugurate the season, which commences on Thursday next with a match v. Endcliffe. A goodly number of members met to contest an interesting match – Married v. Single. The married team was considerably improved by the loan from the single ranks of Messrs. C. M. Bright, J. Mawhood, and Robertshaw; but with this addition they had to succumb to a very crushing defeat of 5 goals to 1. For the married team, Messrs. W. E. and J. C. Clegg seemed to have lost none of their ability to kick accurately, and Hetherington, Robertshaw, and Birkett worked hard to avert defeat. For the victorious eleven all played exceedingly well, Mosforth particularly distinguishing himself by some very timely runs. Teams: Married – W. E. Clegg, J. C. Clegg, W. W. Hetherington, J. W. Birkett, J. Robertshaw, Gibson, A. T. Wright, and Ludlam, with C. M. Bright, J. Mawhood, and Robertshaw. Single – H. H. Podoski, W. Gregory, Walter Teather, H. Fletcher, J. Simpson, W. Mosforth, H. Newbould, W. H. England, B. B. Brown, F. H. Dix, and W. Thompson Teather." (243)

Albion's most famous player was William 'Billy' Mosforth who played for them from age fourteen through to age twenty. (William Clegg and his brother Charles Clegg both also played occasionally for Albion). Mosforth also made appearances in this period for Hallam FC, Providence FC and Heeley FC. He was known as the 'Little Wonder' because he was only 5" 3', 11 stone in weight and started competing as a runner at the many Athletic sports days held in Sheffield. He was also a regular for Hallam cricket club and regularly entered the Hallam FC Annual Sports. In 1880, following his breaking of the Albion FC club rules (see below) he joined the Wednesday, where he stayed for eight years before joining Sheffield United in their first season in 1889. A knee injury meant he retired from football after one season but he played for United long enough to take the

Billy Mosforth wearing an S.U.F.C. shirt

CHAPTER FIVE

record as the first ever player to play and score for both Sheffield Wednesday and Sheffield United. He won nine caps for England, the first aged nineteen; all his fellow England teammates were upper class gentlemen, so Billy, an engraver by trade, was the England team's first working class player. He had a long life; born January 2nd 1858, he died aged 71 in Firvale hospital on the 11th July 1929 and is buried in the Crookes cemetery. Billy also played for the Zulus FC (more later) where his 'flexibility' towards receiving payments caused him problems. In November 1880 Billy had his first run-in with Sheffield authority in the form of Pierce Dix:

"Football. Albion Football Club. At a special general meeting held on Tuesday, under the presidency of Mr. W. Pierce Dix, at Mr. Wright's Sheffield moor, called in accordance with rule 17 of the club a resolution was unanimously agreed upon, proposed by Mr. W. H. England, seconded by Mr. C. M. Bright, condemning the action of Mr. W. Mosforth in relation to the cup tie, and resolving to strike his name off the list of members." [244]

Tantalisingly, the exact nature of Billy's crime is not described but it must have been serious to be sacked at the time when he was probably their best player. His final match for Albion FC was on 11th October 1880 against Heeley FC. He joined Wednesday FC and seven years later would be instrumental in Wednesday FC's change to professionalism.

Eldon St Jude's FC (Sheffield, Yorkshire 1872-1879)
- Equal Twenty-fourth Oldest Sheffield Football Club
- Equal seventy-sixth Oldest Football Club in England

Origin: Church. St. Jude's was built in 1848 near the foot of Eldon street, in the centre of Sheffield and closed in 1999.

According to the 1880 Football Annual
Founded: 1872
Number of members: 46
Club Ground: Brocco Bank
Dressing room: On the ground
Code: Sheffield Association
Hon. Sec.: C. Appleby, 78 William Street, Sheffield
Colours: Red and black

"Sharrow Rangers v. St. Jude's (Eldon) Clubs – Played on Saturday (*1876*) on the ground of the former, and resulted in a victory for the St. Jude's by three goals to two. The Rangers commenced well by scoring the first two goals, kicking up the hill. This roused their opponents' metal, and they put their shoulders to the wheel in good earnest, and eventually won easily. Messrs. Skinner, Gresham, Brown, Foster, and Cole played well for St. Jude's; as also Messrs. Thompson and Sykes for the Rangers." [245]

St. Jude's joined the New Association in 1877 and played Sheaf United FC in a Cup tie. Sheaf United were another minor club that did not feature in the Football Annuals but was formed to play both cricket and football at the new Sheaf House ground from around 1874, until 1879, when the match reports ceased. The following match is a New Association Cup tie:

"ST. JUDE'S (ELDON) v. SHEAF UNITED This match was played on the ground of St. Jude's Club, and won by them by one goal to nothing. The St. Jude's soon had the ball at their opponents' end, but although they made several very good attempts, no score was obtained up to half-time. The Sheaf United supposed on changing ends- kicking down hill- they would hold the advantage, but the reverse proved to be the case for the play was mainly in their territory, and soon after half-time a goal was kicked by C. Foster for the St. Jude's. This put the Sheaf on their mettle. Shortly before time was called the ball was kicked out of the boundary on the top side. This was duly announced by the umpire, but some of the Sheaf United players went on playing, and kicked the ball just to the off-side of the St. Jude's goal, where one of their friends who was watching the game kindly put it through for them, which of course, was disallowed." [246]

Pye Bank FC (Sheffield, Yorkshire 1872-1886)
- Equal Twenty-fourth Oldest Sheffield Football Club
- Equal seventy-sixth Oldest Football Club in England
- Losing finalists of the 1881–82 Sheffield Association Challenge Cup but were the winners of the inaugural Sheffield New Association Challenge Cup in 1877/78

Origin: Unknown. The club lists its ground as Fox Street: Pye Bank is between Burngreave and Parkwood Springs and Fox Street and Pye Bank Road are less than half a mile apart. The only institution called Pye Bank of note in this era that may have formed a football team, is the United Methodist Free Church that opened in 1871 on Pitsmoor Road.

When Sheffield New Association broke away to form a rival Football Association in 1877/78 they played a 12-match competition for the prize of their inaugural Challenge Cup. Pye Bank beat Rising Star 1 goal to 0 in the final, after playing three drawn games.

According to the 1879 Football Annual
Founded: 1872
Number of members: 52
Club Ground: Fox Street
Hon. Sec.: W.J. Worrall, 45 Fitzalan Street
Colours: Navy blue

In the 1880 edition, the information was the same as 1879, except that T. E. Masdin, 129 Nottingham Street, Sheffield, was the new Hon. Sec.

At the 1879 A.G.M.:
"PYE BANK FOOTBALL CLUB.- At the annual general meeting, the following were the elected officers for the ensuing season:- President, Mr. T. Firth: Vice-presidents, Messrs. W. Lyons, H. Fletcher, and R. Hildrick; treasurer, Mr. W. J. Worrall: secretary, Mr. T. E. Masdin, 129, Nottingham Street: committee Messrs. R. Kirk, H. Rodgers, T. Ambler, J. Rimmer, J. Vazson, D. Bilby, J. Eames, T. Kirk, C. Green: delegate to Sheffield Old Football Association, Mr. H. Fletcher: sub-delegate, Mr. A Thornton." [247]

Pye Bank's near-neighbours, All Saint's Victoria FC, (its biggest rival) was formed the year before and played just down the road:

"PYE BANK v. ALL SAINTS VICTORIA (1st Teams). -The Pye Bank Club opened their season on Saturday (1880), at Fox street, with a match against their old antagonists, the All Saints. Neither of the clubs mustered their full strength. A good match was, however played, some excellent play being shown on both sides. The home team scored three goals to their opponents' one during the first half, and at the call of time had placed four more to their credit, whilst the visitors failed to augment theirs, the home team thus winning by several goals to one. The goals were kicked by R. Kirk, three; H. Rodgers, 2; W. J. Worral, 1; and H. Fairest, 1, for the home team and C. H. Green for the visitors. Players: - Pye Bank: T. Kirk (goal), H. Fletcher,

CHAPTER FIVE

J. Simpson, J. Stevens, G. Bownes, W. J. Worrall, R. Kirk, H. Rodgers, C. Hall, T. Masdin, H. Fairest. All Saints: J. Roebuck, B. Bennett, T. Bramwell, E. Holyhead, C. H. Green, J. Toyne, R. Clarke, T. Driver, G. Altlat, R. Hibberd, and O. Cotterill." [248]

Pye Bank FC followed its success in the New Association Challenge Cup by making the final of the 1881/82 Sheffield Association Challenge Cup, but lost 5-0 to Heeley FC at Bramall Lane:

"The final tie for Sheffield Association Challenge cup was played on Saturday at Bramall lane ground. The weather was very unfavourable, a brisk wind blowing over the ground and a drizzling rain falling. No doubt these circumstances combined to considerably reduce the attendance; but there was a very large assembly, notwithstanding, some three or four thousand spectators putting in an appearance. The ground had been well rolled previous to the commencement of the game, but the going soon became extremely soft, notwithstanding. The Heeleyites were strong favourites, odds of 6 and 7 to 4 being freely wagered in their favour; but still the 'Pyebankers' were not without friends, and there were not a few of the onlookers who predicted that even if they did not quite pull through, they would at any rate, make a strong fight for it. Anticipations in this respect were most signally upset, as the Heeleyites, after scoring a goal in the first half, had matters mostly their own way in the second, and ultimately won by five goals to none." [249]

As previously mentioned the Surrey FC players were 'coached' in 1875; ten years later in 1885 Pyebank FC trained for a week in anticipation for the Cup final, imitating Jack Hunter's approach that had paid dividends in the F.A. Cup, two years before:

"We believe the result was not entirely unexpected by the Pyebank team themselves. They had been practicing nearly the whole time of the previous week, but had not an extreme amount of fancy in their own favour. They however entered the field fully determined to try their utmost, and, though defeated, it is highly honourable to their club that they were so successful as to get into the final at all. We rather suspect too, that some of their men hardly played up to their usual form on Saturday. Whether it was that they were somewhat strange to the ground, or that the going was too soft for them, we cannot say; but we certainly expected to see Rhodes, Green, and Rodgers play better than they did. They tried their best, no doubt, and perhaps hardly got so much opportunity of performing as they might have done. Betts, Stevens, Jones, and R. Kirk, in our opinion, excelled for the losers, and it might have been, if all had exhibited the dash of Betts and Kirk, that the result would not have been quite so serious. Hulley, Simpson, and Hall played fairly and no more, and as to the remainder they scarcely maintained their previous reputation." [249]

Despite Pyebank's professional approach, Heeley FC finally broke its longstanding Cup Final jinx:

"There can be no doubt the Heeley victory was well deserved. They have in previous years struggled hard to secure the Cup, having no fewer than three times got into the final without absolutely obtaining their great object. It was quite evident that they were bent on winning on Saturday. Hunter, W. Moss, Whittam, Winterbottom, R. Martin. Jacques, and others played in magnificent style for them, and after the first half the result of the match was never in doubt. The victory is a decided 'feather in the cap' of the Heeley team, and their prominent supporters, Mr. John. D. Harrison, Mr. John Barton, and others are thoroughly to be congratulated upon the manner in which, through thick and thin, they have stuck to the fortunes of the old club. The following were the teams, and as will be gathered by the initiated, both clubs had got their most formidable representatives together: -

HEELEY. - J. Tomlinson (goal), J. Hunter (captain), W. Moss, T. Moss, A. Tomlinson, W. E. Jacques, R. Martin, J. Wyld, I. Swallow, J. Whitham, H. Winterbottom.

PYEBANK. - T. Kirk (goal), J. Stevens, W. Betts, M. P. Jones, J. Simpson, C. Hall, C. Green, R. Kirk, E. Rhodes, T. Hulley, H. Rodgers (captain). UMPIRES. - Messrs. J. C. Clegg and W. E. Clegg; referee, Mr. W. P. Dix." [249]

1873

In this year, twenty-four Association clubs were formed nationally: Cambridge University AFC, Gainsborough Trinity FC, Chichester FC, Bournemouth Rovers FC and Worksop Town FC which are all extant.

The Cambridge University AFC's current Facebook site says 'C.U.A.F.C. is the football club of the University of Cambridge and is unofficially the oldest football club in the world' with a foundation date of 1856. This claim is based on the Cambridge Football Club and the Cambridge Rules written in 1848, of which no copy survives, but the 'University Rules', circa 1856, still exists in the Library of Shrewsbury School. As discussed in Chapter One, that early Cambridge club has been discounted in this classification because of its very short life. The current C.U.A.F.C. does not appear until the Football Annual of 1873. I appreciate that this 1873 foundation date will cause controversy, not least because it makes C.U.A.F.C. slightly younger that their Oxford Rivals. Credit, however, must be given to the Cambridge University Association Football Club for the effect it had on modernising the game; in 1882 Cambridge was described as the first 'combination' team in which each player was allotted an area of the field and played as part of a team in a game that was based upon passing. In a discussion by Charles W. Alcock on the history of a 'definite scheme of attack' and 'elaborate combination' in early football playing styles (which included references to 'Northern' teams, such as Glasgow's Queen's Park FC), he stated in 1891:

"The perfection of the system which is in vogue at the present time however is in a very great measure the creation of the last few years. The Cambridge University eleven of 1883 were the first to illustrate the full possibilities of a systematic combination giving full scope to the defence as well as the attack." [250]

I will cause further controversy by suggesting **Worksop Town FC** has an 1873 foundation date. The club's website and local press are convinced that it is the world's fourth oldest football club, with a foundation date of 1861, but I can find no evidence to substantiate the claim. Worksop Cricket Club was understandably playing very early in 1850, but the earliest sign of a Worksop football game is a Rugby match against a school on 15th March 1873:

"Perhaps the first football match ever played in Worksop, took place last Saturday between gentlemen of Worksop and neighbourhood and the team of the Pestalozzian school...As the rules of Rugby Union were followed, the superior weight of the Worksop team told greatly against the school team in the scrimmages." [251]

There are no earlier press reports for a Worksop FC and no mentions at all in the Football Annuals for any Worksop club between 1857 and 1889.

Seven of the twenty-four newly formed clubs in 1873 were from Yorkshire and five of those were from Sheffield.

CHAPTER FIVE

Owlerton FC (Sheffield, Yorkshire 1873-1897)

- Twenty-Fifth Oldest Sheffield Football Club
- Equal eighty-second Oldest Football Club in England
- Founder member of the Sheffield and District Football League in 1889/90
- 1892 amalgamated with the Montrose Club, becoming 'Owlerton and Montrose FC'

Origin: Unknown. Probably cricket as Owlerton Cricket Club was first mentioned in 1853.

Football Annual	Ground	Foundation Date	Hon. Sec.	Members	Colours	Dressing Room
1875	Rawson's Meadow	1873	W. H. Carr, Barrow Lees Owlerton*	140	Scarlet and black hoops	Victoria Hotel Owlerton
1876	Rawson's Meadow	1873	W.H. Carr, Barrow Lees, Owlerton	140	Scarlet and black hoops	Victoria Hotel Owlerton
1877	Rawson's Meadow	1873	John Webster, Burrow Lees, Owlerton	140	Scarlet and black hoops	Victoria Hotel, Owlerton
1878	x					
1879	Rawson's Meadow	1873	John Helliwell, Burrow Lees, Owlerton	80	Scarlet and black hoops	Victoria Hotel, Owlerton
1880	Rawson's Meadow	1873	W.H. Allan, Burnell Road, Owlerton	90	Scarlet and black hoops	Victoria Hotel Owlerton
1881	x			Reporting stopped in 1881 edition		
1882	x					
1883	x					
1884	x					
1885	x					
1886	x					
1887	Owlerton	1869	A. Dixon, Hillsborough, Sheffield		Blue and white stripes	Crown Inn
1888	Owlerton	1869	A. Dixon, Hillsborough, Sheffield		Blue and white stripes	Crown Inn
1889	Owlerton	1869	A. Dixon, Hillsborough, Sheffield		Blue and white stripes	Crown Inn

* William Henry Carr was a Wednesday player in 1871 and played in goal for the Sheffield v. London match at Bramall Lane in 1876.

Rawson's Meadow, by definition has to be beside a river in Owlerton, which must be the Don. Its changing rooms were at the Victoria Hotel, 923 Penistone Rd, which is less than half a mile away from the current Wednesday ground. Mike Bradbury in his book 'Lost Teams of the North' has pinpointed a football pitch on an 1890 map, suggesting the ground was outlined by the A61, Bastock Road and the river Don, less than 200 yards from the current Hillsborough stadium.

From 1899, Sheffield Wednesday played home matches at their Owlerton ground (later renamed the Hillsborough Stadium) and Owlerton FC has other similarities to Wednesday FC, including the blue and white stripes (three years before Wednesday adopted them). However in my research I could find no formal link or merger, just a categoric 'Wednesday never played at Owlerton.' [252]

The earliest press report I found was from 1874:

"Owlerton Football Club – The following have been elected officers – President, Mr. Thomas Denton; Vice-president, Mr. Henry Margereson; treasurer, Mr. Ellis Cropper; honorary secretary, Mr. William Henry Carr; Committee, Messrs. John Motley, Thomas Charles Worth,

Wm. Buttery, John Webster, Thos. Lint, Vincent Crookes, Thos. Crookes, Thos. Crookes, jun., and Thos. Mallinson. It was also resolved to join the Football Association, Mr. John Webster being elected delegate. Mr. Thomas List was also elected delegate to the Football Accident Society." [253]

Owlerton F.A. Cup Record 1871-1888
1887/88	1	Eckington Works	H	2-1
	2	Sheffield Heeley	H	1-0
	3	Derby County	A	2-6

In 1892 Owlerton FC amalgamated with the Montrose Club:

"Amalgamation of local clubs. At the Queen Street Hotel, last night there was a meeting at which it was decided that the Owlerton Football Club should amalgamate with the Montrose Club, and in future it will be known as the 'Owlerton and Montrose Football Club' The clubs ground will be at Owlerton, and Mr. J. H. Young, who was elected hon. Secretary, was instructed to enter the club for the English Cup, the Sheffield Challenge Cup, and the Minor Cup. The club is now on a firm basis, and has every prospect of success in the future." [254]

Philadelphia FC (Sheffield, Yorkshire 1873- 1877)
- Twenty-Sixth Oldest Sheffield Football Club
- Equal eighty-third Oldest Football Club in England

Origin: Workplace. Philadelphia Steel Works was formed around 1857 in an area subsequently badly affected by the Great Flood of 1864. They played at the non-specific ground of 'Hillsborough', which is approximately two miles away from the works district of Philadelphia.

According to the 1875 Football Annual –
Founded: 1873
Code: Sheffield Association
Number of members: 70
Club Ground: Hillsborough
Hon. Sec.: H. Swift, 4 Orchard Place, Langsett Road
Colours: Blue caps

The above information was repeated in the 1876 edition and the 1877 edition with the exception that the Hon. Sec. was then S. Marston of 20 Watery Street, Sheffield. Match reports with team line-ups are extremely rare for Philadelphia FC, but this away match report in Rotherham in 1877 gave a full team line-up. It was against yet another Rotherham team, this one called 'West End' and the game was played on their ground at the Boston Castle; Philadelphia FC won by 2 goals to 1: "Rotherham West End: R. Price, A.M. Cobbett, Thurell, Shirt, Jakes, Harris, Wood, Cutts, Rhodes, Baywood, Taff, Price and Cooper.Philadelphia: J. Roberts, T. Ambler, R. Bumby, W. Barker, R. Kirk, G. Kirk, J.T. Reaney, A. Ambler, H. France, J. Schofield, J. Cooper, H. Torry, G.W.B. Wheatcroft. Umpire. J. Askwith." [255]

Endcliffe FC (Sheffield, Yorkshire 1873-1881)
- Twenty-Seventh Oldest Sheffield Football Club
- Equal eighty-fourth Oldest Football Club in England
- Amalgamated with Brincliffe FC in April 1879

Origin: Unknown

CHAPTER FIVE

Football Annual	Ground	Foundation Date	Hon. Sec.	Members	Colours
1876	Ecclesall Road	1873	W.H. Booth, Hospital, West Street	120	Navy blue
1877	Banner Cross	1873	E. Barber of Broomhall Pk.	Limited to 60	Navy blue
1878	x				
1879	Banner Cross	1873	E. Barber of Broomhall Pk.	Limited to 50	Navy blue
1880	Banner Cross	1873	F.J. Baines of West Grove, Winter Street	60	Navy blue

Game reports must not have been submitted to the Sheffield press because there does not seem to be the same coverage for Endcliffe FC as other clubs, but in 1879 they played Albion FC:

"Football. Endcliffe v. Albion. First teams representing the above important clubs contested yesterday, at Hunter's Bar, in the presence of a large number of spectators, who watched the game with considerable interest. Neither club had its full strength, but the play was very fast, especially in the second half. Albion had the advantage of kicking down-hill during the first part of the match, and chiefly owing to the spirited play of Mosforth, R. Gregory, England, and W. E. Clegg, they succeeded in scoring twice, both goals being obtained by Gregory. Ends being changed, Endcliffe were not long in equalising matters, the Messrs. Barber and Pawson being very prominent. Directly following they obtained another goal, and it looked as if they were about to leave their opponents a long way behind, especially as the ball was almost immediately afterwards again put through. Not to be easily defeated, however, the Albion forwards 'came again' toward the finish, Mosforth doing some very clever work on the left side, while England was at all times busy and useful. Gregory likewise laboured hard, and ultimately their combined labours were rewarded with a third goal – this time uphill. The battle was fought out with great vigour to the finish, and the result was a victory for Endcliffe by four goals to three, where all played well it is invidious to mention names, but we think Herbert Barber and Pawson shone best for Endcliffe (all the Barbers were in form), and Mosforth and Gregory for Albion." [256]

In 1881 they advertised in the press for members and the match reports ceased from that point onwards.

One of the Yorkshire's, (non-Sheffield football clubs), formed in 1873 was **Rawmarsh FC**, situated north of Rotherham.

According to the 1876 Football Annual –
Founded: 1873
Code: Sheffield Association
Number of members: 150
Club Ground: Rawmarsh
Hon. Sec.: J.D. Blythe, Rawmarsh
Colours: Red white and blue
The above facts were repeated in the 1877 edition and then the reporting stopped.
In 1876 they played and beat a military team:

"15th Regiment v Rawmarsh – This match was played at Rawmarsh on Monday. It may be said that the Rawmarsh players and their friends have looked forward to this match with extreme interest, and were determined to give the military a warm welcome. In this they were successful. A great number of people turned out to see the match, and they loudly applauded and exceptionally good kick or dribbling. The 15th first kicked downhill. The ball, when once in motion, changed sides frequently. A splendid shot, made by a soldier just went over the bar. The ball was soon again near the Rawmarsh goal, and another fine shot was made, but the ball went below. Rawmarsh quickly passed the ball up the field, Ardron, Schofield, and Willey working hard, the last named making a good shot at the military goal, but the ball was capitally stopped by Colour-sergeant Popple, the custodian. Just at this time each goal was alternately threatened. The ball was afterwards taken up to the visitors goal, and another good shot by one of the Rawmarsh men made, but the goal-keeper once more proved invincible, and by a huge kick sent the ball flying to the far side of the field. Up to half time neither side scored. After changing ends the ball was taken up by the soldiers to their opponents' goal, but 'Little Ted' the Rawmarsh captain, was there, and as quickly returned it. After an interval, this was repeated by 'Ted,' who this time ran it down to the military stronghold, where one of the soldiers; backs fouled it fairly in front of his own goal. The Rawmarsh captain afterwards sent the ball through the posts. Rawmarsh thus won by one to nothing. The match was most pleasant throughout. Every soldier worked with a will. Among those who distinguished themselves were Captains Ingall, Brown, and Garnett, and Lieutenant Reynard. The three first, together with Corporal Cowan, Privates Kelly, Fitzpatrick, and Lee, played admirably. The goal-keeping of Colour-sergeant Popple was capital." (257)

Sharrow Rangers FC (Sheffield, Yorkshire 1873-1882)
- Twenty-Eighth Oldest Sheffield Football Club
- Equal eighty-fifth Oldest Football Club in England

Origin: Unknown

Football Annual	Ground	Foundation Date	Hon. Sec.	Members	Colours
1877	Crescent Road, Sharrow	1873	H.N. Moss, Sharrow	70	Blue and black
1878	x				
1879	Crescent Road, Sharrow	1873	H.C. Wells, Glen Road, Nether Edge	100	Blue and black
1880	Crescent Road, Sharrow	1873	H.C. Wells, Glen Road, Nether Edge	80	Blue and black
1881	Crescent Road,	1873	H. Norton Moss, Sharrow, Sheffield	Reporting stopped in 1881 edition	Chocolate and magneta

The first match report I found was for 1876 covering a match that was played on a Thursday, when their opponents were available to play:

"Sharrow Rangers v Thursday Wanderers – These clubs met on Thursday afternoon on the ground of the former at Hunter's Bar. Both sides were well represented, and the match was well contested. The Wanderers, having won the toss, elected to kick towards Sheffield, and at 3.30 Orton kicked off for the Rangers. The ball was at once carried into the Wanderers' territory, and a good shot made into goal by F. Butler, but the danger was averted by the goal keeper. The play now became very fast, each side holding an advantage alternately. The fine play of Messrs. Orton, Byrd, and Butler, for the Rangers, and that of Messrs. Barber, Sorby, and Beardshaw for the Wanderers was most noticeable. A foul having been obtained for the Rangers in the mouth of the enemy's goal, Orton was entrusted with the kick, and, by a well-directed shot, landed the ball well into the goal but the custodian defended his post well and placed the ball out of danger. The Wanderers goal was now kept in a constant state of siege, and just before half-time B. Cooks, by a good kick, scored the first goal for the Rangers. On again resuming, the play continued very even up to half time. On changing ends the Rangers had the advantage of the ground, but the Wanderers were playing well together, and by some fine all-round play the ball was taken past the Rangers backs, and C. Atkin scored an easy goal for the Wanderers, thus making matters equal. Both sides now tried hard to decide the match, and after a short time it became evident that the Rangers held the advantage, and numerous attempts were made as the Wanderers' goal by Messrs. Byrd and Anthony, but they were unable to score for a time. At length J. Byrd, by a splendid screw kick, scored a second goal for the Rangers. Time was now played out without any further result, and the Rangers won a very pleasant match by two goals to one, having had rather the best of the play throughout. In addition to those already mentioned Messrs. Coombe and Bright rendered good service for the Wanderers, and for the Rangers Messrs. Loukes, Booker, and Thornhill played well." [258]

Another club from Rotherham was formed this year, **Holmes FC,** who logically enough played at the Holmes, Kimberworth, near Rotherham. Could Holmes FC be linked to Holmes Hall, the residence of the Earl of Effingham?

According to the 1879 Football Annual –
Founded: 1873
Number of members: 50
Club Ground: Holmes
Hon. Sec.: A. Woodcock, Holmes
Colours: Red and white

The above 1879 facts were repeated in the 1880 edition and then the reporting ceased.

Holmes FC played in one of the first Association matches to be played in Leeds in 1877 (See Hunslet FC):

"HUNSLET v. HOLMES. - This match was played on the ground of the former at Woodhouse Hill Cricket Ground on Monday. The first half of the game was exceedingly good, but a little in favour of Hunslet, who obtained one goal, which was disputed on account of the offside rule. The second half time was in favour of Holmes, who obtained one goal. Ogden, Mills, and Frith played exceedingly well for Hunslet, as also did A. Woodcock, Cooper, and A. Walker for Holmes, the latter proving victorious by one goal to nil. Players: Hunslet- J. Coates, J. Clarke, A. Mills, W. Hill, F. Hinde, W. H. Stacey, J. B. Ogden, F. Frith, C. Shaw, R. Hudson, and W. Gilston. Holmes- A. Woodcock, T. Lee, A. Walker, J. Walker, T. Cobbett, T. Flynn, J. Woodcock, P. Cooper, J. Tan, J, Shirtlaff, D. Hopkinson, and R. Neill." [259]

Ecclesfield FC (Sheffield, Yorkshire 1873 –1894)

- Twenty-Ninth Oldest Sheffield Football Club
- Equal eighty-sixth Oldest Football Club in England
- Losing finalists in the Sheffield Challenge Cup in 1882 and 1888, against Wednesday on both occasions
- Founder member of the Sheffield and District Football League in 1889/90

Origin Unknown.

They are entered twice in the 1879 Football Annual; once on page 100 in the Sheffield Clubs section and once on page 155 as a provincial club. (The page 155 details in brackets)

Founded: 1873 (1872)
Number of members: 40 (40)
Club Ground: Fairham's Croft, Ecclesfield (Fayram's Croft)

Hon. Sec.: W. Stringer, Ecclesfield (W. Stringer, Ecclesfield)
Colours: Amber and black (Black and orange)

With contradicting accounts, I have gone with the 'page 100' version, as that would have been submitted by the Sheffield Association representative and hopefully he knew what he was doing! (In the 1880 edition the same facts as 1879 page 100 were repeated except F. Greaves was then the Hon. Sec).

The first match report I found was from 1873 but without a team line-up:

"WALKLEY v. ECCLESFIELD (1st Teams). - This match was played at Hillsbro' on Monday. Play commenced at three o'clock, and at half-past Walkley had succeeded in obtaining two goals. Ecclesfield then commenced playing on the defensive, and so well did they succeed, that no other goal could be obtained, although their goal was many times in danger. Walkley thus won by 2 goals to 0." [260]

Later the same year, some players' names were mentioned in the next match report:

"HALLAM v. ECCLESFIELD. - A match was played on Monday at Ecclesfield, between the first teams of Hallam and Ecclesfield, and after a very keen contest resulted in a draw, neither side scoring. The partisans of Ecclesfield mustered in strong force. T. Beet, J. Gregory, T. Turton, W. Hague, and Mr. Vesey distinguishing themselves for Ecclesfield; whilst F. Keel, W. J. Bentley, A. Reaney, S. Ridge, and E. Sarson did effectual service for Hallam." [261]

By 1874 there were bad feelings between the Ecclesfield and Hallam teams:

"Hallam v. Ecclesfield. To the editor of the Sheffield Daily Telegraph. Sir, On behalf of the Ecclesfield Football Club, I beg to deny the statements of the Hallam Secretary in your issue on the 3rd of February. With respect to the charging from behind which he refers to, and the kicking when the man was down, such a circumstance never took place. Then with regard to wrangling, out of 15 matches played this season, this match is the only one not played out. The fact of the matter is this, the Hallamites claimed a foul without any grounds whatever, which being disallowed, and they left the field. This was within seven minutes of closing time; each club having scored one goal. – Apologising for trespassing on your space, yours, &c." [262]

Ecclesfield FC - F.A. Cup Record 1871-1888

| 1887/88 | 1 | Derby Midland | H | 4-1 |
| | 2 | Derby County | A | 0-6 |

Ecclesfield FC played Chesterfield in September 1894, but based on the following 1896 article, the club folded at some point between then and 1896, and reformed with the involvement of some 'old pros' as seen below:

"Ecclesfield F. C. – It has been decided to re-establish the Ecclesfield Old Football Club, and subscriptions to the amount of £10 have been promised. The following have been elected – President, Mr. H. J. Hawthorn; secretary, Mr. G. Doncaster, Blind Lane, Ecclesfield; and a committee of 13 several of the old players will be found in their ranks, including J. Stringer (Birdwell), C. Dawson (late United), D. Woolhouse (late Sheffield Wednesday) and M. Stringer (late United and Barnsley St. Peter's); also, several promising young players from the junior clubs of the district. The club has entered for the Alliance and the Sheffield Challenge Cup." [263]

CHAPTER FIVE

1874

Thirty-Six Association Clubs started in 1874, including ten current clubs: West Bromwich Albion FC (7th Oldest League Club), Grantham Town FC, Aston Villa FC (8th Oldest League Club), Northwich Victoria FC, Blackburn Rovers FC (=9th Oldest League Club), Bolton Wanderers FC (=9th Oldest League Club), Walsall FC (=10th Oldest League Club), Burnley FC (=10th Oldest League Club), Bishop's Stortford FC and Stockport FC.

I should explain here that Stockport County FC has an official start date of 1883 but under my reclassification (Appendix 2) a club can take on an earlier foundation date from a club with which they amalgamate. This means that Stockport can claim an 1874 foundation date, because in 1903 the Association club took on the debts of the Rugby club, which was formed in 1874. The reason the League clubs formed in 1874 are ranked differently above is because I sort clubs formed in the same year, by when they first played Association football.

The game's first well-known referee (as opposed to an umpire) was John Lewis; he was three times appointed the referee in F.A. Cup Finals (1895, 1897 and 1898), but he is more famous as the co-founder of Blackburn Rovers FC (1874). To much amusement, he had a 'penalty' awarded against him in court in 1894:

"FOOTBALL REFEREE IN THE POLICE COURT. At Blackburn, yesterday, Mr. John Lewis the well known football referee, was summoned for not having an abstract of the Factories Act posted in his works. In answer to Dr. Morley, J. P., the defendant said the notice had been torn down by some means. Amid audible remarks in court about 'penalty kicks', which created much amusement, the chairman said the penalty would be 10s. and costs." [264]

The third F.A. Cup final of 1874 was contested between the military and a university: Oxford University and the Royal Engineers. The 'Sappers' were based in Chatham, Kent and joined the F.A. on the 8th December 1863; it is ranked in equal 15th position on my main listing as the 5th oldest surviving Association football club. Francis Arthur Marindin captained the Royal Engineers in their first F.A. Cup final on 16th March 1872 which they lost 1-0 to the Wanderers. He next captained them to another final on 14th March 1874 but they lost 2-0 to Oxford University. Between 1871/72 and 1874/75, 86 games were played by the Royal Engineers; 74 were won, 9 were drawn and just 3 were lost. The Royal Engineers were the first southern club side to play northern opponents (Sheffield Football Association, Derbyshire Football Association and Nottingham Forest FC) in 1873, making it the first ever football club tour; Sheffield FC (and the ladies) clearly relished the opportunity to meet up in 1874:

"ROYAL ENGINEERS v. SHEFFIELD. The whole of the visiting team arrived safely at the Victoria station at 5.30 last night, the train being an hour behind time. The Sheffield Football Association Committee having learnt that several ladies are anxious to see the match, have decided to erect a large marquee for their accommodation and shelter. To meet the extra expense, a slight extra charge will be made, which will doubtless be cheerfully paid by all who study comfort. It is a step in the right direction, and reflects credit for the thoughtfulness of the committee for the pleasure of their patrons. The position in football achieved by our antagonists naturally causes them to be made hot favourites. Should our little band succeed in turning tables, and reversing their last year's defeat they will receive such an ovation as has not yet been accorded to them, but such a result is anything but probable." [265]

They lost 1-2 in in a tightly contested match and displayed the much vaunted 'bottom' that Sheffield footballers had become famous for:

"The visit of the Royal Engineers to the cutlery town should be looked out by the Sheffield

Association as a tribute to the standing amongst the football institutions of the country. It is also evident that the redoubtable 'sappers' by visiting Sheffield a second time consider that the team in connection with the northern organisation is worthy of their steel, and that is no small feat to lower the colours of those who have come off victorious in many a hard-fought contest. When the officers of the scientific branch of the service mentioned above visited Sheffield about this time last year, they gave our townsmen an unmistakeable drubbing, winning by the large majority of four goals to none. The Engineers play according to the code of the London Association, and as no return match was arranged, half time was played under each set of rules. They scored two goals whilst observing the Sheffield system, and two more on the metropolitan code. There are many who thought Sheffield was out of form, and we certainly never saw them more disorganised. This defeat has made them anxious to meet their military friends once more, and if possible, turn the tables on them. There were many disappointed by being unable to witness the match on account of the fixture being in the *'bull week', but it was unavoidable, as we believe the military gentlemen are unable to conveniently visit Sheffield at any other time." (265)

'Bull week'* was the period before Christmas when the workers were encouraged to work as many hours as possible to maximise their wages in time for the festive break. The absent spectators missed an excellent match:

"The match as an exhibition of football, was the finest ever seen in Sheffield, the play being the fastest and best it has been our lot to witness. The 'dash' and 'go' of the Engineers were exemplified in a remarkable degree, and the 'bottom' of the Hallamshire men was shown in the decided advantage they had over their opponents in the latter part of the game when the London Laws were in force. The Engineers eventually won by 2 goals to 1. Without wishing to detract in the slightest degree from the success of the visiting team, we cannot but think that Sheffield were rather unlucky, considering the repeated pepperings they had at the goal." (265)

Only four of the thirty-six clubs started in 1874 were from Sheffield, as clubs from the Midlands and Lancashire started to overtake the dominance of Sheffield as a footballing hub.

Providence FC (Sheffield, Yorkshire 1874- 1896)

- Equal thirtieth Oldest Sheffield Football Club
- Equal ninety-forth Oldest Football Club in England

Origin: Church. The Providence Chapel, Cricket Road, Park.

The following three clubs, Exchange FC (1867-1882), Providence FC (1874-1882) and Perseverance FC (1870-1882), merged to become Grange Park in 1882 and played in the F.A. Cup 1887, under that name. In 1889, Park Grange FC changed its name (back) to Exchange FC.

The table below is for Providence FC:

Football Annual	Ground	Foundation Date	Hon. Sec.	Members	Colours
1876	Sharf road (Sheaf?)	1874	R. Hare, 9 Hampton Street Park	80	Red and white
1877	Norfolk Road	1874	W.H. White, 85 Bernard Lane park, Sheffield	80	Red and white
1878	x				
1879	Norfolk Road	1871	R. Hare, Pye Bank, Sheffield	80	Red and grey
1880	Hyde Park	1871	J.R. Harvey, 206 South Street, Sheffield	110	
1881	Hyde Park	1871	H. Hobson, 51 Talbot Street, Sheffield	Reporting stopped in 1881 edition	Crimson and grey

Providence FC changed their name to Park Grange FC for the 1882/83 season:

"A SHEFFIELD football club, which occasionally makes a raid into Lancashire, heretofore known as the Providence Club, has changed its name, and will henceforward be known as Park Grange." (266)

It is interesting to see Billy Mosforth add another club to his C.V., against Midlands' opposition in 1882:

"PARK GRANGE. - C. Hobson, goal; W. and T. Moss, backs; T. Bingley, J. Stevens, and J. Simpson, half-backs; W. Mosforth, H. Hobson, G. H. Bown, H. Winterbottom, and J. Selwood, forwards; umpires, Mr. G. Cropper.

WEDNESBURY OLD ATHLETIC. - C. Kent goal; W. H. Moon and J. Nicholls, backs; J. Holden, J. Cliffe, and T. Hodgkiss, half-backs; G. H. Holden (captain), R. Morley, A. Woodcock, J. Woodcock, and J. Roberts, forwards; umpire, Mr. R. Pinney; referee, Mr. W. H. Stacey." (267)

For Park Grange FC to be playing a prestigious club like Wednesbury Old Athletic FC (1874-1924) that had won the inaugural Birmingham and District Cup in the 1876/77 season, shows that they had ambitious hopes for the club's relaunch under its new name.

Park Grange FC played at the top of Park Hill Lane which was 'always dry and in good condition' according to a report on a game with Lockwood Brothers. (268)

In November 1885, the club took on Heeley FC at the Sheaf House ground, in 'rough and uncomfortable weather' in front of 1,500 spectators; Heeley won by 2 goals to 1. The teams were:

"Heeley – C. E. Knowlson, M. P. Jones, G. A. Lawson, H. Stokes, G. Sykes, C. Hiller, G. A. Shaw, and H. Frank.

Park Grange – G. H. Wood, F. Shipman, G. Crawshaw, G. Jepson, J. Swallow, G. Waller, H. Hobson, A. Harrison, A. Waite, F. Lee, and W. Stansfield. Umpires: Messrs. J. Wild and J. Goddard. Referee, Mr. J. C. Clegg." (269)

Park Grange FC entered the F.A. Cup just once in 1887/88 and lost to Long Eaton Rangers away by 3 goals to 6. Park Grange still existed in 1888 and was an entrant in the Sheffield Challenge Cup. By 1889 they were known again as the Exchange FC. An 1889 press report says 'players of ability' have been recruited in anticipation of the new season: A. Jackson, W. Jackson, G. Crawshaw, H. M'Watt and R. Holroyd. (270)

Match reports ceased in 1896 for the (new) Exchange FC in 1896.

Handsworth Woodhouse FC (Sheffield, Yorkshire 1874- 1877)

- Equal thirtieth Oldest Sheffield Football Club
- Equal ninety-fourth Oldest Football Club in England

Origin: Unknown. The fact that a surgeon played for the club in 1875, perhaps suggests a team composed of middle class men.

According to the 1876 Football Annual –
Founded: 1874
Code: Sheffield Association
Number of members: 140
Club Ground: Handsworth, Woodhouse
Hon. Sec.: W. Shepherd, Handsworth, Woodhouse
Colours: Orange and violet

In the 1877 edition, the above details were repeated with the exception that J. Morton of Handsworth, Woodhouse was the new Hon. Sec.:

"ASTON v. HANDSWORTH. - Serious Accident. - This match was played last Saturday at Aston, the latter club playing a man short. After three-quarters of an hour's splendid play Handsworth obtained one goal. Immediately after this had been secured a serious accident occurred. Kelly, of Handsworth, and Leishman, of Aston, came into violent collision, the result being that both were thrown violently to the ground. Kelly sustained a severe cut on the forehead, and Leishman's injuries brought on concussion of the brain. It was a fortunate circumstance that amongst the Handsworth team Mr. Harrison, surgeon, was playing. This gentleman devoted his attention to the sufferers, and so successful were his efforts in Kelly's case that he was enabled to resume play. Leishman's injuries were, however, far more serious, and he was removed from the field in an insensible state. Handsworth was only able to play nine men during the latter part of the match, but in spite of this they cleverly secured another goal, thus winning the match by two goals to nothing. The play throughout the match on both sides was splendid." [271]

Carnforth FC (Sheffield, Yorkshire 1874-1880)
- Thirty-First Oldest Sheffield Football Club
- Ninety-Fifth Oldest Football Club in England

Origin: Workplace. This club caused initial confusion as Carnforth is near Lancaster and Carnforth FC (Lancaster) is an early Rugby club, yet this Carnforth FC had their club meeting in Sharrow and joined the Sheffield Association. Further investigation found that it was in fact a Sheffield Works team from Carnforth Works, Rockingham Lane, Sheffield.

According to the 1879 Football Annual –
Founded: 1874
Number of members: 60
Club Ground: Sharrow Vale Road
Hon. Sec.: J. Lancaster, 5 Pomona street
Colours: Blue and black hoops

Carnforth FC's last inclusion in the Football Annuals came in 1880 which carried the same details as the 1879 edition, except that H. Anderton of 43 Asline Road was the new Hon. Sec. The Carnforth Works business went up for sale in 1880; the steam engine could be run without any experience, which cannot have helped their future health and safety record:

"CARNFORTH WORKS, Rockingham lane, Sheffield. Established 1862. Owner Retiring from Business. - To be Sold, the STEAM ENGINE. Turning Lathes, Vices, Models, Patterns, &c. To a small Capitalist this is an opportunity that seldom occurs. No previous knowledge of the trade required." [272]

Woodseats FC (Sheffield, Yorkshire 1874-1881)
- Thirty-Second Oldest Sheffield Football Club
- Ninety-Sixth Oldest Football Club in England

Origin: Public House

In the 1869 and 1870 Football Annuals, a short-lived club called 'Norton Woodseats', was listed with little information, except that they had 50 members and that their Hon. Sec. was William Jackson living in 'Woodseats.' There were no match reports in the press but games must have been played in 1869 and 1870 for it to exist in the Football Annuals. I can find no link between Norton Woodseats FC and this Woodseats FC playing in 1874, except for the surname of Jackson, which reappears below. (To add to the confusion, a 'W. Jackson' played for Norton FC in 1867 in the Youdan Cup.) In the absence of any press evidence or membership of the Sheffield Football Association, I have not included Norton Woodseats FC in this classification. If local research can find a link proving they are one and the same club, then Woodseats FC could be moved back to a foundation date of 1869.

The Football Annual details for Woodseats FC appear in the 1879 edition:
Founded: 1876
Number of members: 61
Club Ground: Woodseats
Dressing room: Woodseats Hotel
Hon. Sec.: J. Gilliott, Woodseats
Colours: Green, white cap

All the above details were repeated in the 1880 edition except that the membership had increased to 80 members and T. Rogers from Woodseats was the new Hon. Sec. It seems that the Football Annual foundation date given was wrong, because according to the press they played Garrick FC as early as February 1874. They are not mentioned as early members of the Sheffield Association and played their matches predominantly in Derbyshire and south Sheffield.

The exception to this is this 1874 game against Garrick FC; perhaps that relationship is based on the fact that they were both formed around public houses?

"Garrick v. Woodseats. - The first team of these clubs met once more on the ground of the former on Abbeydale road, on Saturday. The home team won the toss and elected to kick with the wind slightly in their favour, but after about five minutes' play E. Shaw scored the first goal for Woodseats. On changing ends the home team had the best of the play, owing to the Woodseats captain playing too many of his men back. However, he soon discovered his mistake and on rearranging the field the visitors had the play more to their advantage, and obtained a second goal, about a quarter before time, kicked by E. Shaw. When time was called nothing more had been scored. Thus, Woodseats proved victorious by two goals to nothing." [273]

In 1876 Woodseats FC played their southern neighbours:

"WOODSEATS v. DRONFIELD. - This match was played on the ground of the former on Saturday. The Woodseats captain won the toss, and elected to kick with the wind, towards Sheffield. About 3.30 the Dronfield captain set the ball in motion, when the Woodseats men worked it down to their opponents' goal, and constantly made repeated attacks at the Dronfield citadel, but without any result. After half-time the Dronfield men had the wind in their favour, and got the ball well in front of the Woodseats goal, where Mather was lying in wait, and steered it neatly through. The match ended in favour of Dronfield by two goals to nothing, although Woodseats had the best of the play throughout." [274]

In December 1876, the name 'Jackson' crops up again; Woodseats FC clearly had in him a marketing man, as he described a game against Wirksworth FC on New Year's Day 1877, as the 'Match of the Season' in a press advert. This game was to be played at Mr. Jackson's Woodseats Hotel, presumably with the hope to sell some refreshments at the same time. [275]

In 1879 the composition of their committee was as follows:

"WOODSEATS FOOTBALL CLUB. - A meeting of this club was held on Tuesday evening, when they arranged to play their opening match on Saturday next. The following are the officers: - Mr. Twigg, president; Mr. Jackson, treasurer; committee, Messrs. J. Wilson, J. Elliott, H. Elliott, C. Womack, W. Thorpe, M. Biggin, V. Shaw, L. Shaw, H. Rodgers, A. Elshaw, and T.

Barker, with A. Rodgers, secretary." (276)

According to the 1880 Football Annual they were members of the breakaway Sheffield New Association but match reports ceased after 1881. The Woodseats Hotel closed in 2010 and was converted into an Indian restaurant called the Viraaj.

In 1874, a second club started in Chesterfield, Derbyshire, eight years after the first one that was formed in 1866, this time called **Spital FC** (also known as **Spital United**)

According to the 1879 Football Annual –

Founded: 1874
Number of members: 80
Club Ground: Spital Vale
Hon. Sec.: W.H. Crofts, 21 Eyre Street, Chesterfield
Colours: Royal blue and red hoops

The entry for 1880 is the same as 1879 except that G.S. Mason of Spital was then the Hon. Sec. There were then no entries in the Football Annuals until 1885, which was the last mention of Spital FC:

Founded: 1874
Club Ground: Spital
Hon. Sec.: C.L. Mason and T. Piggott, Spital Mills, Chesterfield.
Changing: Eagle Hotel
Colours: Union Jack body, blue sleeves

Spital FC played in the inaugural challenge Cup of the Derbyshire Football Association in 1883/84 and also the following year 1884/85. If the following press article is to be believed, then by 1886 Spital FC were ambitious enough to pay for their future success:

"Staveley Football Club. Indignation meeting. A special meeting of the above club was held at the Crown Inn, Staveley, on Wednesday, where there was a large attendance. The question brought forward had reference to the tempting monetary offers which are alleged to have been made by certain gentlemen connected with the Spital Football Club to several well-known players of the Staveley team as an inducement to them to transfer their service. One of the Staveley players – namely, Marshall, the goal keeper – is reported as now acting in that capacity for the Spital team, and another prominent member of the Staveley eleven had, it is said, promised to play for the club which the gentlemen referred to are so anxious to bring into prominence. The following resolution was proposed, seconded, and passed unanimously – "This meeting desires to express its utter indignation with regard to the section which certain gentlemen connected with the Spital Football Club are pursuing in making monetary inducements to several prominent members of the Staveley team to leave the ranks of the latter club, and the meeting further expresses the hope that the Press will give publicity to this resolution, as it is of opinion that such a pernicious system ought not to be allowed to exist." (277)

The then very successful Staveley FC was an attraction to clubs looking to cherry pick their best players, a process that would still be happening when Sheffield United came calling in five years' time for Ernest 'Nudger' Needham. Certainly, Spital FC's recruitment drive must have succeeded as they had the personnel to enter the F.A. Cup for three successive seasons.

Spital FC - F.A. Cup Record 1871-1888

1882/83	1	Wednesbury Old Athletic	H	1-7
1883/84	1r	Rotherham Town	A	2-7
1884/85	2	Sheffield FC	A	1-4

CHAPTER FIVE

1875

J.M. Wilson described Sheffield in 1875 as a divided town with an industrial centre and genteel suburbs:

"Some of the old streets are small, narrow and irregularly built; some of even the new streets are disfigured by forges, furnaces and other ungainly buildings; spacious squares or other large open edificed areas are totally a-wanting; and the dwelling houses of the merchants and the manufacturers are almost all in the outskirts or in the country; so that the town as a whole, especially with the clouds of smoke, cannot be called attractive. Yet it has good shops, good public buildings and some very fine suburbs; is well paved, well drained and well supplied with water; has undergone much recent improvement in its street architecture; and possesses some imposing, semi -public edifices, such as a stately great hotel adjoining the Victoria railway station, and the extensive premises of the Messrs. Rodgers in the renaissance style, both erected in 1861." [278]

Photography had been invented earlier in the century but the very first images printed in modern newspapers were made from engravings, because ink could be applied to engravings in the same manner as it was applied to moveable type on the printing press. The engraving below is of an unknown match from 1875 but importantly it is captioned: 'Association Football: Dribbling.' The first halftone photographic image in a newspaper dates from the 1873, though widespread use didn't happen until the 1880s.

Thirty-four clubs started in 1875 as Association football continued to boom throughout the rest of England, but none of these new clubs was from Sheffield. New clubs had been formed every year in Sheffield since 1860, but 1875 would be first (apart from 1864, the year of the Great Flood) with no new Sheffield clubs.

Six of the thirty-four clubs started in 1875 are still extant: Royston FC, Sudbury FC (AFC Sudbury), Saffron Walden FC*, Eagley FC**, Chorley FC*** and Small Heath Alliance FC which would evolve into Birmingham City FC, which according to my classification is England's eleventh oldest League Club.

* The 1876 Football Annual has a foundation date of 1875 and I can find no evidence of the 1872 claimed at the club website for Saffron Walden FC.

** The club site claims 1874 but I cannot find any evidence to support the Eagley FC claim; according to the 1879 Football Annual, it was founded in 1875.

*** The club list 1883, as that was the date that the Chorley FC changed from Rugby rules to Association. As part of my reclassification (Appendix 2) I decided that as the two codes in football (ball-carrying and ball-dribbling) were in flux and evolving, then the equally clubs must be as well. In the Chorley FC case, there is a clear evolution between the two clubs, so I have applied the earlier date of 1876.

Three clubs formed in 1875 from the immediate vicinity of Sheffield: Elsecar FC, Whittington Moor FC and Staveley FC.

Elsecar FC (near Barnsley 1875-1893).

According to the 1879 Football Annual:

Number of members: 64

Club Ground: Elsecar

Hon. Sec.: I. Newton, Elsecar

Colours: Scarlet and blue

In the 1880 edition of the Football Annual, the details are duplicated with the exception of the Hon. Sec. who was then M. Harrison of Elsecar; the club never played in the F.A. Cup.

The third club from Chesterfield, after Chesterfield FC (1860) and Spital FC (1874) was **Whittington Moor FC (1875-1880)**.

According to the 1879 Football Annual:

Number of members: 46

Club Ground: Whittington Moor

Hon. Sec.: T. Keeling Birch, Whittington Moor

Colours: White

In the 1880 edition, the above details are duplicated and then the mentions cease.

The third near Sheffield neighbour to form in 1875 was **Staveley FC (1875-1895)**; it was an incredibly successful team from a mining community, just thirteen miles south of Sheffield city centre, which joined the F.A. in 1879 as part of Sheffield Association. It would later join the Derbyshire F.A. in 1883 as a founder member playing in the inaugural Challenge Cup of the Derbyshire Football Association in 1883/84, in which it won 2-1 against Derby Midland; it also beat the same team in the final the following year 1884/85, this time 2-0. Staveley FC was the losing finalist in 1885/86 to Heeley FC but won it again in 1886/87 2-1 against Long Eaton Rangers FC.

CHAPTER FIVE

Football Annual	Ground	Foundation Date	Hon. Sec.	Members	Colours	Dressing Room
1879	Staveley	1875	R. Barlow, Staveley	70	Amber and black hoop	Crown Inn, Staveley
1880	Staveley	1875	G.B. Marples, Staveley	70	Amber and black hoop	Crown Inn, Staveley
1881	Recreation ground	1875	J.T. Till, Staveley	Reporting stopped in in 1881 edition	Navy blue	On the ground
1882	x					
1883	x					
1884	x					
1885	x					
1886	Staveley Town	1876	George Hay, Staveley, near Chesterfield		Red and black quarters	On the ground
1887	Staveley Town	1876	George Hay, Staveley, near Chesterfield		Red and black quarters	Crown Inn
1888	Staveley Town	1878	George Hay, Mount Pleasant, Staveley		Red and black	Crown Inn
1889	Staveley Town	1878	George Hay, Mount Pleasant, Staveley		Red and black	Crown Inn

Such was the strength of the team that they also won the Sheffield Association Cup in 1879/80, beating Heeley 3-1 at Sheaf House and then in the 1884/85 season won the Hallamshire Football Association Challenge Cup: Staveley 2 Eckington 1. It won the same trophy again in 1885/86 beating Eckington FC by 3-2, and was in the 1888/89 Sheffield and Hallamshire Association Cup final losing 2-1 to Rotherham Town at Bramall Lane. Staveley FC had a very strong team which was slowly decimated by other clubs poaching its better players as professionalism became more rampant.

Staveley FC was no slouch in the national competition either; it holds the record for the second highest winning margin in F.A. Cup history (1890/91) beating Walkley FC 19-0 in a qualifier, with Ernest 'Nudger' Needham scoring at least one and maybe more as the match report stopped keeping records after the seventh goal went in. [279] (The F.A. record that no team wants to hold is in the proud possession of Hyde FC who lost to Preston North End by 26 goals to nil).

Staveley FC - F.A. Cup Record 1871-1888

1881-82	2	Grantham	H	3-1
	3	Wednesday	A	2-2
	3r	Wednesday	H	0-0
	3r2	Wednesday	N	1-5
1882/83	1	Walsall Town	A	1-4
1883-84	3	Lockwood Brothers	H	1-0
	4	Blackburn Rovers	A	1-5
1884/85	2	Notts County	H	0-2
1885-86	3	Nottingham Forest	H	2-1
	4	Bye		
	5	Blackburn Rovers	A	1-7
1886-87	3	Notts County	H	0-3

(Staveley continued to play in the F.A. Cup until the 1895/96 season)

Staveley FC's high profile success in many Cup competitions attracted the attention of well-off clubs looking for players:

"EXPORTATION OF ANOTHER PLAYER FROM STAVELEY. Yesterday afternoon Tom Hay, in company with two representatives of the Helliwell Football Club, Bolton, journeyed to Staveley for the purpose of enticing A. Kaye, the Staveley goal keeper, to return with them to act as custodian for the above Lancashire Club. The money inducements held out to him were in advance of his present salary, and the men succeeded in taking Kaye back with them. The Staveley team will be very much weakened by the removal of Kaye, as he has proved himself an excellent man at his post. This makes the fourth importation into Lancashire from the Staveley Club. It will remembered that Tom Hay was formerly in the ranks of the Staveley Club as a goal keeper and is now filling the same position for the Bolton Wanderers." [280]

Ernest Needham, was signed by Sheffield United from Staveley FC in 1891 and the following 1892 article suggests an on-going relationship between the two clubs:

"Staveley Football Club. The proceeds of the match Sheffield United v. Staveley played at Bramall Lane for the latter's benefit, amounted to £30 6s. 8d. and a cheque for that amount has been received by the Staveley club's secretary. This substantial sum will enable the village club to meet all its liabilities and still retain a small balance in hand. The United Club for so generously extending a helping hand in the time of need deserve every thanks, and they have it too, without doubt, both from the village club's executive and the football public of Staveley and district. With a fresh start next season, it is to be hoped better luck will attend the efforts of the colliery club, and that one day they will regain their old position as champion village team of the Midlands." [281]

A Staveley FC player and Derbyshire cricketer, William Cropper, made headlines when he died from an on-pitch incident in January 1889, whilst playing against Grimsby Town FC (founded 1878 till present):

"On Saturday, on the Clee Park Ground, Grimsby, an accident that unfortunately ended fatally happened to W. Cropper, of the Staveley eleven, who had been playing with that team against Grimsby Town, in the position of inner right wing forward, and when running down to secure possession of the ball, he was accidently kicked in the lower part of the abdomen. He was carried off the field to a house near, and a doctor was quickly on the spot. He was well attended to, but he never rallied, and expired about eleven o'clock Sunday morning. William Cropper was born at Brimington on December 27th, 1863. Although a good football player and so prominent a member of the Staveley football team as to have gained the honour of being selected to represent Sheffield and Hallamshire against Glasgow on Saturday next, it was as a cricketer that he gained his highest reputation…..In addition to success as a county cricketer, the deceased player has frequently proved himself a tower of strength to the club of his native village of Brimington, both in cup ties and ordinary matches, and in 1886 he fulfilled an engagement as ground bowler at Lord's. All who have seen him on the football field during the present season will agree as to his undoubted ability as a right-wing forward, especially in the matter of neat and clever passing play. William Cropper had many friends amongst cricket and football players, and was well liked by all who enjoyed his acquaintance. His loss to the Staveley Football Club and the Derbyshire county cricket eleven is a heavy one, and his place will not be easy to fill." [282]

Cropper's opponent that day, Daniel Doyle, was exonerated of any wrong doing in the collision with William Cropper at the inquest. Doyle was a Scottish import for Grimsby Town and would later play for Bolton Wanderers, Everton, Celtic and the Scotland national team. In spite of being found innocent, 'Pastime' magazine shockingly said of Doyle:

'He is undoubtedly able to play a scrupulously fair game for he has received unsolicited

CHAPTER FIVE

testimonials to this effect from coroners' juries. On the other hand, he has certainly the power of taking care of himself in the melee, as the disasters which have befallen those who have come into collision with him amply testify.'

Pastime magazine was founded and edited by Nicholas "Pa" Jackson, a strong advocate of amateurism who formed the Corinthian Casuals FC in 1882.

1876

The growing boom in Association football, continued in 1876 with forty-five clubs forming in England. Nine of the forty-five clubs started in 1875 are still extant: Old Foresters FC, Old Salopians FC, Old Wykehamists FC, Hanover United FC (Polytechnic FC), Stourbridge Standard FC and Stafford Rangers FC. The remaining three extant clubs are League clubs: Middlesbrough AFC joined the F.A. in 1879 as a member of the Sheffield Association (12th Oldest League Club), Goldthorn FC - later Wolverhampton Wanderers FC (13th Oldest League Club) and Yeovil FC (14th Oldest League Club). The official Yeovil site gives 1895 as a foundation date but there was an earlier Rugby playing club from 1876, that evolved into the modern-day club.

Football in 1876 from the book 'Football Our Winter's Game' by Charles W. Alcock
Engraving courtesy of the National Football Museum

The game above is unknown but is probably based on a London game, featuring a solid cross bar introduced officially in 1875.

The growing popularity of football was reflected in April 1876 when the Sheffield Portrait Gallery advertised that in their latest edition was a photograph of the Sheffield Football Team, price 2d. If the original image should ever surface it would not be the oldest photograph of a football team; that accolade belongs to an 1862 image of the Charterhouse school team. The oldest ever photograph of an 'open' football club is of Forest FC in October 1863, featuring the two Alcock brothers, so Sheffield FC was off the pace in one area of record keeping.

The photograph (right) is undated and none of the players are named but their single coloured shirts would suggest that this photograph was taken either between 1857 and 1878 or 1881-1882; at all other times, up to 1889, Sheffield FC's shirts were bi-coloured. Therefore, it could be the photograph retailed by the Sheffield Portrait Gallery in April 1876, but in that year both Clegg brothers were still playing and neither seem to be present in this image. If anyone has evidence to help clarify dates and personnel, please get in touch.

The earliest team photograph of Sheffield FC.

Just two of the forty-five new Association clubs were from Sheffield;

Darnall FC (Sheffield, Yorkshire 1876-1895)
- Equal Thirty-third Oldest Sheffield Football Club
- Equal 117th Oldest Football Club in England

> Origin: Unknown
> According to the 1879 Football Annual –
> Founded: 1876
> Number of members: 94
> Club Ground: Shirland Lane
> Hon. Sec.: G.A. Cheetham, Handsworth Lane
> Colours: Puce and white
> According to the 1880 Football Annual –
> Founded: 1876
> Number of members: 90
> Club Ground: Brooker's Field
> Hon. Sec.: G. Taylor, 142 Industry lane, Darnall
> Colours: Puce and white

In 1877 they played a team of clerks from the Manchester, Sheffield and Lincolnshire Railway Company:

"DARNALL v. M. S. AND L. CLERKS. - Played on the Clerks' ground at Darnall. The first-named won the toss and played with the wind and hill in their favour, and up to half time they had scored four goals to none, kicked respectively by G. A. Cheetham, and J. Woodward; their goal-keeper headed one through, and the last was got in a general scrimmage. Although the Clerks tried all possible schemes to equalise matters, they failed to score, and the match ended in favour of Darnall by four goals to none. The following played well for the Clerks: - W. H. Coggan, A. Smith, and Burley, and besides those above-mentioned, J. Bell, A. Bower, and H. Reckless excelled for Darnall." [283]

A week later Darnall FC played a game against a club which combined the joys of football and cycling. The Liverpool Velocipede Club began in 1869 and the interest in cycling had clearly spread over the Pennines by 1877; a strange combination, but it would have made getting to away matches easier:

"SHEFFIELD AND HALLAMSHIRE BICYCLE AND FOOTBALL CLUB v. DARNALL. This return match, between the first teams, was played at Millhouses on Saturday. Darnall won the toss, and J. Schofield, the bicyclist captain, set the ball in motion. After about 20 minutes' play J. Milner sent one through for Darnall, and in less than ten minutes after he sent another clean through. After half time was called the ball was kick off again, and it soon was seen that the Darnall men had not done, although a slight breeze had got up against them. G. Lister got hold of the ball, and put it through, whilst J. Milner charged the goal-keeper, and thus the match ended in favour of Darnall by three goals to none. All through the game the Darnall goal-keeper only touched the ball three times. The following played well for the vanquished: - J. Tunnard, J. Schofield, S. Johnson, and W. Green; for Darnall, J. Herring, J. Bell, and G. A. Cheetham excelled." [284]

Violence between players and fans goes all the way back to that Folk Football game between Sheffield and Norton in 1793 but was unusual in the Association era. I mentioned earlier in this book spectators attacking Pierce Dix in 1881 and the unfortunate accident to William Cropper. Fans fighting opposition fans was a newer phenomenon; after the final of the Cheshire County Cup final between Northwich Victoria and Crewe Alexandra in 1889, both sets of fans found themselves on either side of the railway track at Middlewich railway station:

"They commenced operations by alternately hooting and cheering and then one man challenged an aggressive antagonist to fight. Both leaped on the metals and fought desperately till separated by officials. Then a great number of Northwich men, ran across the line, storming the platform occupied by the Crewe men…The Middlewich police were sent for. Sergeant Wynne and nine policemen arrived, but by that time Northwich had practically gained possession of the platform, the Crewe men who were outnumbered flying left and right. The special then came in and the police guarded them off, many carrying marks that will distinguish them for some time." [285]

The earliest case of hooliganism I have found for south Yorkshire involved Darnall FC and Worksop FC in 1891:

"Disgraceful conduct of local football players. Series of free fights. A case for the Association. On Saturday, the Darnall Football Club's team met the Worksop team on the ground of the latter and retired beaten by four goals to nil. Later in the evening, says a correspondent, the majority of the Darnallites, who were accompanied by a strong contingent of supporters, visited the Old Ship Inn singing room, situated in the Market place, Worksop. Amongst those in the room were R. Eyre and another member of the home team. The visitors, either through charring at their defeat, or having had too much liquor, tried to pick up a quarrel with Eyre, but he declined to have anything to do with them, and moved to another part of the room. The Darnallites being loud in their offers to fight, some of the supporters of the home team present in the room accepted the challenge, and a general melee took place in the singing room alluded to. From 16 to 20 men were all fighting together, and to make matters worse the lights were put out. In the darkness fists, feet, and belts were freely used, one of the Darnall players being knocked down insensible. The Darnall team and their supporters went to the Worksop Railway Station about 9.30pm, with the intention of leaving by the 9.38 train. Eyre, the Worksop player previously mentioned, who lives at Shireoaks, and was going home by the same train, was on the platform. Here the Darnallites surrounded him, knocked him down, and kicked him in a most brutal manner. There being several colliers on the platform, who were also about to return to Shireoaks by the 9.38 train, another hand to hand fight took place, and the platform presented a curious spectacle, there being some 30 men fighting and kicking at the same time, until the engine steamed into the station and the visitors got into the train. Arrived at Shireoaks, Eyre, who could scarcely stand, was helped out of the carriage, but here another scene occurred. The Darnallites got out of their carriages and again kicked and beat Eyre, while those who defended him were also roughly handled, and as the train steamed out of Shireoaks Station a man, named Heathcote, a resident of Shireoaks, was left lying bleeding and insensible on the platform. Our Worksop representative saw Eyre yesterday (Sunday) morning. He has a deep wound to the back of his left ear, which has the appearance of being caused by a kick, his bottom lip is cut through, both eyes are black and nearly stopped up, and his ribs and legs are black and blue from top to bottom." [286]

Newfield FC (Sheffield, Yorkshire 1876-1880)
- Equal Thirty-third Oldest Sheffield Football Club
- Equal 117th Oldest Football Club in England

> Origin: Public House. Newfield Inn on the corner of Penns Road and Denmark Road, Heeley
> According to the 1879 Football Annual
> Founded: 1876
> Number of members: 100
> Club Ground: Gleadless Road
> Hon. Sec.: A. Hall, (Messrs. Hawksley's) Carver Street, Sheffield
> Colours: Blue and black

The above details were repeated in the 1880 edition and then mentions ceased.

By 1877 they were members of the breakaway Sheffield New Association:

"Newfield Football Club – The annual general meeting of the above club was held at the Newfield Inn, on Wednesday, when the following officers were elected: President, Mr. J. H. Berley; treasurer, Mr. H. Stanley; secretary, Mr. J. W. Turtle; committee, Messrs. E. W. Crabb, J. Shaw, Joe Fidler, S. Thompson, G. May, and F. C. Robinson. Delegate to the New Association and Accident Fund, Mr. A. Hall." [287]

They were still members in 1880 [288], but after that the reports dry up.

Mexborough FC (South Yorkshire 1876 – 1900), won the Sheffield & Hallamshire Senior Cup in 1885/86 and 1895/96.

> According to the 1887 Football Annual –
> Founded: 1876
> Club Ground: Mexboro'
> Dressing room: Commercial Hotel
> Code: Association
> Hon. Sec.: W. Sayer, Garden street, Mexboro'
> Colours: Red and white

The above information was duplicated in the 1888 edition and then the reporting stopped.

By 1889 the football and cricket clubs of Mexborough had amalgamated:

"For years, there has been a feeling amongst the members of the Mexborough Football and Cricket Clubs that, for the mutual advantage of both, they should become amalgamated. The principle difficulty to be overcome is the confliction of interests that will ensue when the details are discussed. By means of amalgamation it is believed that funds would be forthcoming for much-needed improvement of the ground, both for cricketing and footballing purposes. The subject has been discussed at a general meeting of the football club, and the opinion was much in favour of amalgamation. A communication was ordered to be forwarded to Mr. W. Nicholson,

CHAPTER FIVE

the cricket club secretary, who doubtless will call his committee or a general meeting together to take it into consideration, and Mr. P. S. Macliver, a candidate for the Doncaster division, has forwarded a subscription of £1 to the funds of the football club." [289]

Mexborough FC got into debt in 1901 and was not seen thereafter in any press reports:

"MEXBOROUGH FOOTBALL CLUB. HEALTHIER OUTLOOK. There is every indication of the debt of £113, which remained on the Mexborough Football Club at the conclusion of last season, being speedily wiped out. Following the meeting of supporters, a few weeks ago, the chief creditor has called the others together, and an arrangement has been effected, whereby they have agreed to accept half their accounts in full settlement. The cricket club to whom £25 was owing for rent, have very generously reduced this amount to £10. It is proposed to promote an archery tournament for Easter, and other means are suggested for the purpose of clearing off the deficiency. At the commencement of the present season the acting committee decided not to run another team until all liabilities had been got rid of." [290]

A new club, Mexborough Town FC was formed in 1903 and changed its name to Mexborough Athletic in 1926, but failed in 1936. Another 'Mexborough Town FC' was the third attempt to maintain Association football in the town but this too folded in 1993.

An interesting works team was founded in 1876 in Rotherham, called **Phoenix Bessemer FC**, which submitted its details to the 1879 Football Annual:

Founded: 1876
Number of members: 40
Club Ground: The Ickles, near Sheffield
Hon. Sec.: H. Fields, Eastwood Vale, Rotherham
Colours: Navy blue

By the following 1880 edition of the Football Annual, the numbers had increased to 50 and the Hon. Sec. was F. Dunstan of 64 Clun Road, Sheffield, otherwise the information remained the same. The Phoenix Bessemer Steel Works opened in 1872 making steel through the use of the Bessemer process. The football club the entered the Sheffield Association Cup in 1879:

"Phoenix Bessemer v Kimberworth – this match was played on Saturday on the ground of the former Clifton lane, Rotherham. Phoenix Bessemer won the toss, and elected to kick downhill. During the first half of the game the Bessemer team got one goal scored. However, on changing ends, the ball was almost exclusively confined to the visitors' goal, Bessemer quickly putting two more goals to their score, but it now became so dark and misty that it was impossible to distinguish the players or see the ball across the field. Eventually Bessemer won by three goals to two. For Bessemer, the play of W. Scott, C. Douglas, T. Cooper and E. Rhodes was excellent, while for Kimberworth T. and M. Corbett, W. Nixon, J. Peters, and C. Wilson worked hard to save defeat. The teams were as follows: Phoenix Bessemer: E. Rhodes (captain), W. Cutts, T. Cooper, C. Douglas, W. Scott and J. McCormick, forwards; J. Simms, J. Rawlin, T. Hetherington and W. Bagnall, backs; T. Moody, goal; umpires, E. Pinner.

Kimberworth: T. Corbett (captain), M. Corbett, J. Peters, M. Richardson, W. Nixon, J. Roddison, R. Beale, C. White, T. Tyler, G. Mitchell, W. Hague. Umpire, F. Hall; referee, Mr. T. Banks." [291]

In 1882/83 Phoenix Bessemer entered the F.A. Cup, eventually losing to Notts County in the third round:

Round 1   Grantham – walkover
Round 2   Grimsby Town   A   9-1   Round 3   Notts County   A   1-4

176

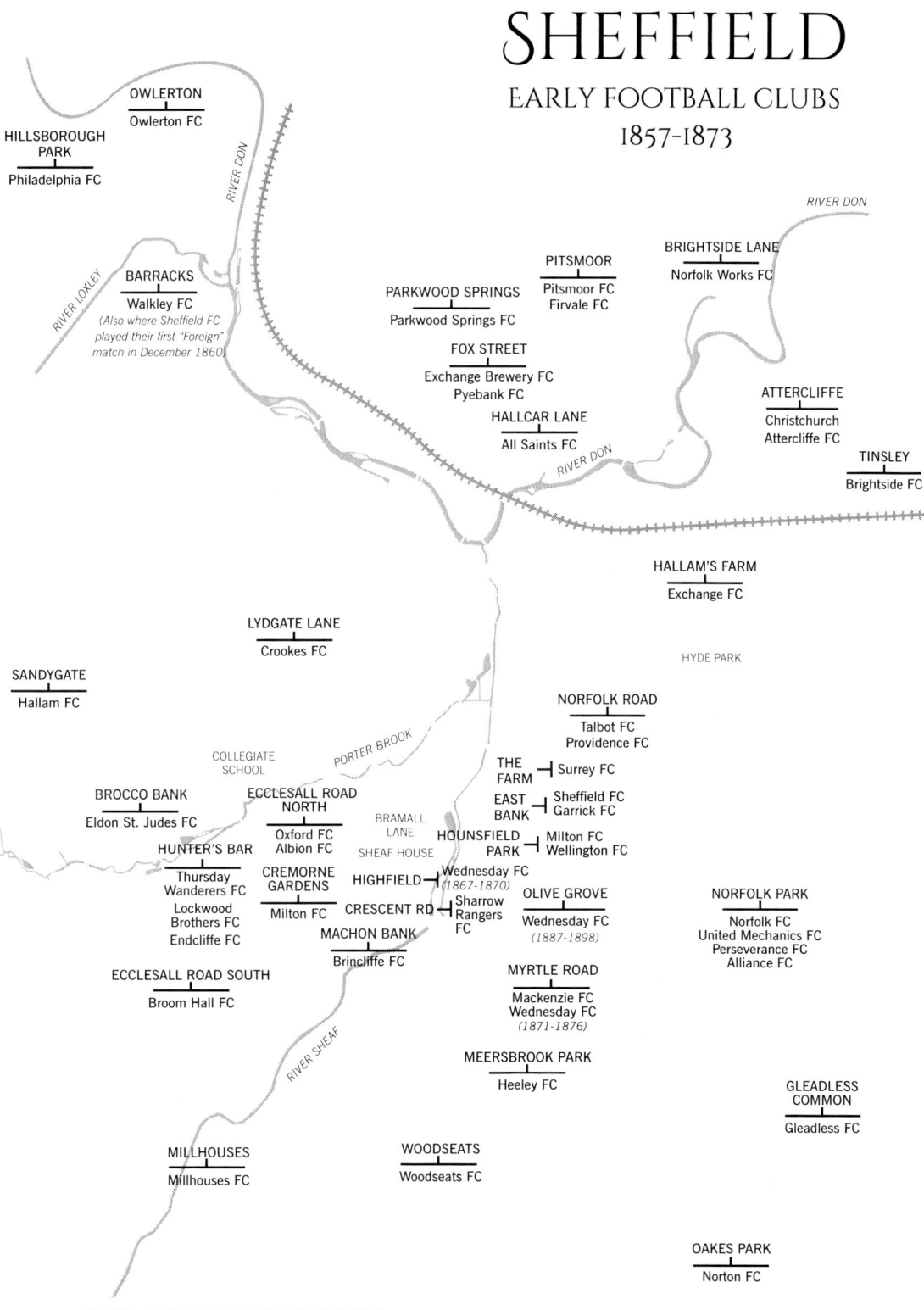

CHAPTER SIX

The Decline of the Old Order 1877-1887

Only four Sheffield clubs formed between 1877 and 1889: White Cross FC (1879) a club in Crookes, the Zulus (1879) a charity club used later as a route for players to receive appearance money, Sheffield Wanderers FC (1879) a brief professional outfit and Sheffield United (1889) a purpose built professional club designed to play at Bramall Lane. Six new Association clubs would appear in the south Yorkshire and north Derbyshire between 1877 and 1887.

In the rest of England, a total of fifty-one Association clubs formed in 1877 alone, of which eighteen came from Lancashire. Seven of those fifty-one clubs are still with us: Burnham FC, Lancing Old Boys, Newmarket Town FC, Buxton FC, Horsham FC, Clitheroe Central FC and Crewe Alexandra FC; the latter claims the title of 15th Oldest League Club.

Professionalism was the new force in football, driven by the football clubs of the north west, a wind that would buffet the Sheffield and London Football Associations until payments to players were legalised. Sheffield had led the way in Association football for twenty years, but from 1877 there was change in the air that would culminate in the legalisation of professionalism on 20th July 1885; after this amateur footballers and their clubs would begin their slow decline. This dramatic fall was mirrored in the other boom areas of amateur football: London, the Home Counties and the Midlands.

Initially, the middle and upper class Sheffield amateurs of the 1860s did not let working men play for their football clubs and the working classes were too busy working to play sports.

As mentioned in Chapter Five, the first Sheffield football clubs sprang up around cricket clubs, the church and the Temperance Movement. The first exception was Garrick FC, perhaps the first club for the working man in 1866 based around a public house. Sheffield's first club for the non-manual working man was Thursday Wanderers FC, started by banking clerks. It was a probable change in their work hours that freed them to play football; right across England the rise of the professional player coincided with the gradual but increasing amount of leisure time given by various changes in employment law. In 1850, textile workers were granted an early finish on Saturdays at 2 o' clock, which went back by another hour in 1874. The Saturday half day holiday would be the norm for the majority by the early 1870s, freeing up the time available to play football. The hour or so that the game required fitted in with their Saturday afternoon. Their game of choice could only be football (or Rugby, north of Sheffield); - cricket required all day to play and so would remain the domain of the middle and upper classes.

If Thursday Wanderers FC was Sheffield's first club for office workers, then Lockwood Brothers FC was the first club for industrial workers. It was created by the owners, but the players were the factory employees of the file, steel and cutlery firm. When Lockwood Brothers FC formed in 1870, there was no appetite from the majority of Sheffield workers to question the amateur status quo. The establishment figures who ran Sheffield football followed the amateur ethos and when working class players were invited to play, they happily followed the rules to avoid upsetting their employers. The difference in Lancashire was that the men who ran

CHAPTER SIX

the football clubs, ran them commercially, and the players happily followed their lead.

Sheffield football's cosy relationship between gentlemen and players lasted until 1879, coming to a head with the confrontation between Zulu FC and the Sheffield Football Association. (more later in this Chapter).

Sheffield, the old home of Association football, was replaced from 1877 by Lancashire; this ultimately led to the launch of the Football League in 1888. The existing football establishments of Sheffield, London and the Midlands had bet on the old ways and fought against the evil that they perceived professionalism to represent, and lost.

The first sign that the old order of Sheffield football was changing in 1877 did not come from a mill worker playing for Blackburn Olympic, but from closer to home.

1877

Sheffield New Football Association

Whilst only three Sheffield clubs would form in this period of 1877- 1887, it does not mean that football was not played in Sheffield at this time; very many small clubs were launched and many joined the breakaway Sheffield New Football Association that was formed in April 1877. Faced with an influx of new football clubs in this year the Sheffield Football Association either didn't want to admit them, or it couldn't cope with new members. Its solution was not to allow any club under two years old to become a member, which forced the hand of the fledgling clubs into forming their own organisation.

Chapter Four covered how quickly the Sheffield New Football Association grew, with twelve clubs on launch and forty-nine by the 1880 edition of the Football Annual. This, at a time when the Sheffield Football Association could only claim thirty-three clubs. The majority of these clubs stayed loyal to the 1867 organisation, in spite of the fact that it was in decline with its longstanding clubs starting to close down. It is quite puzzling why the Sheffield Football Association didn't embrace these new members as it would have given the old organisation an important shot in the arm at a critical time. The reason was not because the new organisation would be run on professional lines, because they were as committed to amateurism as the Sheffield Football Association. The New Association's ethos was a reaction to the status quo of the existing football establishment: 'It was formed for the purpose of bringing out new talent.' [1] The relationship between the two Associations was a little frosty in 1879, as characterised by an exchange of letters printed in the Sheffield Telegraph:

> "THE NEW FOOTBALL ASSOCIATION. To the editor of the Sheffield Daily Telegraph. Sir, - Will you kindly allow the Executive of the Sheffield Football Association, through the medium of your columns, to lay before the public the following correspondence, which will clearly show that the earnest desire of the above association to help the distressed poor of our town has been frustrated through the (old) Sheffield Football Association failing to take up the challenge: -
>
> To Mr. Peirce Dix, Hon. Sec. Sheffield Football Association.
>
> Respected Sir, - I have great pleasure in forwarding you the following copy of resolution passed unanimously by the delegates of the Sheffield New Football Association on Wednesday last: - 'That the hon. sec. be instructed to write the Sheffield Football Association conveying a respectful challenge to play a friendly match with this association for the benefit of the Mayor's Distress Fund at as early a date as possible.' Will

THE DECLINE OF THE OLD ORDER 1877-1887

you kindly let the delegates of your association know as early as convenient, and your prompt answer will be esteemed? In order to serve the charitable object we have in view, it is our intention of handling this challenge, together with, we trust, your favourable acceptation, to the newspapers immediately on receipt of the same. –I am, yours truly, W.S. Ibbotson, Hon. Sec. S. N. F. A.

The following reply was received December 23rd, Fargate, December 13th, 1878.

To Mr. W. S. Ibbotson. Sir, - In reply to yours of the 12th inst., I beg on behalf of the committee of this association to decline your challenge. –Yours obediently, W. Peirce Dix.

On the above reply being read over to the New Association delegates, Mr. R. Hildrick moved and Mr. G. W Cooper seconded the following resolution, which was carried: - 'That this association regrets that the old association should reply in so curt a manner to the challenge, without giving any definite reason for refusing, as it was prompted in a friendly spirit, for a good object.' Signed on behalf of the association, FREDK. SANDERSON, President. W.S. IBBOTSON, Hon. Sec., S.N.F.A." [2]

The 1880 edition of the Football Annual shows the New Association with forty-nine clubs, of which only All Saints FC and Perseverance FC had gone over to the new Association from the 1867 Sheffield Association (forty-two of the forty-nine clubs are from Sheffield). The foundation dates below show that the majority of the clubs were recently formed, perhaps because of the fact of the New Association's creation.

Club	Foundation Date	Ground	Hon. Sec.	Notes
All Saints Wanderers	1877	Frith Park	J. Smith, 7 Carwood Lane	Sheffield
Barrow Hill	1876	Staveley Works Ground	J. Benison, 152 Barrow Hill, Staveley	Derbyshire
Brunswick	1877	Baldwin Street, Attercliffe	G. Booth, 21 Andover Street	Sheffield
Burton Star	1876	Spirecliffe Lane	J. Spencer, 2 Ball Street, North	Staffordshire Sheffield New Association Challenge Cup winners in 1879/80 and losing finalists in 1880/81
Clarence	1878	Queen's Road	W. Deane, Royal Standard, St. Mary's Road	Sheffield
Clifton Rangers	1878	Abbeydale Road	G. Jephson, John Street, Highfield	Sheffield
Dronfield Exchange	1872	Studley Lane	A. C. Turner, Holborn, Dronfield	Sheffield border Derbyshire
Dronfield Town	1879	Dronfield	W. Allen, Darmstead Works Dronfield	Sheffield border Derbyshire
Dronfield Wanderers	1878	Dronfield	G. Platt, jnr., High Street Dronfield	Sheffield border Derbyshire
Ebenezer Wesleyan	1879	Wood Hill	T. Stacey, Montgomery Terrace Road	Sheffield
Ebenezer Wesleyan	1879	Grimesthorpe	J. R. Gibson 44 Grimesthorpe Road	Sheffield
Enfield United	1879	Grimesthorpe	W. Oldham, Carbrook Street, Carbrook	Sheffield
Grenoside	1876	Grenoside	J. Smith, Red Lion, Grenoside	Sheffield

CHAPTER SIX

Half-way House	1879	Nr. Killamarsh Station	W. Milner, jnr., Half-way House, Eckington	Sheffield border Derbyshire
Hallamshire	1878	Lydgate Crooks	A. Newbold, 191 Witham Road	Sheffield
Highfield Rangers	1877	Abbeydale Road	H. Leybourne, 2 Beeley Street	Sheffield
Intake	1879	Intake	J. Spotswood, Elm Tree Hill Intake	Sheffield New Association Challenge Cup winners in 1880/81
Killamarsh Red Rose	1878	Upperthorp	J. G. Hawkings, West Thorpe Killamarsh	Sheffield border Derbyshire
Kilnhurst*	1877	Kilnhurst	W. Crieton, Kilnhurst	Mexborough
Marsh Lane United	1876	Marsh Lane	J. Smith, Marsh Lane, near Chesterfield	Derbyshire
Nether	1873	Queen's Road	W. Cawood, 24 Shude Hill, Sheffield	Sheffield
Norton Britannia	1876	Norton	T. Barker, Derbyshire Lane Norton	Sheffield
Old Whittington Revolution	1876	Whittington Moor	F. Creed, Whittington Moor	Derbyshire
Owlerton Broughton	1877	Wadsley Bridge	W. H. Jones, 16 Bournville Street, Sheffield	Sheffield
New Owlerton	1877	Hillsborough	H. Eadon, Burrow Lees Owlerton	Sheffield
Oxford United	1875	Greystone	H. Darwen, Ecclesall Road Sheffield	Sheffield
Parish Church	1878	East Bank Road	J. Brooksbank, 94 Clarence Street	Sheffield
Park Friendly	1876	Manor Lane Park	G. Whittington, 3 Low Street Park	Sheffield
Park Wood Rovers	1880	Recreation Ground	E. Wardle, 106 Wallace Road	Sheffield
Perseverance Temperance	1866	Norfolk Park	E. M. Mushet, Clyde Street Works, Wicker Sheffield	Sheffield
Pitsmoor Christ Church	1878	Shirecliffe Lane	O. Cotterell, Bank Street Sheffield	Sheffield
Portmahon	1878	Hillsborough	A. Marshall, 22 Spring Vale Road	Sheffield
Postal Telegraph	1877	Norfolk Park	C. R. Morton, Gen. Post Office, Sheffield	Sheffield
Princess Street Wesleyan	1877	Bacon Lane, Attercliffe	W. Moffatt, 4 Lovell Street, Attercliffe	Sheffield
Priory Wanderers	1877	Abbeydale Road	J. C. Jenkinson, 64 Culver Road	Sheffield
Red Rangers	1880	Fox House, Attercliffe	T. Hammar, 53 Fowler Street	Sheffield
Rising Star	1875	Queen's Road	A. Chapman, 63 Bridge Street	Sheffield Sheffield New Association Challenge Cup. Losing finalist in 1877/78 to Pye Bank. Winners in 1878/79 against Christ Church
St. Andrews	1874	Hunter's Bar	W. S. Ibbotson, 77 Montague Street	Sheffield

St. John's Park	1879	Cricket Road	J. Rodgers, Lord Street, Park	Sheffield
Saville Street Foundry	1876	Brightside Lane	J. H. Russell, 42 Berkley Street, Attercliffe	Sheffield
Shiregreen	1876	Shiregreen	J. E. Rhodes, Shiregreen	Sheffield
South View Rangers	1877	Banner Cross, Ecclesall	G. Redfern, 104 Franklin Street	Sheffield
Southey Green	1880	Southey Green	G. Lee, Moonshine, Southey Green	Sheffield
Spital	1873	Spital	Ch. Mason, Spital House Chesterfield	Sheffield
Stocksbridge Forester	1878	Spink Hall	A. Elson, Haywood Park	Sheffield
Thorncilffe	1879	Chapel Town	W. E. Fullelove, Whitfield Chapel Town	Sheffield
Whittington Moor Rovers	1874	New Whittington	G. S. Massey, Whittington Moor, Chesterfield	Sheffield
Wild Myrtle	1874	Heeley Park	J. Plant, 41 Harcourt Road, Heeley	Sheffield
Zion Wanderers	1876	Pothouse Lane	166 Carlton Road, Attercliffe	Sheffield

* Kilnhurst FC's claim to fame was that it produced a player called George Wilson. He followed Jack Hunter across the Pennines to join Blackburn Olympic FC in 1882 (but does not appear in the 1882 team photograph on page 89). According to 'Shooting Stars: The Brief and Glorious History of Blackburn Olympic 1878-1889' by Graham Phythian, George Wilson scored thirty-plus goals in the Olympics' F.A. Cup-winning season and transferred to Preston North End FC in September1883, under persuasion from Billy Sudell. By October 1883 he was the proprietor of the Black-a-Moor's Head Inn on Lancaster Road and had married a Preston 'lass' the same month.

In 1881 the New Association changed its name to the Hallamshire Football Association:

"WITH the Earl Fitzwilliam at its head as honorary president, and its founder and parent, Mr. Sanderson as president, the Hallamshire Football Association is anticipating a highly prosperous season. Seven new clubs have this season joined the Association, so that the winter game is not quite played out in the South Yorkshire district." [3]

According to the 1883 Football Annual, the numbers of the Hallamshire F.A. had gone down from forty-nine to thirty-seven, whilst the old Sheffield Association numbered twenty-nine clubs. By 1886 the demarcation between the two Associations was very indistinct and an amalgamation moved closer with a desire to form a single organisation, more capable of winning inter-Association matches:

"I believe it is now no secret that the executives of the Sheffield and Hallamshire Associations are trying to bring about an amalgamation of the two societies. I understand representatives of both associations have met during the past few days, and such was the spirit displayed on the occasion, that if the clubs forming the associations take the matter up in the same give and take way, very little doubt remains that the amalgamation will soon become an established fact. Both associations have played on strictly amateur principles, and the rules are so nearly alike, that very little trouble will be caused in assimilating them. The chief points to be considered by those who are not bound by selfish considerations is, will it conduce to the best interest of the game in this district? For some years, it is a well known fact, that the Sheffield team have not been able to hold their own against combinations that only a short time ago they were able to run over, and it is high time a remedy was found whereby this state of affairs can be changed. The joining together of the two bodies will enable the management to bring into the field a more powerful team then hitherto, and it is just possible that Sheffield may again be able

CHAPTER SIX

to hold its head as high as it did in the early days when football was in its infancy. I hope the scheme will go forward, and that all clubs within a reasonable distance will become members, and thus build up a strong and powerful association." [4]

In 1885 the Sheffield footballing community was shaken further when William Prest died suddenly on the 10th February, aged just 54, of a burst blood vessel, whilst walking down Market street to his wine merchants in the High Street. His time with the Volunteer Movement ensured his loss would be felt throughout Sheffield, not just in the confines of Sheffield FC and the Sheffield Football Association. According to the Sheffield Daily Telegraph, Lieutenant Colonel Prest was buried with full military honours on the 13th February. The funeral procession left from his home at Dam Cottage to the town cemetery and was lined with thousands of onlookers. His coffin was laid on a gun carriage drawn by six horses, led by a 200-strong firing party and four military bands, followed by full contingents of the Hallamshire Rifles, Yeomanry Cavalry, Artillery Volunteers, Sheffield Engineers and private carriages. With the turbulence surrounding the question of professionalism in the game reaching its pinnacle in 1885, the rivalry between the two Sheffield football organisations and the sudden death of the co-founder of Sheffield FC, it must have felt like troubled times for the likes of J.R. Harvey (S.F.A. Hon. Sec) and Charles Clegg (S.F.A. President).

An amalgamation moved closer in October 1886 and the resistance for merger came from the Hallamshire F.A.:

"I notice that in the draw for the Hallamshire Association Cup ties there are over a dozen clubs of the 22 drawn who are members of the Sheffield Football Association as well as the Hallamshire. Now, as the Sheffield Football Association has declared itself in favour of amalgamation and a combined meeting of the two local associations passed a resolution declaring the desirability of a union, there must be some inconsistency lurking somewhere, or the desired goal would have been reached ere this. Is it same as when the matter was first brought up, where some members at the S.F.A. meeting voted in favour of amalgamation and at the H.F.A. voted against it." [5]

Later that year the two rival Associations finally amalgamated and became the Sheffield and Hallamshire Association. The new union was described in the 1887 Football Annual: 'The wisdom of this (amalgamation) was proved in the results of the Association matches. Close upon 60 clubs have entered the association this season. David Haigh. (Hon.Sec.).'

The Sheffield press said the actual number was fifty-six clubs:

"The one and only local association, the outcome of the amalgamation of the Sheffield Football Association and the Hallamshire Football Association, gives promise of a brilliant season. No less than 56 district clubs have sent in their allegiance to the association and two-thirds of them are in for both cups. The entries for the challenge cup number 20, comprising all the most noted teams of the town, whilst for the minor between 30 and 40 clubs have intimated their intention of competing." [6]

At the time of amalgamation, thirty-five clubs belonged to the Hallamshire Football Association and the remaining twenty-one were members of the Sheffield Football Association. The Sheffield and Hallamshire Association is still going strong today, administering to over eight hundred football clubs. It is based at Clegg House, 204 Meadowhall Road - appropriately enough, the head office is named after the man that brokered the amalgamation between the rival organisations back in 1887.

Elsewhere in South Yorkshire was the formation in Barnsley of its first Association - playing team.

Barnsley Wanderers FC (Yorkshire, December 1877-1882)

Barnsley had always been best known for its Rugby teams: Barnsley FC (1873) and Barnsley St. Mary FC (1878). Barnsley Wanderers FC was the first Association club in the town and I cannot find a link from this club to Barnsley St. Peters (1887), which would become modern day Barnsley FC. The formation of Barnsley Wanderers FC is clearly linked to the Sheffield game:

"The first meeting of the Barnsley Wanderers Football Club formed under Sheffield Association rules was held at the Royal Hotel on Tuesday evening last, when the rules were set and a committee formed." [7]

According to the 1879 Football Annual –
Founded: 1877
Number of members: 40
Club Ground: Huddersfield Road
Dressing room: Royal Hotel
Code: Association
Hon. Sec.: M.B. Lawton, Stanley House, Barnsley
Colours: Navy blue with badge

The only difference between the entries for Barnsley Wanderers FC in the 1879, 1880, and 1881 Football Annuals is that by 1881 the membership has increased to 45 and it was now a member of Sheffield Association; all mentions of Barnsley Wanderers ceased from 1882 onwards.

Sharrow Rangers FC players formed the majority of a Sheffield team that went to Barnsley in 1877 to participate in the first Association rules game played in the town:

"Sheffield Scratch team v Barnsley Wanderers. A team composing mostly of Sharrow Rangers FC visited Barnsley on Saturday to meet a new club lately formed there. This was the first time that the association rules had been played in Barnsley, consequently a numerous concourse of spectators assembled to witness the match. Barnsley team: Lawton, Raby, Fox, Beard, Coles, Ledgar, Mallinson, Marsden, Johnson, Lawton and Crawshaw." [8]

Meanwhile, in Derbyshire, the Sheffield game had reached Eckington:

Eckington FC (Derbyshire, 1877-1894)

- Twice winners of the Hallamshire Football Association Challenge Cup

Eckington FC was listed in the 1880 Football Annual as a member of the Sheffield Association; its foundation date is given as 1880 but it never reappears after this in the Football Annuals.

Number of members: 50
Club Ground: Eckington
Dressing room: Royal Hotel
Code: Sheffield Association
Hon. Sec.: T.D. Alsop, Eckington Collieries, near Chesterfield
Colours: Blue and white

It seems that Mr. Alsop got the foundation date of 1880 wrong as there are match reports from 1877: "Swallownest v. Eckington. Played on the ground of the former, and resulted in easy victory for home team by four goals to none." [9]

In 1880 Eckington FC beat Chesterfield FC by 8 goals to nil and an Eckington FC team list was reported for the first time:

CHAPTER SIX

"Eckington: George Paul (goal). C. Levick (captain), H. Levick, T. Levick, J. Hall, F. Elliot, W. Angus, H. Jennings, E. Beaver, T. Nettleship, and M. Wade. Umpire, J. Levick. Chesterfield: C. Blake (goal), A. Naylor (captain), J. Bishop, D. Casey, G. Sanderson, T. Mello, J. Boardman, J. Hancock, J. Duckmanton, T. Severn, and T. Robinson. Umpire, C. Hibbard." [10]

Eckington FC's most successful period came when they joined the breakaway Sheffield New Association and appeared in the final in four consecutive years. They won the first in 1883/84:

"Hallamshire Football Association Challenge Cup 1883/84: Eckington 4 Clinton 3 (a.e.t.) (after the first game ended in a 2-2 tie and after extra time) played at Bramall Lane. The goals scored in the first 90 minutes were scored by: Clinton FC: Wales (1), Hibberd (2). Eckington FC: T. Levick (1), C. Levick (1), J. Smith (1) …Time soon afterwards arrived, but in consequence of the scores being equal (three goals each) it was decided to play ten more minutes each way. Eckington at once secured a corner, and the ball being splendidly directed by C. Levick it was headed through the Clinton posts. At the expiration of the first ten minutes the game stood. Eckington four to Clintons three goals. No score was afterwards obtained by either, so that Eckington won this highly exciting match, which for the year gives them the Hallamshire Cup, by four goals to three. Teams: - Clinton: - R. Bumby (Goal), J. T. Wainwright, B. Wilson, W. E. Jaques, S. Humberstone, H. Robinson, R. Hibberd, T. Kelsey, G. Green, J. Merry, and O. Wales. Eckington: - A. Hancock, L. Smith, T. Wake, E. Fanley, A. Booth, F. Elliot, J. Smith, C. Levick, T. Levick, H. Marples, and S. Croft." [11]

They lost to the all-powerful Staveley FC in the next two finals:

Hallamshire Football Association Challenge Cup Final 1884/85: Staveley 2 Eckington 1

Hallamshire Football Association Challenge Cup Final 1885/86: Staveley 3 Eckington 2

However, Eckington FC won again in 1886/87:

Hallamshire Football Association Challenge Cup Final 1886/87: Eckington 3 Chirton 1

By 1894 though, the club was in financial difficulties:

"THE FINANCIAL POSITION OF THE ECKINGTON FOOTBALL CLUB. Mr E Reeves presided at the annual meeting of the Eckington Football Club. During discussion, the results of the matches played last season were considered fairly satisfactory, but owing to the dispute in the coal trade, the suspension of the ground, and other causes, the financial position of the club was much below previous years. The deficit was stated to be about £19. It was unanimously agreed that each committee man pay 5s and each player 2s 6d towards wiping off the debt. Collectors were also appointed to solicit subscriptions from the general public. The following officers were elected for the ensuing year: President, Mr. W. E. Wells; treasurer, Mr. Samuel Hardwick; secretary, Mr. A. Ferguson, Dronfield road, Eckington; captain, Mr. Enoch Fairley; sub-captain, Mr. John Gyte; auditors, Messrs G Wilson and John Gyte." [12]

The press reports cease completely for Eckington FC after this report and I have set this as their end date even though reports start again in 1898 with a new incarnation of the club.

Like Barnsley, Leeds was a Rugby stronghold; Leeds FC (1864) tried its hand at the Sheffield Association game, but it would be thirteen years later before Hunslet FC was formed.

Hunslet FC (Leeds, Yorkshire 1877-1903)

"Two local Leeds clubs Excelsior and Albion merged under the auspices of Woodhouse Hill cricket club to play on the pitch as Hunslet FC." [13]

It was Hallam FC which did the missionary work on behalf of Association football in Leeds:

"In fact, Sheffield wanted to show the attributes of their own game to the Rugby footballers of West Yorkshire as soon as possible. The opportunity came when Hunslet Cricket Club of south Leeds decided to launch a Hunslet Association Club during October 1877. This decision was largely brought about by the club's cricket professional who hailed from south Yorkshire. At the behest of the Sheffield FA President, 12 members of the Hallam Club travelled to Leeds on 27th December 1877 to play an exhibition match on the Holbeck Recreation ground. Besides their players, Hallam also brought with them their own umpires and their own goal posts." (14)

It seems Hallam FC travelled incognito to the 1877 match, appearing under the name of the 'Blues' team in the Leeds press:

"HUNSLET FOOTBALL CLUB. - BLUES v. WHITES. -This match was played at Woodhouse-hill Cricket Ground on Thursday. The play on both sides was very good, especially that of the whites, who scored four goals to their opponents' nil, owing to the fine play of F. Hinde and W. Hill. Players- Blues: J. Hough, C. Wragg, G. Skeleton, J. Whittam, F. Ellis, A. Barlow, C. Shaw, G. Balme, R. Hudson, J. Atack, W. Mitchell, J. Clarke, and W. Squires. - Whites: F. Hinde, E. Sarson, G. Sampson, G. Hall, G. Ritchins, F. W. Hall, W. Hill, A. Mills, F. W. Brigham, J. Firth, W. Gilston, A. Bronscombe, and W. Hudson." (15)

The 'Blues' are Hallam FC; why was Hallam FC's name not mentioned in the above report? Was the reputation of Association football and the club name of a leading exponent of the game too toxic for the readership of Leeds? The Sheffield press described the fixture more fully as Hunslet v. Hallam (First teams). (16)

Hunslet FC appears in the 1879 Football Annual as members of the Sheffield Football Association:

Founded: 1876
Number of members: 150
Club Ground: Cricket ground, Woodhouse Hill, Hunslet
Dressing room: George the Fourth Inn, Hunslet
Hon. Sec.: F.W. Brigham, 2 Newport Street, Hunslet
Colours: Blue and white

The details were repeated in 1880 Football Annual but then the reporting ceased. (Hunslet also played Holmes FC and a match report is in the 1873 section)

"Leeds City AFC (1904-1919) is really built out of the ashes of the old Hunslet club, which kept the Association game quietly going on at a time when the Leeds public had no eye or ear for anything but the handling code. Hunslet 'went under' but after the lapse of a season, some of its old members foregathered and, being reinforced by many newcomers, the club was resurrected and given the representative name of the 'Leeds City Association Football Club.' At first the enterprise was nebulous and visionary, but the outlook cleared when the Holbeck Northern Union Club became defunct and placed its (Elland Road) ground on the market." (17)

During the First World War, financial irregularities and breaking the ban on paying players during the war, led to the Leeds City AFC's dissolution in 1919.

1878

No new clubs were founded in the Sheffield Football Association in 1878 but the game continued to boom nationally; forty-six new Association clubs were formed throughout England. Only eleven of those clubs still exist today: Hartlepool United FC, Blackpool FC, Matlock FC, Manchester United FC, Chelmsford FC, Grimsby FC, Clapton FC, Everton FC, Preston North End FC, Braintree FC and Coggeshall FC.

CHAPTER SIX

The start of the Passing Game

1878 marked the time when football tactics and formations changed; the game was transformed from the dribbling game and the 1-1-8 formation, as exemplified by the Charles W. Alcock's Wanderers, to the passing game. The Wanderers had won the F.A. Cup for the fifth time in this year but it would be their last ever victory.

"The game began to be played substantially in its present form, and 'passing on' completely superseded dribbling about the same time that the great provincial centres suddenly came to the front, about 1878 or 1879." [18]

From then on, the more typical formation became 2-2-6 under the passing game and lost forever was the rugby style with eight forwards chasing the game. This slowly evolved into 2-3-5 formation (two full-backs, three-half-backs and five forwards) which was first employed by the likes of Cambridge University, Turton FC, Nottingham Forest FC and Sheffield FC. The 2-3-5 formation was also referred to as 'combination play' in which each player was allotted an area of the field and played as part of a team in a game that was based upon passing. It was copied to great effect by Preston North End FC when they remained unbeaten in the inaugural Football League season in 1888. This formation was dominant until 1925 when the Football Association decided to change the offside rule (see Appendix One).

Floodlights at Bramall Lane

The year 1878 marked another landmark for Sheffield Football, with the first football match ever to be staged under electric floodlighting at Bramall Lane; this was organised by Messrs. Tasker. From the press description, the light was provided by 12 lamps, with two at each corner and two behind each goal:

"At each corner of the ground marked off for the players a wooden stage was erected some ten yards high for carrying the lamp and the reflector. Behind each goal was placed a portable engine, each of which drove two Siemen's dynamo machines on for each light. The illuminating power equalled 8,000 standard candles and the cost per hour for each light was about 3 and a ½ pence." [19]

The new lighting proved to be very popular and a new record attendance was set at Bramall Lane for a football match:

"Everybody seemed highly pleased with the result of the experiment, the light being most brilliant and effective. It may be stated that the experiment turned out to be a great financial success, the novelty of the thing drawing together an immense attendance, reaching in our estimation, nearly twenty thousand people. When everything was in readiness, at 7.30 the distinguishing colours of the two sides were clearly visible, although it was rather difficult to discern the individual movement on the top side of the ground." [19]

It was a game between Reds and Blues featuring leading players of the day, with each side captained by a Clegg brother:

"Reds: F. Stacey, J. Housley, J. Hunter, E. Buttery, F. Hinde, J.C. Clegg (captain), W. Mosforth, A. Woodcock, C. Stratford, H.E. Barber, G. Anthony.

Blues; T. Lawson, W.E. Clegg (captain), R. Gregory, T. Buttery, W.H. Stacey, G.B. Marples, A. Malpas, J. Tomlinson, E.H. Barber, T. Bishop, P. Patterson. Umpires: W. Skinner and R.W. Dickinson. Referee W. Pierce Dix." [19]

The Blues won by 2 goals to nil:

"The contest over the difficulty was to leave the ground. Such a concourse has never been seen at Bramall Lane, and as the means of exit are not particularly easy, there was quite a scene when the spectators attempted to leave. Great good temper, however, was exhibited by all, and eventually the great crowd cleared away without, as far as we were able to ascertain, the slightest accident." [19]

1879

Four clubs started in south Yorkshire in 1879, two of which joined the Sheffield Association, the first new members since 1876.

White Cross FC (Sheffield, Yorkshire 1879-1884)
- Thirty-Fourth Oldest Sheffield Football Club
- Equal 143rd Oldest Football Club in England

Origin: Unknown. Crookes was thriving in the early to mid-1880s with four football clubs. Crookes FC played at Lydgate Lane and met at the Ball Inn; Walkley FC also played at Lydgate Lane and met afterwards at the Old Grindstone. A member of the New Football Association, Hallamshire FC, played at Lydgate and all three were joined by White Cross FC, which chose to play at Dark Lane and celebrate afterwards at the Punch Bowl Inn. All this with Hallam FC's Sandygate ground less than a mile away.

According to the 1880 Football Annual –
Founded: 1879
Number of members: 30
Club Ground: Dark Lane, Crookes (now Springvale Road)
Dressing room: Punch Bowl Inn
Hon. Sec.: F. Wolstenholme, 46 Barber Road
Colours: Navy blue

White Cross FC played by modern tactics as displayed by their combination game and crossing prowess in the following report from 1881:

"WHITE CROSS v. ST, STEPHEN'S (1ST TEAMS). This match was played at Dark lane, on Saturday. White Cross, having won the toss, kicked up hill, and, after some good combined played, Beardshaw succeeded in reducing the opposing stronghold. No further score was registered up to half-time. After changing ends, White Cross had matters pretty much their own way, although Foster, Ledger, Styring, and several others strove hard to save defeat. Mappin placed the second goal to the credit of White Cross. Maxfield soon afterwards registered another; and when the ball was kicked off again Swallow secured possession, and quickly put the leather between the opposing posts. Shortly before time was called, Parkin made a splendid shot from more than half the length of the field, which the goal keeper failed to stop. No further score was made until time was called, White Cross thus winning by five goals to nil. All the white Cross team played well, their crossing tactics completely non-plussing their opponent." [20]

Later that year Pilling and Pullen caused problems for Hallam FC by sticking to their proven tactic of crossing the ball into the centre of the goal area:

"HALLAM v. WHITE CROSS First teams representing the above clubs met on Saturday afternoon *(1881)*, at Sandygate, and the weather being fine there was a fair attendance of spectators. White Cross won the toss, and S. Lovell kicked off for Hallam. For a considerable period the ball was kept in the vicinity of the White Cross goal, but it was then transferred to the other end, when excellent crossing play by Pilling and Pullen endangered the Hallam citadel. Half time arrived without either side having scored. On change of ends, the game was hotly contested, but the play was to some extent in favour of Hallam, who eventually succeeded in scoring a goal, the match thus ending in their favour by one goal to none. Five minutes before the call of time the ball burst. Lovell played in grand form for Hallam, and will be worth looking after by the association. Sarson and Dyson also played well; while Richards, Pilling, and Pullen were generally there or thereabouts for White Cross. We regret to state that Albert Slowe (playing for Hallam) sustained a severe accident during the game, and had to retire." [21]

Zulus FC (Sheffield, Yorkshire, 1879-1882)
- Thirty-Fifth Oldest Sheffield Football Club
- 154th Oldest Football Club in England

Origin: Charity. It started off with the best of motives but by 1882 had become embroiled in a stand-off between the Sheffield Football Association and the players agitating for monetary compensation for their playing skills. Mr. Brewer of the Sheffield Guardians suggested the idea of a charity match following the heroic publicity of the defence of the mission station at Rorke's Drift in January 1879 as part of the Anglo-Zulu War. Under the command of Lieutenant John Chard of the Royal Engineers and Lieutenant Gonville Bromhead, of the 2nd Battalion 24th Regiment of Foot, 150 British and colonial troops successfully defended the garrison against an assault by 3,000 to 4,000 Zulu warriors. Eleven Victoria Crosses were awarded to the defenders of Rorke's Drift, seven of them to soldiers of the 2nd/24th Foot, the most ever received for a single action by one regiment:

"One day in 1879 a match was arranged at Bramall Lane to raise funds for the widows and orphans of those lately killed in the Zulu war of that year. The rival teams were Sheffield and the 'Zulus', the latter dressed Zulu-wise in black jerseys, with decorating beads, hair, shields and assegais. The Zulus won by 5-4, continued their activities against such teams as the 'old Pantomime team' with J.W. Rowley, Witty, Watty, Walton etc. with such success that they were never beaten and received an offer to tour South Africa. In 1882 they were banned by the Sheffield Association because it appeared that the players were receiving money which was not going to charity and that, therefore, they were transgressing the strict regulations concerning amateurism." [22]

After beating a Sheffield Association X1, the Zulus also won at Chesterfield, Barnsley and Edinburgh but they lost to Blackburn Olympic in 1880. Sheffield players who took on the 'Zulu' mantle included: J. Slack, J.J.Lang, A. Woodcock, G. Anthony, H. Hinchcliffe, T. Buttery, G. Butcher, A. Malpas, G. Herring, A. Ramsden, Jack Hunter, Earnshaw, W. Moss, T. Cowley, G. Amley, S. Lucas, T. Milner, D. Willey, Jim Taft, R. Bagnall, J. March, W. Hague and Billy Mosforth.

Problems started to occur in 1881, two years after the club's foundation, because players were choosing to play matches for the Zulus rather than their home clubs and the Sheffield Football Association. The reason for their choice was because they were earning appearance money for their charity games. After playing for the Zulus, Jack Hunter and W. Moss were 'debarred' from playing for Heeley FC in the Wharncliffe Charity Cup semi-final against Wednesday on the 24th January 1881. Wednesday also lost a player for the game, Malpas, due to the same controversy. [23] The man who issued the judgement was W. Pierce Dix, the long-standing Hon. Sec. and subsequent Treasurer of the Sheffield Football Association. Heeley's

Hon. Sec. J.E. Deans handed Pierce Dix an official protest before the game commenced but it was after the match that the trouble escalated, as reported by Charles Clegg in a letter to the press. The player bans led to Pierce Dix getting 'hustled and several times kicked' as he was leaving the ground for the dressing room by persons 'who I am satisfied would be ashamed to be seen guilty of such conduct.' [24] After the event Pierce Dix resigned his post of Hon. Sec. of the Sheffield Association but this would not be the end of the trouble caused by Sheffield players wanting to be paid for their time and skill. (see Chapter Eight) Of the two banned players, Malpas, went on to pressurise Wednesday FC to start paying wages, by threatening to move to a new club in 1887 and Jack Hunter moved to Blackburn Olympic FC in 1882, when Zulus FC folded, as player coach. His deal included becoming landlord of the Cotton Tree pub on Birley Street; he later took on the Mason Arms on Northgate, also in Blackburn.

There was some sympathy for the players, as shown in this article reflecting on the Zulu affair:

"The general public will think, and think rightly, that a good football player, or a body of them, have as much right to make money by exhibiting their skill as professional cricketers. This doubtless is so, but unfortunately, they made matches for days anterior to one of the great games of the season, Sheffield v. London, and came up so worn out and jaded that the honour of the town was tarnished by a disastrous defeat. Moreover, many of the best club matches were spoiled by several of their leading men being away playing in such matches. But for these drawbacks-it is not right or just to stop such matches, though some other clubs, it is said, objected to play in Sheffield matches, if their players took part in such matches, as already alluded to. Gentlemen amateurs are rather too nice in their action in such matters." [25]

Another club sprang up later that year called the **Sheffield Wanderers FC,** formed as a new means for the players to receive payment, but was also quickly closed down:

"A number of players having been travelling around the country under the name of the Sheffield Wanderers, and whose sole aim was their own pecuniary advantage, a copy of the following rule was ordered to be sent to each club with the intimation that it would be strictly enforced- 'That in future any player taking part in a Zulu match or in any way receiving remuneration for playing, be debarred from playing in any association contest or cup tie'." [26]

The fourth south Yorkshire club to consider in 1879 is not from Sheffield, but Doncaster.

Doncaster Rovers FC (Yorkshire, 1879 – Present)
- England's 19th Oldest English League Club
- Yorkshire's second oldest League club after Sheffield Wednesday FC

The foundation of Doncaster Rovers FC is complicated. I have found a contradictory tale involving a thriving Rugby culture, a school team and the possibility of two football clubs forming in Doncaster in 1879. Unfortunately, the Doncaster Gazette has only been digitised for the year of 1870, which just leaves the definitive book, 'Donny: Doncaster Rovers FC The Complete History' by Tony Bluff the Club historian, to clarify matters. In an interview in May 2014 for the Doncaster Rovers club website, Tony Bluff said:

"In 1984, I called at the Rovers office and naively asked if I could use their minute books of directors' meetings and any other material such as result books that they may have in their archives as I wished to compile a history of the club. 'What minute books, what archives? Sorry we have nothing on the history of the club.' So the obvious answer was to spend the next ten years researching at Doncaster Library."

CHAPTER SIX

What he learnt in that time in the library about the club's foundation was as follows:

"In September 1879 Albert Jenkins, an 18-year-old fitter at Doncaster LNER Works, got together a group of men to play a game of football against The Yorkshire Institute for the Deaf and Dumb. At half-time, they were losing 4-0 but a rearrangement of the team enabled them to draw level before the close of play. After the game the players decided they would form a football club and would call themselves Doncaster Rovers. The first match under the name was played against Rawmarsh on October 3rd 1879, with the historic line-up: W. Walker, A. Jenkins, J. Mitchell, T. Clark, W. Salman, W. Chadwick, W. Bedford, A. Roper, J. Gosling, W. Simpson and W. Titterington. The match ended in a draw. After this, the team played friendly matches against local clubs."

The book is not referenced and I cannot find the events referred to, in any national database; until the Doncaster Gazette is fully digitised from 1871 onwards, it is impossible for me to present a definitive version of events, but I think the above facts may be wrong. I agree with Tony Bluff's 1879 foundation date but disagree with the personnel involved. Because Doncaster in the 1870s was a Rugby stronghold there are many mentions for a Doncaster FC that would evolve into Doncaster Rugby Football Club which still plays today. The confusion emanates from the fact that the club that would become Doncaster Rovers started out under the same name of 'Doncaster FC'. They only way to differentiate between the two clubs in the match reports is to look at line-ups of the players and the clubs' committees and follow them until it is clear whether one is looking at the Rugby or the Association 'Doncaster FC.'

My research findings into Doncaster football start, as always, with the Football Annual; the 1879 foundation date for 'Doncaster FC' is confirmed in the 1881 Football Annual, for an *Association playing team,* and critically the Hon. Sec is named:

Founded: 1879
Club Ground: Bennethorpe
Dressing room: Salutation hotel
Code: Association
Hon. Sec.: A. Brooke, High Street, Doncaster
Colours: Navy blue gold band

'A. Brooke' is not mentioned in the first line-up quoted by Tony Bluff, which is not crucial as I am looking at 1881, not 1879 at this point. But his presence in future line-ups would absolutely enable me to clarify which club's match reports relate to the future Doncaster Rovers FC.

The Doncaster Association story is muddied by an early Rugby team playing from 1874, that was still going strong in 1877:

"BARNSLEY v. DONCASTER. -On Saturday afternoon, the opening match of the season was played on the Barnsley ground between two sides of Barnsley and Doncaster. The visitors were short numbered, but Barnsley lent them several men. Doncaster, who had to contend against slight odds, played well, and the result of the match was that Doncaster obtained one goal, and Barnsley two, with one try and three touches down." [27]

A year later in 1878 the Rugby club had a meeting and it is worth noting the names of the attendees:

"DONCASTER FOOTBALL CLUB. - A general meeting of the members of the above club was held at Doncaster on Friday evening, when the following were elected office bearers for the opening season: - M. Stirling, Captain: G. Clark, Vice-Captain: W. Tindal, hon-sec: H. Clark, F. Day, H. D. Ellis, and C. Elwis, members of committee." [28]

THE DECLINE OF THE OLD ORDER 1877-1887

In 1879 there was a new Doncaster FC; a match report for 16th October 1879 states that the Doncaster club mentioned, only 'started this season'. I think this is the first match report for the team that would become Doncaster Rovers FC. I have underlined the key names to be aware of:

"BARNSLEY V. DONCASTER. A match between the above clubs was played on the ground of the former, on Thursday, and after a very pleasant game, resulted in a draw. Owing to the late arrival of the visitors, play did not commence until 4.10pm, at which time the ball was started by the Barnsley captain. Almost as soon as play had begun, the home team made a rush together, and scored their first goal. After this the game was very even, and nothing particular happened, until about 10 minutes before half time, when the Doncaster team got their first goal from the foot of W. Clark. On changing ends, both sides played hard, and before long Barnsley scored their second goal to their score- kicked by Palmer, after a run up by Littlewood- which made matters equal. For the Doncaster Club, which has only been started this season. Palmer, Littlewood, and Groom played best, and for Barnsley, Parkinson and H. E. Raley." [29]

(The above report also begs the question- is the opposition Barnsley Wanderers? or an unknown Barnsley Association team?)

Two days later the same Doncaster FC (as above) played on 18th October 1879 against a school team and this time 'A. Brooke' played in the half-back position:

"DONCASTER FOOTBALL CLUB V. DONCASTER GRAMMAR SCHOOL. -This match was played on Saturday, and after some good and fast play, resulted in favour of the town by three goals to none. Special mention should be made of the goal keeping of Bailey. Players: Doncaster- J. Bailey, goal; H. Arthur, Captain, and F. Slaytor, backs L. P. Frith, and A. Brooke, half-backs; Rev. W. Strawbridge, T. Littlewood, F. Tovey, W. Clark, J. Clark, W. Benbow, and E. Green, forwards. School- Hind, goal; T. Hilman, and Solley, backs; G. F. Richards, and F. Fernyhough, half-backs; Rev. R. W. Pitt, A. Hope, S. Fernyhough, Earle, E. Whitfield, J. A. Tweedale, and Davy, forwards." [30]

Six of the above players played against Rothwell two weeks later (and A. Brooke acted as an umpire):

"DONCASTER v. ROTHWWELL. This match was played on Saturday, on the ground of the latter, and resulted in a victory for Doncaster by one goal to nil. When the ball had been started, good play was shown by both sides, and to all appearances the teams were well matched. For Doncaster, A. Thrush, J. Bilsland, and P. Frith worked hard; while Rothwell, Field and Newton excelled. Players:-Doncaster: J. Bailey (goal), H. Athron (captain) and W. Harrison (backs): P. Frith (half-back); Ord, Johnson, Thrush, Bilsland, Benbow, W. Clark, Green (forwards): umpire, Mr. A. Brooke. Rothwell: J. Wobank, E. Benton, J. Chadwick, Blaky, Whitehead, W. Harrison, W. Ward, H. Taylor, S. Newton, J. Adamson, G. Field; umpire, Mr. W. Lambert." [31]

Seven days later the same players were involved in team now called Doncaster Town by the press and it seems A. Brooke's playing days were behind him as he was umpire again.:

"DONCASTER TOWN V. THORNE GRAMMAR SCHOOL. The above clubs met for the first time on Saturday on the ground of the latter. The ball was set in motion by the Doncaster captain, and after some very good play on both sides, the visitors, just before half time, managed to obtain a goal, which was kicked by Thrush. After half time the School team struggled hard to obtain a goal, but failed, thus leaving the Doncaster team victoriously one goal to nil. The following were the players: - Thorne: Goal, Chalk (Captain); backs Cramdge and Constable; half-backs, Fletcher and Smith; forwards, Coggan. J. Raywood, Middleton, Rolett. R. Raywood, Dook, and Proctor. Doncaster: Goal, Bailey; backs. Coward and Hall, half-backs, Duckett and

CHAPTER SIX

Jones: forwards, <u>Athron</u> (captain), <u>Thrush</u>, Bilis, Land, <u>Clark</u>, <u>Tovey</u>, Smith, and Ord. Umpires, Messrs. <u>Brooke</u> and Barrett." [32]

In December 1880, 'Mr Arthur Brooks' is reported as being the 'Hon. Sec. of Doncaster FC'. He wrote to the Sheffield Independent querying a match report in which his team was purported to have lost six nil against the Lunar Rovers, from Rotherham. He claimed no knowledge of the fixture and said the game 'must have been the Doncaster Amateur Club.' [33] This adds another twist to an already confusing story, suggesting that now there were two Association playing teams in Doncaster. Is this the team that Tony Bluff found in his time at the library?

In 1880 Doncaster FC played Hull Town FC by Association rules and team line-up was:

F. Pacey, <u>J. Bailey</u>, F. Keyworth, P. Stirling, J.N. Smith, W. Benbow, <u>F. Tovey</u>, <u>J. Duckitt</u>, <u>W. Clark</u>, N. Elliot, and <u>A. Thrush</u> (captain). By this point, Mr. <u>H. Athron</u> is acting as an umpire, so perhaps his playing days were also behind him at this point. [34]

The 'Arthur Brooks' narrative, to my mind, presents a totally new foundation story, with new personnel for Doncaster Rovers FC. Hopefully this can be confirmed absolutely when the local paper is digitised for the necessary era.

It seems two of the Association-playing Doncaster FC team players were not only 'Rovers' but also (two wheeled) 'Wanderers', having caught the popular cycling bug by 1885:

"'Doncaster Wanderers' Cycling Club. This club held its annual meeting for the election of officers for the present year. President, Mr. C.M. Hartley, Vice President, Mr. W.E. Ord; Captain, <u>Mr. H. Athron;</u> Vice-captain, <u>Mr. F.S.A. Tovey;</u> Hon. Sec. and Treasurer, Mr Joshua Chapman." [35]

Doncaster Rovers FC did not initially join the nearby Sheffield Football Association; it was not a member in 1882 and the earliest mention I can find for the club in the Sheffield Football Association Challenge Cup is 1885, under the name of the Doncaster Rovers. (They won the trophy in 1890/91 and on three subsequent occasions). The first mention I have found in the press for the full Doncaster Rovers FC name is not until five years after their foundation, when they played away against Sheffield Clarence FC in January 1884. [36] In September 1886 Doncaster Rovers FC played Sheffield FC and won a by a goal to nil, scored by W. Bridgewater. [37] Doncaster Rovers FC first played in the F.A. Cup in 1888/89.

1880

The second team from Eckington followed the first three years later, but this time it was a workplace team.

Eckington Works FC (Derbyshire, 1880-1895)

- Founder member of the Sheffield and District Football League in 1889/90

Like its fellow town team Eckington FC (1877), its first allegiance was to the Sheffield Association, but by 1884 had instead joined the Derbyshire Football Association. A colliery town like its successful neighbours, Staveley FC, Eckington FC was officially named after the company that dominated the town - Eckington Collieries FC - which in 1880 had the following personnel:

"President, Mr. J.C. Colver, vice-presidents, Mr. W.E. Wells, G. Mosby, treasurer, Mr. J. Jervis, Hon. Secretaries, J.D. Alsop, Jas. Levick."[38] In the first match of the Derbyshire Association Challenge Cup in 1884, Eckington FC beat New Whittington Rovers by 9 goals to one.[39] At the same time, it had also entered the Cup offered by the Hallamshire Football Association and drawn Portmahon FC.[40] In 1886 they were still members of the Derbyshire and the Hallamshire Associations but were also members of the Sheffield Association. The only player name mentioned was Arthur Booth, the team captain. [41]

Eckington Works FC - F.A. Cup Record 1871-1888

1885/86   1   Sheffield Heeley   A   1-2
1887/88   1   Owlerton   A   1-2

By 1890, Eckington had its own Eckington Town Football Association with its own Challenge Cup, valued at 30 guineas. W.T. Cartwright was the organising secretary of the new competition that excluded players who had competed in a final tie in the previous two years. [42]

Press reports disappear for Eckington Works in the 1890s but they reappear in 1895 when the club played Chesterfield in the first round of the F.A. Cup; after that the reports cease. Match reports reappear in the 20th century for a new Eckington Works FC, but I cannot see a narrative to confirm continuation for that modern club back to an 1880 foundation.

1881-1886 Sheffield resists professionalism

Although new football clubs were not being formed in Sheffield (see Table Two), it did not mean that football had ceased; the clubs continued to play each other and the Challenge Cups continued, but the centre of the world of football had moved from Sheffield to Lancashire. The game's best players at this point were undisputedly Scottish and would play for any club if they were reimbursed sufficiently. England played Scotland eighteen times in official internationals between November 1872 and April 1889, losing eleven times, drawing four times and winning on just three occasions. One of those losses was a 2-3 defeat at Bramall Lane on the 10th March 1883. The Sheffield press was unhappy at the lack of any local talent playing for England and suspected a southern conspiracy surrounding the omission of Billy Mosforth. In fact, the England team was composed of only six southern players, plus one from Villa FC, one from Great Lever FC and three from Notts County. The closest Sheffield involvement was Charles Clegg designated as one of the match umpires. The attendance was only nine or ten thousand, which was blamed on the decision to double the usual admission money to a shilling. When Scottish club teams visited Sheffield, the press was impressed not only with their skill but their athleticism; 'Damn them, they run at the end as they did at the beginning.' [43]

Seeing the talent on display, the clubs of the north west embraced the importation of 'Scotch Professors', whilst the amateur strongholds of Sheffield, London and the Midlands resisted the move. The London F.A., as the game's law keepers, slowly intervened to try and stop payments to players and as they lost that battle, moved to legislate to legitimise the process and control it from within. Whilst this increasingly bitter battle raged between Lancashire and London, Sheffield kept its head down and continued playing by the amateur rules in the absolute knowledge that it was in the right and the arguments did not affect it. Sheffield Football Association's bet on amateurism did not pay off; when they looked up the old order had changed and Sheffield football had been left behind.

In September 1881, the Sheffield Football Association launched a new initiative of trial matches with an aim of finding new playing talent; this was a response to the poor showing in inter-County games in the 1880/81 season. The Sheffield F.A. had played six representative games and only won two of them. At the 1881 A.G.M. it reviewed its record since the Association had been formed in 1867; the Sheffield F.A. had played a total of 53 matches, won 23, lost 22 and drawn three. Illustrating the superiority of Scottish football once more, the Sheffield F.A. had played the Glasgow Association eight times; with the exception of the first drawn match, they had lost all the subsequent games.

CHAPTER SIX

The decline in results affected the attendances, which in turn reduced the old Association's financial strength. The problem was exacerbated by more competition from new Cup Challenges that were springing up everywhere, drawing spectators away from the classic county matches. The New Association meanwhile was doing very well, causing divided loyalties and attracting the better players.

In December 1882, the Sheffield Association played the Lancashire Association; the latter had agreed to play without any 'imported players,' after Sheffield had refused its earlier invitations. 'This step was rendered necessary by the growing tendency on the part of the authorities of the cotton county to engage professional players from all parts of the Kingdom, but chiefly Scotland.' [44] Wednesday players made up five of the Sheffield team and ten of the Lancashire team came from Darwen and Blackburn clubs, resulting in a creditable three - all draw. [44] In October 1883, Sheffield FC passed an unsuccessful resolution calling for the cooperation of the northern clubs, in an effort to have Cup ties played on strictly amateur lines. [45]

In this period, much was made of the fact of the accepted existence of cricket professionals and the hypocrisy of the football authorities in not allowing the same standards for football players. The logic was dismissed in the Sheffield press:

"In this matter cricket and football stand on different positions. The professional cricketer is in the legitimate outcome of a necessity. It cannot be expected that a man who has to depend on the work of his hands or daily bread shall play in cricket matches lasting three days at a stretch without remuneration. He could not do it, for few employers would or could spare their men when the County Committee called them. Therefore a clever cricket player, if he is a poor man, is paid for his services, devotes himself to cricket and has a recognised status as a professional. On the other hand, football matches are usually played on a Saturday afternoon, occupy but a short time, and make no extraordinary call on the time of the footballer. Hence there is no necessity for paying football players. The necessity being absent, the case is not on all fours with that of cricket. Any agitation to keep football as an amateur game is a wholesome and proper agitation, and there is no organisation in Sheffield in a better position for taking it up than is the Sheffield Club." [46]

Professionalism was legalised in 1885 but the Sheffield establishment remained adamantly against the movement. The antagonism reached its lowest point in a match between Wednesday and Bolton Wanders in January 1885 at Bramall Lane:

"Before commencing with our report, we have no hesitation in saying that play on behalf of the visitors was rougher than has ever taken place in Sheffield before. There is no doubt the best team won, but during the period when the local men were a goal in hand, it was at once apparent, that by hook or by crook, by fair means or foul, Bolton must win. We have never seen the Sheffield football public worked up to such a pitch of indignation, and as time went on, it was painfully visible that a few of the Wednesday players were positively frightened of their burley antagonists, and it is no wonder that they won so easily by six goals to two." [47]

The crowd took such exception to the game that the referee was attacked and punched as he retired from the field, an event described as 'unparalleled in the annals of Sheffield football.'

The article concluded:

"Quoting the words of a prominent member of the Bolton team, and one who is well known in this neighbourhood 'I have played in Sheffield many times, but I have never seen or heard anything like this before. We have it often, you know, in Lancashire.' On the whole we are not so much surprised by it because if anything could change the opinions of the most sceptical, as to the evils of professionalism, the play of Saturday must do so. Football pure and simple

THE DECLINE OF THE OLD ORDER 1877-1887

is ignored, the mind's eye being filled to overflowing with the sole idea-win. Under these circumstances, it naturally follows that football under the professional regime would become a huge speculation, and to prevent this practical extinction of the English national winter pastime it behoves everyone to rally around the Sheffield and the kindred associations and support them in their laudable and hitherto successful endeavours to prevent the legalisation." [47]

Football in 1886. Engraving courtesy of the National Football Museum

The game above is unknown but is interesting to see a solid cross bar (introduced 1875), no goal nets (introduced 1890) but puzzlingly what looks like a 12-yard penalty line which was not introduced until 1891.

This chapter began in 1877 with Barnsley's first Association-playing club and it ends in 1887 with a second longer-lived club from Barnsley.

Barnsley St. Peters FC, later Barnsley FC, (Yorkshire, 1887-Present)
- England's 34th Oldest English League Club
- Yorkshire's third oldest League club after Sheffield Wednesday and Doncaster Rovers FC
- Sheffield and Hallamshire Football Association 1888

In all modern records, Reverend Tiverton Preedy is named as founder of Barnsley St. Peters FC. He was certainly instrumental but the records do not confer on him full founder status; from my research it seems a debt is also owed to a schoolmaster called E.B. Stringer.

It was September 1887 that the Reverend Preedy moved to Barnsley St. Peters under a 'licence to curacy' to the Reverend J.L. Brereton.[48] In his book, Peter Lupson has 'the meeting to form the club on Tuesday 6th September 1887' [49] on the same day Reverend Preedy was offered the curacy of St. Peter's. He goes on to say that Preedy became financial secretary while the vicar, the Reverend Brereton, was made president.

So, if club was formed on the 6th of September and according to the official history of Barnsley FC, the first match was on the 17th September 1887 against Manor House at Ward Green.[50] Could Reverend Preedy have founded the club, sourced the players and organised opponents

CHAPTER SIX

in just ten days? Either the newspaper article is wrong, or the chronology of the football team is wrong, or it was founded by Reverend Brereton on his own. Peter Lupson goes on to say that that Reverend Preedy first went to the Barnsley Rugby club 'but when they arranged a game on Good Friday, he quit.' [49] That means he did not start his association with Barnsley St. Peters until Easter 1888 at the earliest, having arrived in Barnsley in September 1887.

In its first season of 1887/88, Barnsley St. Peters played only local teams from Barnsley. By the start of the following season it had joined the Sheffield and Hallamshire Football Association and was drawn away against the Rotherham Baptists in the Minor Cup in the first round. [51] The first full match report I found is for a game Barnsley St. Peters lost 12-0 against Staveley FC in November 1888, featuring the ill-fated William Cropper:

"Rollinson, the Staveley centre had his foot injured and a toe broken the previous Saturday, and was, of course, unable to play. Willis scored for the home team five minutes from the kick- off. Cropper dribbled though all opposition, and passing to Needham, the latter middled, and Marshall headed a second point. The visitors right wing, Walker and Taylor, then beat the Staveley back, and a grand shot was equally well saved by Lilley. A brilliant combined run resulted in Marshall dashing the leather through a third time. The Barnsley goal continued to be the scene of attack, and Wilshaw eventually effected a splendid shot which struck the cross-bar, and went underneath, making the fourth goal, whilst Cropper put the finishing touch on for the fifth point. For a few minutes after half-time the visitors were dangerous, R. Taylor and Beevers both making capital attempts, and the Staveley backs almost paid the penalty of a goal, in consequence of not keeping their places. The home team, however, again asserted a decided superiority, as Cropper registered the sixth and seventh goals in quick succession, and after capital play by Needham and Wilshaw, Marshall made the eighth, followed by a ninth by the same player. Staveley were constantly pressing, and Potter lowered the Barnsley goal, whilst Cropper and Marshall added the eleven and twelfth, Staveley winning as above. Teams: - STAVELEY. - H. Lilley, J. Lievesley, J. Rice, S. Hay, I. Potter, W. Needham, S. Wilshaw, W. Cropper, W. Marshall, A. Willis, J. W. Lilley. BARNSLEY ST. PETER'S. - T. Nixon, J. Jones, T. Hurst, G. H. Needham, W. Berry, J. Wyke, J. Beevers, R. Taylor, G. Walker, G. Taylor, W. Bennett. Umpires, Messrs. W. Young, and W. Hepenstall; referee, Mr. J. Wilkinson, Sheffield." [52]

In the following report from 1891 comes the only mention I have found for the Reverend Preedy playing football with the club:

"FOOTBALL ACCIDENT- A CLERGYMAN INJURED. - A serious and peculiar accident befel the Rev. Tiverton Preedy, of St. Peter's, Barnsley, on Thursday afternoon. Mr. Preedy was practising football along with other members of the St. Peter's Association Club, and whom running in the field he struck his forehead with great violence against a wooden beam. The players conveyed him with all speed to Dr. Sadler's surgery, and it was found he had sustained a severe scalp wound. He was removed to his residence, and is making satisfactory progress. [53]

Reverend Preedy spoke at the 1893 Annual dinner in the year they won the Barnsley Charity Union Challenge Cup:

"BARNSLEY ST. PETER'S FOOTBALL CLUB. The annual dinner of this club was held at the Clarence Hotel, Barnsley, on Thursday evening, when there was a very fair attendance. The Rev. J. L. Brereton, the president, occupied the chair. The challenge cup of the Barnsley Charity Union, won by St. Peter's, adorned the centre table. - The Rev. T. Preedy said the club had had a tremendous past; it had a tremendous future. They had won the cup by legitimate sport, hard work, and great self-denial. He was proud they had been able to establish a sport with which all sportsmen were proud to be connected. He wished the same spirit animated the young men in London, who seemed to think of nothing but girls and drink, whereas football tended to make them decent men immediately. The young men in City road ought to see there was something more worth living for than booze and girls." [54]

The 'booze and girls' problems of London must have stayed on his mind, as two years later in 1895, he left Barnsley to do good work as a curate at St. Clements Church, Islington, London.

In 1897 the club dropped the 'St. Peters' and became Barnsley FC. In 1907 the Yorkshire Post reported that the Reverend attended all the Barnsley games that they played in London:

"But probably the most earnest of all Barnsley supporters is their original founder- the Rev. Tiverton Preedy, now of All Saints' Mission, Pentonville, but formerly curate at St. Peter's, Barnsley. Mr. Preedy may claim the credit of starting the Barnsley St. Peter's Club, which developed into the town club as it is to-day, and, though he has been for 10 or 11 years in London he has never bated one jot or tittle of his interest in the team's fortunes. Whenever the Barnsley players have gone South, say to Woolwich or Clapton, or even to Luton, Mr. Preedy has usually been present with a batch of his schoolboys to encourage his old pupils in the Association game, and during the present Cup-ties he has made a point of coming to Barnsley to witness every match. 'He will be here on Saturday,' said an unofficial expert, in the course of a chat on the match, 'and what is more, he has 'tipped' Barnsley to win. And that, after all, is the great point. When I ventured to inform the speaker that I thought they stood a good chance of getting into the semi-final, he corrected me. 'You mean,' he said, 'to t'Crystal Palace.' [55]

It would be five years before Barnsley FC won the F.A. Cup in 1912 (still held at the Crystal Palace ground) and a letter appeared in the press claiming a Mr. E.B. Stringer was one of the founders of the club:

"Anent the Cup Final, a Hartfield correspondent writes as follows: - 'I always admire the notes of your football reporter, "Wanderer," and there is still hope for the Rangers. It may interest him to know that our esteemed Schoolmaster (Mr. E. B. Stringer) was one of the founders of the Barnsley Club and took the first gate money, 17s. The success of the club has been due to encouraging local talent, and getting the influence of the tradespeople. Originally it was a Church team (Barnsley St. Peter's), and at that time he worked with the Rev. Tiverton Preedy." [56]

E.B. Stringer does not appear as a player in the official records for Barnsley St. Peters but there is a Mr. A. Stringer who was assistant secretary for the Barnsley Charity Association Football Union in 1891 to Rev. Preedy as secretary.

From an interview with Father Preedy the 'Church Times' in 1926:

"Now you can hardly move in the Father's study. He will wave his hand and say, 'Everything here is a gift.' Did ever a room have so many souvenirs of such various persons and occasions? Among the chief treasures is a football, upon which is recorded the fact that it is the ball that won the Cup Final in 1912, when Barnsley beat West Bromwich by one goal to nil. What is it doing, you may ask, in a slum parson's sitting-room in Pentonville? The answer is that it was presented to Fr. Preedy by the club which in the moment of its dizzy glory remembered that it owed much of its early beginnings to the young curate at Barnsley. Fr. Preedy had been a Rugby player, but when the Barnsley team, for which he played on Saturday afternoons, arranged a fixture for Good Friday he resigned in protest and walked down the street to-where some young men at a public- house corner were making plans for their Soccer side. Fr. Preedy joined them, but little thought that the club was destined for such greatness as the years bestowed." [57]

CHAPTER SEVEN

Football Professionalism and the Football League

If a player today is described as a consummate professional, it is taken as a compliment; alternatively, if someone from the terrace describes a player as a total amateur, then it is viewed as an insult. In football these meanings have turned full circle since 1857; then to be a true amateur you were viewed in awe and any hint of professionalism was a terrible accusation. The argument over professionalism never truly really went away until as late the 20th of April 1974 when the last Amateur Cup final was staged in which Bishop's Stortford beat Ilford 4-1. Later that year the F.A. stopped classifying all clubs as either fully professional or fully amateur, and accordingly, the Amateur Cup was abolished after eighty-one years. An echo today from that era is the so called 'professional foul.' In 1991 the International Football Association Board (see Appendix One) decided that a player who committed a foul or handling offence (that denied an obvious goal-scoring opportunity), should be sent off for serious foul play; these decisions were incorporated in its laws in 1997. The phrase 'professional foul' was first coined by Phil Thompson to describe his own tackle on John O'Hare in the 1978 League Cup Final, who was clear on goal, but outside the eighteen-yard area. Bravely the referee Pat Partridge awarded Nottingham Forest a penalty anyway, which John Robertson scored. The one nil win was the first major trophy of Brian Clough's reign at Forest.

Lancashire takes over

As I mentioned earlier in this book, the move to professionalism was led from Lancashire. Ironically, the man considered to the first ever professional footballer, James Joseph 'Jimmy' Lang was signed by the Wednesday, rather than a club from the north west. Jimmy Lang had come to Sheffield from Glasgow in 1876 to play to play for a Glasgow representative XI in their fixture against Sheffield FC on February 19th. Glasgow won 2-0 and the Sheffield representatives were impressed with his display (despite him being blind in one eye), to the extent that they invited him to join Wednesday FC. He was not paid by the club but instead by Walter Fearnchough to 'work' at his Sheffield business in Garden Street that manufactured bayonet spirals, ledger blades and chaff knives. [1] Meanwhile Heeley FC signed Peter Andrews, a Scottish international who had played against England in 1875. [2] Whilst never stated, the assumption was that neither did any work in their respective cutlery firms but were instead being paid to play football. Jimmy Lang would later play for the Zulus FC, a club used as a vehicle by players to receive appearance money.

I mentioned in the Thursday Wanderers FC section (Chapter Five) that in February 1879, a phoney war had broken out between the unpaid importation of amateur Nottingham footballers (Greenhalgh and the Curshams) and a paid professional footballer (Peter Andrews) of Heeley FC. The gentlemen of the Sheffield Football Association, led by Charles Clegg and Pierce Dix, were still virulently opposed to the growing professionalism in the game; and whilst the Sheffield Association took direct action by banning players, the phony war rumbled on between the Lancashire Clubs and the Football Association.

Charles W. Alcock had been on the F.A. committee since 1866; his pragmatic approach had been instrumental in working with Sheffield to create a unified code and he would be the man at the centre of the professionalism storm. Speaking in 1880 he said:

"Whether the introduction of a so serious and almost business like an element into the sport is a healthy one or not, this is not the place to enquire, but there are many old fogies who recount with no small satisfaction the days when football had not grown to be so important as to make umpires unnecessary, and the 'gate' the first subject of conversation." [3]

The football clubs from the north west continued to improve by importing paid players whilst the F.A. took no direct action; slowly footballing success started to move from the south of England to the north:

Football Association Challenge Cup Winners

1871/72	Wanderers	1872/73	Wanderers
1873/74	Oxford University	1874/75	Royal Engineers
1875/76	Wanderers	1876/77	Wanderers
1877/78	Wanderers	1878/79	Old Etonians
1879/80	Clapham Rovers	1880/81	Old Carthusians
1881/82	Old Etonians (beating Blackburn Rovers in the final)		

The year of 1882 was the pivotal moment when the pendulum swung in favour of the north of England. The following research illuminates the backgrounds of the players from the first eleven F.A. Cup finals:

"Of the 158 southern players involved in the F.A. Cup finals (up to 1881) thirty-nine were involved with the law. Thirty-eight were army officers. There were sixteen clergy men, fourteen school masters, eleven in banking and finance, eight brewery directors, managers or wine merchants, six civil servants, two doctors and two professors. Many others were directors of companies or described as gentlemen." [4]

At the beginning of the 1880/81 season, a number of famous clubs failed to enter the FA Cup. A disenchanted Oxford University AFC polled their players about entering the competition and they decided against continuing, (remember this is a team that had made four F.A. Cup final appearances). Cambridge University AFC and the once invincible Wanderers FC both scratched (the Wanderers failed to replace a number of leading players who had left for the Old Etonians in September 1878). The 1881/82 season is the last year a university side (Caius) entered the 1st round of the FA Cup and it was the last year that an amateur side (Old Etonians) won the competition. Since then, only one other university team has made it to the FA Cup first round proper and that was Team Bath in 2003, where they lost to Mansfield Town.

The F.A. Cup changed forever from the 1882/83 season:

1882/83	Blackburn Olympic	1883/84	Blackburn Rovers
1884/85	Blackburn Rovers	1885/86	Blackburn Rovers
1886/87	Aston Villa	1887/88	West Bromwich Albion
1888/89	Preston North End		

CHAPTER SEVEN

The oldest 'Old Boys' club, 'Old Harrovians' who had played at the Oval for four seasons from 1872 and reached the F.A. Cup semi-finals in season 1877/78, would call the Harrow Recreation Ground its home by 1888.

The Lancashire Football Association formed eleven years after the Sheffield Association on 28th September 1878, with 28 clubs. By 1882 it had 74 clubs, and by 1888 an amazing 104 clubs. In 1898 its membership numbers went down as the clubs consolidated to 74 clubs, but by 1908 it had bounced back up to 203 clubs.

Whilst the northern football clubs did all they could to attract spectators, the gentlemen amateurs were against 'spectators,' the providers of the gate money. No idle southern spectators would be allowed to stand looking at the school sides. As the headmaster of the Loretto school put it: 'The sight of the loungers takes the spirit out of the players, and the loungers should be found something to do if they are too feeble for football,' ... spectating 'is the greatest of all football dangers.' Later 'Pa' Jackson in his autobiography described the spectators at Westminster school as 'the Westminster Railings' and 'members of the proletariat of the district who were mainly there to barrack the 'toffs' playing football.'

In the 1883/84 season, the Preston North End annual wage bill was an astounding £1,200. In a letter in Sporting Life from 1883, a correspondent, calling himself 'Mancunian' listed the clubs by the number of imported players; Preston North End and Bolton Wanderers topped the chart with seven players each. He went on to say:

"The teams are waited on like royalty, with 'rubber downs', bag carriers, and even boot cleaners, following them about, even on their longest journey." [5]

In November 1883, the Football Association decided to take its first stand against professionalism by banning a player for receiving a financial sum to join Accrington and expelling Accrington from the Football Association. Accrington's co-defendants, Church FC escaped with just a censure, so the Lancashire F.A. lobbied hard and in December 1883 Accrington was readmitted.

William 'Billy' Sudell
Engraving courtesy of the National Football Museum

After the 19th of January 1884 F.A. Cup tie between Preston North End (Lancashire) and Upton Park (Essex), the latter complained following their one all draw (a.e.t.) about the number of professionals playing for Preston and wanted the result declared void. The Preston secretary, Major William 'Billy' Sudell was upfront about the money and cited Blackburn Olympic as an example of money being used to remunerate the players when they were not working; they had won the Cup as a result the year before. He said he could prove that very nearly every other important club in Lancashire and the Midlands paid their players. Faced with this admission, the Football Association had no option but to disqualify Preston, which prompted Burnley and Great Lever to also withdraw from the competition. At a later F.A. enquiry, Major Sudell said that 'all Preston players are professional but if you refuse to legalise them they will be amateurs and you will be unable to prove us otherwise.' At the same time as Preston North End were paying players and getting disqualified, Upton Park FC had also strengthened their F.A. Cup team by 'recruiting two players from Oxford University and one each from Cambridge University and Sandhurst' without any retribution from the F.A. [6] This left the Football Association open to an accusation of hypocrisy and Charles W. Alcock attempted to broker a deal, as reported in an F.A. Minutes Committee meeting on February 11th 1884:

'It was proposed by Mr. C.W. Alcock and seconded by Mr. Morley that the time has come for the legalisation of professionalism.' Unfortunately, Alcock and Morley's pragmatism was denied. An amendment in the minutes by Mr. J.H. Cofield and Mr. C. Crump (both from the Birmingham and District Association) said simply: 'That the time has not arrived.'

In 1884, the Manchester Guardian presciently commented: "With the introduction of professionals (into amateur ranks) a new departure is taken. The first effect of the change will be to make the Rugby game the aristocratic one, and the Association game will probably die out in the South of England, which is already declining in favour. Again, a fresh excuse will be given for a tendency to exclusiveness which is even now apparent." [7]

The Lancashire Clubs upped the ante and threatened a thirty-one club break away organisation, unless the F.A. legalised professionalism. When the F.A. refused, the northern Clubs carried out their threat and formed the British Football Association in Blackburn, in October 1884. The Sheffield Football Association continued to complain and in a letter from W.F. Beardshaw, dated November 21st 1884, said that the F.A. 'should have full powers to suppress the evil entirely.' The inflammatory language was not limited to private correspondence; it also spilled into the press: 'Employment of the scum of Scottish villages has tended, in no small degree, to brutalise the game.' [8]

There was a more measured response from the 'Football Field': "Let those who sneer at football professionalism over their walnuts and wine with their legs under their own mahogany consider for a moment what it is for a working man to be thrown onto his own resources for several weeks and then let them speak contemptuously if they will about a man who has the misfortune to be a footballer, leaving one town for another to better himself and keep the wolf from the door." [9]

By January 13th 1885, the Athletic News 'believed that in practice nearly 100 players were paid for taking part in the game on behalf of other Clubs.' A Burnley Committee man said in February 1885: 'The public will not go to see inferior players. During the first year we did not pay a single player and nobody came to see us.' [10]

On the 20th July 1885, the Football Association came up with a compromise solution that finally permitted professionalism, but with added strings. The F.A. announced that it was 'in the interests of Association Football, to legalise the employment of professional football players, but only under certain restrictions.' Clubs were allowed to pay players provided that they had either been born or had lived for two years within a six-mile radius of the ground.

The compromise was sufficient for the dissolution of the British Football Association but the Scottish Football Association muddied the waters by declaring north of the border to be a professional-free zone. It banned Scottish clubs from entering the English F.A. Cup and the playing of English teams that might be composed of professional players. As a result, arranged F.A. Cup fixtures between Blackburn Rovers and Queen Park and Preston North End and Third Lanark were cancelled. Without the professionalism row, the F.A. Cup may have still been today a competition for English and Scottish clubs and may have evolved into a fully British contest.

The Scottish F.A. ruling ensured that even more Scottish players moved south looking for a club that would not worry too much about the 'six-mile radius rule' and of course many English clubs were happy to oblige. The geographic restrictions of the 1885 F.A. ruling continued to be undermined and tested by clubs, creating a new set of headaches for the Football Association. Another unintended consequence of permitting professionalism was on the game of Rugby, with the southern-based Rugby Football Union locked in the same debate with the northern and Welsh clubs. It thought the F.A. decision a mistake and declared rugby to be an amateur sport, banning professionalism and outlawing all forms of payment. This started a civil war in the Rugby game that came to a head in 1895, when the leading northern clubs broke away from the R.F.U. and formed the Northern Rugby Football Union; this soon established a completely new form of the sport that became known as Rugby League.

In 1886 unemployment in the United Kingdom was at its highest for forty years, which created another imperative for gifted players to earn an income playing football; the die was now cast for professional Association football and the beneficiaries were the working-class players employed by the commercially orientated clubs. The Amateur club's final death knell came in 1888 with the formation of the Football League by Aston Villa's William McGregor.

The Football League

A successful football club needed quality players, which necessitated an enclosed ground in order to generate gate receipts to pay the wages. To maintain the gate revenue the clubs required regular quality fixtures to ensure the payment of wages. Unfortunately, lucrative friendlies were regularly cancelled with opponents' F.A. Cup or County Cup matches taking precedence. William McGregor took action after seeing five consecutive Aston Villa matches cancelled. McGregor's original idea for the name of the organisation was the 'Association Football Union', which was eventually rejected as it might be confused with the Rugby Football Union. The initial launch was hurried and commenced without the clubs knowing how the point scoring for the League would work; the first matches kicked off on September 8th 1888 but their points scoring system was not finalised until November 21st. But what had been made clear before kick-off was that the Football League rules did not contain the same strict residence rules that the F.A. had insisted upon in 1885.

William McGregor
Image courtesy of the National Football Museum

Fifteen Clubs applied to join the new Football League in 1888 and twelve were accepted: Notts County (1862) was joined by eleven Clubs, Preston North End (1878), Aston Villa (1874), Wolverhampton Wanderers (1876), Blackburn Rovers (1874), Bolton Wanderers (1874), West Bromwich Albion (1874), Accrington (1878), Everton (1878), Burnley (1874), Derby County (1881) and Stoke (1868). 'The decision to allow just twelve clubs was based on the calculation that there were only 22 vacant dates during a season on which fixtures could be fulfilled.' [11]

Only one of the original twelve clubs, Accrington, failed to convert its golden ticket into a permanent opportunity; in the 1892/93 season, Accrington finished fifteenth (of 16) and was relegated after losing a test match 1-0 against Sheffield United which had finished second in the Second Division. This made Sheffield United the first ever team to win promotion in the Football League. Rather than play in the Second Division, Accrington FC resigned from the league to play in the Lancashire League and by 1896 the club had folded.

Preston North End were the Champions that first season, with Notts County finishing in 11th place and Stoke finishing below them. Preston remained unbeaten throughout the inaugural first season of the Football League with a goal difference of +59 in just 22 games, and won the F.A. Cup without conceding a goal, earning the nickname 'the Invincibles.' Preston North End's architect Billy Sudell left the club in 1893 and in 1895 was jailed for three years for embezzling cheques to the value £800. (12)

The Athletic News described the new Football League as a device to generate money for the member clubs:

"Here we have it in one word. The whole thing is a mere money making scheme, a speculation." (13)

Certainly, it is hard to argue against the proposition that Derby County and Notts County didn't bring much more than large enclosures to the table, as part of their application. Notts County had 40 members in 1881 and its playing record in the late 1880s was poor. Like Notts County, Derby County had secured the local cricket ground for its games which appears to have been the deciding factor for Football League membership, whilst older and more successful clubs from the same place, like Derby Midland (1881) and Derby Junction (1870), were ignored. To add insult to injury, just three years later, Derby Midland merged with the newly successful Derby County. Stoke FC's inclusion is also a mystery based on its on-the-field performances; cynics suggested that Stoke FC's, Hon. Sec. Harry Lockett, had helped McGregor launch the fledgling League, which came with the reward of Stoke's inclusion. For good measure Lockett was appointed as the first secretary of the Football League, a position he would hold until 1902.

The three long-standing clubs that missed out on initial membership were Wednesday (1867), Halliwell (1877) and Nottingham Forest (1865). Note that the founding members were all from the northern half of England and the majority had more of a reputation for high crowd attendances rather than previous footballing success, with only Aston Villa, Blackburn Rovers and West Bromwich having previously won the F.A. Cup. According to one source 'Notts County was apparently preferred because its Trent Bridge ground had a better tram service than Forest's Lenton headquarters.' (14)

The Football League started twenty-five years after the formation of the Football Association; 2013 was the 125th and 150th anniversary of each organisation respectively. There had been friction between both from the beginning; the F.A. debarred former professionals from joining any of the F.A. committees and maintained control over wages, contracts and conditions in favour of the clubs, which they maintained should be run on a not-for-profit basis. This was circumvented from July 1888 for the first time by Small Heath FC (later Birmingham City) which set itself up as Limited Liability Company. It was followed in 1890 by Notts County FC and by 1921 all but two of the League's eighty-six clubs had followed suit. Ironically, in 1903 the F.A. also became a limited company.

Catching the zeitgeist of 1887, Charles W. Alcock began to be remunerated for the job of F.A. Secretary for the first time after twenty-one years of being unpaid. In his other capacity as secretary of Surrey C.C.C. he was used to dealing with the separation of professionalism and amateurism in cricket. There is similarity between the birth and residential rules of cricket and what was introduced into Association football in 1885. Whilst unpaid for many years at the F.A. he was rewarded by Surrey Cricket Club in 1881 with £330, a silver inkstand and candlesticks.

The twenty teams that had wanted to join the Football League in 1888, but failed, launched the 'Combination' or 'Second League' competition. Strangely the playing of matches in this League was not compulsory; some teams only played eight times and it failed after one season. The North-East Counties felt disadvantaged geographically and a meeting was held at Durham in late March 1889, to launch a ten-team Northern League; by the middle of April, the Midland Counties League was formed, led by Lincoln City. One of those ten teams was the world's oldest club, Sheffield FC, which had a very difficult first season trying to score League points; it finished bottom of the League and had no wish to continue and was replaced in the Midland Counties League by Sheffield United. It would be 1892 before either Wednesday or United would gain membership of the Football League. The football clubs excluded from the Football League in 1888 quickly realised that the local leagues did not generate the hoped for income and feared for their future. The second nail in the coffin arrived in the same year, when the F.A. made changes to the F.A. Cup rules making it harder for smaller teams to survive. In the 1888/89 season, qualifying rounds were introduced to the F.A. Cup with 22 clubs being exempt from competition until the first round proper. It was an idea created by Richard Gregson, the secretary of the Lancashire F.A., to reduce the number of one-sided ties: "Now instead of the leading clubs being compelled to go through the ordeal of slaughtering the innocents in the initial stages, the innocents will have all the fun to themselves until Christmas...Then the real fight for supremacy will begin." [15]

The third 'coffin nail' in the death of many amateur clubs was the second change to Football Association regulations for the 1889/90 season, regarding the laws on ground enclosures. Peter Holme at the collections department of the National Football Museum managed to find the specific minute books which include the 'Rules of the Football Association Cup Challenge Cup'; there is a subtle change in the wording in 1889/90 from a 'choice' to 'shall' use an enclosed ground, which meant that from that point onwards clubs had to have a fully enclosed ground. The change started with;

"No. 26. A club not having a private ground, and which, having the choice, decides to play its Cup tie on an enclosed ground in which gate money can be charged shall pay the whole cost of such ground. Dated 3/9/88."

F.A. Rule 26 changed again in the following season:

"No. 26. A Club not having a private ground shall provide a private or enclosed ground to which gate money can be charged for Cup ties, free of all charge to the visiting Club, or play on its opponents ground. Dated 7/8/89."

Chatham United FC's website, claims that its successful run in the F.A. Cup (when it reached the quarter-finals 1888/89), was instrumental in the Football Association changing the rules as above. Chatham matches were played at the Army-owned 'The Lines,' and no admission fees could be charged because of Army regulations, forcing the F.A. into the above rule change. Chatham United FC moved to the Maidstone Road site which was owned by a George Winch; he allowed the club to enclose the ground and build a pavilion. Not all clubs were as fortunate as Chatham, in having a rich benefactor.

By 1887 the Football Annual was carrying adverts for pavilions for football grounds.

The Southern clubs that survived, continued to play under amateur status; the first club to turn professional was Royal Arsenal FC in 1891, followed by Millwall FC (1893) and Southampton FC (1894).

Historically, for the footballing amateurs of Sheffield, it had been straightforward to find a public space in which to turn up and play a game unannounced. However as more public space was consumed by industry, the overheads involved in renting a field from a farmer, or negotiating with the cricket club for winter use, was a new and substantial expense. If club members could not pay subscriptions, then a club could not provide a kit for its players and an away match would be beyond its means. Without an enclosed ground, it would not be invited to join the local league. As more clubs closed, it became harder to find opponents, at a time when local cup and County games were in decline. The downward spiral was hastened by the problems of professionalism, where the best players left to play for the clubs who could afford to pay wages.

Thus, many small clubs folded at the end of the 19th century; of the fifty-three Sheffield Football Association clubs that formed between 1857 and 1889, only six would see the start of the new century. The following report on Rotherham Town FC, highlights the financial problems of maintaining a club at the end of the 19th century and the critical importance of gate money:

"The decline of Rotherham town football club. The importance of the meeting which has been summoned for tonight at 8.30 cannot be well over estimated. The Rotherham Club, as all know, is a limited liability company, one out of which dividends have never been earned, but into which the subscribed capital has been sunk with singularly depressing effects. The question, of course, arises whether Rotherham is large enough to support a club whose team appears in such high class and expensive company as that of the League. Taken comparatively, it does not appear to be so. For example, Sheffield – one of the very best sporting towns in the country – looks upon a gate of 15000 as an excellent one, and, indeed, is well pleased with an average of 12000. Yet, Sheffield boasts a population of close upon 340,000 leaving out of the question the large numbers of people resident in other towns that swell these 'gates.' On the same reasoning, the gates of 4,000 which many people think ought to be got at Rotherham for the first team matches argue that Rotherham has a population of 113,000. Which, as Euclid would say, is absurd. Far more likely is it that an average gate of 2,000 would be looked upon as satisfactory by the committee of the Rotherham club – an average, I say – for, by a strict attention to their work in hand, those in charge of the drifting ship have cut away all superfluous weight and waste, and have made things as ship shape as possible. However, the average gate at Clifton Grove has not been 2,000, or, indeed, anything like it. It has been more like 300 or so, especially of late, and even the fine victory a week ago over Leicester Fosse was accomplished in the presence of a gate which reached the startlingly fine figure of £21. How is a Second Division team to be maintained upon such absurd support? You might as well ask a full-grown man to subsist and maintain his vigour on an infant's bottle!" [16]

CHAPTER EIGHT

Sheffield embraces Professionalism

The near extinction of Wednesday FC

In the 1886/87 season, Wednesday FC did not send in the registration paperwork on time to play in the F.A. Cup; determined not to miss out, several Wednesday players temporarily joined the Lockwood Brothers FC campaign. Bolstered by these quality players, Lockwood Brothers reached the 5th round tie against West Bromwich Albion, losing 2–1 on the 29th January 1887. The Wednesday players came back flushed with their success and keen to address the thorny issue of payments to players, so that they could compete with other 'professional' clubs. A few weeks later Wednesday had the opportunity to gauge itself against Lancashire's best in February 1887 and came up short:

"WEDNESDAY v. PRESTON NORTH END. The visit of the North Enders had been looked forward to with considerable interest in this district, so that it was not to be wondered at that 4,000 spectators should put in an appearance at the Bramall lane enclosure yesterday. The Prestonians had not their strongest team, and Brayshaw was an absentee on the Wednesday side. Preston delighted the spectators with their splendid passing qualities and shooting at goal, and had Wednesday been anything like as proficient in the latter quality, the result would have been different from Preston five to Wednesday none." [1]

This was the season before Preston North End memorably remained unbeaten throughout their 'invincible' first season of the Football League, but nevertheless it was painful lesson for the Wednesday players.

Sheffield Rovers FC

Back in 1881, players had formed Sheffield Wanderers FC as a method to receive remuneration, but had been stopped by a hastily-introduced-law, which threatened players with a Sheffield-wide playing ban. Wednesday's players decided to try the same trick again to circumvent the Sheffield Football Association's stringent attitude to professionalism. Some of the Wednesday players started a new football club called the Sheffield Rovers which would be run on a commercial footing; an application to join the F.A. for next year's tournament was sent and was accepted by Charles W. Alcock. Whether the players intended to compete or whether it was a bluff to force Wednesday's President H. Hawksley into opening negotiations about paying the players' wages, is lost to history.

Sheffield Rovers FC only played four games, one of which was in April 1887 against Eckington Works FC; their team was: J. Smith, F. Salkeld, E. Stringer, J. Hudson, T.E. Cawley, E. Brayshaw, W. Mosforth, E.H. Nicholson, H. Howe, W. Ingram and H. Winterbottom. [2]

A month prior to this, the Wednesday FC had played in the final of the Sheffield Association Challenge Cup against Collegiate FC and the following players all featured: J. Smith, J. Hudson E. Brayshaw, W. Mosforth and T.E. Cawley. A month later they were turning out for Sheffield

SHEFFIELD EMBRACES PROFESSIONALISM

Rovers, meaning that these five players were among the chief agitators for change. William "Billy" Mosforth, the 'Little Wonder' or 'The Sheffield Dodger,' had already been struck off Albion FC's list of players for an unknown irregularity and had been active with Zulus FC. One famous story (probably a myth) says that when he ran onto the pitch in Hallam colours someone in the crowd shouted '10 bob and free drinks, Billy, if you'll change your shirt.' He promptly ran back to the dressing room and returned in a Wednesday shirt.

A 1926 history of Wednesday FC looked back on events: "Those footballers and interested folk who had founded the Sheffield rovers were not keen on embracing professionalism, yet they held the view that if players desired pay to help meet expenses they should have it." [3]

The Wednesday player 'Tom' E. Cawley is credited as 'one of the men who saved Wednesday from disaster-possibly from extinction.' [4] He recalled in conversation, a meeting he went to at the Brunswick Hotel, Haymarket with Jack Harvey (*S.F.A. Hon. Sec.*), Sam Hetherington (?), Harry Winterbottom (*player*), Billy Mosforth (*player*), Jack Hudson (*player*), Albert Chapman (?), Albert Marples (?) and G. Cropper (*Wednesday Hon. Sec.*) to discuss the break away to the Sheffield Rovers. Before that critical vote could be taken, which could have caused the end of Wednesday FC, Cawley suggested that first the Wednesday club should have the option on whether they would agree to paying the players. That was agreed and a larger meeting was convened at the Garrick Hotel in Sycamore Street:

"A great discussion took place and pungent comments were made on professionalism. It was pointed out, however, that the Rovers would 'carry on' if the conditions were not accepted, and that would have meant all the best players throwing in their lot with the Rovers. Obviously, that would have broken the backs of any clubs of any standing, even Wednesday's. So Wednesday capitulated and the wages of 5/- for a home match and 7/6 for away games was agreed upon." [4]

The freshly-remunerated Wednesday FC made the quarter finals of the F.A. Cup the following season and the Sheffield Rovers disappeared as quickly as it had arrived. This had been a high stakes standoff and could easily have meant the end of the Wednesday club. It certainly meant that they had to reassess their finances because they had not had to calculate in any wages bills before this point. In his book, 'The Romance of Wednesday 1867-1926', Richard Sparling uses as an example to illustrate the importance of gate receipts in a Cup tie that took place against Notts. County FC in 1882/83 season:

"For every sixpence taken at the gates, Notts. County took 3d. as their right, the Bramall Lane authorities 2d., Wednesday having to be content with the remaining penny. Professionalism made it necessary to obtain a ground where results financially would be more beneficial. So Wednesday secured a field (through which a steam and a footpath ran) off the Queen's Road. It was obtained on a seven years' lease from the Duke of Norfolk. The path was diverted, the brook covered over, the field enclosed and drained, and the pretty name of Olive Grove bestowed upon it. The Olive Grove enterprise probably cost Wednesday £5,000, the ground proved so difficult to drain."

In 1896 the Sheffield Independent looked back at the moment when Wednesday turned professional:

"In those days the prospects of the Wednesday club did not appear very bright, and indeed Sheffield football, which held out against the advance of professionalism, was growing to be of little account in the land. The local competitions amongst the various clubs of the district, which clubs, by the way, were upon a very fair equality in ability, were interesting enough locally to some 3000 or 4000 local football enthusiasts but from a national point of view Sheffield was deteriorating in the world of football." [5]

CHAPTER EIGHT

The article goes on to explain that the solution for Wednesday was to adopt professionalism and secure their own ground at Olive Grove, "making themselves independent of the vagaries of the cricket authorities at Bramall Lane." [5]

"...They openly went in for professionalism, and thereby secured a strong team of local talent. Amongst the friends of other clubs they naturally gained some opprobrium, for by paying players they were enabled to get good men from the ranks of those other clubs who still held onto the old amateurism, and when in September 1887, Olive Grove was opened, Wednesday had very nearly the cream of the local talent of Sheffield in their ranks. But if the other clubs did not like the proceedings, the public generally did, and the team showing very creditable form against most of the clubs they encountered, people began to flock to Olive Grove to see 'good old Wednesday' perform." [5]

Looking for a League

Wednesday FC was mentioned in the Sheffield press as a likely candidate for the Football Combination League (which started at the same time as the Football League) but it did not become a member. The new Combination League's agenda was described in the press:

"To arrange for the formation of a second football league, the new league of twelve clubs not being deemed representative of the interests of English football." [6] The original twelve clubs were: Walsall Town Swifts, Derby Midland, Notts. Rangers, Burslem Port Vale, Leek, Small Heath Alliance, Crewe Alexandra, Newton Heath, Witton, Blackburn Olympic, Long Eaton Rangers and Bootle. It allowed eight more clubs to join making a total of twenty clubs, which ultimately led to its downfall as there were too many teams to play once, let alone twice. It also decided that the individual clubs could arrange their own fixtures without any centralised control and the Football Combination was wound up before the season completed. Newton Heath (Manchester United), Grimsby Town, Crewe Alexandra, Bootle and Small Heath Alliance (Birmingham City), went on to co-found the Football Alliance the following year.

In 1889 the strict birth and residence restrictions were removed by the Football Association which led to an enormous influx of Scottish footballers, with two hundred and thirty players earning their living at English football clubs by 1890. Major Marindin resigned in 1890 as F.A. president over the ongoing issue of professionalism and was replaced by Sheffield's Charles Clegg. By this time the latter was more pragmatic about professionalism but the Football Association still treated the Football League as an upstart organisation that still had to obey the Football Association pronouncements. When Queen Victoria died in January 1901 an emergency three-man committee of the F.A. unilaterally cancelled the F.A. Cup First Round draws, due the following week, without consulting with the Football League. This meant that the clubs would lose two sets of gate receipts as the following weekend was set to be the date of the actual funeral. Charles Sutcliff a committee member of the Football League wrote in a letter to the Athletic News 'that he thought that the League was sufficiently important …to entitle them to some respect, consideration and even some deference.' At the end of its first season in 1889 the Football League allowed the bottom four clubs to apply for re-election, together with nine new applicants vying for the chance to join the successful organisation. The new entrants discovered that the clubs who had finished in the bottom four spots were always going to be re-elected, because they retained a vote in the election process! Six days after that, led by Nottingham Forest and Wednesday FC, the twelve-team Football Alliance League was formed. The 'Alliance' would in turn become Division Two to the First Division in 1892/93.

SHEFFIELD EMBRACES PROFESSIONALISM

Wednesday clearly didn't want its fixtures to run dry, because at the same time as joining the Alliance, it was also involved in the set-up of the short-lived Northern Counties League in 1889. The foundation names included some the clubs that had been involved in the ill-fated Football Combination League: Sunderland FC, Sunderland Albion, Bootle, Darwen, Newton Heath, Grimsby Town, Mitchell St. Georges and the Small Heath Alliance. [7]

The Alliance League ran for three seasons from 1889 until 1892. Wednesday was the Alliance's champion in the first season and was the losing F.A. Cup finalist in the 1889/90 season. Despite finishing bottom of the Alliance in 1890/91, Wednesday was eventually elected to the expanded Football League in 1892.

In August 1889 clubs in Sheffield, other than Wednesday, were looking around for a league competition of their own and the Sheffield and District Football League was formed with eight clubs: Attercliffe, Owlerton, Walkley, Clinton, Exchange, Ecclesfield, Kilnhurst and Eckington Works. [8] For the following season the membership of the Sheffield and District Football League had gone up to eleven clubs, including Heeley FC and Barnsley St. Peters, [9] but it was disbanded in 1895. [10]

Whereas the amateur football clubs formed between 1857 and 1888 had grown out of existing institutions, such as schools, churches, military and the workplace, from 1888 onwards, football clubs would be created for their own sake and be based on solid financial criteria. The final Sheffield club in this period exemplifies that trend.

Sheffield United Cricket and Football Club (Sheffield, Yorkshire, 1889 – Present)

- Thirty-Sixth Oldest Sheffield Football Club
- Equal 35th Oldest Football League Club in England (Fourth oldest in Yorkshire)
- Won the Sheffield Association Challenge Cup in 1891/92 for the first time and has won it ten times since

Origin: Cricket.

An F.A. Cup quarter final at Bramall Lane in the 1888/89 season was the catalyst that created Sheffield United FC. On March 16th 1889 a record crowd filled Bramall Lane for the semi-final between West Bromwich Albion FC and Preston North End FC. The crowd spilled onto the pitch regularly and the final attendance was said to be in excess of 22,000. Charles Clegg's brother, William, had been at the F.A. Cup semi-final, in his capacity as Mayor and had been involved in a 'Brian Clough-type role' of crowd dispersal:

"Immediately afterwards the crowd again encroached, but made no actual interference with the play, and the referee at once sounded his whistle for the cessation of the game. The breaking in, as before was made at Shoreham street end, and a heaving, surging mass of humanity, against which police for a long time strove in vain, surrounded the goal posts and invaded the green. After waiting some time the players made a movement to leave the field, but there was no way out, and they congregated in a group near the boundary on the lower side. At length the well known form of the Mayor, Alderman Clegg, appeared upon the scene, and a determined effort was organised to clear the green. His worship dealt summarily with several intruders, and ultimately thanks to his exertions and those of a distinguished looking gentlemen, with a fierce moustache and a long flowing coat, the police were enabled to clear the actual field of play, though it was quite impossible to force the crowd back into the original position. A quarter of an hour had thus been wasted and only five minutes' play indulged in. There appeared to be

CHAPTER EIGHT

a consultation of players and officials, but no protest was lodged by either side, and the game proceeded as a genuine cup tie." [11]

The match had clearly illustrated the potential of Bramall Lane to generate gate receipts and seven days later it was announced that a new professional team called Sheffield United had been formed to play at the Lane. The meeting took place the offices of J.B. Wostinholme and a small classified press advert announced the event:

"Sheffield United Cricket Club. The committee have decided to form a FOOTBALL CLUB for next season, for Bramall Lane ground. Professionals may send testimonials and on or before, March 30th to Mr. J.B. Wostinholme, 10 Norfolk Row." [12]

The man behind the club's formation was Charles Stokes who had long thought that a permanent football club should be based at Bramall Lane; clearly the spectacle of a packed ground had helped resolve the argument in his favour. Charles Stokes (30/12/1847 - 8/10/13) was by trade a dentist and a prominent Freemason; he was elected a member of the Bramall Lane Bowling Green in 1869, a member of the Ground Committee in 1875, and in 1877 was a member of the Yorkshire County Cricket Club Committee. He had joined Heeley FC in 1864, aged 16 and eventually become the club's president. He was also Hon. Sec. of Milton FC and a prominent member of Broomhall FC. A tireless football administrator, he was on the committee that helped form the Wednesday Football Club in 1867. Charles Stokes, as a member of the Bramall Lane Ground Committee, called upon Charles Clegg (President of the Sheffield Football Association) to solicit his opinion as to the formation of a new football club. Remember that the Bramall Lane rental arrangements had nearly caused the demise of the Wednesday in 1877, so there would have been careful consideration to make sure that this time a club could operate profitably. Wednesday FC had proved that the professional model worked and the Sheffield press response was not at all anti-professional, describing it as: "…an entirely new departure, but no pains will be spared to secure the services of first-class players, and it is hoped to be able to get together a combination equal to anything in the country." [13] Not everybody was enthusiastic about the formation of this new football club; to an 'Old Cricketer,' Sheffield United was a 'new fad':

"SHEFFIELD UNITED FOOTBALL CLUB. A PROTEST. To the editor of the Sheffield daily telegraph. Sir, Is it not about time that the Bramall Lane Committee made a point of reserving their available forces instead of allowing them to be poached by other counties- not that I blame the players for bettering themselves- for season after season have we seen men worthy of being played for the county annexed by other organisations? Had the committee not better attended to putting their houses in order as regards the object for which they were focused, namely, the proper control and management of Yorkshire county cricket, before entering upon their new fad of forming a football club? Results so far as cricket is concerned show incapacity on the part of some of the committee, or we should not habitually lose players who rise prominent point as in other counties. Take the following instances: - Bearmount (Surrey), Robinson (Lancashire), Ward (Lancashire) and others. If the committee fail in a matter which they originally elected for, and of which they should have some knowledge, or, at any rate, experience, how much more disastrous will be the results of dabbling in the new venture, for which players will have to be kept a couple of years before being entitled to take part in cup competitions- the main support which football clubs have to rely upon. As an old cricketer, I strongly protest against this new venture, which can only result in pecuniary loss and ruination to the ground. By inserting this you will oblige, yours truly, OLD CRICKETER." [14]

Sheffield United's strategy to avoid 'pecuniary loss' was to follow the tried and tested

SHEFFIELD EMBRACES PROFESSIONALISM

Lancashire model of importing Scottish talent:

"I hear a whisper that the football team to be engaged by the Bramall lane Ground Committee for next season will be a powerful one, and include five Scotchmen of good repute- two full backs and three forwards. The remainder of the team will probably, with perhaps one exception, be composed of local players, a Sheffield amateur of well known and high ability acting as goal keeper." [15]

United's first practice match took place on the Hallam FC ground:

"SHEFFIELD UNITED FOOTBALL CLUB The first practice of the Sheffield United Football Club took place at Sandygate Cricket Ground last evening. There was a good muster of members, the following taking part:- P. Stupart (Glasgow), W. F. Beardshaw, E. Stringer, W. Hobson, R. Crichton, H. B. Willey, G. H Aizlewood, W. Mosforth, W. J. Wright, C. C. Pilling, N. Ross (Glasgow), R. Gordon (Glasgow), J. Hudson, B. L. Shaw, C. H. Howlett (Gainsbro'), D. Galbraith (Dundee), J. Duncan, (Dundee), W. Robertson (Dundee), and F. A. Tasker." [16]

Another practice match was arranged against Sheffield FC, but apparently the imported Scottish professors needed more practice:

"Last evening a public practice match between the Sheffield United team and eleven of the Sheffield Club took place at Bramall Lane, the practice wickets on the Shoreham street side of the ground being the venue. The United played their full strength, and amongst the Club team were W. F. Beardshaw, G. J. Groves, H. B. Willey, G. H. Aizlewood, W. T. Wright, B. L. Shaw, J. Jeeves, &c. The play lasted about an hour, and the United had rather the best of the game throughout. The form displayed by the members of the new organisation provoked much criticism. The favourites amongst the strangers were evidently the three forwards from Dundee, who showed good combination, but were heavily handicapped in their crossing by the smallness of the ground, the players often being in each other's way. The local men in their new team all showed fair form, but one or two of the Scotchmen appeared rather off colour, and may show to better advantage after a little more practice." [17]

Sheffield United's 22-man squad was made up from three sources: Eleven local amateurs all from Sheffield FC; W.F. Beardshaw, H.B. Willey, R, Crichton, G.H. Aizlewood, W.T. Wright, C.C. Pilling, B.L. Shaw, F.A. Tasker, G.J. Groves, Smith and J. Jeeves.[18] The presence of W.F. Beardshaw is a surprise as he was the man who had described professionalism as an evil that needed suppressing, just five years before he applied for a position with Sheffield's new professional club (see Chapter Seven). Five local professionals: J. Hudson (Wednesday), W. Mosforth (Wednesday), W. Hobson (Owlerton), C.H. Howlett (Gainsborough Trinity) and E. Stringer (Ecclesfield).[18] Six imported Scottish professionals: Robert Gordon (Northern FC (Glasgow), W. Robertson (Dundee), James Duncan (Dundee), Dugald Galbraith (Dundee), P. Stupart (Glanfield FC) and N. Ross (Glasgow). [18]

Analysis of the playing records for the first season using 'Sheffield United Football Club: 1889-1999,' by Denis Clarebrough and Andrew Kirkham, shows that Scottish imports Ross and Stupart never played and Gordon only played one match in that season and presumably left with the other two. The five local professionals fared much better and all played throughout the season, but the worst performing group was the Sheffield FC amateurs; five never played and the remaining six accumulated a total of just eleven appearances over the entire season. United played its first competitive game against Notts. Rangers FC, of the Midland Counties League, on 7 September 1889, losing 4–1 at Meadow Lane; W. Robertson from Dundee, scored United's first ever competitive goal. Following this game Heeley FC was chosen to be the first Sheffield opponents and this match was played on the Sheaf House ground. United won 2-1, the two

213

CHAPTER EIGHT

goals coming from James Duncan and S. Mack (a new import), and the game was watched by 2,200 spectators. [19] The first ever first match at Bramall Lane on the 28th September against Birmingham St. George FC, ended badly with a 4-0 defeat, watched by 4,000 spectators. [20] Having battled through four qualifying rounds of the F.A. Cup in its first season United beat Burnley 2-1 in the first round proper but was drawn against another powerful Lancashire club, Bolton Wanderers FC, who won by thirteen clear goals; this remains United's heaviest ever defeat. Some compensation was gained from being the losing finalist in the replayed final of the Sheffield Association Challenge Cup with Rotherham Town winning by a goal to nil, a game played at the ground of the Rotherham Swifts. In spite of not belonging to an organised League in the first season, United played a total of fifty-seven friendlies and Cup games. In the spring of 1890, over sixty English clubs were involved in some form of Association League competition. This was very detrimental to County games: "The interest in Inter-Association matches has been considerably discounted in the northern districts by the increasing importance of the inter-club contests. The strictly business-like spirit in which the League is conducted has prevented the clubs…from rendering the same amount of assistance to their District Associations as in the past." [21] After the launch of the Football League in 1888 both Wednesday and United sought alternatives to provide regular fixtures, during the four years until they both finally gained admission in 1892/93.

League Name	The Wednesday	Sheffield United
Football Alliance	1889/90 (Champions) 1890/91 1891/92 (Bottom)	
Northern Counties League	1889/90	
Midland Counties League		1890/91 (5th)
Northern League		1891/92 (3rd) 1892/93 (3rd)
Football League First Division	1892/93 (12th)	1893/94 (10th)
Football League Second Division		1892/93 (2nd)
United Counties League		1893/94 (4th) 1894/95 (competition abandoned)

From inception, Sheffield United FC was run by the first chairman Michael J. Ellison, mentioned earlier as the agent of the Duke of Norfolk, who was instrumental in the building of Bramall Lane cricket ground in 1854. He became President of Sheffield United in 1896, at the same time as Charles Stokes was made chairman. Following the death of Michael J. Ellison, Sheffield United Cricket and Football Club became a limited company and bought the freehold of the ground for £10,134 in 1899. This purchase removed the Duke of Norfolk's prior arrangement of retaining one third of the gate takings from any match at the ground, which had made it difficult for clubs using Bramall Lane in the past to make a profit. In the 1898 Sheffield United Cricket and Football Club accounts show that the total expenses were £5,178 (£2,878 being player's wages), with an income of £6,059 (£5,865 were gate receipts); they made a net profit of £871. The timing of the change to a limited company in 1899 was fortuitous, as Sheffield United would win the F.A. Cup in the same season, thus (presumably) retaining a greater share of the gate money generated. The vacant chairmanship, following the death of Ellison, was taken over by Charles Clegg, who eventually became Club President in 1924.

At the time of the book's publication (April 2017), Sheffield United has achieved promotion to the Championship for the 2017/18 season, after six seasons in the third tier.

SHEFFIELD EMBRACES PROFESSIONALISM

The Wednesday reach the F.A. Cup Final 1890

For the first time in Sheffield history a Sheffield team reached the final of the F.A. Cup when Wednesday met Blackburn Rovers in 1890. Interestingly at this point it seems that the nickname of the 'Blades' applied to the Wednesday rather than Sheffield United, who had only started playing a few months previously in September 1889. Wednesday relinquished the Blades sobriquet to take on the 'Owls' name, presumably as they became more settled in their new Hillsborough home ground at Owlerton from 1899 onwards and United then appropriated it for their own use. The two opposing nicknames were defined for the first time memorably in a 1906 cartoon: [22]

Of the eleven Wednesday players who played Blackburn Rovers in the F.A. Cup final, eight were home grown. The local newspaper reviewed all eleven players and I have included the potted biographies as it is interesting in that players were still mentioned as amateur, as opposed to professional:

"J. Smith, the goalkeeper, is 37 years of age, and was born in Sheffield. He has been closely allied with Wednesday for several years, and has always shown himself a clever custodian. He has nothing flashy in his style, but is cool, calculating, and fearless, and ranks as one of the most reliable goalkeepers in the kingdom.

Haydn A. Morley is one of the amateurs of the team, and is now practicing as a solicitor at Derby. He is 26 years of age, and is exceeding slim for a full back, but makes up for the deficiency by his admirable returns and tackling. He is careful to play the game in its true spirit, and was never known to take undue advantage of an opponent. He fell into the breach this season caused by the indisposition of Fred Thompson, and right loyally has he helped out his old club.

Ted Brayshaw, who is 26 years of age, was born in Sheffield, and from his youth has followed the game, and now ranks as one of the best backs in England. He is fearless, has a huge return, but is prone to playing 'the gallery' when his side is leading. Apart from this drawback he is one of the most reliable backs which could be put in the field.

John W. Dungworth is an amateur player and a Sheffielder, and is 23 years of age. As a mile runner, he has taken many prizes, and is never so much in his element as when indulging in athletic exercises. Although so young, he is left half-back, and he is very difficult to pass, being speedy, dodgy, and using his light weight to the best advantage. He plays a reliable and consistent game.

THE BLADE AND THE OWL.

The Bramall Lane Blade: "Had a good Christmas, Owley?"

The Owlerton Owl: "Hardly know what to say—might have been a lot better, any way!"

[Whilst United have added points to their list this week, Wednesday have had to be satisfied with one.]

Image © The British Library Board. All rights reserved. Included with kind cooperation of the British Newspaper Archive (www.britishnewspaperarchive.co.uk)

CHAPTER EIGHT

'Billy' Betts, as he is familiarly called, is 25 years of age, and is also a 'Blade.' He has often skippered the team in which he is so prominent a member, and is a popular favourite amongst the Olivia Grove habitués. He is a hard-working, unselfish player, is speedy, quick on the ball, and can kick in any position, qualities which render him a most formidable opponent.

George Waller, the other half-back, is 26 years of age, and was also born in Sheffield. He is the tallest of the half-backs, and is undoubtedly the most quiet playing member of the team. He is none the less effective, and in his quiet style tackles flashy opponents in a manner which has often deservedly evoked plaudits from spectators. He is also clever at difficult returns, and is always safe.

Harry Winterbottom, who is 28 years of age, is another Sheffielder, and also undertakes the responsible position of captain of the team. His position outside right wing, and worthily fulfils it. He is fast, tricky, unselfish, and centres well, a fact pretty well known to his opponents, judging by the way in which they look after him.

'Billy' Ingram is the partner of Winterbottom on the right wing, and is another local lad. He is 23 years of age, and has rapidly come to the front as one of the best forwards in the North. His fearless, tricky, genuine play is very much admired, and when he gets an opening in front of goal he shoots in a terrific manner.

'Micky' Bennett, who comes in as centre forward for the final tie, is 26 years of age, and was born at Rotherham. He is not particularly clever on the ball, but plays with sound judgment, knows no fear, and is exceedingly useful with his head play.

Mumford, one of the left-wing men, was born in Shropshire, but has for several years, resided in Sheffield. He is the youngest member of the team, being only 23 years of age. He is a sound, reliable forwards, but sometimes lacks dash and go. He is speedy, low weight, knows how to play the game, and should make a forward of which Sheffield would be proud.

The last to be noticed, but by no means the least, is Tommy Cawley, who is 30 years of age, and the oldest member of the team. In Sheffield football circles, there is no more familiar name of figure than that of Cawley, and the way in which he has been appreciated is amply demonstrated by the fact that he will receive about £200 as the result of a benefit match given to him by the Wednesday Club. Cawley is a good dribbler and fast, but is not usually a huge success when shooting at goal." [23]

In spite of the Sheffield talent on show, the result was a 6-1 thrashing; the following excellent report of the trip to the Kennington Oval from 'One of the Crowd' illustrates the Cup Final atmosphere wonderfully. The anonymous reporter was in possession of a special pass courtesy of Charles W. Alcock, so must have been somebody well connected from within the Sheffield Football Association:

"After visiting one or two other objects of interest I made my way to Vauxhall Bridge, and soon found myself one of a stream of people on their way to Kennington Oval, and about half-past two I presented myself at the gate for admission. Being armed with a special pass from Mr. Alcock, the secretary of the Surrey Club, I experienced no difficulty in getting inside, which was more than those could say who had to enter at the turnstiles, which were literally besieged. Once inside the ground it was soon apparent that all the best places for seeing had been taken up by the early birds, but still there was ample room on the raised terraces for several thousand more. Intent on passing the time as pleasantly as possible until half-past three, I made my way to the gas tank end of the ground, where there appeared to be a rather lively lot congregated. Nor was I mistaken, for in a few minutes a gentleman stepped on to the track and delighted his audience by giving them his opinion as to the respective merits of the team, and offering to back his opinion

– but he never put down any money, although frequently entreated to do so. Having shouted himself hoarse he quietly subsided into the crowd, and I departed for fresh fields and pastures new. There was not much fun to be got out of the spectators, a great number being anxious to do a little business in betting line, but the Yorkshiremen were hardly confident enough of the success of their champions to take the tempting odds offered. The concourse of people inside the ground were made up of all sorts and conditions of men, with a very fair sprinkling of ladies. There were Englishmen and foreigners, gentlemen and working men, soldiers in bright uniforms and soldiers in dark uniforms, sailors, &c., all mixed up in one heterogenous mass. Shortly before the commencement of the match I made my way to the enclosure, and by the aid of my talisman got conducted to the roof of the pavilion. The scene from this point was of the most unique description, and the appearance of the crowd gave me the impression of a well-knitted hearthrug, with a very large centre piece of green, the colours of the outside border being mainly composed of black, with patches of red dotted about here and there. Just before half-past three a loud shout greeted the appearance of the Blackburn Rovers on the green, and a right smart lot they looked, dressed all in white. A minute or two afterwards the Wednesday men stepped into the arena, dressed in blue jerseys and white knickers, and they were greeted with a hearty cheer." [24]

Our correspondent glossed over the details of the game as it became clear that the team from Lancashire was going to win easily:

"Some time before this I had become tired of watching the uneven contest, and had turned my attention to the spectators. Looking down in front of the enclosure a beautiful sight met my gaze. On the green there had been placed some wood similar to that used on the pavilion side if Bramall lane, and peacefully reclining there were about a dozen policemen basking in the sun's rays. Up to now the crowd had been one of the most orderly it had been my lot to see, and the policemen's lot had been a very happy one, but their dream of bliss was rudely dispelled. About five minutes before time what I had thought looked like a hearthrug appeared to be suddenly and violently shaken, and a large number of the pieces were immediately thrown across the green and on towards the enclosure. This sudden uprising appeared to completely knock the wind out of the minions of the law, and it was several seconds before they awoke to a sense of their responsibility. It was then with some difficulty that the crowd could be kept off the playing area, and the game had to be stopped during this time. That such an event as this could happen at Kennington Oval I never imagined, and I pinched myself to see if I was awake. Alas, it was too true, but it was especially hard on the southern scribes who last year held up their hands in virtuous indignation when the semi-final between Preston North End and when West Bromwich Albion, at Sheffield, had to be stopped for a similar thing. Time eventually called, much to the relief of everybody, and the Blackburn Rovers received quite an ovation on making their way to the enclosure. The Wednesday men were cheered by some of their most ardent supporters, and Morley (who had played like a little champion all through the game) was carried off the field shoulder high. When the cup was brought out to be presented to the Rovers, the large crowd that had assembled in front of the pavilion began to sway ominously, and several venturesome people attempted to get in the enclosure. It was now that the cockney policemen were seen at their best, and they began to thrust and haul the people back in a most unceremonious manner, catching some by the throat and swinging them round with some life. Probably bearing in remembrance the valiant deeds accomplished by the police at Trafalgar square* the people took it very quietly, and the ceremony of presenting the cup proceeded without further interruption. On making my way out of the ground everybody appeared to be of opinion that it was the worst final tie ever seen for the English Cup. The only consolation afforded the Wednesday men is that they were beaten by one of the finest teams in England; and had the Rovers been pitted against any other club they would just about have won. What the Wednesday men think about their own play I know not, but it is the opinion of 'One of the Crowd' that they have never shown to worse advantage in any match in which they have taken part in this season." [24]

(* Refers to the Trafalgar square riot on the 13th November 1887, known as 'Bloody Sunday', when demonstrators from the Social Democratic Federation and the Irish National League, clashed violently with the London police).

Sheffield FC to amalgamate?

If ever there was a pivotal moment in Sheffield's football history, when the old order was replaced by the new, it was the summer of 1890. Sheffield FC played Derby Junction away on the 3rd May in the last Midland Counties game. After its first season of League football Sheffield FC had finished bottom and was replaced by Sheffield United which played its first Midland Counties game against Burton Wanderers away on September 13th 1890. In between these two matches the two clubs met at Bramall Lane on September 1st and United won by 9 goals to nil:

> "SHEFFIELD UNITED V. SHEFFIELD CLUB. The season proper of 1890-91 in Sheffield was opened yesterday at Bramall Lane with a match between the above noted clubs. The afternoon, though somewhat cold, was delightfully fine, and some 2,000 spectators lined the ropes. The home team was representative, but Sheffield Club were short of several of their noted men. The patience of the spectators was somewhat tried by the start being delayed half an hour after the advertised time, but it is only fair to state that this was through no fault of the United. From the very first it was palpable that Sheffield Club were very much overmatched, the United, after having started the ball, scoring in the first half minute by Bridgewater, from a pass by Clark. United kept up the pressure and secured unproductive corners, but after thirty minutes' play Clark got through and beat Barber, scoring second goal for United. The Sheffield Club forwards broke away, but there was little or no combination, and the United defence had little difficulty in relieving their lines. Before the whistle sounded for the interval Bridgewater and Watson each scored, United standing four goals to none. On crossing over the attack was maintained by United, and after eight minutes' play, almost solely in the Sheffield Club's half Watson cleverly scored goal number five, and the same player subsequently added another point cleverly when close in, but in a difficult position.
>
> Three unproductive corners fell to United in as many minutes, after which they shot through cleverly from the left, and Clark, when close in, shot through, scoring United's eighth goal. Just on the call of time Bridgewater scored from a corner, the game ending: -
>
> SHEFFIELD UNITED ...... 9 goals
> Sheffield Club .... none
>
> United, - Goal, Howlett; Backs, Whittam and Lilley; half-backs, Cross, Howell, and Robertson; forwards, B. L. Shaw, Bridgewater, T. B. A., Clarke, Watson, and Calder.
> Sheffield Club. –Goal, H. Barber; backs, E. C. Benson and A. J. Ward; half-backs, A. H. Mellowes, C. H. Parker, and H. B. Willey; forwards, C. White, P. Creighton, A. D. Barber, S. Hickson, and A. N. Other. Umpires, Messrs. Bairstow and A. J. Baker. Referee, Mr. J. Fox." [25]

SHEFFIELD EMBRACES PROFESSIONALISM

Two years earlier in 1888, Sheffield FC had merged with Collegiate FC as they felt the financial pinch and the gossip in the 1890 paper was that Sheffield FC had been approached to merge with an unnamed professional club:

"Allow me to offer my congratulations to Sheffield Club on their victory over Loughborough in the Midland Alliance match on Saturday. It is quite refreshing to see our one and only amateur club gaming a match, and I trust is it happy augury of further success. I believe that there was a proposal made to the players of the Sheffield Club to link themselves with a professional organisation in the early part of the season, but longer heads and wiser counsels prevailed, so that the old club, whose Sheffield football traditions can never fade remains, as I earnestly hope it never may, the Amateur Sheffield Club. Its members do, and always have, played purely and solely for the love of the game, and not for pot hunting, and they have done well to discard the proposals of those whose only aim seems to be to make a bid for 'cheap popularity.'" [26]

The above article did not state which 'professional organisation' made the proposal. Wednesday may have been willing to absorb them but it seems much more likely, due to the timings, that the plan was for Sheffield FC to be the basis of the new Sheffield United. Sheffield FC did continue but losing eleven players to United on the club's launch, must have dramatically contributed to Sheffield FC's subsequent poor record in the Midland Counties League.

Sheffield FC, the world's oldest football club nearly ceased to exist after just thirty-three years. The 'wise counsels' would have certainly included the officers of the club. At the A.G.M. in May 1889, the following gentlemen composed the committee: "Chairman; H.W. Chambers, Hon. Sec; W.W. Liddell, President; Col. J.E. Bingham, Vice-presidents; Col. Creswick, Col. Vickers, Messrs. Charles Belk, H. Bramley, W. Chesterman, Arthur Jackson, T.W. Jeffcock, W.A. Matthews, J.C. Shaw, F.P. Smith, W.C. Taylor and F. Ward. Hon. Treasurer; Mr. H.B. Willey, Captain of the 1st team; Mr. W.F. Beardshaw, Captain of the 2nd team; Mr. J. F. Smith." [27] These familiar names do not seem to be the kind of men to make a bid for 'cheap popularity.'.

The First United v. Wednesday derby 1890

The first Sheffield *League* derby, when United played Wednesday was October 16th 1893 at Bramall Lane, ended 1-1. However, their first ever non-League match was a friendly played three years earlier on December 15th 1890, which Wednesday won 2-1 at their Olive Grove ground:

"SHEFFIELD WEDNESDAY V. SHEFFIELD UNITED. The match which has created by far the greatest amounts of interest in Sheffield football circles was the one that came off at Olive Grove this afternoon between Sheffield Wednesday and Sheffield United. For weeks, nay for months, the principal theme of conversation whenever those interested in the winter pastime met was as to who would win, and both teams have found a large number of supporters. It is true that Wednesday have been doing anything but well since the commencement, whereas the United team have won a large majority of their matches, and have worked their way into popular favour by their performances at Bramall Lane; but still there was a vast number of people ready to believe, in fact were certain, that the old club could more than hold its own against its rival. The result of this was that the partisans on both sides were ready to back their fancy, even to laying sight odds. As all Sheffield knows the week before Christmas is one in which workmen put in as much time as possible, and had this been an ordinary match the assembly at the Grove would indeed have been a poor one. But this was a contest of such deep interest that even 'cow week' or 'bull week' could not keep them in their hulls and in spite of everything the Sheffielders 'threw off the band' at dinner time and made their way to the field of battle. The game was not announced to start until 2.30, but the gates were thrown open at 1.30, and even then there were a goodly number of enthusiasts waiting, anxious to secure a good position. Both sides distributed favours, which were freely worn in hats and caps of the lookers on, and the time was spent for the most part discussing the merits of the two teams. By two o'clock the four sides of the field were well lined, and when play commenced there were something like 10,000 present. Wednesday played their usual team with the exception of Todd, who took Dungworth's position on the right, while United stood by the eleven which has done service for the club during the season. It was feared that the keen frost on Sunday would have made play almost impossible, but the slight thaw had made the surface soft and although it was playable, the field was in a somewhat treacherous condition. A cheer went up at 2.25 as both teams entered the ground at the same time, Wednesday appearing in new blue and white striped jerseys." [28]

This is the first mention I found for Wednesday wearing blue and white stripes. The 1890/91 season was also the first season Sheffield United wore red and white stripes, after an initial season in white shirts and blue 'knickers'. How appropriate for the first ever derby to be the match when both clubs wore their striped shirts together for the first time. United scored first after 20 minutes through Robertson, then Hodder equalised for Wednesday in the second half, before an unnamed (due to the light) player scored the winner for Wednesday with five minutes left to play. The article concluded with the line-ups:

"Wednesday – Goal, Smith; backs, Brayshaw, F. Thompson; half backs, Cawley, Betts, Todd; forwards, Hodder, Woolhouse, Brandon, Mumford, Winterbottom

United – Goal, Howlett; backs, Whittam, Lilley; half-backs, Cross, Howell, G. J. Groves; forwards, Shaw, Bridgewater, Robertson, Watson, Calder. Umpires, Messrs. W. E. Clegg and W. Liddell. Referee, Mr. J. C Clegg." [28]

Pleasingly for history lovers, the above match came almost exactly thirty years to the day, from when Sheffield's (and the world's) first ever derby took place between Sheffield FC and Hallam FC, on the 26th December 1860.

Professionalism wins an F.A. Cup for Sheffield 1896
After losing in 1889/1890 it would be six more years before Wednesday won the F.A. Cup, by beating Wolves 2-1 at Crystal Palace on 18th April 1896. At a banquet to celebrate the event held in October 1896, the subject of money came up; it seems that the move to professionalism had been a success and was endorsed by Charles Clegg:

"Mr. Alfred Holmes, who had charge of the first toast, made a big hit in his extended references to the city council as the 'landlords' of his club and his allusion to the improvements which the tenants had effected to their property provoked a good deal or merriment. 'We have dug and delved, builded and banked' said Mr. Holmes, and though perhaps it was not precisely what the speaker meant, many of the hearers took the last word literally. As everybody knows the Wednesday Club has 'banked' since the tenancy of Olive Grove was commenced. Indeed, the clubs as Ald. W. E. Clegg afterwards remarked is 'rolling in wealth.' [29]

Charles Clegg the serving chairman of the Football Association followed and gave a very interesting speech showing his distaste of professionalism had mellowed over the years. As Sheffield's most influential player/administrator, it is appropriate to give Charles Clegg the last words in the book:

"Mr. J. C. Clegg, president of the Football Association, submitted the toast of the evening, 'The winning club.' He was sure that no one could have proposed the toast with more earnestness and pride than himself. It was an occasion which they had looked for many years and they were proud now that it was all the greater because the team had not only won the cup, but deserved it. (Hear, hear). He had seen a very good many final cup ties, but he could say without flattery that he had never seen a better one than the last, and in order that there should be no undue elation he had better say that the same club which on that occasion was responsible for the worst final ties he ever witnessed. (Laughter)." [29]

"A lot had been said of professionalism ruining the game of football. ("No, No"). Anyone who knew anything of the game, would know that was complete nonsense, for no other word would express it. He did not mean to say that professional footballers were angels- they would never be here if they were- (laughter) – but the comparisons made between amateur and professionals had no foundation to fact (hear, hear) in deed and professionals would compare favorably with those who were not paid for their services. He had played himself a good many years ago- (hear, hear!) and he knew that at that time he could not have devoted the time to the game to acquire the skill necessary for a position in one of the first teams of to-day. Amateurs could not afford to neglect their ordinary duties, and they had no right to expect the same result from them as from those who, in a manner, made football a business. But that was no reason why reflections should be cast upon those who did make it a business (Hear, hear). And the real grounds of complaint, became fewer and fewer as the seasons rolled on. (Hear, hear). The game was played better now than it had been for years, for both players and spectators were learning to control themselves in exciting matches in a manner which they must certainly do if football was to be played as it should be played, (Applause)." [29]

It would take three years for Sheffield United to emulate Wednesday's feat of lifting the F.A. Cup in 1899 when they beat Derby County 4-1. No match photographs appear to exist of Wednesday's or Sheffield United's early F.A. Cup final appearances, but when United drew 2-2 against Tottenham Hotspur in 1901, a photograph was taken at the Crystal Palace game. I think it shows the moment after a Spur's goal, with goalkeeper Willie Foulkes retrieving the ball. The game looks to have been played with no goal nets, even though they were introduced in 1890. Somewhere in a striped shirt is United captain, Ernest 'Nudger' Needham and the pitch markings show the penalty 'line' that was introduced in 1891. The new 'penalty area' was introduced in the following year. The match was a 2-2 draw and in the replay at Burden Park, Bolton, Tottenham won 3-1.

Association Football and the Men who Made it 1905

Conclusion

In 1872 when Sheffield was leading the world in Association football the qualities that gave a player pre-eminence were described locally as '…speed, science and bottom.'

The qualities of speed and science are as relevant today as they were 160 years ago; players with pace, the pressing game, formation, tactics, player conditioning, coaching, medicine, physiotherapy, nutrition, Opta stats, kit and boot technology, etc. For me, the final element, 'bottom', covers the all-important qualities of resolution and determination, of not knowing when you are beaten and persisting against all the odds. This philosophy paid dividends until the late 1870s but then Sheffield clubs discovered that a fourth element was required. A club needed money to survive and then to succeed, even if you had a speedy team which played scientifically and had plenty of 'bottom.'

In the early days of Association Football there was no place more important than Sheffield and it could be argued that without the Sheffield Association, there would be no Football Association. Of the twenty oldest Association Football clubs in England, ten came from the town of Sheffield, with just eight originating from London or the home counties. Amazingly, ten of the Sheffield clubs formed between 1857 and 1889 competed nationally in the Football Association Cup. This meteoric rise was followed by a slow decline because Sheffield did not embrace professionalism; Wednesday was nearly replaced by the Sheffield Rovers in 1887, Sheffield FC could have been subsumed in 1889 and Hallam FC folded for nearly a year in 1886. Only four of the ninety-five Sheffield clubs playing between 1857 and 1889 still exist today.

Once the professionalism nettle had been grasped, the early 20th century was a success again for the Sheffield Clubs with Wednesday and United winning F.A. Cups and First Division titles, and Sheffield FC lifting the F.A. Amateur Cup in 1903/04.

In the 2016/17 season Sheffield has no Premier League presence; instead it has two League clubs and no non-League sides above level eight in the football pyramid. The last major success of any Sheffield club dates back thirty-six years to 1991 (Wednesday's League Cup win); it is therefore reasonable to say that Sheffield football has been in decline for many years. This is a scandalous outcome for a major city with such an immaculate footballing history. 2017 is an important year of anniversaries for Sheffield football; it is the perfect time for Sheffield's football clubs to show their legendary 'bottom' (combined with the always necessary funding from somewhere) and make some new footballing history.

I hope you have enjoyed my chronological list of Sheffield football clubs and I will leave you with the words of author Nick Hornby, who is also enamoured of both football and lists; for me his words encapsulate the emotions that are involved in being a fan of Sheffield football:

'I fell in love with football as I was later to fall in love with women. Suddenly, uncritically, giving no thought to the pain it would bring.'

Table One: Sheffield Football Clubs

Sheffield Position (National position for all clubs current or defunct)	Team Name (Name change)	Current League Level 2015/16 Or Defunct	Origin Type	Year of foundation	Year of Closure (years survived)	First official Association link	Notes
1 (1)	Sheffield FC (1)	Evo-Stik Northern Premier. First Division South. Pyramid level 8 (2016/17)	School Alumni cricket and the Volunteer Movement	October 24th 1857	Not applicable	1868 Football Annual	FA Amateur Cup Winner 1903/04 Sheffield & Hallamshire Senior Cup Winners 1993/94, 2004/05, 2005/06, 2007/08, 2009/10 F.A.Cup entrant
2 (5)	Hallam FC (2)	Koolsport Northern Counties East League Division 1 Pyramid level 10 (2016/17)	Players from another club (Sheffield FC)	1860	Not applicable	1868 Football Annual	Youdan Cup Winner 1867 Sheffield & Hallamshire Senior Cup Winners 1950/51, 1961/62 1964/65, 1967/68, F.A. Cup entrant
=3 (=8)	Norfolk FC (3)	Defunct	Cricket	1861	1881 (20 years)	1868 Football Annual	
	Pitsmoor FC (4)	Defunct	Cricket	1861	1887 (26 years)	1868 Football Annual	
4 (9)	Norton FC (5)	Defunct	Cricket	1861	1878 (17 years)	1872 Football Annual	
=5 (=13)	Firvale FC (6)	Defunct	Cricket	1862	1894 (32 years)	1868 Football Annual	
	Heeley FC (7)	Defunct	Church	1862	1899 (37 years)	1868 Football Annual	Sheffield & Hallamshire Senior Cup Winners 1881/82 F.A.Cup entrant
	Mackenzie FC (8)	Defunct	Cricket	1862	1872 (10 years)	1868 Football Annual	
	Milton FC (9)	Defunct	Cricket	1862	1870 (8 years)	1868 Football Annual	Instrumental in the foundation of Notts County FC
	Howard Hill Steel Bank FC (10)	Defunct	Public House	1862	1864 (2 years)	Never joined the Sheffield FA	
6 (=16)	Broomhall FC (11)	Defunct	Cricket	1863	1880 (17 years)	1868 Football Annual	
7 (=24)	United Mechanics FC (12)	Defunct	Workplace	1865	1877 (12 years)	1868 Football Annual	
=8 (=29)	Garrick FC (13)	Defunct	Public House	1866	1886 (20 years)	1868 Football Annual	

TABLE ONE: SHEFFIELD FOOTBALL CLUBS

	Wellington FC (14)	Defunct	Unknown	1866	1878 (12 years)	1868 Football Annual	
9 (=29)	The Wednesday FC (15)	Sky Bet Championship Pyramid level 2 (2016/17)	Cricket	1867	Not applicable	1868 Football Annual	3rd Oldest League Club Cromwell Cup Winner 1868 FA Cup Winners 1895/96 1906/07 1934/35 Sheffield & Hallamshire Senior Cup Winners – 1876/77 and have won it in total 14 times Division One Champions: 1902/03, 1903/04, 1928/29, 1929/30 League Cup 1990/91
10 (31)	Exchange FC (16) (Park Grange 1882)	Defunct	Cricket	1867	1896 (29 years)	Joined the F.A. in 1871 as a member of the Sheffield Association	F.A. Cup entrant as Park Grange FC
11 (=32)	Dore FC (17)	Defunct	Unknown	1867	1891 (24 years)	1878 Football Annual	
12 (=37)	Dronfield FC (18)	Defunct	Unknown	1868	1925 (57 years)	1871 Football Annual	
13 (38)	Brincliffe FC (19)	Defunct	Unknown	1868	1881 (13 years)	1872 Football Annual	Amalgamated with Endcliffe FC 1879 (Sheffield Daily Telegraph Monday 28 April 1879)
=14 (=46)	Oxford FC (20)	Defunct	Unknown	1869	1884 (15 years)	1871 Football Annual	
	Parkwood Springs FC (21)	Defunct	Unknown	1869	1880 (11 years)	1871 Football Annual	
=15 (=49)	Christchurch (Attercliffe) FC (22)	Defunct	Church	1870	1904 (34 years)	1871 Football Annual	F.A. Cup entrant
	Surrey FC (23)	Defunct	Church	1870	1882 (12 years)	1871 Football Annual	
16 (=50)	Perseverance FC (24) (Park Grange 1882)	Defunct	Temperance	1870	1896 (26 years)	1872 Football Annual	F.A. Cup entrant as Park Grange FC
=17 (=51)	Walkley New Connexion FC (Walkley FC) (25)	Defunct	Church	1870	1890 (20 years)	1873 Football	
	Crookes FC (26)	Defunct	Cricket	1870	1903 (33 years)	1873 Football Annual	

TABLE ONE: SHEFFIELD FOOTBALL CLUBS

=18 (=52)	(Bankers FC) Thursday Wanderers FC (27)	Defunct	Workplace	1870	1882 (12 years)	1874 Football	Sheffield & Hallamshire Senior Cup Winners - 1878/79
	Gleadless FC (28)	Defunct	Unknown	1870	1880 (10 years)	1874 Football Annual	
=19 (=55)	Lockwood Brothers FC (29)	Defunct	Workplace	1870	1888 (18 years)	1879 Football Annual	Sheffield & Hallamshire Senior Cup Winners-1883/84 and 1884/85 F.A. Cup entrant
	Alliance FC (30)	Defunct	Temperance	1870	1880 (10 years)	1879 Football Annual	
	Talbot FC (31)	Defunct	Cricket	1870	1880 (10 years)	1879 Football Annual	
=20 (=62)	Millhouses FC (32)	Defunct	Unknown	1871	1881 (10 years)	1875 Football Annual	
	Exchange Brewery FC (33)	Defunct	Workplace	1871	1880 (9 years)	1875 Football Annual	
21 (65)	All Saints' Night School FC (All Saints Wanderers (34)	Defunct	School	1871	1883 (12 years)	1879 Football Annual	
22 (72)	Brightside FC (35)	Defunct	Unknown	1872	1879 (7 years)	1874 Football Annual	
=23 (=73)	Norfolk Works FC (36)	Defunct	Workplace	1872	1877 (5 years)	1875 Football Annual	
	Albion FC (37)	Defunct	Unknown	1872	1880 (8 years)	1875 Football Annual	
=24 (=76)	Eldon St. Jude's FC (38)	Defunct	Church	1872	1879 (7 years)	1879 Football Annual	
	Pye Bank FC (39)	Defunct	Unknown	1872	1886 (14 years)	1879 Football Annual	Sheffield New Association Challenge Cup Winners - 1877/78
25 (=82)	Owlerton FC (40)	Defunct	Cricket	1873	1897 (24 years)	1874 Sheffield Football Association	F.A. Cup entrant
26 (=83)	Philadelphia FC (41)	Defunct	Workplace	1873	1877 (4 years)	1875 Football Annual	
27 (=84)	Endcliffe FC (42)	Defunct	Unknown	1873	1881 (8 years)	1876 Football Annual	Amalgamated with Brincliffe FC 1879 (Sheffield Daily Telegraph Monday 28 April 1879)
28 (=85)	Sharrow Rangers FC (43)	Defunct	Unknown	1873	1882 (9 years)	1877 Football Annual	
29 (=86)	Ecclesfield FC (44)	Defunct	Unknown	1873	1894 (21 years)	1879 Football Annual	F.A. Cup entrant

TABLE ONE: SHEFFIELD FOOTBALL CLUBS

=30 (=94)	Providence FC (45) (Park Grange 1882)	Defunct	Church	1874	1896 (22 years)	1876 Football Annual	F.A. Cup entrant as Park Grange FC
	Handsworth Woodhouse FC (46)	Defunct	Unknown	1874	1877 (3 years)	1876 Football Annual	
31 (95)	Carnforth FC (47)	Defunct	Workplace	1874	1880 (6 years)	1877 Sheffield Football Association	
32 (96)	Woodseats FC (48)	Defunct	Public House	1874	1881 (7 years)	1879 Football Annual	
				1875			
=33 (=117)	Darnall FC (49)	Defunct	Unknown	1876	1895 (19 years)	1879 Football Annual	
	Newfield FC (50)	Defunct	Public House	1876	1879 (3 years)	1879 Football Annual	
				1877			
				1878			
34 (=143)	White Cross FC (51)	Defunct	Unknown	1879	1884 (5 years)	1879 Football Annual	
35 (154)	Zulus FC (52)	Defunct	Charity	1879	1882 (3 years)	Unknown	I can find no records of them joining the Sheffield F.A. but as the players were being banned by the organisation, they must have been members in the first place!
				1880			
				1881			
				1882			
				1883			
				1884			
				1885			
				1886			
	Sheffield Rovers FC			1887		Unknown	Formed as a stalking horse by Wednesday players to convince the club to start paying them wages. The club only played four games and can be discounted in the overall totals
				1888			
36	The Sheffield United Cricket and Football Club (53)	Sky Bet League 1. Pyramid level 3 (2016/17)	Cricket	1889	Not applicable	1889 Sheffield Football Association	F.A. Cup Winners 1898/99 1901/02 1914/15 1924/25 Sheffield & Hallamshire Senior Cup Winners - 1890/91 and have won it in total 10 times Division One Champions: 1897/98

Ascertaining the year of a club's closure is difficult and I base it on when on when press reports cease.

Table Two: Sheffield Football Clubs by date of formation

Year formed	Club Name (Members of the Sheffield Football Association)	Club ceased	Net Total of Sheffield Football Association clubs in this year	Club lifetime (as at 2017)	Total of all Sheffield clubs across both Associations	Notes
1857	Sheffield FC	Not applicable	1	160 years		
1858						Sheffield FC had sixty-two members according to the archive sold at Sothebys
1859						
1860	Hallam FC	Not applicable	2	157 years		
1861	Norfolk FC	1881	3	20 years		
	Pitsmoor FC	1887	4	26 years		
	Norton FC	1878	5	17 years		
1862	Firvale FC	1893	6	32 years		'A year before the the Football Association was formed there 15 organised teams playing in Sheffield.' The Romance of Wednesday 1867-1926 by Richard Sparling There was a York FC (1861) who played Rugby but that still only makes 11 clubs based on my research
	Heeley FC	1899	7	37 years		
	Mackenzie FC	1872	8	10 years		
	Milton FC	1870	9	8 years		
	Howard Hill Steel Bank FC (Never appeared in the Football Annual, or as a member of the Sheffield F.A.)	1864	10	2 years		
1863	Broomhall FC	1880	11	17 years		
1864		Howard Hill Steel Bank FC ceases	10			The year of the Great Flood
1865	United Mechanics FC	1877	11	12 years		
1866	Garrick FC	1886	12	20 years		'Sheffield Club had 260 members and the year's receipts amounted to £450,' The Romance of Wednesday 1867-1926 by Richard Sparling
	Wellington FC	1878	13	12 years		
1867	The Wednesday FC	Not applicable	14	150 years		In a letter to the FA in 1867 William Chesterman wrote there were 14 Sheffield clubs with 100 members
	Exchange FC (Park Grange 1882)	1896	15	29 years		
	Dore FC	1891	16	24 years		
1868	Dronfield FC	1925	17	57 years		
	Brincliffe FC	1881	18	13 years		

TABLE TWO: SHEFFIELD FOOTBALL CLUBS BY DATE OF FORMATION

1869	Oxford FC	1884	19	15 years		
	Parkwood Springs FC	1880	20	11years		
1870	Christchurch (Attercliffe) FC	1904	21	34 years		
	Surrey	1882	22	12 years		
	Perseverance FC	1896	23	26 years		
	Walkley New Connexion FC	1890	24	20 years		
	Crookes FC	1903	25	33 years		
	Thursday Wanderers FC	1882	26	12 years		
	Gleadless FC	1880	27	10 years		
	Lockwood Bros FC	1888	28	18 years		
	Alliance FC	1880	29	10 years		
	Talbot FC	1880	30	10 years		
1871	Millhouses FC	1881	31	10 years		
	Exchange Brewery FC	1880	32	9 years		
	All Saint's Night School FC	1883	33	12 years		
1872		Mackenzie FC ceases	32			'Several thousand members and sixteen clubs' Sheffield Independent Tuesday 07 May 1872
	Brightside FC	1879	33	7 years		
	Norfolk Works FC	1877	34	5 years		
	Albion FC	1880	35	8 years		
	Eldon St. Jude's FC	1879	36	7years		
	Pye Bank FC	1886	37	14 years		
1873	Owlerton FC	1897	38	24 years		
	Philadelphia FC	1877	39	4 years		
	Endcliffe FC	1881	40	8 years		
	Sharrow Rangers FC	1882	41	9 years		
	Ecclesfield FC	1894	42	21 years		
1874	ProvidenceFC	1896	43	22 years		
	Handsworth Woodhouse FC	1877	44	3 years		
	Carnforth FC	1880	45	6 years		
	Woodseats FC	1881	46	7 years		
1875	No new clubs were formed in the Sheffield Football Association				'Sheffield Association has 33 clubs with a total of 4,933 members' 1876 Football Annual (season 1875/76)	In December 1875, the Sheffield and Rotherham Independent reported matches involving fifty different clubs taking place over one weekend in Sheffield and surrounding areas
1876	Darnall FC	1895	47	19 years		
	Newfield FC	1879	48	3 years		

TABLE TWO: SHEFFIELD FOOTBALL CLUBS BY DATE OF FORMATION

Year	New Clubs	Clubs Ceasing				Notes
1877	No new clubs were formed in the Sheffield Football Association	United Mechanics FC ceases	47		59	12 new clubs in the New Association
		Norfolk Works FC ceases	46		58	
		Philadelphia FC ceases	45		57	
		Handsworth Woodhouse FC ceases	44		56	
1878	No new clubs were formed in the Sheffield Football Association	Norton FC ceases	43		58	15 new clubs in the New Association Sheffield Daily Telegraph - Thursday 11 April 1878
		Wellington FC ceases	42		57	
1879	White Cross FC		43	5 years	68	10 more clubs have joined the New Association (making a total of 25) Sheffield Independent Saturday 20 September 1879
	Zulus FC		44	3 years	69	
		Brightside FC ceases	43		68	
		Eldon St. Jude's FC ceases	42		67	
		Newfield FC ceases	41		66	
1880*	No new clubs were formed in the Sheffield Football Association	Park Springs FC ceases	40		82	Meanwhile the breakaway New Association numbered 42 clubs from Sheffield. (Meaning a total of 76 clubs across both Associations)
		Gleadless FC ceases	39		81	
		Alliance FC ceases	38		80	
		Talbot FC ceases	37		79	
		Exchange Brewery FC ceases	36		78	
		Albion FC ceases	35		77	
		Carnforth FC ceases	34		76	
1881**	No new clubs were formed in the Sheffield Football Association	Norfolk FC ceases	33		74	New Association is now called Hallamshire Football Association. 41 clubs in total. Sheffield Independent - Saturday 11 September 1880
		Brincliffe FC ceases	32		73	
		Millhouses FC ceases	31		72	
		Endcliffe FC ceases	30		71	
		Woodseats FC ceases	29		70	
1882***	No new clubs were formed in the Sheffield Football Association	Surrey FC ceases	28			
		Thursday Wanderers FC ceases	27			
		Sharrow Rangers FC ceases	26			
		Zulus FC ceases	25			
1883	No new clubs were formed in the Sheffield Football Association	All Saints' Night School ceases	24		61	Hallamshire Football Association has 37 clubs
1884	No new clubs were formed in the Sheffield Football Association	Oxford FC ceases	23			
1885	No new clubs were formed in the Sheffield Football Association					

TABLE TWO: SHEFFIELD FOOTBALL CLUBS BY DATE OF FORMATION

1886	No new clubs were formed in the Sheffield Football Association	Garrick FC ceases Pye Bank FC ceases	22 21			
1887	Sheffield Rovers FC formed as a stalking horse by Wednesday players to convince the club to start paying them wages. The club only played four games and can be discounted in the overall totals.	Pitsmoor FC ceases	20		56	The two rival associations amalgamate and become the Sheffield and Hallamshire Association and have 56 clubs combined. (Meaning the Hallamshire F.A. had 36 clubs)
1888	No new clubs were formed in the Sheffield & Hallamshire Football Association	Lockwood Bros FC ceases	19		53	53 clubs in total belong to S.&H.F.A., with 23 entering the Challenge Cup (Sheffield Independent 2nd May 1888)
1889	The Sheffield United Cricket and Football Club		20	128 years		13 clubs in S.&H.F.A., Challenge Cup first round (Derbyshire Times and Chesterfield Herald 7th September 1889)

* 1880/81. In Chapter Four, the numbers for Cup entries were listed in the Football Annual, that meant that across both Associations a total of 78 clubs existed.

** 1881/82. In Chapter Four, the numbers for Cup entries were listed in the Football Annual, that meant that across both Associations a total of 59 clubs existed.

*** S.F.A. has 29 clubs according to the 1883 Football Annual.

APPENDIX ONE

Rules Chronology

1815: Eton Field Game Rules

1848: Cambridge Rules

1849: Surrey Football Club Rules

1853: Harrow School Rules

1858: Sheffield Rules

1862: Sheffield Rules: second version included references to half way line kick offs and crossbars, albeit occasionally made with tape.

The Simplest Game Rules.

1863: Football Association Laws. The F.A. membership fee in the first year was one guinea. The Football Association laws followed the strict off side rules devised initially at Harrow School.

Cambridge University Rules.

1864: An official show game for the F.A. Laws was arranged for Battersea Park on 9th January; the members of the opposing teams for this game were chosen by the President of the F.A. (Pember) and the Secretary (Morley). This official first game included fourteen players per team.

1866: Charles W. Alcock and Charles Clegg joined the F.A. committee. In 1863 the Football Association did not require a tape between the goal posts but it was introduced in a resolution of February 22 1866. Also, forward passes became permitted, as long as there were three defending players between the receiver and the goal. Catching the ball in any circumstance (apart from the goal keeper) was now illegal. For the first time a specific ball was nominated 'Lillywhites's Number Five'.

Charles W. Alcock claimed the unfortunate distinction of being the first man ruled offside in an official Football Association fixture.

1867: The 1867 'three man' rule which said that the receiving player was not offside if three opponents stood between him and the goal line, meant that the passing game started to evolve. The change did not greatly enhance goal scoring and Sheffield Football Association introduced a one-man offside rule which encouraged more passing into the game, the so-called 'combination' method. In the Sheffield game the only restriction upon the position of any player in the field was that he must not be nearer to his adversaries' goal than the nearest of the defending side. When Sheffield and London amalgamated their rules in 1877, Sheffield adopted the 'three-man' rule, which would stay in place until it became the 'two-man' rule in 1925.

APPENDIX ONE: RULES CHRONOLOGY

1868: Sheffield football abolished 'rouges' [1]; the assumption is that they were replaced by the corner kick, but this was not categorically stated in the Sheffield Rules, until a new edition came out in October 1871.

1869: Goal kicks were introduced in this year, but it would be the following year before goal keepers would be mentioned officially in the laws of the game.

1870: The goal keeper was officially introduced into the laws of the game, distinguishable by a cap, and only he could handle the ball. Most clubs now accepted the eleven-a-side norm.

First ever (unofficial) international football match, England v Scotland, took place on March 5th 1870 and finished in a 0-0 draw at the Kennington Oval in London.

1871: The Rugby Football Union and the Football Association Challenge Cup commenced.

1872: Corner kicks were introduced by the Football Association. It was also agreed the ball must be spherical with a circumference of 27 to 28 inches.

The first ever official international Association football match, Scotland v England, took place on 30th November 1872 at West of Scotland Cricket Club's ground at Hamilton Crescent in Partick, Scotland; the match finished 0–0.

1873: The offside law was changed, so that an offside position was determined when the ball was played by a team-mate, rather than when it was received.

1874: The usual policy in important games was for two umpires to be appointed to referee the game, one nominated by each side. It seems this practice originated in the written rules of the Eton Field Game. Umpires would only make a decision if appealed to by the players. Umpires were first officially mentioned in the laws of the game in 1874, when for the first time they could award free kicks and send players off, or as the regulation of the time put it:
'…in the event of any persistent infringement the umpire, upon an appeal by the captain of the opposite side, shall place the player so offending out of play.'

(Referees were introduced in 1891 to make decisions if the umpires could not agree on a decision. Initially the referee stood on the touchline keeping time and was 'referred' to if the umpires could not agree. Ultimately the two umpires became linesmen and later 'assistant referees' as they are called today.)

1875: A solid cross bar was permitted as an alternative to a tape, but was not obligatory.

1876: Inaugural Sheffield Football Association Challenge Cup Rules: 'No individual shall be allowed to play for more than one competing club, but the members of each representative team may be changed during the series of matches if thought necessary. The play in each contest is to last an hour and a half, and the average circumference of the ball to be from 27 to 28 inches.'

1877: Sheffield Association Rules amalgamated with the Football Association Laws on 28th April. Football Association set the official length of a match at 90 minutes.

1882: The two-handed throw-in was introduced. The tape crossbar was finally abolished by the Football Association at the Manchester Conference of December 6th 1882.

To facilitate the start of a Home Championships Tournament the International Football Association Board (I.F.A.B.) was formed on 6th December 1882 in Manchester. The four home Associations (The F.A., The Scottish F.A., The Football Association of Wales and the Irish F.A.)

APPENDIX ONE: RULES CHRONOLOGY

discussed unification of their Laws. Interestingly there was representation of the Sheffield F.A. in the person of their Treasurer, Mr Pierce Dix, who represented the Football Association (along with Major Marindin). The discussions cannot have gone well as the unification of the Laws was not resolved until the inception of the British Home Championships in 1884. The following points were resolved by I.F.A.B. to be universal across all four nations:

- No more tapes, crossbars only were to be used.
- Touchlines were to be used (previously only boundary flags were compulsory).
- Kick-off had to be in the direction of the opponent's goal line (only amended in 2016).
- It was agreed to dispense with an experimental rule by which the committing of a deliberate handball when a goal would otherwise have been scored, was punished by the award of a goal.
- Throw-in. A two-handed throw-in from above the head, in any direction was agreed upon. Previously the Football Association had allowed a one-handed throw-in any direction whereas the Scottish rule was a two handed above the head throw that had to be at a right angle to the boundary (as in Rugby and previously in the Sheffield Rules).
- A player with their back to the opponent's goal could be charged from behind if, in the opinion of the officials, he was wilfully impeding his opponent.
- There was an addition to the Laws regarding nails in boots, which specified that players breaking the rule could take no further part in the game.

1884: The Football Association passed legislation saying that no more than one day's wages per week could be claimed for time lost through football.

1885: The Football Association legalised professionalism. Clubs were allowed to pay players provided that they had either been born or had lived for two years within a six-mile radius of the ground.

1886: In spite of the agreement of 1884, the Football Associations of England, Scotland, Wales and Northern Ireland still all played by slightly different Laws; the home team rules applied in each match. A meeting of I.F.A.B. took place at the F.A.'s offices on 2nd June 1886 where they decided that they all had equal voting rights. Representing England from the F.A. were Major Marindin and Charles W Alcock, Scotland (S.F.A.) had R. Browne and A. Kennedy, Wales (F.A.W.) Mr. Hunter and Mr. Mills-Robert and Ireland (I.F.A.) was represented by J. Sinclair and J. McAlvery.

1887: An F.A. Committee issued notes of guidance to umpires and referees on pitch markings, suggesting the need for a line running right across the field to divide it into two halves, a semi-circle of one yard radius at the corner flags, and semi-circles of 6 yards radius round each goal post.

1889: The first reported death of an umpire or referee, found in my research, during a match:

> "The Death of Football Umpire. Yesterday before Mr. Commissioner Bosanquet, at the Manchester Spring Assizes, James Tattersall, 18, factory operative, was indicted for the manslaughter of Thomas Mawdsley, at Nyland, near Preston, on the 18th April. Mr. Cooper prosecuted and Mr. Shea defended. On behalf of the prosecution it was stated that in a football match at Leyland, where Mawdsley acted as an umpire, a dispute arose about a goal, and Tattersall, who was among the spectators, went into the field of play and kicked the deceased's brother because he said it was not a goal. Mawdsley

then approached Tattersall, and the latter knocked him down and kicked him in the abdomen. Mawdsley expired on the spot. Dr. F.T. Paul of the Liverpool College, said the appearance of the deceased were quite consistent with sudden death owing to the pressure of a clot of blood on the lungs, or the bursting of a blood vessel in the brain. Mr. Shea said the kick was intended for Mawdsley's shin, and wherever the blow lighted it was not intended to do him any serious injury. The jury returned a verdict of not guilty, and Tattersall was discharged." [2]

The strict residence restrictions surrounding the legalisation of professionalism were removed by the Football Association.

1890: Goal nets were introduced.

1891: Referees were introduced and given the power to send players off, and to award free kicks and for the first-time penalties. The new penalty law required new pitch marking. Two lines were marked across the field, 12 and 18 yards from each goal line, replacing the semi-circles that had been in force since 1887. The penalty was not taken from a spot but anywhere along the 12-yard line until 1902. A penalty kick was awarded for offences occurring 12 yards from the goal line. The other players had to stand behind the ball and at least 6 yards from the kicker, as marked by the 18-yard line, when the kick took place. It was probably this year that the use of the referee's whistle became commonplace.

My research suggest that the first penalty ever awarded, was north of the border at a match between Abercorn and Port Glasgow Athletic on the 8th of August 1891. The referee 'enforced the new football rule' and Connell scored the first penalty for Abercorn; the referee clearly liked the new law and awarded two more in the same match. [3]

1892: 'Even armed with the official rules without the standardisation of referees the rules continued to be flaunted. As late as 1893 anyone could, and in fact did, referee matches in the south. All that was needed to be appointed to some of the most important fixtures was to become acquainted with some official or a member of a council and the thing was done. Rarely was a question asked about a man's fitness or ability. The Laws of the Game were to all intents and purposes unknown. Very few, even of the most prominent men had read them, and a large proportion had never seen them'. (Rennie Carr, 'The Referee').

1893: The occupation of referee was finally recognised with the creation of the Referees Society in March 1893 at a meeting in Andertons's Hotel, London. Charles W. Alcock (Secretary of the F.A.) became President, F.J. Wall (later Chairman of the F.A.) became Chairman and Arthur Roston Bourke became Honorary Secretary. The London Society's prime purpose was to examine the qualification of referees orally and appoint them to matches. (Later the Society would be renamed the Referees' Association).

1895: William Pickford, a Vice President of the Referees Society, produced 'The Referees' Chart, 1895-96'. This contained seventeen Laws and was far more substantial than those drafted in 1863.

1896: The Referees' Association published the Referees' Chart and finally referees had a reliable rule book.

APPENDIX ONE: RULES CHRONOLOGY

1899: The Referees Association had 27 societies and 773 members; the appointment of referees became too great and responsibility was transferred to the Football Association. (4)

1902: The F.A., decided to award penalties for fouls committed in an area 18 yards from the goal line and 44 yards wide and created both the penalty box and penalty spot. Another box designated as the 'goal area' (commonly called the 'six-yard-box', six yards long and 20 wide) replaced the semi-circle in the goalmouth.

1904: The Fédération Internationale de Football Association (F.I.F.A.) was formed in Paris.

1906: The Football Association club subscription was 10 Shillings and sixpence per annum.

1908: On the 9th May the Referees' Union was formed.

1912: Goalkeepers were banned from handling the ball outside the penalty area.

1913: F.I.F.A. joined I.F.A.B.

1920: Players could no longer be offside from a throw-in.

1925: The offside rule was changed so that only two players needed to be ahead of the attacker instead of three.

> Since 1878, the dominant team formation had been 2-3-5 formation (two full-backs, three-half-backs and five forwards); this changed as a result of the offside rule change. To exploit the change, Arsenal player, Charles Buchan suggested to his manager Herbert Chapman, that they should change their shape to 3-4-3. Buchan's thinking was that the centre-half took responsibility for the offside trap, instead of the full backs, who played just in front of the centre-half whilst one of the forwards was brought back into midfield. Initially the formation was known as the 'WM' formation and developed into the counter-attacking game. The next big change came in the 1990s with the adoption of 4-4-2, where the midfielders were expected to do both defensive and offensive work. This season Chelsea's Antonio Conte introduced the 3-4-3 formation and it is credited with the team's transformation from the mid-table outcome of 2015/16 to the heights of the Premier League and has become football's most fashionable formation. Nowadays, much in football is new but Charles Buchan's old idea from 1925 should be remembered and credited.

1937: The 'D' shape was added the edge of the penalty area.

1938: Revision of the Laws of the Game. The 17 Laws were redrafted and updated by Sir Stanley Rous, who would become F.I.F.A. President in 1961.

1958: New voting rights were determined (still the same today) with each British Association having one vote, F.I.F.A. having four, and any proposal needing at least six votes in favour to succeed.

1970: F.I.F.A. allowed two substitutes at World Cup tournaments.

1974: The F.A. stopped classifying all clubs as either fully professional or fully amateur, and as a result the Amateur Cup was abolished, eighty-one years after inception.

1978: The phrase 'professional foul' was first coined.

APPENDIX ONE: RULES CHRONOLOGY

1982: Introduction of the four-step rule; the goalkeeper was given up to four steps to travel while holding, bouncing or throwing the ball in the air and catching it again, without having to release it into play.

1990: The offside rule was altered so an attacker was onside if he was level with the last defender.

1991: International Football Association Board decided that a player who committed a foul or handling offence (that denied an obvious goal-scoring opportunity), should be sent off for serious foul play.

1992: The four-step rule for goalkeepers of 1982 was replaced to stop timewasting in the game; goalkeepers were now banned from handling back passes.

The 'golden goal' rule was introduced to settle matches in extra time, 124 years after it was first played in the final of Sheffield's Cromwell Cup.

1995: Three substitutes were allowed in matches instead of two.

1997: The Laws of the Game were revised for the first time since the 1930s.

1998: Lunging tackles that endangered the safety of opponents was made a red-card offence.

2000: The six-second rule was introduced for goalkeepers in another attempt to stop time wasting.

2004: The 'golden goal' rule was scrapped.

2008: I.F.A.B. authorised the U.E.F.A. to experiment with two extra assistant referees, one behind each goal line.

In 1863 the Football Association had just thirteen Laws composed of 541 words; 154 years later, the Football Association Rules book is now over six hundred pages long.

APPENDIX TWO

Classification Rules for English Football Clubs 1857-1889

One of the many reasons why a chronological history of football clubs has never been written before is because there are so many variables; my task was to decide on a set of logical rules that could be applied across the hundreds of football clubs, ensuring their foundation dates could be measured against each other. There are thousands of football clubs that were formed between 1857 and 1888 making the classification an impossibility, unless I set criteria that would make the numbers more manageable, without losing important clubs along the way. This book is specifically about Sheffield football clubs and their neighbours, but the rules that applied nationally have been applied to the clubs in this book. In the future, I will look at other geographic locations, but the classification rules will be constant.

Because the Sheffield football scene was not complicated by Rugby teams playing in the town and very few mergers and amalgamations occurred, the following rules are mainly theoretical in respect of this book, but are useful to understand in conjunction with the non-Sheffield clubs that are mentioned in the text.

The first non-English Football Club in the world did not happen until 22nd October 1864 (Wrexham), so clubs in this classification with a foundation date earlier than this, are effectively the oldest Football Clubs in the World as well as the oldest in England.

Main qualification
English football clubs (including extant and defunct Clubs, as long as they have run for one season or more and were founded before 1889), are listed if they were included in the Football Annuals between 1868-1889.

They are then divided into either:

Association if:
They listed the club's code as Association (or similar) in the Football Annual between 1868-1889

And/or the club was a founder member of a County F.A. formed before 1889

And/or the club played in the F.A. Cup before 1889

Or Rugby if:
They listed the club's code as Rugby (or similar) in the Football Annual between 1868-1889

Association qualification 1. The club plays Association Football
To be included in this list the clubs should be (or would become) Association code playing.

Association football by definition has to start in December 1863 when the Football Association was formed in London. The problem is that this is just the beginning of the evolution of the Association code; in 1863 the new rules included catching and running with the ball, touchdowns and no forward passing, a game that to modern eyes would look very much like Rugby. The salient point is that 'Association' clubs always tried to represent the ball-dribbling fraternity, as opposed to the ball-carrying crowd, which usually evolved into a Rugby club. I am fortunate in this first book about Sheffield because the Rugby code was more or less non-existent.

Association qualification 2. Inclusion in the Charles Alcock's Football Annual 1868-1899

As part of this research into the period up to 1888, I also analysed the 1889 edition to check for clubs that started in the 1888/89 season. All the annuals that I analysed from 1868 to 1889 featured a section where the clubs are listed, broken down into Metropolitan (London) and Provincial sections. If a Sheffield club is listed here, it is in this book. As the years progressed, reports from the County Associations started to appear in which they would list all the clubs in their Associations but without the breakdown of detail that a main listing would provide. These clubs are not included <u>unless</u> they are one of the founding members of their County Association OR played in the F.A. Cup between 1871-1888.

Association qualification 3. Founding member of a County Football Association

As long as a club is part of the foundation of a new County Football Association in its first year of launch or in the earliest reported list of clubs in the press. It should be included in the book because of its historical significance, even if the club itself may turn out to be short-lived.

Association qualification 4. Entry to the F.A. Challenge Cup between 1871 and 1888 it is included in the list.

Club Types

The usual classification route is to separate football clubs by the definition of whether they were 'Open' or 'Closed'. Simply put, could anyone join the club (open) or was there an entry qualification of some kind that excluded non-members. 'Closed' clubs could be:

    School
    University
    Bank
    Hospital
    Company
    Military

My first instinct was to only include 'open' clubs but classifying clubs using this criterion disqualifies 'Old Boy's' sides and it is impossible to exclude the likes of the Old Etonians in a history of Association football. Of the six types listed above I have decided only to exclude educational and military establishments from my main list. They represent, if you will, pure "closed" clubs as adults could not join a school side and a non-military man would not get very far trying to get a game with the 21st Essex Rifles. However, there are three glittering club exceptions to this rule who appear in the full chronological Association list; Oxford University Association FC (1872), Cambridge University Association FC (1873) and the Royal Engineers FC (1863).

Evolution

Playing rules were evolving from 1857 until 1871 when the Rugby Football Union was formed and there was a clear distinction between Association and Rugby. If the rules were evolving then we must accept that clubs were also evolving. A club that started out playing Rugby and later turned to Association is included in the book and its foundation date is when the club originally formed. (making clubs in Bradford very happy!) Equally if a club that played Association Football for a period of time, but then left to play Rugby, it is included, and its end date is when it leaves to join the R.F.U.

Some football clubs may have originally started as, say, Cricket clubs or Athletic clubs but the date used for this book is not when the original non-football club was formed but when it started playing football (be it Association or Rugby).

Exact foundation months are often missing, so if I only had a year for a foundation date, to sift them further, I have ranked clubs from the same year further by deciding when they fully embraced the Association game. I have done this by taking the earliest date from either of the following:

- When it first appeared in Charles Alcock's Football Annual playing by the Association code.
- When it joined its local County Football Association
- When it played for the first time in the Football Association Cup

Association Qualification 4. Does the club exist in the press of its day?

If a club claims an earlier date than any of the above evidence suggests, then it must appear in the press of their day to confirm that earlier existence. Much later unsubstantiated recollections cannot be used as the only proof for foundation dates. Some famous clubs such as Everton and Stoke suffer from unsubstantiated foundation dates. This happens when recollections of church teams and works teams, are recalled but are not reported in the press. Those teams evolve into proper clubs and the early evidence is missing, but once claimed becomes reinforced through repetition from that point. To be fair to Stoke FC, it is less keen nowadays to claim its 1863 foundation, and in 1928 James Catton was questioning the fact that Everton might be celebrating their jubilee a year early in the Athletic News. It is also worth noting that the very early match reports (like the Football Annual) were self-reported, in that it was up to the captain or the Hon. Sec. to send in the match report after the match to the local press. This, as you can imagine, occasionally caused some animated correspondence from the opposition team, if they felt facts had been misrepresented.

Association Qualification 5. Reforming Clubs, Mergers and Continuity

This final qualification is the most complex and the one that involved me making a judgement call in some cases. Fortunately in the case of south Yorkshire football this rarely happened. The questions that need asking when deciding whether clubs can claim continuity from previous incarnations are:

- Does the new club stay in the same geographic location?
- Is the new club's name substantially similar or dramatically different?
- Were the old club's debts picked up by the new incarnation?
- Does the old club immediately cease playing after merging? (Things can get complicated in a few cases; for example, a schism occurred in some clubs where a new club would be formed and an old club was left behind. This was usually because some players wished to remain amateur and disagreed with a professional future.)
- Do previous players move to the new club?
- Do club Hon. Secs., Presidents, Founders, Workplace employers move to the new club?
- How long a period existed between the two incarnations? A gap of more than a year between old club and new club will be my criteria for failure. (I have made an exception if a world war occurs between the two club incarnations; for example, Chesham Town went from 1915 to Chesham United in 1919)

APPENDIX TWO: CLASSICFICATION RULES ENGLISH FOOTBALL CLUBS 1857-1889

In each case I have had to make an individual judgement call about what it means for that particular club's foundation date and end date.

To explain this subject further it might be good to look at two non-Sheffield examples:

Newton Heath/Manchester United
Manchester United does not put on its website that it formed in April 1902; it states 1878 because it was formed from the remnants of Newton Heath FC. The president of Newton Heath, Mr Healey, was owed £250 by the club which it could not pay so he made a petition to wind up the club in 1902. Five gentlemen including Harry Stafford 'the club's popular player' put in a total of £1,000 to save the club. Their big decision was to change the name dramatically from Newton Heath to Manchester United; this was approved by a public meeting subject to the approval of the Football Association. Looking at my rules above, apart from the dramatic change of name, everything else suggests a continuation of the same club, from Newton Heath to Manchester United.

It gets more complicated and some famous clubs have similar backgrounds but take their foundation date from the changeover date. The classification needed to be consistent so here is much more complicated example.

West Bromwich (Dartmouth)/West Bromwich Strollers/West Bromwich Albion
The West Bromwich Albion website has a foundation date of 1878 and states the fact that it was formed by workers from Salter's Spring Works in West Bromwich, whose first match was a goalless draw against workers from the nearby Hudson soap factory on 23rd November 1878. George Salter played for West Bromwich (Dartmouth) at their Four Acres ground and their club started in <u>1874</u>. George Salter's company is acknowledged as the foundation for the Strollers, which became West Bromwich Albion:

'There was no less than seven Salter's employees in the 1886 West Bromwich Albion cup winning side. It is unclear whether the West Bromwich Strollers was a team formed by workers from Salters as an outside club, or whether the Strollers were actually the Salters works team itself.' (Lost Teams of the Midlands by Mike Bradbury page 273).

West Bromwich Albion took over the Four Acres ground when West Bromwich (Dartmouth) folded in 1882. George Salter went on to be Chairman of the board of directors and honorary president of West Bromwich Albion for many years.

In this case the club stayed in the same geographic location, the name stayed substantially the same and some players (and critically George Salter) moved to the new club. This is much more contentious than the Newton Heath example but my judgement call, moves Albion's foundation date back four years to 1874. I accept that some fans will take exception to having their foundation dates moved earlier or later but surely it is preferable to try and standardise the criteria, so that all clubs can be equally measured?

As more newspapers are digitised, research keeps changing formation dates; this classification is as up to date as possible. I hope that this book will generate interest in the many small and local clubs, and that people will conduct further research at their local level. There will be errors in a book of this scope and I will use the website www.EnglandsOldestFootballClubs.com to continually update relevant information. I hope the book solves a few arguments (and not cause too many). If you have new or different information, please post it at the website's forum.

NOTES

Chapter One: The Search for a Unversal Code
(1) The Romance of Wednesday 1867-1926. Richard Sparling
(2) "Year Book," "Every-Day Book." and "Table Book" (1838 to 1842) William Hone
(3) Ashbourne News 4th March 1927
(4) Football: The first 100 years. The untold story. Adrian Harvey pg.12-14
(5) Rides on a Railway. Samuel Sidney 1851
(6) Eton College Magazine. 1832
(7) Manchester Courier and Lancashire General Advertiser. Tuesday 20 November 1866
(8) Bell's Life in London and Sporting Chronicle. 30th of September 1849
(9) Bell's Life in London and Sporting Chronicle. Sunday 07 October 1849
(10) The Condition of the Working Class in England in 1844. Frederick Engels.
(11) A History of Sheffield. David Ley
(12) Sheffield Independent. Saturday 04 February 1854
(13) Football: The first 100 years. The untold story. Adrian Harvey pg. 116
(14) Lot description for Sotheby's sale in 2011. Richards Tims, Chairman of Sheffield FC
(15) Football: The first 100 years. The untold story. Adrian Harvey pg. 97
(16) Football in Sheffield. Percy M Young 1962 p.20
(17) Sheffield Daily Telegraph. 5 November 1907
(18) Sheffield Independent. Saturday 24 June 1854
(19) Classified advert. Times Newspaper 9th December 1859
(20) Bell's Life in London and Sporting Chronicle. Sunday 16 January 1859
(21 According to J.A. Cruickshank (Harrow 1854-1860, Football X1 1858/9 (captain 1859) and an eventual master at Harrow from 1866 to 1891). As reported in A History of British Football by Percy M. Young 1968
(22) Association Football and the Men who Made it 1905 pg.38
(23) Sporting Life. Wednesday 28 October 1863
(24) The Oxford Companion to Sports and Games 1975
(25) F.A. Minutes
(26) English Illustrated Magazine article January 1891 "Association Football". C.W. Alcock
(27) Bell's Life in London and Sporting Chronicle. Saturday 26 December 1863
(28) Bell's Life in London and Sporting Chronicle. 12th December 1863
(29) Bell's Life in London and Sporting Chronicle. 16 January 1864
(30) Bells Life in London and Sporting Chronicle. 2nd January 1864
(31) Bell's Life in London and Sporting Chronicle. Saturday 29 October 1864
(32) Football in Sheffield. Percy M Young 1962 p.23
(33) Sporting Life. Wednesday 30 January 1867
(34) Bell's Life in London and Sporting Chronicle. Saturday 02 March 1867
(35) F.A. Minutes
(36) The Sportsman. Saturday 04 December 1869
(37) Sheffield Independent. Tuesday 10 October 1871
(38) Sheffield Independent. Thursday 12 October 1871
(39) Sheffield Independent. Saturday 28 April 1877
(40) Rugby's Great Split: Class, Culture and the Origins of Rugby League Football. Tony Collins

Chapter Two: Sheffield Schools
(1) Sheffield Daily Telegraph. Thursday 01 December 1870
(2) The National Gazetteer of Great Britain and Ireland , 1868
(3) Football: The First Hundred Years: The Untold Story by Adrian Harvey
(4) A History of British Football. Percy M. Young, 1968
(5) Sheffield Daily Telegraph. Wednesday 01 February 1865
(6) Sheffield Independent. Saturday 28 May 1853
(7) "SHEFFIELD COLLEGIATE SCHOOL. A PRINCIPAL will be wanted for the above school, at the end of January next, in the place of the Rev. W. W. Grignon, who has been elected to the Head Mastership of Felstead Grammar School, Essex. The School and Principal's House, capable of accommodating 40 Boarders, comprise, together with the Grounds, a site of about 3½ Acres; these have been erected and formed at the cost of upwards of 10,000l., and are pleasantly situated in the neighbourhood of Sheffield. There is also a Laboratory attached to the School, for the study of general and analytical Chemistry, now under the management of an eminent Chemist. It is required that the Principal be a clergyman of the Church of England, a Graduate of Oxford or Cambridge; and that he should not undertake any other Clerical duty. The Salary of the Principal will be 355l. per annum, with the addition of 5l. per annum for every boy attending the School above the number of 80: he will also have the privilege of occupying the Boarding House rent free, together with the use of certain furniture and fixtures belonging to the Proprietors, and will receive the profits of the Boarders, in addition to the Salary, accounting only for the Tuition Fees". Saturday 01 December 1855
(8) Sheffield Independent. Saturday 21 May 1859
(9) Cambridge Chronicle and Journal. Saturday 19 January 1861
(10) The National Gazetteer of Great Britain and Ireland 1868
(11) Sheffield Daily Telegraph. Saturday 07 March 1863

NOTES

(12) Sheffield Daily Telegraph. Monday 28 March 1887
(13) Sheffield Evening Telegraph. Saturday 24 March 1888
(14) In a Class of their Own. A History of English Amateur Football. Terry Morris

Chapter Three: Sheffield Volunteer Movement
(1) The Spectator 12 November 1859, Page 3
(2) Sheffield Daily News, and Morning Advertiser. Saturday 21 May 1859
(3) Sheffield Independent. Saturday 28 May 1859
(4) Sheffield Independent. Saturday 11 June 1859
(5) Sheffield Daily News, and Morning Advertiser. Tuesday 28 June 1859
(6) Sheffield Times. November 24th 1860
(7) Sheffield Independent. Saturday 04 May 1861
(8) Sheffield Daily Telegraph. Saturday 23 November 1861
(9) Sheffield Independent' Tuesday 12 November 1872
(10) Manchester Courier and Lancashire General Advertiser. Saturday 18 August 1866

Chapter Four: Sheffield Football Association
(1) Theory of the evolution of modern sport. Stefan Szymanski
(2) Sporting Life. Wednesday 13 March 1867
(3) Sheffield Independent. Tuesday 07 May 1872
(4) Cambridge Independent Press. Saturday 08 January 1887
(5) The Sheffield & Rotherham Independent. Saturday, March 25 1876
(6) Sheffield Independent. Friday 27 April 1877

Chapter Five: The Golden Age of Sheffield Amateur Football 1857-1876
(1) A review of Charles Kingsley's Two Years Ago (1857) for the Saturday Review, written by the cleric T.C. Sandars
(2) Principal Amateur Clubs of the Past. Article by C.W. Alcock in The Book of Football magazine 1905/06 Amalgamated Press
(3) The Romance of Wednesday 1867-1926. Richard Sparling
(4) Football The Rugby Union Game. Francis Marshall. 1892
(5) Derby Mercury. Wednesday 25 October 1876
(6) Sheffield Independent. Saturday 07 June 1856
(7) Bell's Life in London and Sporting Chronicle. Sunday 30 January 1831
(8) Bell's Life in London and Sporting Chronicle. Sunday 17 March 1844
(9) The Era. Sunday 06 June 1847
(10) According to the 1841 Sheffield and Rotherham Directory, the Creswick family lived at Parkfield House, Highfields, with Nathaniel Creswick Senior (1793- 1855) (occupation of Silver Plater) and his first son Nathaniel Creswick Junior (1831- 1917) (Solicitor); by 1844, he has moved to East Hill House for the birth of his second son Alfred Jubb. In the 1851 census the family is living at 5 Norfolk Road, including the 19-year-old Nathaniel junior. By 1861 with his father dead Nathaniel is living at 29, Park Grange, still with his mother. By 1871 his mother had died and he was living in Handsworth with his wife and daughter. In 1891, still sporting his Volunteer Movement rank, Colonel Nathaniel Creswick is recorded as living at Chantry Grange, Norton Woodseats, Sheffield.
(11) Sheffield Independent. Saturday 25 March 1854
(12) Sheffield Independent. Saturday 21 October 1854
(13) Sheffield Independent. Saturday 25 July 1857
(14) "English Illustrated" Magazine article January 1891 "Association Football" by C.W Alcock
(15) The Sheffield &Rotherham Independent April 10, 1858
(16) The Era Sunday 23 May 1858
(17) Leeds Intelligencer. Saturday 24 April 1858
(18) Bell's Life in London and Sporting Chronicle. December 23, 1860
(19) Sheffield Daily Telegraph. Friday 28 December, 1860
(20) Nottinghamshire Guardian. Tuesday 31 December 1861
(21) Bell's Life in London and Sporting Chronicle. Saturday 24 March 1866
(22) The Romance of Wednesday 1867-1926. Richard Sparling
(23) Sheffield Independent. Tuesday 13 December 1870
(24) Sheffield Daily Telegraph. Monday 27 September 1875
(25) Sheffield Football a History: Volume 1. Keith Farnsworth 1995
(26) Sheffield Independent. Thursday 26 September 1872
(27) Sheffield Daily Telegraph. Wednesday 19 November 1873
(28) Sheffield Daily Telegraph. Monday 31 January 1876
(29) Bell's Life in London and Sporting Chronicle. 23 February 1862
(30) Bell's Life in London and Sporting Chronicle. Sunday 06 March 1859
(31) "English Illustrated" Magazine article January 1891 "Association Football" by CW Alcock
(32) The Countrymen: The History of Hallam FC. John A. Steele
(33) Sheffield Daily Telegraph. Tuesday 27 September 1864
(34) Sheffield Times. July 21 1860
(35) Football in Sheffield. Percy Young. Pg.31
(36) Manchester Courier and Lancashire General Advertiser. Saturday 10 November 1894
(37) Tamworth Herald. Saturday 26 February 1927
(38) Sheffield Independent. Saturday 05 January 1861
(39) Stephen Waterfall (1784-1859) a file manufacturer in Sheffield and his wife Mary (1789-1866) had nine children:
James (1813- 1878)
John (1815- 1891)
Elizabeth (1817-?)
Anne (1819 -1838)
George (1821-1867) Played for Hallam FC v Sheffield December 1861
William (1824- 1904) Played for Hallam FC v Sheffield December 1861
Alfred (1826-1889) Played for Hallam FC v Sheffield December 1861
Samuel (1829=1874)
Henry (1837-1890)
James (1813- 1878) married Sarah Woodhead Marshal (1813-1900) and had five children one of whom was Annie (1840-1893) possibly named after his sister who died only 19, two years before. She married Hallam FC's co-founder John Charles Shaw (1830- 1918) - his first wife, Mary Ann died young, aged just 24.
(40) Sheffield Evening Telegraph. Tuesday 19 October 1915
(41) The Vickers Brothers: Armaments and Enterprise 1854–1914. Clive Trebilcock
(42) Sheffield Independent. Saturday 09 April 1859

NOTES

(43) Sheffield Independent. Saturday 23 March 1861
(44) The Sheffield & Rotherham Independent. Supplement. Saturday, September 28, 1861
(45) Sheffield Independent. Saturday 21 December 1861
(46) Nottinghamshire Guardian. Tuesday 31 December 1861
(47) Sheffield Independent. Tuesday 04 February 1862
(48) Sheffield Daily Telegraph. Saturday 02 February 1867
(49) Sheffield Independent. Tuesday 19 February 1867
(50) Sheffield Daily Telegraph. Monday 18 February 1867
(51) Sheffield Independent. Saturday 16 February 1867
(52) Sporting Life,. Wednesday 20 February 1867
(53) Bell's Life in London and Sporting Chronicle. Saturday 09 March 1867
(54) Sheffield Daily Telegraph. Tuesday 12 March 1867
(55) London and Provincial Entr'acte. Saturday 25 June 1870
(56) London and Provincial Entr'acte. Saturday 22 November 1873
(57) Sheffield Daily Telegraph. Saturday 02 October 1886
(58) Sheffield Daily Telegraph. Tuesday 05 October 1886
(59) Sheffield Independent. Tuesday 12 October 1886
(60) Sheffield Daily Telegraph. Tuesday 27 September 1887
(61) Sheffield Independent. Monday 10 October 1887
(62) Sheffield Daily Telegraph. December 1918
(63) Condition of our chief towns-Sheffield. The Builder 21September 1861
(64) Sheffield Independent. Saturday 04 February 1854
(65) Sheffield Independent. Saturday 16 February 1867
(66) Sheffield Independent. Tuesday 07 April 1863
(67) Leeds Mercury. Saturday 23 December 1865
(68) Sheffield Independent. Wednesday 24 April 1867
(69) Derbyshire Times and Chesterfield Herald. Wednesday 26 November 1873
(70) Sheffield Daily Telegraph. Tuesday 19 March 1872
(71) The Sheffield & Rotherham Independent. Tuesday, November 05, 1861
(72) Sheffield Independent. Monday 09 March 1863
(73) The Sportsman. Tuesday 16 January 1866
(74) Bell's Life in London and Sporting Chronicle. Saturday 24 October 1868
(75) Sheffield Independent. Saturday 25 March 1826
(76) Sheffield Independent. Saturday 13 October 1827
(77) Sheffield Independent. Saturday 17 September 1853
(78) Sheffield Independent. Thursday 05 December 1861
(79) Sheffield Independent. Tuesday 01 April 1862
(80) Sheffield Independent. Saturday 08 October 1864
(81) Sotheby's Catalogue. "22 February 1862-13 January 1866"
(82) The Sportsman. Thursday 28 February 1867
(83) Sheffield Independent. Tuesday 08 August 1871
(84) The Annuls of Yorkshire (1860-1865)
(85) Sheffield Independent. Saturday 08 October 1864
(86) Sheffield Daily Telegraph. Tuesday 23 February 1875.
(87) Shooting Stars: The Brief and Glorious History of Blackburn Olympic 1878-1889 .Graham Phythian . Pg. 15.
(88) Sheffield Independent. Saturday 21 February 1863
(89) Sheffield Independent. Saturday 08 October 1864
(90) Sheffield Independent. Friday 27 September 1867
(91) Sheffield Daily Telegraph. Monday 19 March 1877
(92) Sheffield Daily Telegraph. Wednesday 27 October 1880
(93) The Sheffield & Rotherham Independent. Saturday, March 29, 1884
(94) The York Herald. Saturday, April 26, 1884
(95) Sheffield Independent. Friday 13 February 1891
(96) Sheffield Daily Telegraph. Thursday 20 August 1896
(97) Sheffield Independent. Wednesday 08 October 1862
(98) Lost Teams of the North by Mike Bradbury
(99) Sheffield Independent. Friday 02 October 1863
(100) Sheffield Daily Telegraph. Monday 04 January 1864
(101) Sheffield Independent. Saturday 29 April 1865
(102 Sotheby's Catalogue "22 February 1862-13 January 1862"
(103) Bell's Life in London and Sporting Chronicle. Saturday 21 December 1867
(104) http://www.nottscountyfc.co.uk/news/article/notts-county-fc-history-209591.aspx
(105) Nottinghamshire Guardian. Friday 28 November 1862
(106) Sporting Life. Saturday 06 December 1862
(107) Sheffield Daily Telegraph. Saturday 14 October 1865
(108) Notts County FC and the birth of modern football: The Early Years of the Oldest Professional Club in the World. Darrin Foss
(109) Sheffield Independent. Tuesday 20 January 1863
(110) Sheffield Independent. Tuesday 06 November 1877
(111) Sheffield Independent. Saturday 03 September 1870
(112) Sheffield Daily Telegraph. Saturday 04 March 1865
(113) Sheffield Daily Telegraph. Monday 21 November 1864
(114) Sheffield Daily Telegraph. Wednesday 22 September 1869
(115) Sheffield Independent. Friday 28 November 1862
(116) Sheffield Independent. Wednesday 04 March 1863
(117) Sheffield Independent. Saturday 10 October 1863
(118) Leicester Journal. Friday 25 December 1863
(119) Sporting Life. Wednesday 30 January 1867
(120) Sheffield Independent. Saturday 17 October 1863
(121) Sheffield Independent. Monday 16 April 1866
(122) Sheffield Independent. Wednesday 01 March 1876
(123) Website http://www.mick-armitage.staff.shef.ac.uk/sheffield/maps.html
(124) Sheffield Independent. Monday 14 March 1864
(125) The Sportsman. Saturday 25 November 1865
(126) Leeds Mercury. Saturday 23 December 1865
(127) Sheffield Independent. Saturday 04 February 1865
(128) Polytechnic FC claim an1875 foundation but this is contradicted by the Football Annuals
(129) Sheffield Daily Telegraph. Saturday 07 December 1861
(130) Sheffield Daily Telegraph. Saturday 28 October 1865
(131) Sheffield Independent. Thursday 04 January 1866
(132) Sheffield Independent. Saturday 16 February 1867
(133) Sheffield Independent. Wednesday 03 June 1868
(134) Sheffield Independent. Tuesday 07 May 1872
(135) Cricketing Reminiscences and Personal Recollections. W. G. Grace
(136) Sheffield Daily Telegraph. Monday 08 March 1869
(137) The Victorians and Sport. Mike Huggins
(138) The Sportsman. Thursday 10 October 1867
(139) The Sportsman. Saturday 04 January 1868
(140) The Romance of Wednesday 1867-1926 Richard Sparling
(141) Sheffield Independent. Tuesday 04 January 1870
(142) Sheffield Daily Telegraph. Thursday 04 January 1872
(143) Sheffield Independent. Saturday 19 November 1870
(144) F.A. Cup semi-final between West Bromwich Albion and Preston North End March 1889

NOTES

(145) Sheffield Independent. Tuesday 16 February 1886
(146) Sheffield Independent. Monday 29 March 1869
(147) Website http://www.chesterfield-fc.co.uk/club/club-history/
(148) Football Weekly Book of 100 Famous Football Clubs produced by the Amalgamated Press 1930's
(149) Sheffield Daily Telegraph. Thursday 20 February 1868
(150) Sheffield Daily Telegraph. Friday 27 December 1872
(151) Sheffield Daily Telegraph. Friday 06 September 1867
(152) The Romance of Wednesday 1867-1926. Richard Sparling
(153) Sheffield Independent. Saturday 04 January 1868
(154) Sheffield Independent. Tuesday 13 September 1887
(155) Sheffield Independent. Monday 12 March 1877
(156) Sheffield Independent. Saturday 11 December 1869
(157) Sheffield Independent. Tuesday 24 October 1871
(158) Sheffield Daily Telegraph. Friday 03 January 1873.
(159) Sheffield Daily Telegraph. Saturday 29 February 1868
(160) Sheffield Daily Telegraph. Wednesday 11 March 1868
(161) Sheffield Daily Telegraph. Saturday 21 March 1868
(162) Sheffield Daily Telegraph. Tuesday 18 May 1869
(163) Derbyshire Times and Chesterfield Herald. Saturday 03 January 1891
(164) Derbyshire Times and Chesterfield Herald. Friday 15 November 1935
(165) Sheffield Daily Telegraph. Thursday 16 January 1868
(166) Sheffield Independent. Thursday 02 January 1868
(167) Website http://www.clubwebsite.co.uk/dronfieldtownfc/History
(168) Sheffield Daily Telegraph. Saturday 29 February 1868
(169) Sheffield Daily Telegraph. Monday 28 December 1868
(170) Sheffield Independent. Monday 07 December 1868
(171) Sheffield Daily Telegraph. Saturday 09 October 1869
(172) Sheffield Independent. Monday 05 February 1872.
(173) The Sheffield & Rotherham Independent. Tuesday, April 13, 1875
174) The Eton College Chronicle
(175) Sheffield Independent. Tuesday 07 December 1869
(176) Sheffield Independent. Tuesday 24 January 1871
(177) Sheffield Daily Telegraph. Friday 03 January 1873
(178) Sheffield Independent. Saturday 02 October 1869
(179) Sheffield Independent. Saturday 26 February 1870
(180) Sheffield Daily Telegraph. Friday 14 March 1873.
(181) Sheffield and Rotherham Independent. 11th November 1875
(182) Sheffield Independent. Thursday 12 October 1871
(183) The Sheffield & Rotherham Independent. Supplement, Saturday, January 19, 1884
(184) The York Herald. Tuesday, January 29, 1884
(185) Sheffield Independent. Wednesday 26 October 1870
(186) Sheffield Daily Telegraph. Friday 03 January 1873
(187) Website http://www.rotherhamweb.co.uk/area/sport/rufc.htm
(188) The Sheffield & Rotherham Independent, Tuesday, December 27, 1870
(189) Sheffield Daily Telegraph. Wednesday 05 February 1873
(190) Derbyshire Times and Chesterfield Herald. Saturday 12 January 1878
(191) Sheffield Independent. Tuesday 02 January 1877
(192) Blackburn Standard. Saturday 20 April 1895
(193) Lost Teams of the North Mike Bradbury
(194) Sheffield Daily Telegraph. Tuesday 25 April 1871
(195) Burnley Express. Saturday 18 October 1884
(196) Sheffield Daily Telegraph. Tuesday 18 October 1870
(197) Sheffield Independent. Tuesday 13 December 1870
(198) Sheffield Daily Telegraph. Tuesday 27 April 1875
(199) Sheffield Independent. Saturday 08 September 1888
(200) Sheffield Independent. Wednesday 07 May 1873
(201) The Sheffield & Rotherham Independent Tuesday, April 13, 1875
(202) Sheffield Daily Telegraph. Tuesday 17 October 1876
(203) Sheffield Independent. Friday 15 March 1872
(204) Sheffield Independent. Wednesday 30 September 1874
(205) Sheffield Independent. Tuesday 27 October 1874
(206) Sheffield Daily Telegraph. Friday 04 December 1874
(207) Sheffield Independent. Thursday 13 February 1879
(208) Sheffield Independent. Wednesday 20 December 1882
(209) Sheffield Independent Tuesday 24 January 1871
(210) Sheffield Daily Telegraph. Tuesday 08 October 1872
(211) Sheffield Daily Telegraph. Tuesday 01 July 1873
(212) Sheffield Daily Telegraph. Tuesday 25 November 1879
(213) Sheffield Daily Telegraph. Wednesday 04 January 1888
(214) Sheffield Independent. Wednesday 12 February 1873
(215) Sheffield Independent. Monday 08 September 1879
(216) Sheffield Daily Telegraph. Monday 20 October 1873
(217) The Sheffield & Rotherham Independent Tuesday, April 13, 1875
(218) Sheffield Independent. Wednesday 09 February 1876
(219) Sheffield Daily Telegraph. Tuesday 17 October 1876
(220) Sheffield Independent. Thursday 23 November 1876
(221) Sheffield Independent. Tuesday 29 October 1872
(222) Sheffield Daily Telegraph. Tuesday 28 April 1874
(223) Sheffield Independent. Tuesday 08 October 1878
(224) Sheffield Independent. Thursday 05 December 1878
(225) Sheffield Independent. Tuesday 27 January 1874
(226) Sheffield Independent. Monday 12 November 1877
(227) Sheffield Independent. Thursday 25 May 1871
(228) Sheffield Independent. Saturday 27 January 1872
(229) Sheffield Independent. Tuesday 12 September 1876
(230) Sheffield Independent. Tuesday 16 February 1875
(231) Sheffield Daily Telegraph. Wednesday 24 November 1875
(232) Sheffield Daily Telegraph. Tuesday 17 October 1876
(233) Sheffield Daily Telegraph. Tuesday 27 December 1881
(234) Sheffield Independent. Tuesday 31 December 1872
(235) Sheffield Daily Telegraph. Tuesday 13 January 1874
(236) Sheffield Independent. Tuesday 24 November 1874
(237) Website http://www.gracesguide.co.uk/Main_Page
(238) Sheffield Daily Telegraph. Saturday 11 September 1875
(239) Sheffield Daily Telegraph - Tuesday 17 October 1876
(240) A Century of Sheffield 1835 to 1935 -Folio 3
(241) Sheffield Daily Telegraph. Tuesday 08 October 1872
(242) The Sheffield & Rotherham Independent. Saturday, April 15, 1876
(243) Sheffield Independent. Tuesday 30 September 1879
(244) Sheffield Independent. Thursday 04 November 1880

NOTES

(245) Sheffield Daily Telegraph. Tuesday 17 October 1876
(246) Sheffield Daily Telegraph. Wednesday 07 November 1877
(247) Sheffield Independent. Saturday 30 August 1879
(248) Sheffield Independent. Tuesday 05 October 1880
(249) Sheffield Independent. Monday 27 February 1882
(250) "English Illustrated" Magazine article January 1891 "Association Football" by C.W. Alcock
(251) Sheffield Daily Telegraph. Wednesday 19 March 1873
(252) The Romance of Wednesday 1867-192. Richard Sparling
(253) Sheffield Daily Telegraph. Saturday 19 September 1874
(254) Sheffield Daily Telegraph. Friday 15 April 1892
(255) Sheffield Independent. Tuesday 13 February 1877
(256) Sheffield Independent. Friday 10 October 1879
(257) Sheffield Daily Telegraph. Wednesday 06 December 1876
(258) Sheffield Daily Telegraph. Saturday 21 October 1876
(259) Leeds Mercury. Wednesday 26 December 1877
(260) Sheffield Independent. Wednesday 22 January 1873
(261) Sheffield Independent. Wednesday 05 March 1873
(262) Sheffield Daily Telegraph. Friday 06 February 1874
(263) Sheffield Evening Telegraph. Wednesday 26 August 1896
(264) Manchester Courier and Lancashire General Advertiser. Friday 21 December 1894
(265) Sheffield Independent. Monday 21 December 1874
(266) Athletic News. Wednesday 27 September 1882
(267) Sheffield Independent. Tuesday 07 November 1882
(268) Sheffield Independent. Tuesday 09 October 1883
(269) Sheffield Independent. Monday 30 November 1885
(270) Sheffield Independent. Monday 26 August 1889
(271) Sheffield Daily Telegraph. Tuesday 02 February 1875
(272) Sheffield Independent. Saturday 06 March 1880
(273) Sheffield Daily Telegraph. Tuesday 01 December 1874
(274) Sheffield Daily Telegraph. Wednesday 15 November 1876
(275) Sheffield Daily Telegraph. Saturday 23 December 1876
(276) Sheffield Independent. Thursday 18 September 1879
(277) Sheffield Independent. Friday 08 October 1886
(278) Imperial Gazetteer. J.M. Wilson. 1875
(279) Sheffield Independent. Monday 06 October 1890
(280) Sheffield Daily Telegraph. Thursday 30 October 1884
(281) Sheffield Daily Telegraph. Monday 15 February 1892
(282) Sheffield Independent. Monday 14 January 1889
(283) Sheffield Independent. Tuesday 06 February 1877
(284) Sheffield Independent. Tuesday 13 February 1877
(285) Derbyshire Courier. Saturday 06 April 1889
(286) Sheffield Independent. Monday 23 February 1891
(287) Sheffield Independent. Friday 14 September 1877
(288) Sheffield Daily Telegraph. Saturday 11 September
(289) Sheffield Daily Telegraph. Friday 20 September 1889
(290) Sheffield Daily Telegraph. Thursday 03 January 1901
(291) Sheffield Daily Telegraph. Tuesday 09 December 1879

Chapter Six: The Decline of the Old Order 1877-1887
(1) Sheffield Daily Telegraph. Thursday 11 April 1878
(2) Sheffield Daily Telegraph. Monday 06 January 1879
(3) Athletic News. Wednesday 27 September 1882
(4) Sheffield Independent. Tuesday 11 May 1886
(5) Sheffield Daily Telegraph. Tuesday 05 October 1886
(6) Sheffield Daily Telegraph. Monday 12 September 1887

(7) The Sheffield & Rotherham Independent. Thursday, December 06, 1877.
(8) The Sheffield & Rotherham Independent. Tuesday, December 18, 1877
(9) Sheffield Daily Telegraph. Thursday 12 April 1877
(10) Sheffield Daily Telegraph. Monday 01 November 1880
(11) Sheffield Independent. Tuesday 01 April 1884
(12) Derbyshire Times and Chesterfield Herald. Saturday 26 May 1894
(13) Rugby's Great Split: Class, Culture and the Origins of Rugby League Football. Tony Collins
(14) The Code War. Graham Williams
(15) Leeds Times. Saturday 29 December 1877
(16) Sheffield Independent. Thursday 26 December 1878.
(17) The Book of Football (Amalgamated Press Magazine 1905)
(18) Montague Shearman Athletics and Football 1887
(19) Sheffield Independent. Saturday 19 October 1878
(20) Sheffield Independent. Tuesday 11 January 1881
(21) Sheffield Independent. Monday 03 October 1881
(22) Football in Sheffield. Percy M Young 1962
(23) Sheffield Daily Telegraph. Tuesday 25 January 1881
(24) Sheffield Independent. Wednesday 26 January 1881
(25) Sheffield Daily Telegraph. Thursday 07 April 1881
(26) Sheffield Daily Telegraph. Thursday 16 November 1882
(27) Sheffield Independent. Tuesday 09 October 1877
(28) Yorkshire Post and Leeds Intelligencer. Monday 19 August 1878
(29) Sheffield Independent. Saturday 18 October 1879
(30) Sheffield Independent. Tuesday 21 October 1879
(31) Sheffield Independent. Tuesday 11 November 1879
(32) Sheffield Independent. Tuesday 18 November 1879
(33) Sheffield Independent. Wednesday 17 November 1880
(34) Sheffield Daily Telegraph. Wednesday 22 December 1880
(35) Yorkshire Gazette. Saturday 31 January 1885
(36) Sheffield Independent. Tuesday 22 January 1884
(37) Sheffield Independent. Monday 20 September 1886
(38) Derbyshire Times and Chesterfield Herald. Wednesday 25 August 1880
(39) Derbyshire Times and Chesterfield Herald. Saturday 08 November 1884
(40) Sheffield Daily Telegraph. Thursday 30 October 1884
(41) Sheffield Daily Telegraph. Wednesday 01 September 1886
(42) Sheffield Independent. Tuesday 05 August 1890
(43) Sheffield Daily Telegraph. Monday 16 February 1880
(44) Sheffield Independent. Monday 18 December 1882
(45) Sheffield Daily Telegraph. Tuesday 02 October 1883
(46) Sheffield Daily Telegraph. Tuesday 02 October 1883
(47) Sheffield Daily Telegraph. Monday 26 January 1885
(48) Yorkshire Post and Leeds Intelligencer. Wednesday 07 September 1887
(49) Thank God for Football. Peter Lupson
(50) Barnsley Football Club: The official history 1887-1998. Brian Dennis, John Daykin and Derek Hyde
(51) Sheffield Daily Telegraph. Wednesday 05 September 1888.
(52) Sheffield Independent. Monday 05 November 1888
(53) Yorkshire Post and Leeds Intelligencer. Saturday 12 December 1891
(54) Sheffield Independent. Saturday 03 June 1893
(55) Yorkshire Evening Post. Wednesday 06 March 1907

NOTES

(56) Kent & Sussex Courier. Friday 19 April 1912
(57) The Church Times. June 4, 1926

Chapter Seven: Football Professionalism and the Football League
(1) Football in Sheffield. Percy Young 1962 p.40
(2) Football in Sheffield. Percy Young 1962 p.41
(3) The Football Annual 1880
4) Researching the Game's past. Keith Warsop
(5) Sporting Life. Monday 10 December 1883
(6) The Code War. Graham Williams
(7) Manchester Guardian. November 30 1884
(8) The Athlete. January 30 1884
(9) The Football Field .12th October 1884
(10) Athletic News. February 1885
(11) All Sports Weekly by J.A.H Catton. 12/2/1927
(12) Yorkshire Gazette. Saturday 13 April 1895
(13) Athletic News April 16th 1888
(14) The Association Game. Matthew Taylor
(15) Athletic News May 7th 1888
(16) Sheffield Evening Telegraph. Monday 27 January 1896

Chapter Eight: Sheffield embraces Professionalism
(1) Sheffield Daily Telegraph. Wednesday 23 February 1887
(2) Sheffield Daily Telegraph. Tuesday 19 April 1887
(3) The Romance of Wednesday 1867-1926. Richard Sparling Pg. 74
(4) The Romance of Wednesday 1867-1926. Richard Sparling pg. 74
(5) Sheffield Independent. Monday 20 April 1896
(6) Sheffield Independent. Saturday 28 April 1888
(7) Sheffield Daily Telegraph. Friday 10 May 1889
(8) Sheffield Independent. Thursday 22 August 1889
(9) Sheffield Independent. Monday 01 September 1890
(10) Sheffield Independent. Wednesday 17 July 1895
(11) Sheffield Independent. Monday 18 March 1889
(12) Sheffield Evening Telegraph. Saturday 23 March 1889
(13) Sheffield Independent. Saturday 23 March 1889
(14) Sheffield Daily Telegraph. Thursday 16 May 1889
(15) Sheffield Independent. Tuesday 04 June 1889
(16) Sheffield Independent. Wednesday 21 August 1889
(17) Sheffield Independent. Friday 23 August 1889
(18) Sheffield Independent. Monday 26 August 1889
(19) Sheffield Evening Telegraph. Saturday 14 September 1889
(20) Sheffield Daily Telegraph. Monday 30 September 1889
(21) The Football Annual 1890
(22) Sheffield Evening Telegraph. Saturday 29 December 1906 Cartoon
(23) Sheffield Independent. Saturday 29th March 1890
(24) Sheffield Independent. Monday 31 March 1890
(25) Sheffield Daily Telegraph. Tuesday 02 September 1890
(26) Sheffield Daily Telegraph. Monday 29 September 1890
(27) Sheffield Independent. Tuesday 14 May 1889
(28) Sheffield Evening Telegraph. Monday 15 December 1890
(28) Sheffield Daily Telegraph. Thursday 08 October 1896

Football Rules Chronology
(1) Football in Sheffield. Percy Young pg. 24
(2) Sheffield Evening Telegraph. Friday 17 May 1889
(3) Greenock Telegraph and Clyde Shipping Gazette. Monday 10 August 1891
(4) The Referees' Association website

BIBLIOGRAPHY

Newspapers and magazines
   Sheffield Daily Telegraph
   Sheffield Independent
   The Sheffield & Rotherham Independent
   Bell's Life in London and Sporting Chronicle
   The Book of Football 1905/06
   Football Weekly Book of 100 Famous Football Clubs. Amalgamated Press 1930's
   Athletic News
   Sporting Life
   The Athlete
   The Football Field
   All Sports Weekly
   Northern Review
   Ashbourne News
   Manchester Courier and Lancashire General Advertiser
   English Illustrated Magazine
   The National Gazetteer of Great Britain and Ireland
   The Spectator
   Eton College Magazine
   Cambridge Chronicle and Journal
   Saturday Review
   Derby Mercury
   The Era
   English Illustrated
   Leeds Intelligencer
   Leeds Mercury
   Yorkshire Post and Leeds Intelligencer
   Nottinghamshire Guardian
   Tamworth Herald
   London and Provincial Entr'acte
   Derbyshire Times and Chesterfield Herald
   The York Herald,
   The Eton College Chronicle
   Blackburn Standard
   Kent & Sussex Courier
   Church Times
   The Builder

BIBLIOGRAPHY

Books

Football Annuals 1868-1899. Originally entitled as John Lilywhite's Football Annual, edited by the F.A. Secretary, Charles W. Alcock and 'Published with the sanction of the Football Association.', priced at 1s.6d. After the first edition, Charles W. Alcock left his cousin John Lillywhite and it became his sole responsibility, together with a new publisher 'Sportsman.'

The Romance of Wednesday 1867-1926. Richard Sparling. Printed by Sir W.C. Leng & Co., 1926

Football in Sheffield. Percy M. Young. Published by Stanley Paul, London, England (1962)

Football: The first 100 years. The untold story. Adrian Harvey. Routledge (28 Sept. 2005)

Association Football and the Men who Made it. Alfred Gibson and William Pickford. Caxton (1905)

Sheffield United Football Club: 1889-1999. Denis Clarebrough and Andrew Kirkham. Sheffield United Football Club (16 Jan. 1999)

Lost Teams of the North. Mike Bradbury. Xlibris (22 Oct. 2013)

The Oxford Companion to Sports and Games. Oxford University Press; (Jun. 1975)

In a Class of their Own. A History of English Amateur Football. Terry Morris Chequered Flag Publishing (2 Nov. 2015)

Sheffield Football a History: Volume 1. Keith Farnsworth Hallamshire Publications Ltd (Jun. 1995)

The Countrymen: The History of Hallam FC. John A. Steele

The Vickers Brothers: Armaments and Enterprise 1854–1914. Clive Trebilcock. Europa Publications, 1977.

The Association Game. Matthew Taylor. Routledge; 1 edition (16 Aug. 2007)

The Annuls of Yorkshire (1860-1865)

Sheffield and Rotherham Directory

Notts County FC and the birth of modern football: The Early Years of the Oldest Professional Club in the World. Darrin Foss. CreateSpace Independent Publishing Platform (19 Aug. 2013)

Barnsley Football Club: The official history 1887-1998. Brian Dennis, John Daykin and Derek Hyde. Yore Publications; (11 Oct. 1998)

Soccer's Missing Men (Sport in the Global Society). J.A. Mangan Routledge (8 Oct. 2015)

Donny: Doncaster Rovers FC. The Complete History' Tony Bluff. Yore Publications (12 Nov. 2011)

A History of Sheffield. David Ley. Carnegie Publishing Ltd; 3rd Revised edition (3 Aug. 2010)

Researching the Game's past. Keith Warsop. Soccer History 2002

Shooting Stars: The Brief and Glorious History of Blackburn Olympic 1878-1889. Graham Phythian. Tony Brown (1 Mar. 2007)

Cricketing Reminiscences and Personal Recollections. W. G. Grace. Published by Hambledon Press London (first published 1899)

Football: The Rugby Union Game. Francis Marshall. 1892 (HardPress Publishing.1 Aug. 2012)

Rugby's Great Split: Class, Culture and the Origins of Rugby League Football. Tony Collins. Routledge; 2nd Edition (14 July 2006)

The Code War. Graham Williams. Yore Publications; First Edition (10 May 1994)
Athletics and Football. Montague Shearman. Longmans Green 1887
Thank God for Football. Peter Lupson. SPCK Publishing (1 July 2006)

Acknowledgements
British Library
http://www.bl.uk/collection-guides/british-newspaper-archive
Richard Tims at The World's First Football Club, Sheffield FC
Peter Holme at the National Football Museum
David Barber at the Football Association
Deborah Mason at the Rugby Football Union
Janet Ring at the Sheffield Library
Robin Wiltshire at the Sheffield Archive
Anne Marples: Crookes historian
Ray King and David Westby for good advice at crucial times
Reading, proofing and support: Judith Gear, Elise Gear, Leila Gear, Mason Gear and Charlie Moreton
Internet and website: Malcolm Bailey
Book design: John Griffiths

Website: EnglandsOldestFootballclubs.com
Email: Martin@EnglandsOldestFootballclubs.com

INDEX

Full club team lists of player's names are not included. If you would like a specific name searched in the book contact me by email.

A
Accrington FC, 202,204
Adelphi Hotel, 19,75,81, l08,115
Ainger, A.C., 41
Albion FC, 150-152
Alcock, Charles William, 21,28,31,35,37,38,4852,54,58,66,68, 101,107,172,201,203,205,208,216,231
Alcock, John Forster (F.A. meeting 26/10/1863),26
Aldershot FC,28
All Saints' Night School FC,146-148,181
Alliance FC, 141-142
Andrews. Peter, 137,200
Ash, H. (Sheffield F.A. v. London F.A. 2/1871), 38,86,110,149
Ashbourne, 12
Aston Villa FC, 65,162,201,204
Athletic Sports, 32,56,59,60,61,62,72,82,106
Attercliffe FC, 127-128

B
Ball Inn, Crookes, 134,189
Bankers FC (see Thursday Wanderers FC)
Barnes FC, 26,27,28,36
Barnsley St. Peters FC (Barnsley FC), 197-199
Barnsley Wanderers FC, 185
Beardshaw, W.J. (S.F.C. Hon. Sec.), 42,54,120,137,138,139,203,213,
Bell, Theodore (F.A. meeting 26/10/1863), 26
Bell (Dingley Dell) (F.A. meeting 26/10/1863), 27
Birmingham F.A., 51,76,203
Birmingham and District Cup, 76,164
Bishop's Stortford FC, 162
Blackburn Meadows, 149
Blackburn Olympic FC, 89,124,191,201,202
Blackburn Rovers FC, 133,162,201,216-218
Blackheath FC, 26, 27,28
Blackheath Proprietary School, 26,27,28
Blackpool FC, 187
Blades, 215
Bolton Wanderers FC, 162,196, 214
Bournemouth Rovers FC, 155
Bradford FC, 104
Braintree FC,187
Bramall Lane, 19,37,45,78,80,81,99,101,111,116,121,188,209,214

Brereton, Reverend J.L., 197,198
Brightside FC,148-149
Brincliffe FC, 122-124
British Football Association, 203
Brooke, Arthur, 193,194
Broomhall FC, 74,101-103
Brown, Bayley and Dixon FC, 143,144
Buchan, Charles, 235
Bull week, 163,219
Burngreave Victoria FC, 147
Burnham FC, 179
Burnley FC, 162
Bury St Edmunds FC, 148
Buttery, T. (Featured in 1874 engraving), 52,144,188,190
Buxton FC, 162

C

Cambridge Rules, 14,15
Cambridge University AFC,155
Cambridge University, 40
Cambridge University Rules, 19,24,25
Campbell, Francis Maule (F.A. meeting 26/10/1863), 26,27
Carnforth FC,165
Carr, W.H. (Featured in 1874 engraving), 38,52,84,127,156,
Catton, J.A.H., 55,239
Cawley, Tom E., 208,209,216,220
Chambers, Ernest, 58
Chambers, Geoffrey, 58
Chambers, Harry Junior, 58
Chambers, Harry Waters, 31,43,47,48,52,54,56-66,137,219
Charterhouse School, 25,27,172
Chatham United FC, 206
Chelmsford FC, 187
Chesterfield FC, 82,112-114
Chester le Street, 12
Chesterman, William, 20,27,33,34,62,219
Chichester FC, 155
Cholera Ground, 129
Chorley FC, 169
Church FC, 202
Clapham Rovers, 107,201
Clapton FC, 187
Clegg, John Charles (Sheffield F.A. v. London F.A.), 2/1871), 49,50,51,52,63,64,66,99,118,123,124,132,
    137,142,151,184,188,191,210,212,214,220,221,231
Clegg, William Edwin (Sheffield F.A. v. London F.A. 2/1871) ,52,63,118,124,137,142,151,188,211,220
Clinton FC, 186
Clitheroe Central FC, 179
Clough, Brian, 200,211
Clyde of Glasgow FC, 141
Coaching, 124,154
Coggeshall FC,187
Collegiate FC, 208
Collegiate School, 40-43,46,95,101,140
Combination football, 30,155,188,189
Combination League, 205,210,211

INDEX

Congleton FC, 68
Conservative Party, 69,80
Corinthian Casuals FC,172
Cremorne Gardens, 97,98,99,115
Creswick Nathaniel, 19,20,41,42,45,46,56-66,70,73,88,219
Crewe Alexandra FC, 174,179
Cromwell Cup, 76,110,116,119
Crookes FC, 134-136
Cropper, William, 171,172,198
Crown Inn, 90
Crusaders FC, 26,28,34
Crystal Palace, 199
Crystal Palace FC, 26,27
Cursham, Arthur William, 137,138,139
Cursham, Henry 'Harry', 57,65,137,138,139

D

Daft, Richard, 57
Darnall FC, 173-175
Day, Francis (F.A. meeting 26/10/1863), 26
Deans, J.E., 90,92,93,102,105,110,117,191
Derbyshire Football Association, 114,138,169,194,
Derby Junction FC, 205
Derby Midland FC, 169,205
Denison William,16
Denton, John (S.F.C. Hon. Sec.), 54
Dingley Dell FC, 26,27,34,67
Dix, Pierce (S.F.C. Hon. Sec.), 49,89,150,151,152,180,190,191
Doncaster Rovers FC, 191-194
Dore FC, 121
Doyle, Daniel, 171
Dronfield FC, 115,122
Duke of Norfolk, 80,81,209

E

Eagley FC, 169
Earl of Effingham, 160
East Bank, 53,54,58,109
Ecclesfield FC, 160-161
Ecclesall College, 40,151
Eckington FC, 185,186
Eckington Collieries FC,194
Eckington Works FC, 194-195
Eldon St Jude's FC,152-153
Ellison, Michael J., 19,72,81,214
Elsecar FC, 169
Endcliffe FC, 157-158
Engineers FC, 46,123,134
Engravings, 168,197
Eton school, 13,14,15,21,40
Everton FC, 187
Exchange FC, 119-121
Exchange Brewery FC, 145-146

INDEX

F

Firth, Thomas, 150
Firvale FC, 74,87-88
Folk Football, 11,12
Football Alliance, 210,214
Football Annual, 35-36
Football Association, 30,31,32,36,38,39,47,64,202,203,206,210
Football Association Amateur Cup, 66,67
Football Association Challenge Cup, 26,38,64,65,215-218
Football Association Laws, 28,29
Football League, 204-207,210,214
Football Players' Accident Society, 64
Forest FC, 26,27,28,68,146,172
Floodlights, 111,188-189
Free Wanderers FC, 111

G

Gainsborough Trinity FC, 155
Garden Street FC, 142
Garratt, Richard, 99
Garrick FC, 74,108-111,166
Grantham Town FC, 162
Gitanos FC, 67
Glasgow Football Association, 195,200
Gleadless FC, 139-140
Goldthorn FC, (Wolverhampton Wanderers FC), 147
Gordon, Henry William (F.A. meeting 26/10/1863), 26
Grace, W. G., 107
Great Lever FC, 195
Gregory, R. (Featured in 1874 engraving), 52,155,188
Gregory Thomas Dyson (F.A. meeting 26/10/1863), 26
Great Flood, 55,103
Greenhalgh, Ernest Harwood, 138,139
Grignon, Reverend William Stanford, 41
Grimsby FC, 171,187
Grinders, 18,36
Gymnastic society, 16

H

Hacking, 13,14,28,31,32
Haigh, David (S.F.A.), 184
Haigh, John, 51,50
Hall, J.F. (S.F.A.), 49,118,149
Hallam Cricket club, 69
Hallam FC, 36,46,54,60,61,68-79,186,187
Hallamshire Football Association, 183,184
Hallamshire Proprietory Bowling Club, 135
Hallamshire Rifles, 45,46,184
Halliwell FC, 205
Handsworth Woodhouse FC, 164-165
Hanover United FC (Polytechnic FC), 105,147
Harrow Chequers FC, 36,146
Harrow School, 14,16,21,40
Hartlepool United FC,187
Hartshorne, Bertram Fulke (F.A. meeting 26/10/1863), 27

INDEX

Harvey, J.R. (S.F.A.), 50,51,163,184
Hat-trick, 123
Heading, 125
Heeley FC, 88-94,154,155,213
Heeley Friends FC, 94
Heeley Victoria FC, 143
Hemsworth, B., 49
Hemsworth FC, 91
Hertfordshire Rangers, 58
Highfields, 56,89,96,97,98,99,115,116
Hillsborough, 133,157
Hillsborough Stadium, 156
Hogg, Quintin, 146
Holmes FC, 160
Hooliganism, 174
Hollingworth, J. (Sheffield F.A. v. London F.A. 2/1871), 38
Hornby, Nick, 222
Horsham FC, 179
Hounsfield Park, 99,100 (Houndsfields Park (sic) 112)
Howard Hill Steel Bank FC, 100-101
Houseman, C. W., 37
Hulme Athenaeum FC, 101,110
Hunslet FC, 104,160,186,187
Hunter's Bar, 116,123,140
Hunter, John 'Jack', 89,92,124,135,154,190
Hyde Park, 56,83,120

I

Ibbotson, W. S. (Hon. Sec. N.F.A.), 181,182
Ilderton, 12
Ipswich FC, 127

J

Jackson, Nicholas "Pa", 172,202

K

Kennington Oval, 78
Kensington School, 26,28
Kettering FC, 148
Kidderminster FC, 148
Kilhamite Methodists, 133
Kilnhurst FC, 183
Kimberworth FC, 143-144
Kinnaird. A.F. (Lord), 146
Kirkham, 12

L

Lancashire F.A., 51,55,76,179,180,196,202
Lancing Old Boys, 179
Lang, James Joseph 'Jimmy', 137,200
Lausanne FC, 107
Laxton, 12
Leeds, 59
Leeds City AFC,187
Leeds FC, 104

INDEX

Lewis, John, 162
Liddell W.W. (S.F.C. Hon. Sec.), 54,123,220
Lillywhites, 22,35
Limited Liability Company, 205
Lincoln City FC, 205
Lincoln FC, 28,80
Liverpool FC, 55
Liverpool Velocipede Club, 173
Lockwood Brothers FC, 119,140-141,179
Lockwood, George Francis, 140
Lockwood, Jnr W. (Sheffield F.A. v. London F.A. 2/1871), 38,62,140
Lord's Cricket Ground, 67
Lydgate Lane, 134,135
Lunar Rovers FC, 129

M

M.C.C., 12,48,67
Macclesfield FC, 44,148
Mackenzie, Alfred Westwood (F.A. meeting 26/10/1863), 26
Mackenzie, FC (F.A. meeting 26/10/1863), 42,74,94-96
Mackintosh, William John (F.A. meeting 26/10/1863), 26
Maidenhead United FC, 78
Maidenhead FC,127
Malpas, A., 148,188,190,191
Manchester United FC, 187,240
Mansfield Greenhalgh FC, 138
Mansfield Town FC, 138
Marindin, Francis Arthur, 162,210,233
Marlow FC, 127
Marsh, John. (Sheffield F.A. v. London F.A. 2/1871) (Featured in 1874 engraving), Wednesday Hon. Sec., 38,52,62,115,122,137
Matlock FC, 187
Matthews, W.A. (S.F.C. Hon. Sec.), 45,54,62,65,137,138,219
McGregor, William, 204,205
Meersbrook Park, 90
Mexborough FC, 175-176
Middlesbrough FC, 77,92,93,128
Midland Counties League, 205
Midland Railway Station, 37
Mills, C. (Sheffield F.A. v. London F.A. 2/1871), 38,86,96,120
Millhouses FC, 144-145
Millwall FC, 207
Milton FC, 74,96-100
Mincing Lane FC, 58,68,79
Montrose FC, 156,157
Moore, Frederick Henry (F.A. meeting 26/10/1863), 26
Morley, Ebenezer Cobb (F.A. meeting 26/10/1863), 25,26,27,28,33,203
Mosforth, William 'Billy', 89,92,151,164,190,209,213
Muscular Christianity, 80
Myrtle Road (Ball Inn), 95,98,115,116

N

N.N Kilburn FC, 25,27,28
Needham, Ernest 'Nudger', 170,171
Newfield FC, 175

INDEX

Newmarket Town FC, 179
Norfolk FC, 74,80-83
Norfolk Park, 129
Norfolk Works FC, 149-150
Northern Counties League, 211,214
Northern League, 205
Northwich Victoria FC, 44,162,174
Norton Bible Class FC, 142
Norton FC, 74,85-87,113
Notts. County FC, 36,44,96,97,137,138,204
Nottingham Forest FC, 36,37,83,105,205
Notts. Rangers FC, 210,213

O

Oakes Park, 85,86
Old Carthusians FC, 104,124,201
Old Etonians FC, 104,201
Old Foresters FC, 172
Old Forge Ground (Brightside Lane), 50,51,54,128
Old Grindstone Inn, Crookes, 134,189
Old Harrovians FC, 104,202
Old Rossallians FC, 138,139
Old Salopians FC, 172
Old Wykehamists FC, 172
Olive Grove, 116,209,210,219
Outrages, 107,108
Overend, Wilson, 44,45,46,59,
Owlerton FC, 156-157
Owls, 215
Oxford FC, 124-125
Oxford University AFC, 70,148,201

P

Pantomimists, 111
Parker's Piece, 78
Parkfield House, 30,56,58
Parkwood Springs FC, 126-127
Partridge, Pat, 200
Passing Game, 30,188,231
Pastime magazine, 171,172
Pedestrianism, 56,58,63
Pember, Arthur (F.A. meeting 26/10/1863), 27,28,31
Perceval House FC, 26,28
Perseverance FC, 132-133,181
Photography, 168,173,221
Pitsmoor FC, 70,74,83-84
Philadelphia FC, 157
Phoenix Bessemer FC, 176-177
Preedy, Reverend Tiverton, 197,198,199
Prest, William, 19,41,42,45,46,56-66, 72,81,184
Preston North End FC, 187,188,201,202,203,204,205,208
Professionalism, 131,170,179,195,196,197,200-204,208-211,220-221
Providence FC, 163-164
Punch Bowl Inn, Crookes, 189
Pye Bank FC, 153-155

256

INDEX

Q
Queen's Park FC, 114
Queen Victoria, 53,210
Quibell's Field, 82,83,120

R
Rawmarsh FC, 158-159
Rawson's Meadow, 156
Reading FC, 143
Red Lion Public House, 90
Reigate Priory FC, 78,127
Remnants FC, 67
Richmond FC, 28
Rodgers, Joseph and Sons, 45
Rotherham FC, 129-132
Rotherham County FC, 129
Rotherham Swifts FC, 131
Rotherham Town FC, 129,130,131,207
Rotherham United FC, 129,130,131
Rotherham Wanderers FC, 129
Rouges, 23
Royal Arsenal FC, 207
Royal Engineers FC, 162,163,201
Royal Naval School FC, 28
Royston FC, 169
Rugby Football Union, 204
Rugby League, 204
Rugby school, 13,14,21,28

S
Saffron Walden FC, 169
Sale FC, 36
Saltley Teacher Training College FC, 146
Sampson, G.H. (Sheffield F.A. v. London F.A. 2/1871), 38,123,129,187
Sanderson, Frederick (President N.F.A.) (Garrick team captain in 1867?), 48,181,183
Sandford, Reverend G., 41
Sandygate, 68, 70,71,72,77,78,79,213,
Saturday half day holiday, 108,179
Scarborough, 12
Scottish F.A., 76, 203
Screw kick, 88
Sellars, (Featured in 1874 engraving), 52, 82
Sharrow Rangers FC, 159-160
Shaw, John Charles, 37,49,50,52,69,72,79,80,118,137
Sheaf House, 49,94,98,99,102,112,116,141,145,152,170,213
Sheaf United FC, 152
Sheffield Association Challenge Cup, 42,48,76,91
Sheffield and District Football League, 119, 127,133,134,156,160,194,211
Sheffield FC, 28,32,33,36,37,38,47-52,114,179,190,195,207
Sheffield Football Association, 33,36,37,38,47-52,114,179,190,195,207
Sheffield Gymnasium, 56,57
Sheffield and Hallamshire Association, 49-52,184
Sheffield New Football Association, 48-52,180-184
Sheffield Rovers FC, 208-209
Sheffield Rules, 19,20,22,32,36,37,38

INDEX

Sheffield United Cricket club, 56
Sheffield United Cricket and Football Club, 94,131,171,204,206,211-221
Sheffield United Gymnastic Club, 62
Sheffield Wanderers FC, 191
Shillingford, George William (F.A. meeting 26/10/1863), 26
Shropshire Wanderers FC, 65
Simplest Game Rules, 23
Small Heath Alliance FC (Birmingham City FC), 169,205
Sorby, R. A., 65,136,137
Sorby, T. H., 137
Sotheby's, 20,58,70
South Derbyshire Association (later Derbyshire Football Association), 37,47,86
Spital FC, 113,114,167
St. Marie's Catholic Cathedral, 128,129
St. Mark's College FC, 146
Stacey, W.H. (Featured in 1874 engraving), 52,117,118,146,160,164,188
Stafford Rangers FC, 172
Staveley FC, 167,169-172,198
Steam Clock Inn, 54
Steward, Herbert Thomas (F.A. meeting 26/10/1863), 26
Stockport FC, 162
Stoke Ramblers FC (later Stoke City FC), 122, 204,205
Stokes, Charles, 94,115,212
Stoneyhurst, 12
Stourbridge Standard FC, 172
Stringer, E.B., 197,199
Sudbury FC, 169
Sudell, William 'Billy', 183,202,205
Surbiton FC, 26,28
Surrey FC (Sheffield), 128-129
Surrey Football Club Rules ,16,17
Surrey County Cricket Club,16, 205
Swifts FC, 67

T

Talbot FC, 142-143
Temperance, 132,141
Thompson, Phil, 200
Thornhill FC, 129,130,131
Thring, John Charles, 14,23
Thurlstone Crystal Palace FC, 136,137
Thursday Wanderers FC, 136-139,179,200
Tingle, B., (Featured in 1874 engraving), 52,125
Tottenham Hotspur FC, 221
Turner, James (F.A. meeting 26/10/1863), 26
Turton FC, 78

U

United Mechanics FC, 74,105-107
Uppingham School, 24,28
Upton Park FC, 202

INDEX

V
Vickers, Albert, 72
Vickers, Thomas E. (Colonel Tom), 44,45,46,69,72
Vincent Square, 78
Volunteer Movement, 44-46,68

W
Wanderers FC, 65,68,201
Wake, W.R. (S.F.C. Hon. Sec.), 54,65,117,118,123
Walkley New Connexion FC, 133-134
Walsall FC, 162
War Office (later Civil Service FC), 27,28,36,105
Ward, Reverend E. D., 58
Ward, Frederick (S.F.C. President), 58
Ward, Thomas Asline, 58
Waterfall, William, 69,73
Wawn, George Twizell (F.A. meeting 26/10/1863), 27
Wednesbury Old Athletic FC, 164
Wednesday FC, 36,70,98,114-119,152,156,196,205,208,209,210
Wellington FC, 74,112-114
Wellsbrook Park, 90
Welsh F.A., 76
Wesley College, 40,56
West Bromwich Albion FC, 162,201,240
Westminster School, 78
Wharncliffe Charity Cup, 92,190
Whistle, use of, 83,234
Whitby, 12
White Cross FC, 189-190
White Lion Public House, 90
Whittington Moor FC, 169
Wilkinson, W. (Featured in 1874 engraving), 52,149
Willey, H.B. (S.F.C. Hon. Sec.), 42,213,218,219
Willey, T.C. (Sheffield F.A. v. London F.A. 2/1871), 38,62,65,123,124,138
Wilson, George, 183
Wimbledon School, 27,28
Winchester School, 13,14
de Winton, Henry, 14
Wood, A. (Sheffield F.A. v. London F.A. 2/1871) (Featured in 1874 engraving), 38,52,123,127,149
Woodseats FC, 165-167
Worksop Town FC, 155,174
World's Oldest Football Ground, 78, 104
Wrexham FC, 79,104

X

Y
Yeovil FC, 172
York Athletic Sports and Football Club, 42
Yorkshire County Cricket Club, 101
Youdan Cup, 62,64,73-76,86,95,101,112

Z
Zulus FC, 89,124,190-191

Soccerbilia

Soccerbilia - the home of British football magazines

We have thousands of football magazines in stock covering 90 different publications. This includes, among others, complete runs of Charles Buchan's Football Monthly, Soccer Star, Jimmy Hill's Football Weekly, World Soccer and the first twenty odd years of Shoot. We also have a very good selection of bound magazines from as early as 1920.

We were recently able to help the National Football Museum in Manchester source some difficult to obtain newspapers from the early 1900s. We recently added 50 editions of the very rare 'Pastime' newspaper from 1894 onwards that we are very proud of. The site offers many first issues of other famous football magazines

'I came across Soccerbilia while researching for my own football collection and have been very pleased with the quality of the items I have purchased. The site is informative and well set out. Martin Westby clearly has a feeling for football and its memorabilia.'
Martin Tyler, Football Commentator, Sky Sports.

As well as being a site where football memorabilia collectors can fill the gaps on their magazine of choice, it is also a place where visitors can use the continuous run of magazines from 1909 to the present day, to buy unique birthday presents for their friends and family members who love 'soccer.

'Martin has done a fantastic job here and long may it continue, I found the website very informative and shall certainly be revisiting in the near future. In fact, I am now tempted to bring my collection of soccer magazines down from the loft to see what I might be missing!'
News from the Net by Kevin Artlett May 2014.

www.soccerbilia.co.uk
Telephone: 01202 259155
Email: office@soccerbilia.co.uk